Fodor's 2000

San Francisco

D0885128

金山銀行

LIPPOBANK

Fodor's Travel Publications, Inc. • New York, Toronto, London, Sydney, Auckland
www.fodors.com/sanfrancisco

CONTENTS

MAPS

Circled letters in text correspond to letters on the photographs. For more information on the sights pictured, turn
to the indicated page number ⒶↃ on each photograph.

DESTINATION
SAN FRANCISCO

Few cities enchant their guests like San Francisco. Many of its residents were once visitors who came to see the sights and then, smitten, returned to look for a job and a place to live. However you define the good life—or the great vacation—you can find it here, abandoning yourself to the wonderful food and wine, the arts, shopping, café-sitting, people-watching, and the outdoors. The venues for these activities range from Fisherman's Wharf to Baker Beach and are invariably surrounded by a sublime marriage of man-made and natural beauty that is unique to the city.

HILLS AND VIEWS

Ⓐ 55

Wherever you are around San Francisco and Marin County, you're never far from a dazzling view. One classic is the panorama from Berkeley and Oakland over the Ⓓ**Bay Bridge** and the San Francisco skyline—it's particularly magical after dark. Or head to the top of 180-foot Ⓔ**Coit Tower,** the vintage landmark that's one of the city's favorite viewpoints. Or try taking the ferry to Ⓐ**Alcatraz Island:** you can see the city, Marin County, and the East Bay en route. The views from the notorious penal island aren't too bad either. Years ago, Ⓒ**cable car** passengers on Hyde Street, which runs down to Fisherman's Wharf at the base of the hill, must have found all that water between them and the residents of Alcatraz very comforting. The hills of Angel Island, the trail-crossed, bay-washed state

Ⓑ 45

© 19

Ⓓ 29

Ⓔ 41

park beyond Alcatraz, provide stunning views as well. The steep hills that make for such great views define the cityscape and make for better sightseeing. And just when the steep inclines threaten to wear you out, you'll come upon some secret stairway, such as the Filbert Street steps on Telegraph Hill, that will help you scuttle up and down. The sinuous alpine-style switchbacks of ⑧**Lombard Street** between Hyde and Leavenworth, ornamented by bright flowers, have made this byway a sightseeing attraction. It's one of the key sights for every first-timer in town—and in this town, that's saying a lot.

Ⓐ▷ 83

If you miss the city's neighborhoods you will miss much of its soul. In Ⓐ**Haight-Ashbury,** the '60s still echo (if faintly), and murals in Ⓑ**Balmy Alley** in the heavily Latino and increasingly hipster Mission District add color to this already vibrant area. The Ⓒ**Chinatown Gate** marks the entrance to 14 blocks of exotic bustle. The great charm of this city is its offer of community to all. Anyone, from banker to biker to bohemian, gay or straight, from Nob Hill to the Castro, can find a haven here.

COMMUNITIES

Ⓑ▷ 74

Ⓒ▷ 37

Ⓐ▷194

Ⓑ▷108

Ⓒ▷170

DINING

Bay Area residents view good food as a birthright. The sheer number and variety of restaurants make the senses reel. Although fresh ingredients were always at hand, it took Berkeley's Alice Waters, of Ⓐ**Chez Panisse,** to build a cuisine around them, and her café is now the nucleus of an enclave called the Gourmet Ghetto. That said, food is not the only draw—the ocean view from the Ⓑ**Beach Chalet** is as compelling as the frothy drinks and freshly brewed beer. Nor is the food always Californian. At Ⓒ**Molinari Delicatessen** and Ⓓ**Rose Pistola** in North Beach, the accent is definitely Italian. And all over town you'll find Indian, Chinese, Vietnamese, French, and Mexican fare, and just about any other cuisine you can name.

Ⓓ▷102

SHOPPING

Ⓐ▷171

Given San Francisco's rich patchwork of neighborhoods and lifestyles, shopping for clothing, crafts, art, or just about anything else is as much a travel experience as a transaction. Want something tie-dyed? Head for the Haight. Need a ginseng pick-me-up? Try Chinatown. Fine collectibles? Visit the venerable Ⓐ**Gump's** or the dealers in gentrified Jackson Square.

Ⓑ▷164

Boutiques, antiques, and an air of chic dominate Ⓑ**Union Street,** where browsers can have as much fun as buyers. Note that window-shoppers here often find themselves reaching irresistibly for their plastic. (This is a peril, too, for those who venture into the fancy Union Square shopping zone.) Objects of extraordinary beauty, from kites to kimonos, can be acquired at the Ⓒ**Japan Center.** Wherever you shop, from the Castro to Pacific Heights, you're certain to discover a fascinating new face of the city.

Ⓒ▷51

THE ARTS

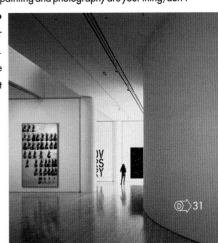

Ⓐ⟩ 148

Ⓑ⟩ 64

Ⓒ⟩ 80

In San Francisco the lively arts sometimes get downright frisky. A case in point is Club Fugazi, home to *Beach Blanket Babylon,* a long-running send-up of all things San Franciscan. Then there are the refined pleasures of performances by the Ⓐ**San Francisco Symphony,** led by Michael Tilson Thomas, or of productions at the War Memorial Opera House. Contemplative pleasure is the order of the day at the Ⓑ**Asian Art Museum.** Cinemaphiles flock to the Ⓒ**Castro Theatre.** It specializes in flicks your local video store probably doesn't stock, and its programs are eclectic and thoughtfully assembled. There are film festivals all over town, as well as a generous share of movie houses whose selections are decidedly noncommercial. If contemporary painting and photography are your thing, don't miss the Ⓓ**San Francisco Museum of Modern Art,** or SFMOMA to its many friends. Its Mario Botta–designed home is as arresting as the works that hang within it.

Ⓓ⟩ 31

Ⓐ▷62

OUTDOORS

Ⓑ▷43

In San Francisco you are never far from the great outdoors. The sea air and California sunshine alone are worth the trip to the city. Don't worry: You will see fog, too. The best place to enjoy them is Ⓐ**Golden Gate Park,** one of the world's great urban preserves. Gloriously landscaped, it's home to some equally glorious biking and jogging as well as a conservatory, a Dutch windmill, a Japanese tea garden, and a paddock full of buffalo. The

Ⓒ▷184

Pacific, which pounds the park on the west, also washes the windswept beaches of the sprawling Golden Gate National Recreation Area, to the north. Smaller green spaces are scattered all over town; locals greet the day with tai chi in Ⓑ**Washington Square.** When the water beckons, rent a sailboat in Sausalito if you're up to handling the tricky winds, or just head for Ⓒ**Tiburon,** in Marin County, to sit on the deck of a bay-view restaurant and watch other people's boats bobbing hither and yon on the glittering waters.

SIDE TRIPS

San Francisco puts you within striking distance of many other memorable destinations. Marin County, on the north end of the Golden Gate Bridge, is full of drowsy towns with lovely restaurants, good bookstores, and abundant natural beauty. Ⓐ**Point Reyes National Seashore** has a famous lighthouse and secluded beaches, and Ⓑ**Muir Woods** is home to a redwood grove that includes trees dating back more than a thousand years. Farther north in the Wine Country, you'll encounter graceful architecture like that at Ⓒ**Robert Mondavi** winery, as well as lovely inns, some of the country's most creative restaurants, and fabulous wines by the score.

Ⓒ▷ 246

Ⓑ▷ 187

GREAT ITINERARIES

San Francisco in 5 Days

Much of San Francisco's appeal springs from the distinct personalities of its neighborhoods, so allow as much time as possible to soak up the city's ambience. Five days is enough to see highlights of the city by the bay: Fisherman's Wharf, Union Square, Alcatraz, North Beach, Chinatown, and the Golden Gate Bridge.

☺ *So you don't show up somewhere and find the doors locked, shuffle the itinerary segments with closing days in mind.*

are worth a look. After a few hours of browsing swank shops, take in an evening of culture on Geary Street's theater row or quaff a cocktail and watch the sun set at one of the square's sky-view lounges.

☺ *Best on weekdays.*

DAY 2

Devote the day to two of the most important cultures in the city's history. Head to North Beach, the Italian quarter, and join locals from the old country for breakfast Italian-style: an espresso and pastry at an outdoor café along Columbus Avenue. Allow an hour or two to wander this small area filled with tempting delis, bakeries, and pasta houses. You'll see beat-era landmarks like City Lights Bookstore and reminders of

DAY 1

Spend the day checking out San Francisco's bustling centers of commercial activity. In the morning explore Fisherman's Wharf and its jumble of tourist shops, street performers, and artists. Pier 39 is a consumer extravaganza; a double-decker carousel shares space with touristy shops and Underwater World, a fascinating walk-through glimpse of ocean life. Don't miss the antics of the hundreds of sea lions basking in the sun. Jump a cable car (the Powell-Hyde line is the most dramatic) at the wharf and take in sweeping views of the bay, Alcatraz, and the Golden Gate Bridge as you rattle your way to Union Square, ground zero for sophisticated shopping. Maiden Lane's charming galleries and boutiques

the city's bawdy past in the steamy shops and clubs of Broadway. Be sure to walk up Telegraph Hill to Coit Tower. You'll be rewarded with breathtaking views of the bay and the city's tightly stacked homes. Spend the afternoon exploring labyrinthine Chinatown, where tea and herb shops, live fish markets, and exotic-produce stalls spill onto the street. Then take the California Street cable car up blue-blood Nob Hill and top off the evening with a tropical concoction at the Tonga Room, the Fairmont Hotel's kitschy-chic Polynesian lounge, or take in the quirky musical revue of San Francisco, Ⓐ*Beach Blanket Babylon*, back in North Beach.

☺ *If Beach Blanket Babylon is on your list, this won't work on Monday or Tuesday.*

DAY 3

Today you'll hit the city's outdoor highlights. Take a morning ferry from Pier 41 to the infamous prison Alcatraz. When the boat docks back at the pier, head toward the Marina neighborhood, home to young professionals and exclusive boutiques and bistros. Along the way, catch a glimpse of San Francisco's nautical history at the National Maritime Museum. If you love chocolate, stop off at Ghirardelli Square, a shopping center and home to the tempting Ghirardelli Chocolate Factory. Make a beeline for the end of the Marina and the stunning Palace of Fine Arts. Don't

miss the Palace's wacky and wonderful hands-on science museum, the Exploratorium. Before dusk, bundle up and head to the Golden Gate Bridge to catch the sunset.

☺ *The Exploratorium is closed on Monday.*

DAY 4

Dedicate the morning to art and the rest of the day to funk. Start south of Market at the San Francisco Museum of Modern Art to take in works by local, Mexican, and European masters. While you're in the area, don't miss Ⓑ*Yerba Buena Gardens* and its Center for the Arts. Then take the antique-streetcar

Ⓐ ➤ 137

SAN FRANCISCO BAY

To Alcatraz

Pier 41/
Alcatraz Ferry

Powell-Hyde
Cable Car

Pier 39/
Underwater World

Fisherman's
Wharf

National
Maritime
Museum

Jefferson St.

Beach St.

Marina Blvd.

Palace of Fine Arts/
Exploratorium

THE
SIDIO

Ghirardelli
Square

MARINA

Columbus
Ave.

Telegraph Hill/
Coit Tower

NORTH
BEACH

Filbert St.

Green
St.

Beach Blanket
Babylon

Broadway

City Lights
Bookstore

Jackson St.

Chinatown

Fairmont
Hotel

(California St.
Cable Car)

NOB
HILL

Maiden
Lane

Geary St.

Union
Square

San Francisco
Museum of
Modern Art

SOMA

Yerba Buena
Gardens/
Center
for the Arts

Market Street
"F"-line

"F"-line down Market Street to the colorful, gay-friendly Castro, brimming with shops and cafés. A double feature at the Castro Theatre makes for a great afternoon diversion. Head to the mural-filled Mission District, home to twentysomething hipsters and working-class Latino families. Simple Mission Dolores, built in 1776, is San Francisco's oldest standing structure. In the evening check out some of the Mission's trendy watering holes and restaurants.
⊘ Avoid Wednesday, when the Museum of Modern Art is closed.

swing through the California Academy of Sciences, the city's famed natural-history museum, or spend the rest of the afternoon strolling the park, around Stow Lake and all the way to the Dutch Windmill on the park's coastal edge. Head up to the Cliff House for dinner or a drink and a view of the Pacific sunset.
⊘ Never on Monday, when the museums are closed.

Haight St.

Haight-Ashbury

Ashbury St.

Market St.

Mission
Dolores

Castro
Theatre

CASTRO

16th St.

Castro St.

MISSION

Valencia St.

Square and the gorgeous Art Deco Paramount Theatre. The wineries of Napa and Sonoma counties are also within reach.

DAY 5

Step back into San Francisco's hippie days and explore its most glorious green space. Start out in Haight-Ashbury, the epicenter of 1960s counterculture, whose streets are lined with excellent music and book shops and groovy vintage-clothing stores. In the afternoon join in-line skaters, joggers, and walking enthusiasts in picnic-perfect Golden Gate Park—more than 1,000 acres of greenery stretching from the Haight to the Pacific. Among the botanical gardens and playing fields, you'll find the American art–filled M. H. de Young Memorial Museum, the Asian Art Museum, and the serene Japanese Tea Garden. Then either take a

If You Have More Time

Drive over the Golden Gate Bridge to the dramatic coastline of the Marin Headlands or to redwood-rich ©Muir Woods. Or head across the Bay Bridge and explore formerly radical, still-offbeat Berkeley. A visit to diverse Oakland also makes a great afternoon; don't miss waterfront Jack London

If You Have 3 Days

If it's your first visit, follow the suggestions for the first day: See Fisherman's Wharf and Pier 39 in the morning and Union Square in the afternoon, then head to the San Francisco Museum of Modern Art. On the second day, begin with a walk on the Golden Gate Bridge, then explore North Beach and Chinatown in the afternoon. Begin the third day with a ferry to Alcatraz. Spend the rest of the day in the neighborhood most appealing to you, either the Castro, the Mission, or Haight-Ashbury.

© ▷ 87

1 EXPLORING SAN FRANCISCO

Brace yourself for the brilliant colors of ornately painted, bay-window Victorians; the sounds of foghorns and cable car lines; and the crisp, salty smell of the bay. San Francisco's world-famous landmarks—the Golden Gate Bridge, Alcatraz, the Transamerica Pyramid—provide an unforgettable backdrop for its eclectic neighborhoods, from bustling Chinatown and bacchanalian North Beach to the left-of-center Castro district and the city's new cultural center, SoMa.

YOU COULD LIVE IN SAN FRANCISCO a month and ask no greater entertainment than walking through it," wrote Inez Hayes Irwin, the author of *The Californiacs*, an effusive 1921 homage to the state of California and the City by the Bay. Her claim remains true today: As in the '20s, touring on foot is the best way to experience this diverse metropolis.

Revised by
Daniel Mangin

San Francisco is a relatively small city. About 750,000 residents live on a 46.6-square-mi tip of land between San Francisco Bay and the Pacific Ocean. San Franciscans cherish the city's colorful past; many older buildings have been spared from demolition and nostalgically converted into modern offices and shops. Longtime locals rue the sites that got away—railroad and mining boom–era residences lost in the 1906 earthquake, the baroque Fox Theater, and Playland at the Beach. Despite acts of God, the indifference of developers, and the mixed record of the city's planning commission, much of the architectural and historical interest remains. Bernard Maybeck, Julia Morgan, Willis Polk, and Arthur Brown Jr. are among the noteworthy architects whose designs remain.

San Francisco's charms are great and small. First-time visitors won't want to miss Golden Gate Park, the Palace of Fine Arts, the Golden Gate Bridge, or a cable car ride over Nob Hill. But a walk down the Filbert Steps or through Macondray Lane, or a peaceful hour gazing east from Ina Coolbrith Park can be equally inspiring.

The neighborhoods of San Francisco retain strong cultural, political, and ethnic identities. Locals know this pluralism is the real life of the city. Experiencing San Francisco means visiting the neighborhoods: the colorful Mission District, the gay Castro, countercultural Haight Street, swank Pacific Heights, exotic Chinatown, and still-bohemian North Beach.

Exploring involves navigating a maze of one-way streets and restricted parking zones. San Francisco's famed 40-plus hills can be a problem for drivers who are new to the terrain. Cable cars, buses, and trolleys can take you to or near many attractions.

UNION SQUARE AREA

Much of San Francisco may feel like a collection of small towns strung together, but the Union Square area bristles with big-city bravado. The city's finest department stores do business here, along with exclusive emporiums like Tiffany & Co. and big-name franchises like Niketown, Planet Hollywood, Borders Books and Music, and the Virgin Megastore. Several dozen hotels within a three-block walk of the square cater to visitors. The downtown theater district and many fine arts galleries are nearby.

Numbers in the text correspond to numbers in the margin and on the Downtown San Francisco map.

A Good Walk

Begin three blocks south of Union Square at the **San Francisco Visitors Information Center** ①, on the lower level of Hallidie Plaza at Powell and Market streets. Up the escalators on the east side of the plaza, where Powell dead-ends into Market, lies the **cable car terminus** ② for two of the city's three lines. Head north on Powell from the terminus to Geary Street, make a left, and walk west 1½ blocks into the theater district for a peek at the **Geary Theater** ③. Backtrack on the north side of Geary Street, where the sturdy and stately **Westin St. Francis Hotel** ④ dominates Powell between Geary and Post streets. **Union Square** ⑤ is across Powell from the hotel's main entrance. You can pick up discount and full-price event tickets at the **TIX Bay Area** ⑥ booth in the square.

From the square head south on Stockton Street to O'Farrell Street and take a spin through **F.A.O. Schwarz** ⑦ (also on Stockton are Planet Hollywood and the Virgin Megastore). Walk back toward Union Square past Geary Street and make a right on **Maiden Lane** ⑧, a two-block alley directly across Stockton from Union Square that runs east parallel to Geary. When the lane ends at Kearny Street, turn left, walk 1½ blocks to Sutter Street, make a right, and walk a half block to the **Hallidie Building** ⑨. After viewing this historic building, reverse direction and head west 1½ blocks up Sutter to the fanciful beaux-arts–style **Hammersmith Building** ⑩, on the southwest corner of Sutter Street and Grant Avenue. In the middle of the next block of Sutter stands a glorious Art Deco building at **450 Sutter Street** ⑪. From here, backtrack a half block east to Stockton Street and take a right. In front of the the Grand Hyatt hotel sits **Ruth Asawa's Fantasy Fountain** ⑫. Union Square is a half block south on Stockton.

TIMING

Allow two hours to see everything around Union Square. Stepping into the massive Macy's department store or browsing boutiques can eat up countless hours. If you're a shopper, give yourself extra time.

Sights to See

⓿ ❷ **Cable car terminus.** San Francisco's cable cars were declared National Landmarks (the only ones that move) in 1964. Two of the three operating lines begin and end their runs here. The Powell–Mason line climbs up Nob Hill, then winds through North Beach to Fisherman's Wharf. The Powell–Hyde line also crosses Nob Hill but then continues up Russian Hill and down Hyde Street to Victorian Park, across from the Buena Vista Café and near Ghirardelli Square. Buy your ticket ($2 one-way) on board, at nearby hotels, or at the police/information booth near the turnaround.

Depending on your disposition, you'll find the panhandlers, street preachers, and other regulars at the Powell and Market terminus daunting or diverting. Either way you'll wait longer here to board a cable car than at any other stop in the system. If it's just the experience of riding a cable car you're after, board the less-busy California line at Van Ness Avenue and ride it down to the Hyatt Regency Hotel (☞ SoMa and the Embarcadero, *below*). ⊠ *Powell and Market Sts.*

⓿ ❼ **F.A.O. Schwarz.** The prices are not Toys 'R Us, but it's worth stopping by this three-floor playland to look at the 6-ft-tall stuffed animals and elaborate fairy-tale sculptures. Among the wares are a large Barbie section, an astounding supply of stuffed animals (the priciest is a whopping $15,000), and just about every other toy imaginable. ⊠ *48 Stockton St.,* ☎ *415/394–8700.* ☺ *Mon.–Sat. 10–7, Sun. 11–6.*

⑪ **450 Sutter Street.** Handsome Mayan-inspired designs adorn the exterior and interior surfaces of this 1928 Art Deco skyscraper, a masterpiece of terra-cotta and other detailing. ⊠ *Between Stockton and Powell Sts.*

❸ **Geary Theater.** The American Conservatory Theater (ACT), one of North America's leading repertory companies (☞ Theater *in* Chapter 4), uses the 1,035-seat Geary as its main venue. Built in 1910, the Geary has a serious neoclassic design lightened by colorful carved terra-cotta columns depicting a cornucopia of fruits. Damaged heavily in the 1989 earthquake, the Geary has been completely restored to highlight

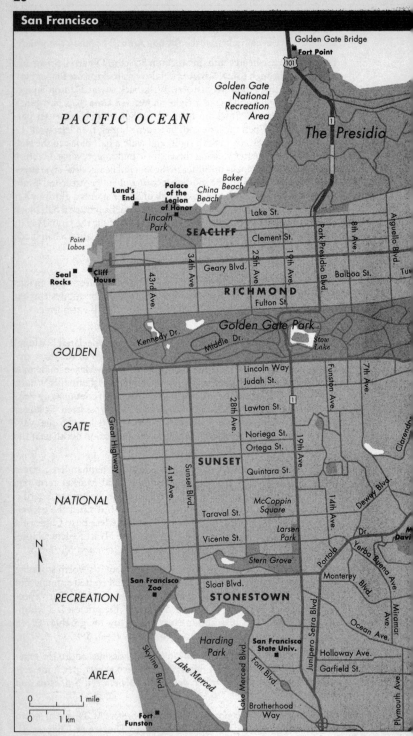

PACIFIC OCEAN

Golden Gate Bridge
Fort Point

Golden Gate
National
Recreation
Area

The Presidia

Baker
Beach

Palace
of the
Legion
of Honor

China
Beach

Land's
End

Lincoln
Park

SEACLIFF

Lake St.

Clement St.

Park Presidio Blvd.

8th Ave.

Arguello Blvd.

Point
Lobos

34th Ave.

Geary Blvd.

25th Ave.

19th Ave.

Balboa St.

Seal
Rocks

Cliff
House

43rd Ave.

RICHMOND

Fulton St.

Golden Gate Park

GOLDEN

Kennedy Dr.

Middle Dr.

Stow
Lake

7th Ave.

GATE

Lincoln Way

Judah St.

28th Ave.

Lawton St.

Funston Ave.

19th Ave.

Noriega St.

Ortega St.

Claresndn

SUNSET

Quintara St.

41st Ave.

Sunset Blvd.

McCoppin
Square

14th Ave.

Dewey Blvd.

NATIONAL

Taraval St.

Larsen
Park

Dr.

Davi

Vicente St.

Portola

Yerba Buena Ave.

Miramar

Stern Grove

Monterey Blvd.

Ave.

Great Highway

RECREATION

San Francisco
Zoo

Sloat Blvd.

STONESTOWN

Ocean Ave.

Junipero Serra Blvd.

Harding
Park

San Francisco
State Univ.

Holloway Ave.

Skyline Blvd.

Lake Merced

Lake Merced Blvd.

Font Blvd.

Garfield St.

Plymouth Ave.

AREA

N

Brotherhood
Way

0   1 mile

0   1 km

Fort
Funston

San Francisco Bay

Marina Green
Fort Mason
Fisherman's Wharf
Pier 39
MARINA
NORTHERN WATERFRONT
Bay St.
NORTH BEACH
Coit Tower
Palace of Fine Arts
Lombard St.
RUSSIAN HILL
Columbus Ave.
The Embarcadero
TELEGRAPH HILL
101
FILLMORE
Broadway
Larkin St.
Hyde St.
Polk St.
(tunnel)
CHINATOWN
Ferry Building
101
PACIFIC HEIGHTS
Washington St.
NOB HILL
California St.
Powell St.
Grant Ave.
FINANCIAL DISTRICT
San Francisco-Oakland Bay Bridge
Sacramento St.
Gough St.
Van Ness Ave.
Laguna St.
80
Pine St.
Bush St.
JAPAN TOWN
Post St.
Geary St.
UNION SQUARE
1st St.
2nd St.
Yerba Buena Center
Geary St.
Divisadero St.
Steiner St.
Turk St.
Franklin St.
CIVIC CENTER
Mission St.
5th St.
6th St.
2nd St.
3rd St.
Presidio Ave.
Golden Gate Ave.
HAYES VALLEY
SOMA
8th St.
9th St.
Folsom St.
Harrison St.
Brannan St.
Bryant St.
Townsend St.
Masonic Ave.
Fulton St.
Hayes St.
WESTERN ADDITION
Market St.
7th St.
Brannan St.
King St.
Berry St.
Geary St.
Fell St.
Haight St.
10th St.
Central Basin
IGHT-BURY
Dubace Ave.
7th St.
280
Buena Vista Park
Castro St.
Central Freeway
7th St.
Clayton St.
17th St.
Potrero Ave.
Mariposa St.
Pennsylvania Ave.
Indiana St.
3rd St.
India Basin
Market St.
Dolores Park
MISSION
20th St.
Harrison St.
Van Ness Ave.
POTRERO
CASTRO
Dolores St.
Guerrero St.
Mission St.
San Francisco General Hospital
NOE VALLEY
24th St.
Twin Peaks
25th St.
Cesar Chavez St.
Islais Cr. Channel
Diamond St.
BERNAL HEIGHTS
280
Oakdale Ave.
India Basin
Bosworth St.
Quesada Ave.
Hunters Point
nterey Blvd.
Fwy.
Silver Ave.
Southern
San Jose Ave.
GLEN PARK
Felton St.
3rd St.
Balboa Park
Alemany Blvd.
Excelsior Ave.
Mission St.
Persia Ave.
Moscow St.
Mansell St.
Gilman Ave.
Jamestown Ave.
France Ave.
John McLaren Park
101
South Basin
Geneva Ave.
3Com Park

Downtown San Francisco

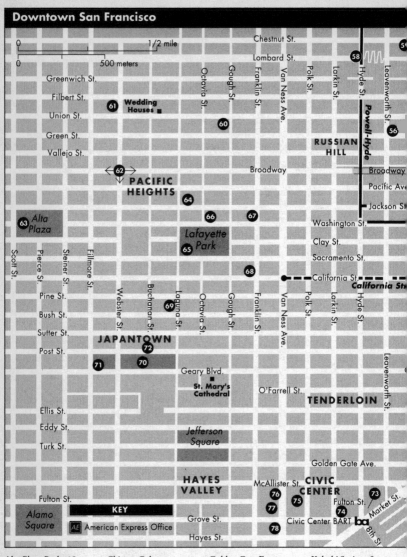

San Francisco Bay

its historic, gilded splendor. ⊠ *415 Geary St. (box office at 405 Geary St.),* ☎ *415/749–2228.*

❾ Hallidie Building. Named for cable car inventor Andrew S. Hallidie, this 1918 structure is best viewed from across the street. Willis Polk's revolutionary glass-curtain wall—believed to be the world's first such facade—hangs a foot beyond the reinforced concrete of the frame. The reflecting glass, decorative exterior fire escapes that appear to be metal balconies, and Venetian Gothic cornice are worth noting. Ornamental bands of birds at feeders stretch across the building on several stories. ⊠ *130 Sutter St., between Kearny and Montgomery Sts.*

❿ Hammersmith Building. Glass walls and a colorful design distinguish this four-story beaux-arts–style structure, built in 1907. The Foundation for Architectural Heritage once described the building as a "commercial jewel box." Appropriately, it was originally designed for use as a jewelry store. ⊠ *301 Sutter St.*

NEED A BREAK?   You can nibble on sampler plates or have a full meal at the **E & O Trading Co.** (⊠ 314 Sutter St., ☎ 415/693–0303). The ambience is late 19th-century Asian trading post, but the chow is strictly modern Pan-Asian.

❽ Maiden Lane. Known as Morton Street in the raffish Barbary Coast era (☞ The Heart of the Barbary Coast, *below*), this former red-light district reported at least one murder a week during the late 19th century. After the 1906 fire destroyed the brothels, the street emerged as Maiden Lane, and it has since become a semi-chic pedestrian mall stretching two blocks, between Stockton and Kearny streets. Traffic is prohibited most days between 11 and 5, when the lane becomes a patchwork of umbrella-shaded tables. Masses of daffodils and balloons lend a carnival mood during the annual spring festival, when throngs of street musicians, arts-and-crafts vendors, and spectators emerge.

With its circular interior ramp and skylights, the handsome brick 1948 structure at **140 Maiden Lane,** the only Frank Lloyd Wright building in San Francisco, is said to have been his model for the Guggenheim Museum in New York. The **Folk Art International/Boretti Amber/ Xanadu** (☎ 415/392–9999) galleries, showcases for Baltic, Latin-American, and African folk art, occupy the space. ⊠ *Between Stockton and Kearny Sts.*

⑫ Ruth Asawa's Fantasy Fountain. Local artist Ruth Asawa's sculpture, a wonderland of real and mythical creatures, honors the city's hills, bridges, and architecture. Children and friends helped Asawa shape the hundreds of tiny figures from baker's clay; these were assembled on 41 large panels from which molds were made for the bronze casting. ⊠ *In front of Grand Hyatt at 345 Stockton St.*

❶ San Francisco Visitors Information Center. A multilingual staff operates this facility below the cable car terminus. Staff members answer questions and provide maps and pamphlets. You can also pick up discount coupons—the savings can be significant, especially for families—and hotel brochures here. ⊠ *Hallidie Plaza, lower level, Powell and Market Sts.,* ☎ *415/391–2000.* ☺ *Weekdays 9–5:30, Sat. 9–3, Sun. 10–2.*

❻ TIX Bay Area. This excellent service provides half-price day-of-performance tickets (cash or traveler's checks only) to all types of performing arts events, as well as regular full-price box office services for concerts, clubs, and sporting events (credit cards accepted). Telephone reservations are not accepted for half-price tickets. Half-price tickets for Sunday and Monday events are sold on Saturday. Also sold at the booth is the **Golden Gate Park Explorer Pass** ($14; good for discount admission

HOW CABLE CARS SPARED THE CITY'S HILLS AND HORSES

GAZE UP FROM THE BASE of Nob or Russian hill, and you won't have trouble figuring out why the Society for the Prevention of Cruelty to Animals became an early supporter of Andrew Smith Hallidie's proposal to add cable cars to San Francisco's mass transit mix. Conductors of horse-drawn streetcars heading up these and other peaks in the 1850s and 1860s screamed at and fiercely whipped the animals, vainly encouraging them to muster the strength to halt their slides back *down* to the base.

The "sorrowful plight" of the horses may have been one of Hallidie's inspirations, but he was also in the business of selling wire cable. He was first person to manufacture it in California, beginning during the Gold Rush. Hallidie, a Scotsman, had come to California seeking gold. He didn't find much, but he did strike it rich selling his cable and building suspension bridges and mine conveyances. The technology for cable cars had been used for decades in mines, but it was Hallidie who successfully applied it to an urban environment.

Drop by the Cable Car Museum (☞ Nob Hill and Russian Hill, *below*) on Nob Hill, and you'll see how breathtakingly simple Hallidie's system, eventually employed by more than a dozen cities around the world, is. Four sets of cables—one for each of the streets (Powell, Hyde, Mason, and California) on which the cars now travel—spin on huge powerhouse wheels, making a continuous circuit beneath city streets. When the conductor wants to put a car in motion, he or she operates a handgrip, the end of which grabs the cable, allowing the car to move along with the cable. When the conductor releases the grip, the car comes to a halt. Brakes are also involved when the vehicle is on an incline.

San Francisco's system dates from 1873, when Hallidie demonstrated his first car on Clay Street. It's said that no one was brave enough to operate the car back down Nob Hill, so the inventor took the helm himself, guiding the car safely back to the base of Portsmouth Plaza (now Square) at Kearny Street. Historians have pointed out that without cable cars the city's hills might well have been leveled, or at least reduced in height, as happened in Manhattan and other urban areas that expanded before the cars were invented. As it turned out, the cars made previously uninhabited or sparsely populated crests a magnet for the wealthy. The rich folk on Nob Hill built their own line, the California Street leg, in operation to this day, to convey them between the Financial District and their mansions.

THE HEYDAY OF CABLE CARS was the two decades after their introduction. At the dawn of the 20th century, 500 cable cars zipped along a network of more than 100 mi. Today a few dozen cars travel on three lines, and the network covers just 9½ mi. Most of the cars date from the last century, though the cars and lines had a complete overhaul during the early 1980s and the cables are replaced every three to six months. Hallidie, who was considered a civic hero in his day, fittingly has his name on the Hallidie Building, an innovative skyscraper built in 1918.

— Daniel Mangin

to the main attractions in Golden Gate Park) and Muni Passports and adult Fast Passes for use on the transit system. ⊠ *Union Square,* ☎ *415/433–7827.* ☉ *Tues.–Thurs. 11–6, Fri.–Sat. 11–7.*

⑤ Union Square. The heart of San Francisco's downtown since 1850, the 2.6-acre square takes its name from the violent pro-union demonstrations staged here prior to the Civil War. At center stage, the *Victory Monument,* by Robert Ingersoll Aitken, commemorates Commodore George Dewey's victory over the Spanish fleet at Manila in 1898. The 97-ft Corinthian column, topped by a bronze figure symbolizing naval conquest, was dedicated by Theodore Roosevelt in 1903 and withstood the 1906 earthquake. After the earthquake and fire of 1906, the square was dubbed "Little St. Francis" because of the temporary shelter erected for residents of the St. Francis Hotel. Actor John Barrymore, the grandfather of actress Drew Barrymore and a notorious carouser, was among the guests pressed into volunteering to stack bricks in the square. His uncle, thespian John Drew, remarked, "It took an act of God to get John out of bed and the United States army to get him to work."

Once the jewel of downtown, the square looks rather dowdy in the late 20th century, but it is scheduled for a makeover during 2000, so you may find portions of it closed. After the renovations the same kaleidoscope of characters will likely return: office workers sunning and brown-bagging, street musicians, the occasional preacher, and a fair share of homeless people. The square often hosts public events such as fashion shows, free noontime concerts, and noisy demonstrations. Union Square covers a convenient but costly four-level underground garage. For cheaper parking try the nearby Sutter-Stockton Garage. ⊠ *Between Powell, Stockton, Post, and Geary Sts.*

❹ Westin St. Francis Hotel. The second-oldest hotel in the city, established in 1904, was conceived by railroad baron and financier Charles Crocker and his associates as a hostelry for their millionaire friends. Swift service and sumptuous surroundings—glass chandeliers, a gilt ceiling, and marble columns—have always been hallmarks of the property. After the hotel was ravaged by the 1906 fire, a larger, more luxurious Italian Renaissance–style residence was opened in 1907 to attract loyal clients from among the world's rich and powerful. The hotel's checkered past includes the ill-fated 1921 bash in the suite of the silent-film comedian Fatty Arbuckle, at which a woman became ill and later died. Arbuckle endured three sensational trials for rape and murder before being acquitted, by which time his career was kaput. In 1975 Sara Jane Moore, standing among a crowd outside the hotel, attempted to shoot then-president Gerald R. Ford. As might be imagined, no plaques commemorate these events in the lobby. The ever-helpful staff will, however, direct you to tea (daily from 3 to 5) or champagne and caviar in the **Compass Rose** (☎ 415/774–0167) lounge. Elaborate Chinese screens, secluded seating alcoves, and soothing background music make this an ideal rest stop after frantic shopping or sightseeing. Reservations are not required, but walk-ins should expect a wait during December and on weekends. ⊠ *335 Powell St., at Geary St.,* ☎ *415/397–7000.*

SOUTH OF MARKET (SOMA) AND THE EMBARCADERO

Key players in San Francisco's arts scene migrated to the area south of Market Street along the waterfront and west to the Mission District in the 1990s. At the heart of the action in this area, known as SoMa, are the San Francisco Museum of Modern Art (SFMOMA) and the Center for the Arts at Yerba Buena Gardens.

SoMa's emergence as a focal point of San Francisco's cultural life was more than three decades in the making. Huge sections of this former industrial neighborhood were razed in the 1960s to make way for an ambitious multiuse redevelopment project, but squabbling over zoning and other issues delayed construction well into the 1970s. In the meantime, alternative artists and the gay leather crowd set up shop. A dozen bars frequented by the latter group existed alongside warehouses, small factories, and art studios. Although many artists moved farther southwest within SoMa or to the Mission District when urban renewal began in earnest, they still show their work at the Center for the Arts at Yerba Buena Gardens and other galleries.

SoMa was once known as South of the Slot, in reference to the cable car slot that ran up Market Street. Beginning with tents set up in 1848 by Gold Rush miners, SoMa has played a major role in housing immigrants to the city; except for a brief flowering of elegance during the mid-19th century, these streets were reserved for newcomers who couldn't yet afford to move to another neighborhood. Industry took over most of the area when the 1906 earthquake collapsed most of the homes into their quicksand bases.

Today the mood is upscale industrial. The gentrifying South Park area is where the cybercrowd from *Wired* magazine and other new media tank up on lattes and toasted baguettes. Even with the influx of money, the neighborhood still has an edge that keeps it interesting.

Numbers in the text correspond to numbers in the margin and on the Downtown San Francisco map.

A Good Walk

The **San Francisco Museum of Modern Art** ⑬ dominates a half block of 3rd Street between Howard and Mission streets. Use the crosswalk near SFMOMA's entrance to head across 3rd Street into Yerba Buena Gardens. To your right after you've walked a few steps, a sidewalk leads to the main entrance of the **Center for the Arts** ⑭. Straight ahead is the East Garden of Yerba Buena Gardens and beyond that, on the 4th Street side of the block, is the **Metreon** ⑮ entertainment, retail, and restaurant complex. A second-level walkway in the southern portion of the East Garden, above the Martin Luther King Jr. waterfall, arches over Howard Street, leading to the main (south) entrance to **Moscone Convention Center** ⑯ and the **Rooftop@Yerba Buena Gardens** ⑰ facilities. Exit the rooftop near Folsom Street, cross 4th Street, turn right, and head back toward Howard Street. In the middle of the block, across from the rooftop, is the **Ansel Adams Center for Photography** ⑱. From the Adams gallery continue north up 4th Street to Mission Street; a half block west on Mission is the **Cartoon Art Museum** ⑲. From here backtrack east on Mission (toward SFMOMA) past the monolithic San Francisco Marriott, also known as the "jukebox" Marriott because of its exterior design. East of the Marriott is dour-looking St. Patrick's Catholic Church, a Gothic Revival structure completed in 1872 and rebuilt after the 1906 earthquake and fire. Cross 3rd Street and continue a third of a block to the headquarters of the **California Historical Society** ⑳.

Backtrack a few steps on Mission to 3rd Street, where you can walk north and cross over Market Street to where 3rd, Market, Kearny, and Geary streets converge. In the traffic triangle here stands historic **Lotta's Fountain.** Walk back to the south side of Market Street from the fountain and head east (left, toward the waterfront) to the **Palace Hotel** ㉑. Enter via the Market Street entrance, checking out the Pied Piper Bar, Garden Court restaurant, and main lobby. Exit via the lobby and make a left, which will bring you back up to Market Street. Turn right and you'll see several unusual **Market Street buildings** as you walk to the waterfront. Toward the end of Market a three-tier pedestrian mall connects the five buildings of the **Embarcadero Center** ㉒ office-retail complex. Embarcadero 5, at the very end of Market Street, houses the **Hyatt Regency Hotel** ㉓. On the waterfront side of the hotel is Justin Herman Plaza.

Across the busy Embarcadero roadway from the plaza stands the port's trademark, the **Ferry Building** ㉔. Near here slithers a portion of the 5-ft-wide, 2½-mi-long glass-and-concrete Promenade Ribbon, which spans the waterfront from the base of Telegraph Hill past the Ferry Building to the South Beach area.

The ornate Audiffred Building, on the southwest corner of the Embarcadero and Mission Street, houses Boulevard restaurant on the ground floor of the 1889 structure. Head west on Mission Street along the side of Boulevard and cross Steuart Street. In the middle of the block is the entrance to the historic sections of **Rincon Center** ㉕, worth seeing for the famous murals and the old Rincon Annex Post Office. Continue south within the center to its newer portions and make a left as you exit through the doors near Chalkers Billiards. Across Steuart Street you'll see the Jewish Community Federation Building, which houses the **Jewish Museum** ㉖.

If you need a drink after all this walking, pop into the plush but welcoming bar at the Harbor Court Hotel at 165 Steuart, a few doors south of the Jewish Museum, or continue south on Steuart and then the Embarcadero to Harrison Street and the cheerily postmodern Gordon Biersch Brewing Co. restaurant and microbrewery. In the center island of the Embarcadero across from Gordon Biersch you can catch the N-Judah light-rail train, which winds around the Embarcadero and up Market Street.

TIMING
The walk above takes a good two hours, more if you visit the museums and galleries. SFMOMA merits about two hours, the Center for the Arts, the Cartoon Art Museum, and the Ansel Adams Center 45 minutes each.

Sights to See

⑱ **Ansel Adams Center for Photography.** Ansel Adams created this center in Carmel in 1967, and some of his work is always on display. Recent exhibits have included works by contemporary Native-American photographers and images of a World War II–era Japanese internment camp shot by Adams, Dorothea Lange, and Toyo Miyataki. ✉ 250 4th St., ☎ 415/495–7000. ☞ $5. ⊙ Daily 11–5, 1st Thurs. of month 11–8.

⑳ **California Historical Society.** The society, founded in 1871, administers a vast repository of Californiana—500,000 photographs, 150,000 manuscripts, thousands of books, periodicals, and paintings as well as Gold Rush paraphernalia. The airy sky-lit space has a central gallery, two adjacent galleries, the North Baker Research Library (accessible by appointment only), and a well-stocked bookstore. ✉ 678 Mission St., ☎ 415/357–1848. ☞ $2; free 1st Tues. of month. ⊙ Tues.–Sat. 11–5 (galleries close between exhibitions).

⑲ **Cartoon Art Museum.** Krazy Kat, Zippy the Pinhead, Batman, and other colorful cartoon icons greet you as you walk in the door to the Cartoon Art Museum. In addition to a 12,000-piece permanent collection, a 3,000-volume library, and a CD-ROM gallery, changing exhibits examine everything from the impact of underground comics to the output of women and African-American cartoonists. The museum store carries a wide range of books on popular and underground strips and animated movies. ⊠ *814 Mission St., 2nd Floor,* ☎ *415/227–8666.* 🖭 *$5 (pay what you wish 1st Wed. of month).* ☉ *Wed.–Fri. 11–5, Sat. 10–5, Sun. 1–5.*

⑭ Center for the Arts. The dance, music, theater, visual arts, films, and videos presented at this facility in Yerba Buena Gardens range from the community-based to the international. At the outdoor performance stage there's often music at midday between April and October. ⊠ *701 Mission St.,* ☎ *415/978–2787.* 🖭 *Galleries $5; free 1st Thurs. of month 6 PM–8 PM.* ☉ *Galleries and box office: Tues.–Sun. 11–6 (until 8 PM 1st Thurs. of month).*

㉒ Embarcadero Center. John Portman designed this five-block complex built during the 1970s and early 1980s. Shops and restaurants abound on the first three levels; there's ample office space on the floors above. Louise Nevelson's 54-ft-high black-steel sculpture, *Sky Tree,* stands guard over Building 3 and is among 20-plus artworks throughout the center. The indoor–outdoor **SkyDeck** atop Embarcadero 1 (buy tickets on the ground floor and take the mezzanine-level elevator) provides an enticing 360-degree view of the city and interactive multimedia presentations about San Francisco history and culture. Tickets ($6) to the deck, which is open daily 9:30–9, sometimes sell out days in advance for certain hours; call the hot line for information. ⊠ *Clay St. between Battery St. (Embarcadero 1) and the Embarcadero (Embarcadero 5),* ☎ *800/733–6318 for Embarcadero Center information; 888/737–5933 for SkyDeck hot line; 415/772–0591 for SkyDeck ticket booth.*

NEED A
BREAK?

On sunny days **Justin Herman Plaza** (⊠ Market St. and the Embarcadero, east of Embarcadero 5) is a nice place to enjoy a snack from one of Embarcadero Center's dozen or so take-out shops. The plaza plays host to arts-and-crafts shows, street performers, and skateboarders on weekends year-round (almost daily in summer). An ice rink is set up during winter.

㉔ Ferry Building. The beacon of the port area, erected in 1896, has a 230-ft clock tower modeled after the campanile of the cathedral in Seville, Spain. On April 18, 1906, the four great clock faces on the tower, powered by the swinging of a 14-ft pendulum, stopped at 5:17—the moment the great earthquake struck—and stayed still for 12 months. The Ferry Building contains the offices of the Port Commission and the World Trade Center, though plans surface periodically for more high-profile uses of this prime real estate. A waterfront promenade that extends from the piers on the north side of the Ferry Building south to the Bay Bridge is great for jogging, in-line skating, watching sailboats on the bay, or enjoying a picnic. Ferries behind the building sail to Sausalito, Larkspur, Tiburon, and the East Bay. ⊠ *The Embarcadero at the foot of Market St.*

㉓ Hyatt Regency Hotel. John Portman designed this hotel noted for its 17-story hanging garden. Christmas is the best time to see it, when strands of tiny white lights hang down above the lobby starting at the 12th floor. The four glass elevators facing the lobby are fun to ride, unless you suffer from vertigo. The Hyatt played a starring role in the 1970s disaster movie *The Towering Inferno.* ⊠ *Embarcadero 5,* ☎ *415/778–1234.*

OFF THE
BEATEN PATH

SS *JEREMIAH O'BRIEN* – A participant in the D-Day landing in Normandy during World War II, this Liberty Ship freighter is one of two such vessels (out of 2,500 built) still in working order. To keep the 1943 ship in sailing shape, the steam engine (which appears in the film *Titanic*) is operated dockside nine times a year on special "steaming weekends." Cruises take place twice a year, in May and October. During the summer the ship is docked at Pier 45. ⊠ *Pier 32, the Embarcadero at Brannan St.,* ☎ *415/441–3101.* ⊑ *$5.* ☉ *Daily 10–7.*

㉖ **The Jewish Museum.** The exhibits at this small museum survey Jewish art, history, and culture. The museum was open only sporadically in 1999, but its operators expect to resume regular hours in 2000. ⊠ *121 Steuart St.,* ☎ *415/543–8880.* ⊑ *$5; free 1st Mon. of month.* ☉ *Mon.–Wed. noon–6, Thurs. noon–8, Sun. 11–6. Hrs may vary.*

Lotta's Fountain. San Franciscans gather each April 18, the anniversary of the 1906 earthquake, at this quirky monument, given in 1875 to the city by entertainer Lotta Crabtree. The exploits of this Madonna prototype so enthralled San Francisco's early population of miners that they were known to shower her with gold nuggets and silver dollars after her performances. The fountain, whose peculiar and a bit clunky design she had a hand in, was her way of saying thanks to her fans. The fountain was being restored in 1999, and it should be reinstalled by 2000. Lotta Crabtree is depicted in one of the Anton Refregier murals in Rincon Center (☞ *below*). ⊠ *Traffic triangle at intersection of 3rd, Market, Kearny, and Geary Sts.*

Market Street buildings. Market Street, which bisects the city at an angle, has consistently challenged San Francisco's architects. One of the most intriguing responses to this challenge sits diagonally across Market Street from the Palace Hotel. The tower of the **Hobart Building** (⊠ 582 Market St.) combines a flat facade and oval sides and is considered one of Willis Polk's best works in the city. East on Market Street is another classic solution, Charles Havens's triangular **Flatiron Building** (⊠ 540–548 Market St.). Farther on at **388 Market** is a sleek modern variation on the flatiron theme by Skidmore, Owings, and Merrill. Holding its own against the skyscrapers that tower over this intersection is the **Donahue Monument** (⊠ Market and Battery Sts.). This homage to waterfront mechanics, which survived the 1906 earthquake (a famous photograph shows Market Street in ruins around the sculpture) was designed by Douglas Tilden, a noted California sculptor who was deaf. The plaque below the monument marks the spot as the location of the San Francisco Bay shoreline in 1848. ⊠ *Market St. between New Montgomery and Beale Sts.*

☝ ⑮ **Metreon.** Kid-play meets the 21st century at this Sony entertainment center with interactive play areas based on books like Maurice Sendak's *Where the Wild Things Are* and a three-screen, three-dimensional installation that illustrates principles discussed in architect David Macauley's *The Way Things Work*. There's also a 15-screen multiplex, an IMAX theater, retail shops, and restaurants. ⊠ *4th St. between Mission and Howard Sts.,* ☎ *800/METREON (800/638–7366).*

⑯ **Moscone Convention Center.** The site of the 1984 Democratic convention, Moscone is distinguished by a contemporary glass-and-girder lobby at street level (all convention exhibit space is underground) and a column-free interior. ⊠ *Howard St. between 3rd and 4th Sts.*

㉑ **Palace Hotel.** The city's oldest hotel, a Sheraton property, opened in 1875. Fire destroyed the original Palace following the 1906 earthquake despite the hotel's 28,000-gallon reservoir fed by four artesian wells; the current building dates from 1909. President Warren Harding died at the Palace while still in office in 1923, and the body of King Kalakaua of Hawaii spent a night chilling here after he died in San Francisco in 1891. The managers play up this ghoulish past with talk of a haunted guest room. Free guided tours (☎ 415/557–4266) of the hotel's grand interior take in the glass-dome Garden Court restaurant, mosaic-tile floors in Oriental-rug designs, and Maxfield Parrish's wall-size painting, *The Pied Piper,* the centerpiece of the Pied Piper Bar. Glass cases off the main lobby contain memorabilia of the hotel's glory days. ⊠ *2 New Montgomery St.,* ☎ *415/512–1111.* ☉ *Tours Tues. and Sat. 10:30 AM, Thurs. 2 PM.*

㉕ Rincon Center. A sheer five-story column of water resembling a mini-rainstorm stands out as the centerpiece of the indoor arcade at this mostly modern office-retail complex. The lobby of the Streamline Moderne–style former post office on the Mission Street side contains a Works Project Administration **mural by Anton Refregier.** The 27 panels depict California life from the days when Native Americans were the state's sole inhabitants through World War I. Completion of this significant work was interrupted by World War II and political infighting. The latter led to some alteration in Refregier's "radical" historical interpretations; they exuded too much populist sentiment for some of the politicians who opposed the artist. A permanent exhibit below the murals contains photographs and artifacts of life in the Rincon area in the 1800s. ⊠ *Between Steuart, Spear, Mission, and Howard Sts.*

★ ☙ **⑰ Rooftop@Yerba Buena Gardens.** Fun is the order of the day among these brightly colored concrete and corrugated-metal buildings atop Moscone Convention Center South. A historic **Looff carousel** ($1 per ride) twirls from Wednesday to Sunday between noon and 6. South of the carousel is **Zeum** (☎ 415/777–2800), a high-tech interactive arts and technology center ($7 adults, $5 kids ages 5–18) geared to children ages 8 and over. Kids can make claymation videos, work in a computer lab, and view exhibits and performances. Zeum is open from Wednesday to Friday between noon and 6 and on weekends between 11 and 5. Also part of the rooftop complex are gardens, an ice-skating rink, and a bowling alley. ⊠ *4th St. between Mission and Howard Sts.*

★ **⑬ San Francisco Museum of Modern Art (SFMOMA).** Mario Botta designed the striking SFMOMA facility, completed in early 1995, which consists of a sienna brick facade and a central tower of alternating bands of black and white stone. Inside, natural light from the tower floods the central atrium and some of the museum's galleries. A black-and-gray stone staircase leads from the atrium to four floors of galleries. Works by Matisse, Picasso, O'Keeffe, Kahlo, Pollock, and Warhol form the heart of the diverse permanent collection. The photography holdings are also strong. The adventurous programming includes traveling exhibits and multimedia installations. The café, accessible from the street, provides a comfortable, reasonably priced refuge for drinks and light meals. ⊠ *151 3rd St.,* ☎ *415/357–4000.* ▨ *$8; free 1st Tues. of each month; ½-price entry Thurs. 6–9.* ☉ *Memorial Day–Labor Day, Fri.–Tues. 10–6, Thurs. 10–9; Labor Day–Memorial Day, Fri.–Tues. 11–6, Thurs. 11–9.*

OFF THE BEATEN PATH   **SEA CHANGE** – The 10-ton, 70-ft-tall *Sea Change* sculpture, a bright red, steel work with a crown that moves gracefully in the wind, soars above South Beach Park. The artist, Mark di Suvero, came to San Francisco in 1941 as an eight-year-old immigrant from Shanghai—his father was a naval attaché for the Italian government—and later worked as a welder on the city's waterfront. A half block southwest of the sculpture is Pacific Bell Park, scheduled to open in April 2000 as the new home of the San Francisco Giants baseball team. ⊠ *The Embarcadero near Townsend St.*

★ **Yerba Buena Gardens.** The centerpiece of the SoMa redevelopment area is the two blocks that encompass the Center for the Arts, Moscone Center, Metreon, and the Rooftop@Yerba Buena Gardens (☞ *above*). A circular walkway lined with benches and sculptures surrounds the East Garden, a large patch of green amid this visually stunning complex. The waterfall memorial to Martin Luther King Jr. is the focal point of the East Garden. Powerful streams of water surge over large, jagged stone columns, mirroring the enduring force of King's words that are carved on the stone walls and on glass blocks behind the waterfall. Above the memorial are two restaurants and an overhead walkway to Moscone Convention Center's main entrance. ⊠ *Between 3rd, 4th, Mission, and Folsom Sts.* ☉ *Sunrise–10 PM.*

THE HEART OF THE BARBARY COAST

"The slums of Singapore at their foulest, the dens of Shanghai at their dirtiest, the waterfront of Port Said at its vicious worst—none of these backwaters of depravity and vice . . . achieved the depths of utter corruption that typified the 'Barbary Coast.' " So screamed the breathless dust jacket of Herbert Asbury's 1933 account of San Francisco's days as a brawling, extravagant upstart of a town in the latter half of the 19th century.

It was on Montgomery Street, in the Financial District, that Sam Brannan proclaimed the historic gold discovery that took place at Sutter's Mill on January 24, 1848. The Gold Rush brought streams of people from across America and Europe, transforming the onetime frontier town into a cosmopolitan city almost overnight. The population of San Francisco jumped from a mere 800 in 1848 to more than 25,000 in 1850, and to nearly 150,000 in 1870. Along with the prospectors came many other fortune seekers. Saloon keepers, gamblers, and prostitutes all flocked to the so-called Barbary Coast (now Jackson Square and the Financial District). Underground dance halls, casinos, bordellos, and palatial homes sprung up as the city grew into a world-class metropolis. Along with the quick money came a wave of violence. In 1852 the city suffered an average of two murders and one major fire each day. Diarists commented that hardly a day would pass without bloodshed in the city's estimated 500 bars and 1,000 gambling dens, and "houses of ill-repute" proliferated. As one Frenchman noted: "There are also some honest women in San Francisco, but not very many."

By 1917 the excesses of the Barbary Coast had fallen victim to the Red-Light Abatement Act and the ire of church leaders—the wild era was over, and the young city was forced to grow up. Since then the red-light establishments have edged upward to the Broadway strip of North Beach, and Jackson Square evolved into a sedate district of refurbished brick buildings decades ago. Only one remnant of the era remains. Below Montgomery Street between California Street and Broadway, underlying many building foundations along the former waterfront area (long since filled in), lay at least 100 ships abandoned by frantic crews and passengers caught up in gold fever.

Numbers in the text correspond to numbers in the margin and on the Downtown San Francisco map.

A Good Walk

Bronze sidewalk plaques mark the street corners along the 50-site, 3.8-mi-long Barbary Coast Trail. The trail begins at the Old Mint, at 5th and Mission streets, and runs north through downtown, Chinatown, Jackson Square, North Beach, and Fisherman's Wharf, ending at Aquatic Park. For information about the sites on the trail, pick up a brochure at the San Francisco Visitors Information Center (☞ Union Square Area, *above*).

To catch the highlights of the Barbary Coast Trail and a glimpse of a few important Financial District structures, start at Montgomery and Market streets (above the Montgomery BART/Muni station). Walk east on Market Street toward the Ferry Building to Sansome Street and turn left. At 155 Sansome Street is the Stock Exchange Tower. Around the corner (to the left) on Pine Street is the **Pacific Stock Exchange** ㉗ building. Continue north on Sansome. Turn left on California and right on Montgomery Street. Between California and Sacramento streets is the **Wells Fargo Bank History Museum** ㉘.

Two blocks north on Montgomery from the Wells Fargo museum stands the **Transamerica Pyramid** ㉙, between Clay and Washington streets. A tranquil redwood grove graces the east side of the pyramid. Walk through it, and you'll exit on Washington Street, across which you can see Hotaling Place to your left. Walk west (left) to the corner, cross Washington Street, and walk back to Hotaling. This historic alley is your entrance to **Jackson Square** ㉚, the heart of the Barbary Coast. Of particular note here are the former A. P. Hotaling whiskey distillery, on the corner of Hotaling Place, and the 1850s structures around the corner in the **700 block of Montgomery Street.** To see these buildings, walk north on Jackson from the distillery and make a left on Montgomery. Continue south on Montgomery to Washington Street, make a right, and cross Columbus Avenue. Head north (to the right) up Columbus to the **San Francisco Brewing Company** ㉛, the last standing saloon of the Barbary Coast era and a place overflowing with freshly brewed beers and history.

TIMING

Two hours should be enough time to see everything on this tour—unless you plan on trying all the homemade beers at the San Francisco Brewing Company. The Wells Fargo Museum (open only on weekdays) deserves a half hour. Evenings and weekends are peaceful times to admire the distinctive architecture. If you want to see activity, go on a weekday around lunchtime.

Sights to See

㉚ **Jackson Square.** Here was the heart of the Barbary Coast of the Gay '90s. Though most of the red-light district was destroyed in the 1906 fire, old redbrick buildings and narrow alleys recall the romance and rowdiness of the early days. Some of the city's earliest business buildings, survivors of the 1906 quake, still stand in Jackson Square, between Montgomery and Sansome streets.

By the end of World War II most of the 19th-century brick structures had fallen on hard times. But in 1951 a group of preservation-minded designers and furniture wholesale dealers selected the area for their showrooms, turning Jackson Square into the interior design center of the West. In 1972 the city officially designated the area—bordered by Columbus Avenue on the west, Broadway and Pacific Avenue on the north, Washington Street on the south, and Sansome Street on the east—San Francisco's first historic district. When property values soared, many of the fabric and furniture outlets fled to Potrero Hill. Advertising agencies, attorneys, and antiques dealers now occupy the Jackson Square area structures.

Restored 19th-century brick buildings line Hotaling Place, which connects Washington and Jackson streets. The lane is named for the head of the **A. P. Hotaling Company** whiskey distillery (⌗ 451 Jackson St., at Hotaling Pl.), which was the largest liquor repository on the West

Coast in its day. The Italianate Hotaling building reveals little of its infamous past, but a plaque on the side of the structure repeats a famous query about its surviving the quake: IF, AS THEY SAY, GOD SPANKED THE TOWN FOR BEING OVER FRISKY, WHY DID HE BURN THE CHURCHES DOWN AND SAVE HOTALING'S WHISKEY?

The **Ghirardelli Chocolate Factory** once occupied 415 Jackson Street. It was quite common for the upper floors of these buildings to be used as flats by owners and tenants; Domenico Ghirardelli moved his growing business and his family into this property in 1857. By 1894 the enterprise had become large enough to necessitate the creation of what's now **Ghirardelli Square** (☞ The Northern Waterfront, *below*), near Fisherman's Wharf.

With the gentrification, it takes a bit of conjuring to evoke the Barbary Coast days when viewing the Gold Rush–era buildings in the **700 block of Montgomery Street.** But much happened here. Writer Bret Harte wrote his novel *The Luck of Roaring Camp* at Number 730. He toiled as a typesetter for the spunky *Golden Era* newspaper, which occupied Number 732 (now part of the building at Number 744). The late ambulance-chaser extraordinaire, lawyer Melvin Belli, had offices in Numbers 722–728. The lawyer's headquarters were in the former Melodeon Theater at Number 722, where Lotta Crabtree—she of Lotta's Fountain (☞ South of Market and the Embarcadero, *above*) fame—performed. ☒ *Jackson Square district: Between Broadway and Washington and Montgomery and Sansome Sts.*

㉗ Pacific Stock Exchange. Ralph Stackpole's monumental 1930 granite sculptural groups, *Earth's Fruitfulness* and *Man's Inventive Genius*, flank this imposing structure, which dates from 1915. The Stock Exchange Tower, around the corner at 155 Sansome Street, is a 1930 modern classic by architects Miller and Pfleuger, with an Art Deco gold ceiling and a black marble wall entry. ☒ *301 Pine St. (tower around corner at 155 Sansome St.).*

㉛ San Francisco Brewing Company. Built in 1907, this pub looks like a museum piece from the Barbary Coast days. An old upright piano sits in the corner under the original stained-glass windows. Take a seat at the mahogany bar and look down at the white-tile spittoon. In an adjacent room look for the handmade copper brewing kettle used to produce a dozen beers—with names like Pony Express—by means of old-fashioned gravity-flow methods. ☒ *155 Columbus Ave., ☎ 415/ 434–3344.*

㉙ Transamerica Pyramid. The city's most photographed high-rise is the 853-ft Transamerica Pyramid. Designed by William Pereira and Associates in 1972, the initially controversial icon has become more acceptable to most locals over time. A fragrant redwood grove along the east side of the building, replete with benches and a cheerful fountain, is a placid patch in which to unwind. ☒ *600 Montgomery St.*

㉘ Wells Fargo Bank History Museum. There were no formal banks in San Francisco during the early years of the Gold Rush, and miners often entrusted their gold dust to saloon keepers. In 1852 Wells Fargo opened its first bank in the city, and the company established banking offices in the mother-lode camps, using stagecoaches and pony express riders to service the burgeoning state. (California's population boomed from 15,000 to 200,000 between 1848 and 1852.) The museum displays samples of nuggets and gold dust from mines, a mural-size map of the Mother Lode, original art by western artists Charles M. Russell and Maynard Dixon, mementos of the poet bandit Black Bart ("Po8," as he signed his poems), and an old telegraph machine on which you can practice sending codes. The showpiece is the red Concord stagecoach, the likes of which carried passengers from St. Joseph, Missouri, to San Francisco in three weeks during the 1850s. ⊠ *420 Montgomery St.,* ☎ *415/ 396–2619.* 🖷 *Free.* ⏱ *Weekdays 9–5.*

OFF THE
BEATEN PATH

BANK OF AMERICA BUILDING – This 52-story polished red granite-and-marble building takes up nearly an entire downtown block. A massive, abstract black-granite sculpture designed by the Japanese artist Masayuki commands the corner of the complex at Kearny and California streets. The work has been dubbed the "Banker's Heart" by local wags. On top of the building is the **Carnelian Room** (☎ 415/433–7500), a chic cocktail lounge and restaurant—open daily from 3 to 11 and for Sunday brunch from 10 to 1:30—with a view of the city and the bay. This is a perfect spot for a sunset drink; until mid-afternoon the room is the exclusive Banker's Club, open only to members or by invitation. ⊠ *Between California, Pine, Montgomery, and Kearny Sts.*

CHINATOWN

Prepare to have your senses assaulted in Chinatown. Pungent smells waft out of restaurants, fish markets, and produce stands. Good-luck banners of crimson and gold hang beside dragon-entwined lampposts, pagoda roofs, and street signs with Chinese calligraphy. Honking cars chime in with shoppers bargaining loudly in Cantonese or Mandarin. Add to this the visual assault of millions of Chinese-theme goods spilling out of the numerous shops lining Grant Avenue, and you get an idea of what Chinatown is all about.

Bordered roughly by Bush, Kearny, and Powell streets and Broadway, Chinatown is home to one of the largest Chinese communities outside Asia. The area is tightly packed, mostly because housing discrimination in the past kept residents from moving outside Chinatown. There was nowhere to go but up and down—thus the many basement establishments in Chinatown. The two main drags of Chinatown are Grant Avenue, jammed with kitschy tourist shops, and Stockton Street, where the locals do their business.

Many of Chinatown's earliest residents came from southern China, and they brought their cuisine with them. Nowadays Cantonese cooking exists alongside spicier Szechuan, Hunan, and Mandarin specialties. In the windows of markets on Stockton Street and Grant Avenue you can see roast ducks hanging, fish and shellfish swimming in tanks, and strips of Chinese-style barbecued pork shining in pink glaze.

Merely strolling through Chinatown and its many bazaars, restaurants, and curio shops yields endless pleasures, but you'll have a better chance of experiencing an authentic bit of one of the world's oldest cultures by venturing off the beaten track. You needn't be shy about stepping into a temple or an herb shop: Chinatown has been a tourist stop for more than 100 years, and most of its residents welcome guests.

You may find the noisy stretches of Grant Avenue and Stockton Street difficult to navigate, especially by car. Park outside the area, as a spot here is extremely hard to find and traffic is impossible.

Numbers in the text correspond to numbers in the margin and on the Downtown San Francisco map.

A Good Walk

The Bus 30-Stockton, which travels north and south on Stockton Street, will get you from downtown or Fisherman's Wharf to Chinatown. While wandering through Chinatown's streets and alleys, don't forget to look up. Above street level, many older structures—mostly brick buildings that replaced rickety wooden ones destroyed during the 1906 earthquake—have ornate balconies and cornices. The architecture in the 900 block of Grant Avenue (at Washington Street) and Waverly Place (north of and parallel to Grant Avenue between Sacramento and Washington streets) is particularly noteworthy, though some locals decry it and similar examples as inauthentic adornment meant to make their neighborhood seem "more Chinese."

Visitors usually enter Chinatown through the green-tile **Chinatown Gate** ㉜, at Bush Street and Grant Avenue. Shops selling souvenirs, jewelry, and home furnishings line Grant north past the gate. Pop into Dragon House (☞ Antique Furniture and Accessories *in* Chapter 6), at Number 455. A veritable museum, the store sells centuries-old antiques rather than six-month-old goods made in Taiwan. **Old St. Mary's Cathedral** ㉝ towers over the corner of Grant Avenue and California Street. Continue on Grant to Clay Street and turn right. A half block down on your left is **Portsmouth Square** ㉞. A walkway on the eastern edge of the park leads over Kearny Street to the third floor of the Holiday Inn, where you'll find the **Chinese Culture Center** ㉟.

Backtrack on the walkway to Portsmouth Square and head west up Washington Street a half block to the **Old Chinese Telephone Exchange** ㊱ (now the Bank of Canton), and then continue west on Washington Street. Cross Grant Avenue and look for Waverly Place a half block up on the left. One of the best examples of this alley's traditional architecture is the **Tin How Temple** ㊲. After visiting Waverly Place and Tin How, walk back to Washington Street. Several herb shops do business in this area. Two worth checking out are Superior Trading Company at Number 837 and the Great China Herb Co. at Number 857. These Chinese pharmacies carry everything from tree roots and bark to over-the-counter treatments for impotence.

Across Washington Street from Superior is Ross Alley. Head north on Ross toward Jackson Street, stopping along the way to watch the bakers at the **Golden Gate Fortune Cookies Co.** ㊳. Turn right on Jackson. When you get to Grant Avenue, don't cross it. If you'd like to sample some aromatic teas, turn right on Grant and visit the Ten Ren Tea Co., a few doors away at Number 949. For some of Chinatown's best pastries, turn left and stop by Number 1029, the Golden Gate Bakery, where the moon cakes are delicious.

The markets in the 1100 block of Grant Avenue carry intriguing delicacies. You can often spot braised pig noses or ears in the window of Four Sea Supermarket, on the northeast corner of Grant and Pacific avenues.

Head west (up the hill) on Pacific Avenue to Stockton Street, turn left, and walk south past Stockton Street's markets. At Clay Street make a right and head halfway up the hill to the **Chinatown YWCA** ㊴. Return to Stockton Street and make a right; a few doors down is the **Kong Chow Temple** ㊵, and next door is the elaborate **Chinese Six Companies** building.

TIMING

Allow at least two hours to see Chinatown. Brief stops will suffice at the cultural center and temples. The restaurants don't invite lingering, so if you're lunching, a half hour should be adequate unless you choose one of the higher-end places.

Sights to See

32 Chinatown Gate. Stone lions flank the base of this pagoda-top gate, the official entrance to Chinatown and a symbolic and literal transition from the generic downtown atmosphere to what sometimes seems like another country altogether. The male lion's right front paw rests playfully on a ball; the female's left front paw tickles a cub lying on its back. The lions and the glazed clay dragons atop the largest of the gate's three pagodas symbolize, among other things, wealth and prosperity. The fish whose mouths wrap tightly around the crest of this pagoda symbolize prosperity. The four Chinese characters immediately beneath the pagoda represent the philosophy of Sun Yat-sen (1866–1925), the leader who unified China in the early 20th century. Sun Yat-sen, who lived in exile in San Francisco for a few years, promoted the notion of friendship and peace among all nations based on equality, justice, and goodwill. The vertical characters under the left pagoda read "peace" and "trust," the ones under the right pagoda read "respect" and "love." ⊠ *Bush St. and Grant Ave.*

39 Chinatown YWCA. Julia Morgan, the architect known for the famous Hearst Castle and the first woman in California to be licensed as an architect, designed this handsome redbrick building, which originally served as a meeting place and residence for Chinese women in need of social services. The YWCA building will be closed for several years for seismic retrofitting and other structural repairs. ⊠ *965 Clay St.*

35 Chinese Culture Center. The San Francisco Redevelopment Commission agreed to let Holiday Inn build in Chinatown if the chain provided room for a Chinese culture center. Inside the center are the works of Chinese and Chinese-American artists as well as traveling exhibits relating to Chinese culture. Walking tours ($15; make reservations one week ahead) of historic points in Chinatown take place on most days at 10:30 AM and on Saturday at 2 PM. ⊠ *Holiday Inn, 750 Kearny St., 3rd Floor,* ☎ *415/986–1822.* ⌸ *Free.* ☉ *Tues.–Sun. 10–4.*

**OFF THE
BEATEN PATH**

CHINESE HISTORICAL SOCIETY – Chinatown is spilling into North Beach these days, so it's fitting that this small museum documenting the lives of Chinese-Americans has joined the march. One interesting focus of the collection of photographs and other artifacts is the disparity between the lives early Chinese immigrants led and the perceptions non-Chinese Americans had about those lives. ⊠ *644 Broadway, Suite 402 (take elevator in restaurant lobby),* ☎ *415/391–1188.* ⌸ *Free.* ☉ *Mon. 1–4, Tues.–Fri. 10:30–4, Sat. 10–2.*

Chinese Six Companies. Several fine examples of Chinese architecture can be spotted along Stockton Street, but this is the most noteworthy. With its curved roof tiles and elaborate cornices, the imposing structure's oversize pagoda cheerfully calls attention to itself. The business leaders who ran the six companies dominated Chinatown's political and economic life for decades. ⊠ *843 Stockton St.*

38 Golden Gate Fortune Cookies Co. The workers at this small factory sit at circular motorized griddles. A dollop of batter drops onto a tiny metal plate, which rotates into an oven. A few moments later out comes a cookie that's pliable and ready for folding. It's easy to peek in for a moment here. A bagful of cookies (with mildly racy "adult" fortunes or more benign ones) costs $2 or $3. ⊠ *56 Ross Alley (north of and parallel to Grant St. between Washington and Jackson Sts.),* ☎ *415/781–3956.* ☉ *Daily 10–7.*

40 Kong Chow Temple. The god to whom the members of this temple pray represents honesty and trust. You'll often see his image in Chinese stores and restaurants because he's thought to bring good luck in business. Chinese immigrants established the temple in 1851; its congregation moved to this new building in 1977. Take the elevator up to the fourth floor where incense fills the air. Your party can show its respect by placing a dollar or two in the donation box. Amid the statuary, flowers, orange offerings, and richly colored altars (red wards off evil spirits and signifies virility, green symbolizes longevity, and gold majesty) are a couple of plaques announcing that MRS. HARRY S. TRUMAN CAME TO THIS TEMPLE IN JUNE 1948 FOR A PREDICTION ON THE OUTCOME OF THE ELECTION. . . . THIS FORTUNE CAME TRUE. The temple's balcony has a good view of Chinatown. ⊠ *855 Stockton St.,* ☎ *415/434–2513.* 🎫 *Free.* 🕐 *Mon.–Sat. 9–4.*

㊱ Old Chinese Telephone Exchange. Most of Chinatown burned down after the 1906 earthquake, and this was the first building to set the style for the new Chinatown. The intricate three-tier pagoda was built in 1909. The exchange's operators were renowned for their prodigious memories, about which the San Francisco Chamber of Commerce boasted in 1914: "These girls respond all day with hardly a mistake to calls that are given (in English or one of five Chinese dialects) by the name of the subscriber instead of by his number—a mental feat that would be practically impossible to most high-schooled American misses." ⊠ *Bank of Canton, 743 Washington St.*

NEED A BREAK?   Dim sum is the Chinese version of a smorgasbord. In most dim sum restaurants women navigating stacked food-service carts patrol the premises. Customers choose dishes and the cost is stamped on the bill. Dim sum is served at the garishly fancy **New Asia** (⊠ 772 Pacific Ave., ☎ 415/391–6666) from 9 AM to 3 PM (no credit cards taken for dim sum). More down-to-earth and inexpensive, **Kay Cheung Seafood Restaurant** (⊠ 615 Jackson St., ☎ 415/989–6838) serves dim sum from 9 to 2:30 (some credit cards taken). It's best to arrive at both restaurants before 1 PM for the best selection.

㉝ Old St. Mary's Cathedral. This building, whose structure includes granite quarried in China, was dedicated in 1854 and served as the city's Catholic cathedral until 1891. The cathedral hosts Noontime Concert, a notable chamber-music series on Tuesday and Thursday at 12:30; each October the theme is music by Russian emigrés. The church needs to undergo seismic retrofitting or be demolished. When sufficient funds are raised, it will close for a few years. Across California Street in **St. Mary's Park** the late local sculptor Beniamino (Benny) Bufano's 12-ft-tall stainless-steel and rose-color granite statue of Sun Yat-sen towers over the site of the Chinese leader's favorite reading spot during his years in San Francisco. ⊠ *Grant Ave. and California St.,* ☎ *415/288–3840 (concert line).* 🎫 *$3 suggested donation for concert series.*

㉞ Portsmouth Square. Captain John B. Montgomery raised the American flag here in 1846, claiming the area from Mexico. The square—a former potato patch—was the plaza for Yerba Buena, the Mexican settlement that was renamed San Francisco. Robert Louis Stevenson, the author of *Treasure Island,* lived on the edge of Chinatown in the late 19th century and often visited this site, chatting up the sailors who hung out here. Some of the information he gleaned about life at sea found its way into his fiction. Bruce Porter designed the bronze galleon that sits on top of a 9-ft granite shaft in the northwestern corner of the square in the writer's memory. With its pagoda-shape structures, Portsmouth Square is a favorite spot for morning tai chi. By noon dozens of men huddle around Chinese chess tables, engaged in not-always-legal competition. Undercover police occasionally rush in to break things up, but this ritual, like tai chi, is an established way of life. Children scamper about two playgrounds within the square, which has rest room facilities. ⊠ *Bordered by Walter Lum Pl. and Kearny, Washington, and Clay Sts.*

★ ㊲ **Tin How Temple.** Day Ju, one of the first three Chinese to arrive in San Francisco, dedicated this temple to the Queen of the Heavens and the Goddess of the Seven Seas in 1852. Climb three flights of stairs—on the second floor is a mah-jongg parlor whose patrons hope the spirits above will favor them. In the temple's entryway, elderly ladies can often be seen preparing "money" to be burned as offerings to various Buddhist gods or as funds for ancestors to use in the afterlife. Red-and-gold lanterns adorn the ceiling—the larger the lamp the larger its donor's contribution to the temple—and the smell of incense is usually thick. Oranges and other offerings rest on altars to various gods. The gold-leaf wood carving suspended from the ceiling depicts the north and east sides of the sea, which Tin How (Tien Hau or Tien Hou in Cantonese) and other gods protect. A statue of Tin How sits in the middle of the back of the temple, flanked on one side by a red lesser god and the right by a green one. Photography is not permitted, and visitors are asked not to step onto the balcony. ⊠ *125 Waverly Pl., ☎ no phone. ⊡ Free (donations accepted). ⊙ Daily 10–4.*

NORTH BEACH AND TELEGRAPH HILL

Novelist and resident Herbert Gold calls North Beach "the longest-running, most glorious American bohemian operetta outside Greenwich Village." Indeed, to anyone who's spent some time in its eccentric old bars and cafés or wandered the neighborhood, North Beach evokes everything from the Barbary Coast days to the no-less-sedate beatnik era. Italian bakeries appear frozen in time, homages to Jack Kerouac and Allen Ginsberg pop up everywhere, and the modern equivalent of the Barbary Coast's "houses of ill-repute," strip joints, do business on Broadway.

More than 125,000 Italian-American residents once lived in North Beach, but now only about 2,000, most of them elderly, do. Much of the neighborhood is Chinese now. But walk down narrow Romolo Place (off Broadway east of Columbus) or Genoa Place (off Union west of Kearny) or Medau Place (off Filbert west of Grant) and you can feel the immigrant Italian roots of this neighborhood. North Beach is still the number one place for cappuccino and biscotti, after which you can pop into that icon of the beat era, the City Lights Bookstore (☞ *below*).

Like Chinatown, this is a neighborhood where eating is unavoidable. Several Italian restaurants specialize in family-style full-course meals at reasonable prices; other eateries serve pricey nuovo-Italian dishes. A local delicacy is focaccia—spongy, pizzalike bread slathered with olive oil and chives or tomato sauce—sold fresh from the oven at places like **Danilo Bakery** (⊠ 516 Green St., near Grant Ave., ☎ 415/989–1806). Eaten warm or cold, focaccia is the perfect walking food. Many other aromas fill the air: coffee beans, deli meats and cheeses, Italian pastries, and—always—the pungent smell of garlic.

Seafood is usually associated with nearby Fisherman's Wharf, but fishing was North Beach's first industry. The neighborhood truly was a beach at the time of the Gold Rush—the bay extended into the hollow between Telegraph and Russian hills. Among the first immigrants to Yerba Buena during the early 1840s were young men from the northern provinces of Italy. The Genoese started the still-active fishing industry in the newly renamed boomtown of San Francisco, as well as a much-needed produce business. Later, Sicilians emerged as leaders of the fishing fleets and eventually as proprietors of the seafood restaurants lining Fisherman's Wharf. Meanwhile, their Genoese cousins established banking and manufacturing empires. Less than a square mile, North Beach is the most densely populated district in the city—and among the most cosmopolitan.

Numbers in the text correspond to numbers in the margin and on the Downtown San Francisco map.

A Good Walk

Stand on the northwest corner of Broadway and Columbus Avenue to get your bearings. To the southwest is Chinatown—the Chinatown portion of Grant Avenue intersects Broadway a few steps west of Columbus before changing character completely after it crosses Broadway and Columbus in North Beach. The Financial District skyscrapers loom overhead to the south of the intersection of Columbus and Broadway, though one of the earliest and shortest examples, the triangular Sentinel Building, where Kearny Street and Columbus Avenue meet at an angle, grabs the eye with its unusual shape and mellow green patina. (The building's owner, filmmaker Francis Ford Coppola, has the penthouse office.)

East across Columbus is the Condor, where in 1964 local celeb Carol Doda became the nation's first dancer at a nightclub to go topless. (These days Doda runs a lingerie shop at 1850 Union Street and the Condor is a sports bar.) Around the same time, North Beach was a nexus of comedy. Bill Cosby, Phyllis Diller, Dick Gregory, the Smothers Brothers, and other talents cut their teeth at clubs like the hungry i and the Purple Onion.

To the north of Broadway and Columbus is the heart of Italian North Beach. A few doors north of the Condor, Grant Avenue heads to the northeast, toward Telegraph Hill. Columbus shoots north past Washington Square to Fisherman's Wharf.

Walk south on Broadway across Columbus to **City Lights Bookstore** ㊸, where you can pick up a book by one of the beat writers or just soak up the ambience. Three of the most atmospheric bars in San Francisco are near here: Vesuvio, across Jack Kerouac Alley from City Lights; Specs, across Columbus from City Lights at 12 William Saroyan Place; and, a few steps south of Specs' at 242 Columbus, Tosca, where opera tunes stock the jukebox. For joltingly caffeinated espresso drinks, also to the tune of opera, head north on Columbus a block and a half on the same side of the avenue as City Lights to Caffè Puccini, at Number 411. By now, you've been in North Beach for a couple of hours and hardly gone anywhere. There are sights to see, but relaxing and enjoying life is what North Beach is all about.

Head up the east side of Columbus Avenue (the same side as the Condor) past Grant Avenue. On the northeast corner of Columbus and Vallejo Street is the Victorian-era **St. Francis of Assisi Church** ㊷. Go east on Vallejo Street to Grant Avenue and make another left. Check out the the eclectic shops and old-time bars and cafés between Vallejo and Union streets.

Turn left at Union Street and head west to **Washington Square** ㊸, an oasis of green amid the tightly packed streets of North Beach. At Union and Stockton streets is San Francisco's oldest Italian restaurant, Fior d'Italia, which opened in 1886. After the 1906 earthquake and fire, the restaurant operated out of a tent until its new quarters were ready. On the north side stands the double-turreted **Saints Peter and Paul Catholic Church** ㊹.

After getting your fill of North Beach, head up **Telegraph Hill** ㊺ from Washington Square. Atop the hill is **Coit Tower** ㊻. People in poor health will not want to attempt the walk up the steep hill; Coit Tower can be reached by car (though parking is very tight) or public transportation—board Muni Bus 39-Coit at Washington Square. To walk, head east up Filbert Street at the park; turn left at Grant Avenue and go one block north, then right at Greenwich Street and ascend the steps on your right. Cross the street at the top of the first set of stairs and continue up the curving stone steps to Coit Tower.

On the other side of Coit Tower, the Greenwich steps take you down the east side of Telegraph Hill, with stunning views of the bay en route. At Montgomery Street, perched on the side of the hill, is **Julius' Castle** ㊼ restaurant. A block to the right at **1360 Montgomery Street,** where the Filbert steps intersect, is a brilliant Art Deco apartment building. Descend the Filbert steps amid roses, fuchsias, irises, and trumpet flowers—courtesy of Grace Marchant, who labored for nearly 30 years to transform a dump into one of San Francisco's hidden treasures in the 1900s. At the foot of the hill is the serene **Levi Strauss headquarters** ㊽.

TIMING

It takes a little more than an hour to walk the tour, but the point in both North Beach and Telegraph Hill is to linger—set aside at least a few hours.

Sights to See

★ ㊶ **City Lights Bookstore.** The hangout of beat-era writers—Allen Ginsberg and Lawrence Ferlinghetti among them—remains a vital part of San Francisco's literary scene. ✉ *261 Columbus Ave.,* ☎ *415/362–8193.*

★ ㊻ **Coit Tower.** Among San Francisco's most distinctive skyline sights, the 210-ft-tall Coit Tower stands as a monument to the city's volunteer firefighters. During the early days of the Gold Rush, Lillie Hitchcock Coit (known as Miss Lil) was said to have deserted a wedding party and chased down the street after her favorite engine, Knickerbocker Number 5, while clad in her bridesmaid finery. She was soon made an honorary member of the Knickerbocker Company, and after that always signed her name as "Lillie Coit 5" in honor of her favorite fire engine. Lillie died in 1929 at the age of 86, leaving the city $125,000 to "expend in an appropriate manner . . . to the beauty of San Francisco."

Inside the tower, 19 Depression-era murals depict economic and political life in California. The government commissioned the murals, and the 25 artists who painted them were each paid $38 a week. Some were fresh from art school; others had found no market for art in the early 1930s. The radical Mexican painter Diego Rivera inspired the murals' socialist-realist style, with its biting cultural commentary, particularly about the exploitation of workers. At the time the murals were painted, clashes between management and labor along the waterfront and elsewhere in San Francisco were widespread.

Ride the elevator to the top of the tower to enjoy the view of the San Francisco–Oakland Bay Bridge and the Golden Gate Bridge; due north is famous Alcatraz Island. Artists are often at work in Pioneer Park, at the foot of the tower. For a modest price you can often pick up a small painting of the view you're witnessing. *Discoverer of America,* the impressive bronze statue of Christopher Columbus, was a gift from the local Italian community in 1957. ✉ *Telegraph Hill Blvd., at Greenwich St. or Lombard St.,* ☎ *415/362–0808.* 🎫 *$3.75.* ☉ *Daily 10–6.*

Grant Avenue. Originally called Calle de la Fundación, Grant Avenue is the oldest street in the city. Here you'll find dusty bars (the Saloon, Grant & Green Blues Club), odd curio shops, unusual import stores, atmospheric cafés, and authentic Italian delis. A June street fair celebrates the area's Italian culture. ⊠ *Between Columbus Ave. and Filbert St.*

NEED A BREAK?

Cafés are a way of life in North Beach. A must-visit spot is **Caffe Trieste** (⊠ 601 Vallejo St., at Grant Ave., ☎ 415/392–6739), where the Giotta family presents a weekly musical (patrons are encouraged to participate) every Saturday at 2 PM; arrive by 1 or 1:15 to secure seats. The program ranges from Italian pop and folk music to operas. A neighborhood favorite since 1956, this was once the headquarters of the area's beat poets, artists, and writers. If you'd rather be surrounded by the sights and smells of Sicily, drop in for a glass of red wine at **Caffe Sport** (⊠ 574 Green St., near Columbus Ave., ☎ 415/981–1251), where bright artifacts from the old country decorate the walls.

㊼ Julius' Castle. Every bit as romantic as its name implies, this contemporary Italian restaurant commands a regal view of the bay from its perch high up Telegraph Hill. An official historic landmark, whose founder, Julius Roz, had his craftsmen use materials left over from the 1915 Panama–Pacific International Exposition, the restaurant has a dark-paneled Victorian interior that befits the elegant setting. Ask for a table on the upper floor's outside terrace, where the views are especially dazzling. ⊠ *1541 Montgomery St.,* ☎ *415/392–2222.* ⊘ *Daily 5 PM–10 PM.*

㊽ Levi Strauss headquarters. This carefully landscaped complex appears so collegiate it is affectionately known as LSU (Levi Strauss University). Grassy knolls complement the redbrick buildings, providing a perfect environment for brown-bag and picnic lunches. At **Fuel Juice Bar** (⊠ 1255 Battery St., ☎ 415/362–7622), inside the complex, bins brimming with fresh fruits and veggies hint at the flavors you'll taste in the café's fresh juices, smoothies, and sandwiches. ⊠ *Levi's Plaza, 1155 Battery St.*

㊷ St. Francis of Assisi Church. This 1860 building stands on the site of the frame parish church that served the Catholic community during the Gold Rush. Its solid terra-cotta facade complements the many brightly colored restaurants and cafés nearby. ⊠ *610 Vallejo St.,* ☎ *415/983–0405.* ⊘ *Daily 11–5.*

㊹ Saints Peter and Paul Catholic Church. Camera-toting tourists focus their lenses on the Romanesque splendor of what's often called the Italian Cathedral. Completed in 1924, the cathedral has Disney-esque stone-white towers that are local landmarks. On the first Sunday of October a mass followed by a parade to Fisherman's Wharf celebrates the Blessing of the Fleet. Another popular event is the Columbus Day pageant in North Beach. ⊠ *666 Filbert St., at Washington Square.*

㊺ Telegraph Hill. Telegraph Hill got its name from one of its earliest functions—in 1853 it became the location of the first Morse Code Signal Station. Hill residents command some of the best views in the city, as well as the most difficult ascents to their aeries (the flower-lined steps flanking the hill make the climb more than tolerable for visitors, though). The Hill rises from the east end of Lombard Street to a height of 284 ft and is capped by Coit Tower (☞ *above*). ⊠ *Between Lombard, Filbert, Kearny, and Sansome Sts.*

OFF THE
BEATEN PATH

1360 MONTGOMERY STREET – In the 1947 film *Dark Passage*, Humphrey Bogart plays an escaped prisoner from San Quentin convicted of killing his wife. His real-life wife, Lauren Bacall, befriends him and lets him hole up in her apartment, inside this fantastic Art Deco building. From the street you can view the etched-glass gazelles and palms counterpointing a silvered fresco of a heroic bridge worker. ⊠ *Montgomery St., between Union and Filbert Sts. (near the top of the Filbert Steps).*

43 **Washington Square.** Once the daytime social heart of Little Italy, this grassy patch has changed character numerous times over the years. The beats hung out in the 1950s, hippies camped out (sometimes literally) in the 1960s and early 1970s, and nowadays you're just as likely to see kids from Southeast Asia tossing a Frisbee as Italian men or women chatting about their children and the old country. In the morning elderly Asians perform the motions of tai chi, but by mid-morning groups of conservatively dressed Italian men in their 70s and 80s begin to arrive. Choose your line of sight carefully, and you might swear you've drifted back to the early 20th century. Lillie Hitchcock Coit, in another of her shows of affection for San Francisco's firefighters, donated the statue of two firemen with a child they've rescued. ⊠ *Bordered by Columbus Ave. and Stockton, Filbert, and Union Sts.*

NOB HILL AND RUSSIAN HILL

Once called the Hill of Golden Promise, this area was officially dubbed Nob Hill during the 1870s when "the Big Four"—Charles Crocker, Leland Stanford, Mark Hopkins, and Collis Huntington, who were involved in the construction of the transcontinental railroad—built their hilltop estates. The lingo is thick from this era: Those on the hilltop were referred to as "nabobs" (originally meaning a provincial governor from India) and "swells," and the hill itself was called Snob Hill, a term that survives to this day. By 1882 so many estates had sprung up on Nob Hill that Robert Louis Stevenson called it "the hill of palaces." But the 1906 earthquake and fire destroyed all the palatial mansions, except for portions of the Flood brownstone. Though Nob Hill lacks the quirky flavor of other San Francisco neighborhoods, it exudes history.

Just nine blocks or so from downtown and a few blocks north of Nob Hill, Russian Hill has long been home to old San Francisco families, who were joined during the 1890s by bohemian artists and writers that included Charles Norris, George Sterling, and Maynard Dixon. Several stories explain the origin of Russian Hill's name, though none is known to be true. One legend has it that during San Francisco's early days, the steep hill (294 ft) was the site of a cemetery for unknown Russians; in another version Russian farmers raised vegetables here for Farallon Islands seal hunters; and a third attributes the name to a Russian sailor of prodigious drinking habits who drowned when he fell into a well on the hill. An astounding array of housing covers the hill: simple studios, spiffy pieds-à-terre, Victorian flats, Edwardian cottages, and boxlike condos. The bay views here are some of the city's best.

Numbers in the text correspond to numbers in the margin and on the Downtown San Francisco map.

A Good Walk

The Van Ness–California cable car line runs up to Nob Hill. If you're not up for a strenuous walk, this is the best way to get here from the Financial District or the Embarcadero (from downtown take any of the Powell Street cars). Begin on California and Taylor streets at the

Masonic Auditorium ㊾. Across California Street is the majestic **Grace Cathedral** ㊿. From the cathedral walk east (toward Mason Street and downtown) on California Street to the **Pacific Union Club** ㉑. Across Mason Street from the Pacific Union Club is the lush **Fairmont Hotel** ㉒. Directly across California Street from the Fairmont is the **Mark Hopkins Inter-Continental Hotel** ㉓, famed for panoramic views from its Top of the Mark lounge. Head east down the hill one block to Powell Street to the **Renaissance Stanford Court Hotel.** From here walk north on Powell Street three blocks to Washington Street and then west one block to Mason Street to the **Cable Car Museum** ㉔.

From the Cable Car Museum continue four blocks north on Mason Street to Vallejo Street, turn west, and start climbing the steps that lead to the multilevel **Ina Coolbrith Park** ㉕. At the top, you can see the **Vallejo steps area** across Taylor Street from the park. The Flag House, one of several brown-shingle prequake buildings in this area, is to your left at Taylor Street. Cross Taylor Street and ascend the Vallejo steps; the view east takes in downtown and the Bay Bridge. Continue west from the top of the Vallejo steps to two secluded Russian Hill alleys. Down and to your left is Florence Place, an enclave of 1920s stucco homes, and down a bit farther on your right is Russian Hill Place, with a row of 1915 Mediterranean town houses designed by Willis Polk. After reemerging on Vallejo Street from the alleys, walk north (right) on Jones Street one short block to Green Street. Head west (left) halfway down the block to the octagonal **Feusier House** ㉖. Backtrack to Jones Street, and head north to **Macondray Lane** ㉗. Walk west (to the left) on Macondray and follow it to Leavenworth Street. Head north (to the right) on Leavenworth to the bottom of **Lombard Street** ㉘, the "crookedest street in the world." Continue north one block on Leavenworth and then east on Chestnut Street to the **San Francisco Art Institute** ㉙.

TIMING

The tour above covers a lot of ground, much of it steep. If you're in reasonably good shape you can complete this walk in 3½ to 4 hours, including 30-minute stops at Grace Cathedral and the Cable Car Museum. Add time for gazing at the bay from Ina Coolbrith Park or enjoying tea or a cocktail at one of Nob Hill's grand hotels.

Sights to See

★ ㉔ **Cable Car Museum.** San Francisco once had more than a dozen cable car barns and powerhouses. The only survivor, this 1907 redbrick structure, an engaging stopover between Russian Hill and Nob Hill, contains photographs, old cable cars, signposts, ticketing machines, and other memorabilia dating from 1873. The massive powerhouse wheels that move the entire cable car system steal the show. The design is so simple it seems almost unreal. You can also go downstairs to the sheave room and check out the innards of the system. A 15-minute video describes how it all works—cables must be replaced every three to six months—or you can opt to read the detailed placards. The gift shop sells cable car paraphernalia. ⊠ *1201 Mason St., at Washington St.,* ☎ *415/474–1887.* ▨ *Free.* ☉ *Oct.–Mar., daily 10–5; Apr.–Sept., daily 10–6.*

㉒ **Fairmont Hotel.** The Fairmont's dazzling opening was delayed a year by the 1906 quake, but since then the marble palace has hosted presidents, royalty, movie stars (Valentino, Dietrich), and local nabobs. Things have changed since its early days, however: On the eve of World War I you could get a room for as low as $2.50 per night, meals included. Nowadays, prices go as high as $8,000, which buys a night in the eight-room, Persian art–filled penthouse suite that was showcased regularly in the TV series *Hotel* (the exterior and some of the interiors of the

Fairmont also appeared in the show). On Friday and Saturday from 3 to 6 and on Sunday from 1 to 6, afternoon tea is served in the plush lobby, all done up Gold Rush style with flamboyant rose-floral carpeting, lush red-velvet chairs, gold faux-marble columns, and gilt ceilings. Don't miss an evening cocktail (the ambience demands you order a mai tai) in the kitschy **Tonga Room,** complete with tiki huts, a sporadic tropical rainstorm, and a floating (literally) bandstand.

Across from the Fairmont, **Brocklebank Apartments,** on the northeast corner of Sacramento and Mason streets and viewable only from a distance, is also a media star. In 1958 it was a major location in Alfred Hitchcock's *Vertigo* and in the 1990s popped up in the miniseries *Tales of the City,* Armistead Maupin's homage to San Francisco. ✉ *950 Mason St.,* ☎ *415/772–5000.*

(56) **Feusier House.** Octagonal houses were once thought to make the best use of space and enhance the physical and mental well-being of their occupants. A brief mid-19th-century craze inspired the construction of several in San Francisco. Only the Feusier House, built in 1857 and now a private residence surrounded by lush gardens, and the Octagon House (☞ Pacific Heights, *below*), remain standing. Across from the Feusier House is the **1907 Firehouse** (✉ 1088 Green St.). Local art patron Mrs. Ralph K. Davies bought it from the city in 1956. It's closed to the public, so view from outside. ✉ *1067 Green St.*

NEED A BREAK? Take a break from walking the hills at the original **Swensen's Ice Cream** (✉ Union and Hyde Sts., ☎ 415/775–6818). A neighborhood favorite, it opened in 1948.

(50) **Grace Cathedral.** The seat of the Episcopal Church in San Francisco, this soaring Gothic structure, erected on the site of Charles Crocker's mansion, took 53 years to build. The gilded bronze doors at the east entrance were taken from casts of Ghiberti's Gates of Paradise, which are on the baptistery in Florence, Italy. A black-and-bronze stone sculpture of St. Francis by Beniamino Bufano greets visitors as they enter.

The 35-ft-wide Labyrinth, a large, purplish rug, is a replica of the 13th-century stone labyrinth on the floor of the Chartres Cathedral. All are encouraged to walk the ¼-mi-long labyrinth, a ritual based on the tradition of meditative walking. There's also a terrazzo outdoor labyrinth on the church's north side. The AIDS Interfaith Chapel, to the right as you enter Grace, contains a sculpture by the late artist Keith Haring and panels from the AIDS Memorial Quilt. Especially dramatic times to view the cathedral are during Thursday-night evensong (5:15) and during holiday special programs. ✉ *1100 California St., at Taylor St.,* ☎ *415/749–6300.* ⏲ *Sun.–Fri. 7–6, Sat. 8–6.*

(55) **Ina Coolbrith Park.** This attractive park is unusual because it's vertical—that is, rather than one open space, it's composed of a series of terraces up a very steep hill. A poet and Oakland librarian whose uncle was the Mormon prophet Joseph Smith, Ina Coolbrith (1842–1928) introduced Jack London and Isadora Duncan to the world of books. For years she entertained literary greats in her Macondray Lane home near the park. In 1915 she was named poet laureate of California. ✉ *Vallejo St. between Mason and Taylor Sts.*

★ (58) **Lombard Street.** The block-long "Crookedest Street in the World" makes eight switchbacks down the east face of Russian Hill between Hyde and Leavenworth streets. Join the line of cars waiting to drive down the steep hill, or walk down the steps on either side of Lombard. You'll take in super views of North Beach and Coit Tower whether you walk or drive—though if you're the one behind the wheel, you'd better keep your eye on the road lest you become yet another of the many folks who ram the garden barriers. ⊠ *Lombard St. between Hyde and Leavenworth Sts.*

❺❼ Macondray Lane. Enter this "secret garden" under a lovely wooden trellis and walk down a quiet cobbled pedestrian street lined with Edwardian cottages and flowering plants and trees. A flight of steep wooden stairs at the end of the lane leads down to Taylor Street—on the way down you can't miss the bay views. If you've read any of Armistead Maupin's *Tales of the City* or sequels, you may find the lane vaguely familiar. It's the thinly disguised setting for part of the series' action. ⊠ *Jones St. between Union and Green Sts.*

❺❸ Mark Hopkins Inter-Continental Hotel. Built on the ashes of railroad tycoon Mark Hopkins's grand estate (which was built at his wife's urging; Hopkins himself preferred to live frugally), this 19-story hotel went up in 1926. A combination of French château and Spanish Renaissance architecture, with noteworthy terra-cotta detailing, it has hosted statesmen, royalty, and Hollywood celebrities. From the 1920s through the 1940s, Benny Goodman, Tommy Dorsey, and other top-drawer entertainers appeared here regularly. The 11-room penthouse was turned into a glass-walled cocktail lounge in 1939: The **Top of the Mark** (☞ Skyline Bars *in* Chapter 4) is remembered fondly by thousands of World War II veterans who jammed the lounge before leaving for overseas duty. Wives and sweethearts watching the ships depart gave the room's northwest nook its name—Weepers' Corner. With its 360-degree views, the lounge is a wonderful spot for a nighttime drink. ⊠ *1 Nob Hill, at California and Mason Sts.,* ☎ *415/392–3434.*

❹❾ Masonic Auditorium. Formally called the California Masonic Memorial Temple, this building was erected by Freemasons in 1957. A selection of brochures by the entrance explains the beliefs of Freemasonry: Only men can join, atheists are forbidden, patriotism and love of family are central tenets, and so on. (Readers of Tolstoy will remember Pierre's painful ambivalence about Freemasonry in *War and Peace*.) The auditorium is the site of occasional musical events (Van Morrison, Natalie Cole), as well as lectures, conventions, and seminars. The impressive lobby mosaic, done mainly in rich greens and yellows, depicts the Masonic fraternity's role in California history and industry. There's also an intricate model of King Solomon's Temple in the lobby. ⊠ *1111 California St.,* ☎ *415/776–4917.* ☉ *Lobby weekdays 8–5.*

❺❶ Pacific Union Club. The former home of silver baron James Flood cost a whopping $1.5 million in 1886, when even a stylish Victorian like the Haas-Lilienthal House (☞ Pacific Heights, *below*) cost under $20,000. All that cash did buy some structural stability. The Flood residence (to be precise, its shell) was the only Nob Hill mansion to survive the 1906 earthquake and fire. The Pacific Union Club, a bastion of the wealthy and powerful, purchased the house in 1907 and commissioned Willis Polk to redesign it; the architect added the semicircular wings and third floor. (The ornate fence design dates from the mansion's construction.) Art shows frequently take place in Huntington Park, west of the house. ⊠ *1000 California St.*

Renaissance Stanford Court Hotel. In 1876 Leland Stanford, a California governor and founder of Stanford University, was the first to build an estate on Nob Hill. The only part that survived the earthquake was a basalt-and-granite wall that's been restored; it can be seen on the eastern side of the hotel. In 1912 an apartment house was built on the site of the former estate, and in 1972 the present-day hotel was constructed from the shell of that building. The lobby contains a stained-glass dome and sepia-tone murals depicting scenes of early San Francisco. ⊠ *905 California St.,* ☎ *415/989–3500.*

NEED A
BREAK?
A harpist plays the classics and other tunes during afternoon tea at the **Ritz-Carlton, San Francisco** (⊠ 600 Stockton St., at California St., ☎ 415/296–7465). Hours vary throughout the year but it's generally served from 2:30 to 4:30 on weekdays and from 1 to 4:30 on weekends.

59 **San Francisco Art Institute.** A Moorish-tile fountain in a tree-shaded courtyard immediately draws the eye as you enter the institute. The highlight of a visit is Mexican master Diego Rivera's *The Making of a Fresco Showing the Building of a City* (1931), in the student gallery to your immediate left once inside the entrance. Rivera himself is in the fresco—his back is to the viewer—and he's surrounded by his assistants. They in turn are surrounded by a construction scene, laborers, and city notables such as sculptor Robert Stackpole and architect Timothy Pfleuger. *The Making of a Fresco* is one of only three Bay Area murals painted by Rivera.

The older portions of the Art Institute were erected in 1926. Ansel Adams created the school's fine-arts photography department in 1946, and school directors established the country's first fine-arts film program. Notable faculty and alumni have included painter Richard Diebenkorn and photographers Dorothea Lange, Edward Weston, and Annie Leibovitz. **McBean Gallery** exhibits the often provocative works of established artists. ⊠ *800 Chestnut St.,* ☎ *415/771–7020.* 🎟 *Galleries free.* ☉ *McBean Gallery Tues.–Sat. 10–5 (Thurs. until 8), Sun. noon–5; student gallery daily 9–9.*

Vallejo steps area. Several Russian Hill buildings survived the 1906 earthquake and fire and remain standing. Alert firefighters saved what's come to be known as the **Flag House** (⊠ 1652–56 Taylor St.) when they spotted the American flag on the property and doused the flames with seltzer water and wet sand. The owner, a flag collector, fearing the house would burn to the ground, wanted it to go down in style, with "all flags flying."

The Flag House, at the southwest corner of Ina Coolbrith Park (☞ *above*), is one of a number of California Shingle–style homes in its neighborhood, several of them designed by Willis Polk, who also laid out the Vallejo steps, which climb the steep ridge across from Taylor Street from the Flag House. Polk designed the **Polk-Williams House** (⊠ 1013–19 Vallejo St.) and lived in one of its sections, and **1034–1036 Vallejo,** across the street. ⊠ *Taylor and Vallejo Sts. (steps lead up toward Jones St.).*

PACIFIC HEIGHTS

Some of the city's most expensive and dramatic real estate—including mansions and town houses priced at $2 million and up—is in Pacific Heights. Grand Victorians line the streets, and from almost any point in this neighborhood you get a magnificent view.

Old money and new, personalities in the limelight, and those who prefer absolute media anonymity live here. Few visitors see anything other than the pleasing facades of Queen Anne charmers, English Tudor imports, and baroque bastions, but that's reason enough for a stroll. You'll notice that few of the homes in Pacific Heights have large gardens. Space has always been at a premium in San Francisco, even in such a wealthy neighborhood.

Numbers in the text correspond to numbers in the margin and on the Downtown San Francisco map.

A Good Walk

Pacific Heights lies on an east–west ridge along the city's northern flank from Van Ness Avenue to the Presidio and from California Street to the bay, but a few important sights are in the lowlands (still technically Pacific Heights). The first stop is the **Octagon House** ⑥⓪, at the corner of Gough (rhymes with "cough") and Union streets. Stroll west through the upscale shopping district of Union Street. The modest **Wedding Houses** sit on the north side of Union Street just before Buchanan Street. Continue one block farther to Webster Street and then one block north to Filbert Street. You can't miss the elaborate, schizophrenically styled **Vedanta Society** ⑥①, on the southwest corner of Filbert and Webster streets.

Prepare for a steep climb as you head south up Webster Street. At the crest of the hill, four notable **Broadway and Webster Street estates** ⑥② stand within a block of each other. Two are on the north side of Broadway to the west of the intersection, one is on the same side to the east, and the last is south a half block on Webster Street. After viewing the estates, continue south on Webster to Pacific Avenue and turn right (west). You'll pass some apartment buildings in the first block and a half, then single-family homes. The Italianate gem at 2475 Pacific Avenue sat on a 25-acre farm in the 1850s. Several Queen Anne homes stand tall on the south side of the 2500 block (between Steiner and Pierce streets); a three-story circular glass-walled staircase distinguishes the more modern home at Number 2510, on the north side. Continue west on Pacific to Scott Street, and walk south into **Alta Plaza Park** ⑥③.

Catch your breath at the park, and then walk east on Jackson Street several blocks to the **Whittier Mansion** ⑥④, on the corner of Jackson and Laguna streets. Make a right on Laguna and a left at the next block, Washington Street. The patch of green that spreads east from here is **Lafayette Park** ⑥⑤. Walk on Washington along the edge of Lafayette Park past the formal French **Spreckels Mansion** ⑥⑥, at the corner of Octavia Street, and continue east two more blocks to Franklin Street. Turn left (north); halfway down the block stands the handsome **Haas-Lilienthal House** ⑥⑦. Head south on Franklin Street, stopping to view several **Franklin Street buildings** ⑥⑧. At California Street, turn right (west) to see more **noteworthy Victorians** ⑥⑨ on that street and Laguna Street.

TIMING

Set aside about two hours to see the sights mentioned here, not including the tours of the Haas-Lilienthal House and the Octagon House. Unless you're in great shape, it'll be a slow walk up extremely steep Webster Street from the Union Street sights, and although most of the attractions are walk-bys, you'll be covering a good bit of pavement.

Sights to See

⑥③ **Alta Plaza Park.** Landscape architect John McLaren, who also created Golden Gate Park, designed Alta Plaza in 1910, modeling its terracing on the Grand Casino in Monte Carlo, Monaco. From the top you can see Marin to the north, downtown to the east, Twin Peaks to the south, and Golden Gate Park to the west. ⊠ *Between Clay, Steiner, Jackson, and Scott Sts.*

⑥② **Broadway and Webster Street estates.** Broadway uptown, unlike its garish North Beach stretch, is home to some prestigious addresses. At 2222 Broadway is a three-story palace with an intricately filigreed doorway built by Comstock silver mine heir James Flood and later donated to a religious order. The Convent of the Sacred Heart purchased the Grant House at 2220 Broadway. These two buildings, along with a

Flood property at **2120 Broadway**, are all used as school quarters. A gold mine heir, William Bourn II, commissioned Willis Polk to build the nearby mansion at **2550 Webster St.**

68 **Franklin Street buildings.** Don't be fooled by the **Golden Gate Church** (✉ 1901 Franklin St.)—what at first looks like a stone facade is actually redwood painted white. A Georgian-style residence built in the early 1900s for a coffee merchant sits at **1735 Franklin.** On the northeast corner of Franklin and California streets is a **Christian Science church**; built in the Tuscan Revival style, it's noteworthy for its terracotta detailing. The **Coleman House** (✉ 1701 Franklin St.) is an impressive twin-turreted Queen Anne mansion built for a Gold Rush mining and lumber baron. Don't miss the large stained-glass window on the house's north side. ✉ *Franklin St. between Washington and California Sts.*

67 **Haas-Lilienthal House.** A small display of photographs on the bottom floor of this elaborate 1886 Queen Anne house, which cost a mere $18,500 to build, makes clear that it was modest compared with some of the giants that fell victim to the 1906 earthquake and fire. The Foundation for San Francisco's Architectural Heritage operates the home, whose carefully kept rooms provide an intriguing glimpse into late 19th-century life. Volunteers conduct one-hour house tours two days a week and an informative two-hour tour of the eastern portion of Pacific Heights on Sunday afternoon. ✉ *2007 Franklin St., between Washington and Jackson Sts.,* ☎ *415/441–3004.* 🖅 *$5.* ☉ *Wed. noon–4 (last tour at 3), Sun. 11–5 (last tour at 4). Pacific Heights tours ($5) leave the house Sun. at 12:30.*

65 **Lafayette Park.** Clusters of trees dot this four-block-square oasis for sunbathers and dog-and-Frisbee teams. During the 1860s a tenacious squatter, Sam Holladay, built himself a big wooden house in the center of the park. Holladay even instructed city gardeners as if the land were his own and defied all orders to leave. The house was finally torn down in 1936. On the south side of the park, **2151 Sacramento**, a private condominium, was the site of a home occupied by Sir Arthur Conan Doyle in the late 19th century. ✉ *Between Laguna, Gough, Sacramento, and Washington Sts.*

69 **Noteworthy Victorians.** Two **Italianate Victorians** (✉ 1818 and 1834 California St.) stand out on the 1800 block of California. A block farther is the Victorian-era **Atherton House** (✉ 1990 California St.), whose mildly daffy design incorporates Queen Anne, Stick-Eastlake, and other architectural elements. The oft-photographed **Laguna Street Victorians**, on the west side of the 1800 block of Laguna Street, cost between $2,000 and $2,600 when they were built in the 1870s. ✉ *California St. between Franklin and Octavia Sts.;* ✉ *Laguna St. between Pine and Bush Sts.*

60 **Octagon House.** This eight-sided home sits across the street from its original site on Gough Street. It's full of antique American furniture, decorative arts (paintings, silver, rugs), and documents from the 18th and 19th centuries. The deck of revolutionary-era hand-painted playing cards takes an anti-monarchist position: In place of kings, queens, and jacks, the American upstarts substituted American statesmen, Roman goddesses, and Indian chiefs. White quoins accent each of the eight corners of the pretty blue-gray exterior. An award-winning Colonial-style garden completes the picture. ✉ *2645 Gough St.,* ☎ *415/441–7512.* 🖅 *Free; donations encouraged.* ☉ *Feb.–Dec., 2nd Sun. and 2nd and 4th Thurs. of each month, noon–3; group tours weekdays by appointment.*

66 Spreckels Mansion. This estate was built for sugar heir Adolph Spreckels and his wife, Alma. Mrs. Spreckels was so pleased with her house that she commissioned George Applegarth to design another building in a similar vein: the California Palace of the Legion of Honor (☞ Lincoln Park and the Western Shoreline, *below*). One of the city's great iconoclasts, Alma Spreckels was the model for the bronze figure atop the Victory Monument in Union Square. ⊠ *2080 Washington St., at Octavia St.*

61 Vedanta Society. A pastiche of Colonial, Queen Anne, Moorish, and Hindu opulence, with turrets battling onion domes and Victorian detailing everywhere, this 1905 structure was the first Hindu temple in the West. The highest of the six Hindu systems of religious philosophy, Vedanta maintains that all religions are paths to one goal. Although the Vedanta Society's main location is at Vallejo and Fillmore streets, the Webster Street temple is the organization's heart. ⊠ *2963 Webster St.,* ☎ *415/922–2323.*

Wedding Houses. These identical white double-peak homes (joined in the middle) were erected in the late 1870s or early 1880s by dairy rancher James Cudworth as wedding gifts for his two daughters. These days, the buildings house businesses and an English-style pub. ⊠ *1980 Union St.*

64 Whittier Mansion. This was one of the most elegant 19th-century houses in the state, with a Spanish-tile roof and scrolled bay windows on all four sides. An anomaly in a town that lost most of its grand mansions to the 1906 quake, the Whittier Mansion was built so solidly that only a chimney toppled over during the disaster. ⊠ *2090 Jackson St.*

JAPANTOWN

About 1860 a wave of Japanese immigrants arrived in San Francisco, which they called Soko. After the 1906 earthquake and fire, many of these newcomers settled in the Western Addition. By the 1930s they had opened shops, markets, meeting halls, and restaurants and established Shinto and Buddhist temples. Known as Japantown, this area was virtually deserted during World War II when many of its residents, including second- and third-generation Americans, were forced into so-called relocation camps. Today Japantown, or "Nihonmachi," is centered on the southern slope of Pacific Heights, north of Geary Boulevard between Fillmore and Laguna streets. The Nihonmachi Cherry Blossom Festival is celebrated on two weekends in April.

Japantown doesn't feel much different from other parts of the city. Most shops and restaurants are Japanese-oriented, but the majority are tidily lined up in the Japan Center rather than spilling out onto the streets. And though it contains Japanese touches, the architecture in the area is fairly generic. That said, there are plenty of authentic treasures to be found in the shops and restaurants of Japantown. About three dozen restaurants serve Japanese, Chinese, and Korean food. Following the practice in Japan, plastic replicas of the various dishes are on view.

Though Japantown is a relatively safe area, the Western Addition, which lies to the south of Geary Boulevard, can be dangerous; after dark also avoid straying too far west of Fillmore Street just north of Geary.

Numbers in the text correspond to numbers in the margin and on the Downtown San Francisco map.

A Good Walk

Several key components of San Francisco's history intersect at Geary Boulevard and Fillmore Street. The three-block **Japan Center** ⑦ sits on a portion of the area settled by Japanese and Japanese-Americans in the early 20th century. The stretch of Fillmore on either side of Geary Boulevard was a center of African-American culture during the mid-20th century. The part to the south remains so today, though the many blues and other music clubs that once thrived here have closed.

Near the southwest corner of Geary and Fillmore is the entrance to the legendary Fillmore Auditorium, where 1960s bands like Jefferson Airplane and the Grateful Dead performed. Two doors west of the Fillmore was the People's Temple (since demolished), the headquarters of the cult run by the Reverend Jim Jones, whose flock participated in a mass suicide in Guyana in November 1978.

Kabuki Springs & Spa ⑦ is on the northeast corner of Geary and Fillmore. Head north on Fillmore to Post Street and make a right. Pass the entrance to the eight-screen AMC Kabuki theater and enter the Japan Center mid-block, in the Kinokuniya Building. Among the shops of note are the Kinokuniya Bookstore (☞ Booksellers *in* Chapter 6) and Ma-Shi'-Ko Folk Craft (☞ Handicrafts and Folk Art *in* Chapter 6), both on the second floor.

A second-level bridge spans Webster Street, connecting the Kinokuniya and Kintetsu buildings. Make a right after you cross the bridge and then a left. There are usually several fine ikebana arrangements in the windows of the headquarters of the Ikenobo Ikebana Society of America. A few doors farther along at May's Coffee Stand you can pick up a lemonade and a tasty fish-shape waffle filled with red-bean paste. If you're hungrier, make two more lefts (heading back toward the bridge) to the noodle shop Mifune.

After exiting the Kintetsu Building, pop across Post Street to the open-air **Japan Center Mall** ⑦, a short block of shoji-screened buildings on Buchanan Street between Post and Sutter streets.

TIMING

The distance covered in the tour is extremely short. Not including a visit to Kabuki Springs & Spa, an hour will probably suffice.

Sights to See

⑦ **Japan Center.** The noted American architect Minoru Yamasaki created this 5-acre complex that opened in 1968. The development includes a hotel (the Radisson Miyako, at Laguna and Post streets); a public garage with discounted validated parking; shops selling Japanese furnishings, clothing, cameras, tapes and records, porcelain, pearls, and paintings; an excellent spa; and a multiplex cinema.

Between the Miyako Mall and Kintetsu Building are the five-tier, 100-ft-tall **Peace Pagoda** and the Peace Plaza, where seasonal festivals are held. The pagoda, which draws on the 1,200-year-old tradition of miniature round pagodas dedicated to eternal peace, was designed by Yoshiro Taniguchi to convey the "friendship and goodwill" of the Japanese people to the people of the United States. ⊠ *Bordered by Geary Blvd. and Fillmore, Post, and Laguna Sts.,* ☎ *415/922–6776.*

NEED A BREAK?   At **Isobune** (☎ 415/563–1030), on the second floor of the Kintetsu Building, "sushi boats" float by customers, who take what they want and pay per dish at the end of the meal.

⓻ **Japan Center Mall.** The buildings lining this open-air mall are of the shoji school of architecture. Seating in this area can be found on local artist Ruth Asawa's twin origami-style fountains, which sit in the middle of the mall; they're squat circular structures made of fieldstone, with three levels for sitting and a brick floor that is also a drain. ⊠ *Buchanan St. between Post and Sutter Sts.*

★ ⓻ **Kabuki Springs & Spa.** Japantown's house of tranquility got a complete makeover in 1999. The feel is less Japanese than before. Balinese urns decorate the communal bath area, and you're just as likely to hear soothing flute or classical music as you are Kitaro. The massage palette has also expanded well beyond the traditional shiatsu technique. The experience is no less relaxing, however, and the treatment regimen now includes facials, salt scrubs, and mud and seaweed wraps. You can take your massage in a private room with a bath or in a curtained-off area. The communal baths ($10 before 5 PM, $15 after 5) contain hot and cold tubs, a large Japanese-style bath, a sauna, a steam room, and showers. The baths are open for men only on Monday, Tuesday, Thursday, and Saturday, and for women only on Wednesday, Friday, and Sunday. Men and women can reserve private rooms daily. A 90-minute massage-and-bath package with a private room costs $90. A package that includes an hour-long massage and the use of the communal baths costs $75. ⊠ *1750 Geary Blvd.,* ☎ *415/922–6000.* ☉ *Daily 10–10.*

OFF THE
BEATEN PATH

ST. MARY'S CATHEDRAL – Affectionately known as Our Lady of the Maytag for its resemblance to a washing-machine agitator, this Catholic house of worship was designed by a team of local architects and Pierre Nervi of Rome; it was dedicated in 1971. The interior is as unusual as the exterior: Seven thousand aluminium ribs cascade powerfully above the marble altar, which is backed by purple and blue cloth partitions and brightly colored lights. Four stained-glass windows cross in the massive dome and represent the four elements: the blue northern windows, water; the light-color southern windows, sun; the red western windows, fire; and the green eastern windows, earth. ⊠ *1111 Gough St., at Geary Blvd. (from Japan Center head east on Geary),* ☎ *415/567–2020.*

CIVIC CENTER

The Civic Center—the Beaux-Arts complex between McAllister and Grove streets and Franklin and Hyde streets that includes City Hall, the War Memorial Opera House, the Veterans Building, and the old Public Library (slated to become the Asian Art Museum and Cultural Center by 2002)—is a product of the "City Beautiful" movement of the early 20th century. City Hall, completed in 1915, is the centerpiece. The new main library on Larkin Street between Fulton and Grove streets, completed in 1996, is a modern variation on the Civic Center's architectural theme.

The Civic Center area may have been set up on City Beautiful principles, but illusion soon gives way to reality. The buildings may be grand, but there's a stark juxtaposition of the powerful and the powerless here. On the streets and plazas of Civic Center, many of the city's most destitute residents eke out an existence.

Despite the social problems, there are areas of interest on either side of City Hall. East of City Hall is United Nations Plaza, a carnival of bright colors during the twice-weekly farmers' market. The handsome new main library is just a block west of the plaza. On the west side of City Hall are the opera house, the symphony hall, and other cultural institutions. A few upscale restaurants in the surrounding blocks cater to the theater/symphony crowd.

Numbers in the text correspond to numbers in the margin and on the Downtown San Francisco map.

A Good Walk

Start at **United Nations Plaza** ⑦, set on an angle between Hyde and Market streets. BART and Muni trains stop here, and the Bus 5-Fulton, Bus 21-Hayes, and other lines serve the area. Walk west along the plaza toward Fulton Street, which dead-ends at Hyde Street, and cross Hyde. Towering over the block of Fulton between Hyde and Larkin streets is the Pioneers Monument. The new main branch of **San Francisco Public Library** ⑦ is south of the monument. North of it is the old library. The patch of green west of the library is Civic Center Plaza, and beyond that is **City Hall** ⑦. If City Hall is open, walk through it, exiting on Van Ness Avenue and turning right. If the building's closed, walk around it to the north—to the right as you're facing it—and make a left at McAllister. Either way you'll end up at McAllister Street and Van Ness Avenue. Looking south (to the left) across the street on Van Ness, you'll see three grand edifices, each of which takes up most of its block. On the southwestern corner of McAllister and Van Ness Avenue is the **Veterans Building** ⑦. A horseshoe-shape carriage entrance on its south side separates the building from the **War Memorial Opera House** ⑦. In the next block of Van Ness Avenue, across Grove Street from the opera house, is **Louise M. Davies Symphony Hall** ⑦. From Davies, head west (to the right) on Grove Street to Franklin Street, turn left (south), walk one block to Hayes Street and turn right (west). A hip strip of galleries, shops, and restaurants lies between Franklin and Laguna streets. Like Japantown, the Civic Center borders the Western Addition; it's best not to stray west of Laguna at night.

TIMING

Walking around the Civic Center shouldn't take more than about 45 minutes. Another half hour or more can be spent browsing the shops along Hayes Street. On Wednesday or Sunday allot some extra time to take in the farmers' market in United Nations Plaza.

Sights to See

⑦ **City Hall.** This masterpiece of granite and marble was modeled after St. Peter's cathedral in Rome. City Hall's bronze and gold-leaf dome, which is even higher than the U.S. Capitol's version, dominates the area. Arthur Brown Jr., who also designed Coit Tower (☞ North Beach and Telegraph Hill, *above*) and the War Memorial Opera House (☞ *below*), was trained in Paris; his classical influences can be seen throughout the structure. The building was spruced up and seismically retrofitted in the late 1990s, but the sense of history remains palpable. Some noteworthy events that have taken place here include the marriage of Marilyn Monroe and Joe DiMaggio (1954), the hosing—down the central staircase—of civil rights and freedom of speech protesters (1960), the murders of Mayor George Moscone and openly gay Supervisor Harvey Milk (1978), the torching of the lobby by angry members of the gay community in response to the light sentence (eight years for manslaughter, eventually reduced to 5½ years) given to the former supervisor who killed them (1979), and the weddings of scores of gay couples in celebration of the passage of San Francisco's Domestic Partners Act (1991). Because the retrofitting project went $50 million over budget, the reopening festivities in 1999 were subdued. If the building's open, inspect the palatial interior, full of grand arches and with a sweeping central staircase. Across Polk Street is Civic Center Plaza, with lawns, walkways, seasonal flower beds, a playground, and an undergroundparking garage. ✉ *Between Van Ness Ave., Polk, Grove, and McAllister Sts.*

78 Louise M. Davies Symphony Hall. Fascinating and still futuristic looking after two decades, this 2,750-seat hall is the home of the San Francisco Symphony. The glass wraparound lobby and pop-out balcony high on the southeast corner are visible from the outside. Henry Moore created the bronze sculpture that sits on the sidewalk at Van Ness Avenue and Grove Street. The hall's 59 adjustable Plexiglas acoustical disks cascade from the ceiling like hanging windshields. Concerts range from typical symphony fare to more unusual combinations, such as pop-rock singer Elvis Costello performing with a string quartet. San Francisco Symphony leader Michael Tilson-Thomas is the only U.S.-born conductor for a major American orchestra. Scheduled tours (75 minutes), which meet at the Grove Street entrance, take in Davies and the nearby opera house and Herbst Theatre. ✉ *201 Van Ness Ave.,* ☎ *415/552–8338.* 🎫 *Tours $5.* ☯ *Tours Mon. (except holidays) hourly 10–2.*

NEED A BREAK?

For a quick pizza or reasonably priced designer salad, dash over to **Spuntino** (✉ 524 Van Ness Ave., ☎ 415/861–7772), open weekdays from 7 AM to 8 PM and Saturdays from 11:30 to 8.

---

74 San Francisco Public Library. The main library, which opened in 1996, is a modernized version of the old Beaux-Arts library that sits just across Fulton Street. The several specialty rooms include centers for the hearing and visually impaired, a gay and lesbian history center, and African-American and Asian centers. Also here are an auditorium, an art gallery, a café, and a rooftop garden and terrace. The San Francisco History Room and Archives contains historic photographs, maps, and other city memorabilia. At the library's core is a five-story atrium with a skylight, a grand staircase, and murals painted by local artists. Tours of the library are conducted daily at 2:30 PM. ✉ *100 Larkin St. between Grove and Fulton Sts.,* ☎ *415/557–4400.* ☯ *Mon. 10–6, Tues.–Thurs. 9–8, Fri. 11–5, Sat. 9–5, Sun. noon–5.*

73 United Nations Plaza. Brick pillars listing various nations and the dates of their admittance into the United Nations line the plaza, and its floor is inscribed with the goals and philosophy of the United Nations charter, which was signed at the War Memorial Opera House in 1945. On Wednesday and Sunday a farmers' market fills the space with homegrown produce and plants. ✉ *Fulton St. between Hyde and Market Sts.*

76 Veterans Building. Performing and visual arts organizations occupy much of this 1930s structure. **Herbst Theatre** (☎ 415/392–4400) hosts lectures and readings, classical ensembles, and dance performances, along with City Arts and Lectures events. Past City Arts guests have included author Tom Wolfe and playwright-performer Anna Deavere Smith. Also in the building are two galleries that charge no admission. The street-level **San Francisco Arts Commission Gallery** (☎ 415/554–6080), open from Wednesday to Saturday between noon and 5, displays the works of Bay Area artists. The **San Francisco Performing Arts Library and Museum** (☎ 415/255–4800) occupies part of the fourth floor. A small gallery hosts interesting exhibitions, though the organization functions mainly as a library and research center, collecting, documenting, and preserving the San Francisco Bay Area's rich performing arts legacy. The gallery is open during the afternoon from Wednesday through Saturday. ✉ *401 Van Ness Ave.*

⓿ **War Memorial Opera House.** During San Francisco's Barbary Coast days, opera goers smoked cigars, didn't check their revolvers, and expressed their appreciation with "shrill whistles and savage yells," as one observer put it. All the old opera houses were destroyed in the quake, but lusty support for opera continued. The opera didn't have a permanent home until the War Memorial Opera House was inaugurated in 1932 with a performance of *Tosca*. Modeled after its European counterparts, the building has a vaulted and coffered ceiling, marble foyer, two balconies, and a huge silver Art Deco chandelier that resembles a sunburst. The San Francisco Opera performs here from September to December, and the San Francisco Ballet from February to May, with December *Nutcracker* performances. ⊠ *301 Van Ness Ave.,* ☎ *415/ 621–6600.*

THE NORTHERN WATERFRONT

For the sights, sounds, and smells of the sea, hop the Powell–Hyde cable car from Union Square and take it to the end of the line. The views as you descend Hyde Street down to the bay are breathtaking—tiny sailboats bob in the whitecaps, Alcatraz hovers ominously in the distance, and the Marin Headlands form a rugged backdrop to the Golden Gate Bridge. Once you reach sea level at the cable car turnaround, Aquatic Park and the National Maritime Museum are immediately to the west, and the commercial attractions of the Fisherman's Wharf area are to the east. Bring good walking shoes and a jacket or sweater for mid-afternoon breezes or foggy mists.

Years pass for most San Franciscans between visits to Fisherman's Wharf, whose diversions are decidedly tourist-oriented. But the area is not without cultural and historical points of interest, and it is the departure point for the ferry ride to the deservedly popular Alcatraz Island. Even if you abhor schlock you can have a good time here if you pay attention.

Each day street artists—jewelers, painters, potters, photographers, and leather workers—and others offer their wares for sale. Beauty, of course, is always in the eye of the beholder, but some of the items may be overpriced and of questionable quality. Bargaining is always possible.

Numbers in the text correspond to numbers in the margin and on the Northern Waterfront/Marina and the Presidio map.

A Good Walk

Begin at Polk and Beach streets at the **National Maritime Museum** ①. (Walk west from the cable car turnaround; Bus 19 stops at Polk and Beach streets, and Bus 47-Van Ness stops one block west at Van Ness Avenue and Beach Streets.) Across Beach from the museum is **Ghirardelli Square** ②, a complex of shops, cafés, and galleries in an old chocolate factory. Continue east on Beach to Hyde Street and make a left. At the end of Hyde is the **Hyde Street Pier** ③. South on Hyde a block and a half is the former Del Monte **Cannery** ④, which holds more shops, cafés, and restaurants. Walk east from the Cannery on Jefferson Street to **Fisherman's Wharf** ⑤. A few blocks farther east is **Pier 39** ⑥.

TIMING

For the entire Northern Waterfront circuit, set aside three or four hours, not including boat tours, which will take from one to three hours or more. All the attractions here are open daily.

Sights to See

★ **Alcatraz Island.** The boat ride to the island is brief (15 minutes) but affords beautiful views of the city, Marin County, and the East Bay.

The audio tour, highly recommended, includes observations of guards and prisoners about life in one of America's most notorious penal colonies. A separate ranger-led tour surveys the island's ecology. Plan your schedule to allow at least three hours for the visit and boat rides combined. Reservations, even in the off-season, are recommended. ⊠ *Pier 41,* ☎ *415/773–1188 (boat schedules and information); 415/705–5555 or 800/426–8687 (credit-card ticket orders); 415/705–1042 (park information).* ⌨ *$11 or $7.75 without audio ($18.50 for evening tours, which includes audio); add $2 per ticket to charge by phone.* ☉ *Ferry departures Sept.–May 23, daily 9:30–2:15 (4:20 for evening tour); May 24–Aug., daily 9:30–4:15 (6:30 and 7:30 for evening tour).*

Angel Island. For an outdoorsy adventure, consider a day at Angel Island, northwest of Alcatraz. Discovered by Spaniards in 1775 and declared a U.S. military reserve 75 years later, the island was used from 1910 until 1940 as a screening ground for Asian immigrants, who were often held for months, even years, before being granted entry. In 1963 the government designated Angel Island a state park. Today people come for picnics and hikes—a scenic 5-mi path winds around the perimeter of the island—as well as guided tours that explain the park's history. Twenty-five bicycles are permitted on the regular ferry on a first-come, first-served basis, and you can rent mountain bikes for $10 per hour or $25 per day at the landing. ⊠ *Pier 41,* ☎ *415/435–1915 for park information and ferry schedules; 415/705–5555 or 800/426–8687 for tickets.* ⌨ *$10.* ☉ *Ferry sailing days and departure times vary; call for schedule.*

❹ Cannery. This three-story structure was built in 1894 to house what became the Del Monte Fruit and Vegetable Cannery. Today the Cannery is home to shops, art galleries, a comedy club (Cobb's), and some unusual restaurants. The **Museum of the City of San Francisco** (☎ 415/928–0289), on the third floor, displays historical items, maps, and photographs, as well as the 500-pound head of the Goddess of Progress statue, which crowned the City Hall building that crumbled during the 1906 earthquake. Admission to the museum is free. ⊠ *2801 Leavenworth St.,* ☎ *415/771–3112.*

NEED A BREAK? The mellow **Buena Vista Café** (⊠ 2765 Hyde St., ☎ 415/474–5044) claims to be the first U.S. establishment to have served Irish coffee. The late San Francisco columnist Stan Delaplane is credited with importing the Celtic concoction. The café opens at 9 AM weekdays, 8 AM weekends, and serves a great breakfast. It is always crowded, but try for a table overlooking nostalgic Victorian Park with its cable car turntable.

Ferries. Alcatraz Island and Angel Island are just two of the destinations served by the **Blue and Gold Fleet** (⊠ Pier 41, ☎ 415/705–5555). Alcatraz is the best deal—you get all the fun of bay cruise and a great tour of the prison. But the boats are a fine way to day-trip to Sausalito and Tiburon. Blue and Gold also runs ferries to Oakland, Alameda, and Vallejo. The Vallejo boat docks near Six Flags Marine World (☞ On and Around the Bay *in* Chapter 7). The **Red and White Fleet** (⊠ Pier 43½, ☎ 415/447–0591 or 800/229–2784) operates bay and other cruises.

⏱ ❺ Fisherman's Wharf. Ships creak at their moorings; seagulls cry out for a handout. By mid-afternoon the fishing fleet is back to port. The chaotic streets of the wharf are home to numerous seafood restaurants, among them sidewalk stands where shrimp and crab cocktails are sold in disposable containers. T-shirts and sweats, gold chains galore, redwood furniture, acres of artwork (precious little of it original), and gener-

Northern Waterfront/Marina and the Presidio

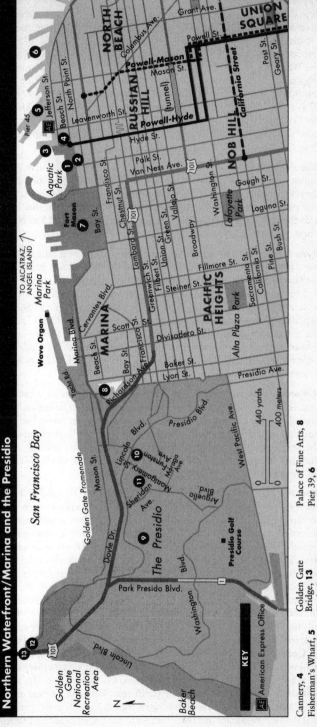

Cannery, **4**
Fisherman's Wharf, **5**
Fort Mason, **7**
Fort Point, **12**
Ghirardelli Square, **2**

Golden Gate
Bridge, **13**
Hyde Street Pier, **3**
National Maritime
Museum, **1**

Palace of Fine Arts, **8**
Pier 39, **6**
Presidio, **9**
Presidio Museum, **10**
Presidio Visitor
Center, **11**

KEY

AE American Express Office

TO ALCATRAZ,
ANGEL ISLAND

San Francisco Bay

440 yards
400 meters

ally amusing street artists also beckon visitors. Everything's over-priced, especially the so-called novelty museums, which can provide a diversion if you're touring with antsy kids. The best of the lot, though mostly for its kitsch value, is **Ripley's Believe It or Not** (⌂ 175 Jefferson St., ☎ 415/771–6188). King Tut and latter-day celebs populate the **Wax Museum** (⌂ 145 Jefferson St., ☎ 415/885–4975). For an intriguing if mildly claustrophobic glimpse into life on a submarine during World War II, drop by the USS *Pampanito* (⌂ Pier 45, ☎ 415/775–1943). The sub, open daily from 9 to 6 (until 8 between Memorial Day and Labor Day), sank six Japanese warships and damaged four others. Admission is $7. ⌂ *Jefferson St. between Leavenworth St. and Pier 39.*

❷ Ghirardelli Square. Most of the redbrick buildings in this early 20th-century complex were part of the Ghirardelli chocolate factory. Now they house name-brand emporiums, restaurants, and galleries that sell everything from crafts and knickknacks to sports memorabilia. Placards throughout the square describe the factory's history. ⌂ *900 North Point,* ☎ *415/775–5500.*

❸ Hyde Street Pier. The pier, one of the wharf area's best bargains, always crackles with activity. Depending on the time of day, you might see boatbuilders at work or children manning a ship as though it were still the early 1900s. The highlight of the pier is its collection of historic vessels, all of which can be boarded: the *Balclutha,* an 1886 full-rigged three-masted sailing vessel that sailed around Cape Horn 17 times; the *Eureka,* a side-wheel ferry; the *C. A. Thayer,* a three-masted schooner; and the *Hercules,* a steam-powered tugboat. ⌂ *Hyde and Jefferson Sts.,* ☎ *415/556–3002 or 415/556–0859.* ⊡ *$4.* ⊙ *Daily 9:30–5; summer, daily 10–6.*

❶ National Maritime Museum. You'll feel as if you're out to sea when you step inside this sturdy, rounded structure. Part of the San Francisco Maritime National Historical Park, which includes Hyde Street Pier, the museum exhibits ship models, maps, and other artifacts chronicling the development of San Francisco and the West Coast through maritime history. ⌂ *Aquatic Park at the foot of Polk St.,* ☎ *415/556–3002.* ⊡ *Donation suggested.* ⊙ *Daily 10–5.*

☝ ❻ Pier 39. This is the most popular—and commercial—of San Francisco's waterfront attractions, drawing millions of visitors each year to browse through its dozens of shops. Ongoing free entertainment, accessible validated parking, and nearby public transportation ensure crowds most days. Check out the **Marine Mammal Store & Interpretive Center** (☎ 415/289–7373), a quality gift shop and education center whose proceeds benefit Sausalito's Marine Mammal Center, and the **National Park Store** (☎ 415/433–7221), with books, maps, and collectibles sold to support the National Park Service. Brilliant colors enliven the double-decker **Venetian Carousel,** often awhirl with happily howling children. The din on the northwest side of the pier comes courtesy of the hundreds of sea lions that bask and play on the docks. At **Underwater World** (☎ 415/623–5300 or 888/732–3483), moving walkways transport visitors through a space surrounded on three sides by water filled with indigenous San Francisco Bay marine life, from fish and plankton to sharks. The **California Welcome Center,** inside the Citibank Cinemax Theater, is open from 9 to 5:30 daily. Parking is at the Pier 39 Garage, off Powell Street at the Embarcadero. ⌂ *Beach St. at the Embarcadero.*

THE MARINA AND THE PRESIDIO

The Marina district was a coveted place to live until the 1989 earthquake, when the area's homes suffered the worst damage in the city—largely because the Marina is built on landfill. Many home owners and renters fled in search of more solid ground, but young professionals quickly replaced them, changing the tenor of this formerly low-key neighborhood. The number of upscale coffee emporiums skyrocketed. A bank became a Williams-Sonoma and the local grocer gave way to a Pottery Barn. On weekends, a fairly homogeneous well-to-do crowd frequents these and other establishments. One unquestionable improvement was the influx of contemporary cuisine in this former bastion of coffee shops and outdated Italian fare. Even before the quake, though, the Marina Safeway, at Laguna Street and Marina Boulevard, was a famed pickup place for young heterosexual singles.

West of the Marina is the sprawling Presidio, a former military base. In 1996 President Clinton signed a bill placing the Presidio in the hands of a trust corporation as part of a novel money-generating experiment. The trust is leasing buildings and allowing limited development in hopes of making enough money to cover some of the Presidio's operating costs. Whether this arrangement is a worthy model for national parks of the future—or the first step in the crass commercialization of a public resource—remains to be seen. Whatever the outcome, the Presidio will still have superb views and the best hiking and biking areas in San Francisco; a drive through the area can also be rewarding.

Numbers in the text correspond to numbers in the margin and on the Northern Waterfront/Marina and the Presidio map.

A Good Drive

Though you can visit the sights below using public transportation, this is the place to use your car if you have one. You might even consider renting one for a day to cover the area, as well as Lincoln Park, Golden Gate Park, and the western shoreline.

Start at **Fort Mason** ⑦, whose entrance for automobiles is off Marina Boulevard at Buchanan Street. If you're coming by bus, take Bus 30-Stockton heading north (and later west); get off at Chestnut and Laguna streets and walk north three blocks to the pedestrian entrance at Marina Boulevard and Laguna. To get from Fort Mason to the **Palace of Fine Arts** ⑧ by car, make a right on Marina Boulevard. The road curves past a small marina and the Marina Green. Turn left at Divisadero Street, right on North Point Street, left on Baker Street, and right on Bay Street, which passes the Palace's lagoon and dead-ends at the Lyon Street parking lot. Part of the Palace complex is the **Exploratorium,** a hands-on science museum. (If you're walking from Fort Mason to the Palace, the directions are easier: Follow Marina Boulevard to Scott Street. Cross to the south side of the street—away from the water—and continue past Divisadero Street to Baker Street, and turn left; you'll see the Palace's lagoon on your right. To take Muni, walk back to Chestnut and Laguna streets and take Bus 30-Stockton continuing west; get off at North Point and Broderick streets and walk west on North Point.)

The least confusing way to drive to the **Presidio** ⑨ from the Palace is to exit from the south end of the Lyon Street parking lot and head east (left) on Bay Street. Turn right (north) onto Baker Street, and right (west) on Francisco Street, taking it across Richardson Avenue to Lyon Street. Turn south (left) on Lyon and right (west) on Lombard Street, and go through the main gate to Presidio Boulevard. Turn right on Presidio, which becomes Lincoln Boulevard. Make a left at Montgomery Street; a half block up on the right is the **Presidio Visitor Center** ⑪. (To take the bus to the Presidio, walk north from the Palace to Lombard Street and catch Bus 28 heading west; it stops on Lincoln near the visitor center.) Nearby is the **Presidio Museum** ⑩.

From the visitor center head north a half block to Sheridan Avenue, make a right, and make a left when Sheridan runs into Lincoln Boulevard. Lincoln winds through the Presidio past a large cemetery and some vista points. After a couple of miles you'll see a parking lot marked FORT POINT on the right. Park and follow the signs leading to **Fort Point** ⑫, walking downhill through a lightly wooded area. To walk the short distance to the **Golden Gate Bridge** ⑬, follow the signs from the Fort Point parking lot; to drive across the bridge, continue on Lincoln Boulevard a bit and watch for the turnoff on the right. Bus 28 serves stops fairly near these last two attractions; ask the driver to call them out.

TIMING

The time it takes to see this area will vary greatly depending on whether you'll be taking public transportation or driving. If you drive, plan to spend at least three hours, not including a walk across the Golden Gate Bridge or hikes along the shoreline—each of which will take a few hours. With or without kids, you could easily pass two hours at the Exploratorium.

Sights to See

★ ⓒ **Exploratorium.** The curious of all ages flock to this fascinating "museum of science, art, and human perception" within the Palace of Fine Arts. The more than 650 exhibits focus on sea and insect life, computers, electricity, patterns and light, language, the weather, and much more. "Explainers"—often high school students on their days off from school—provide help and demonstrate scientific principles (lasers, dissection of a cow's eye). Reservations are required to crawl through the pitch-black, touchy-feely **Tactile Dome,** an adventure of 15 minutes. The object is to crawl and climb through the space relying solely on the sense of touch. ⊠ *3601 Lyon St. at Marina Blvd.,* ☎ *415/561–0360 for general information; 415/561–0362 for Tactile Dome reservations.* ⊡ *$9; free 1st Wed. of month; Tactile Dome admission $3 extra.* ☉ *Memorial Day–Labor Day, daily 10–6, Wed. 10–9; Labor Day–Memorial Day, Tues., Thurs.–Sun., and most Mon. holidays 10–5, Wed. 10–9.*

❼ **Fort Mason Center.** Originally a depot for the shipment of supplies to the Pacific during World War II, Fort Mason was converted into a cultural center in 1977. In business here are the popular vegetarian restaurant Greens and shops, galleries, and performance spaces, most of which are closed on Monday.

The **Mexican Museum** (⊠ Bldg. D, ☎ 415/441–0404) showcases Mexican, Mexican-American, and Chicano art—everything from pre-Columbian Indian terra-cotta figures and Spanish colonial religious images to exhibits about Mexican-American and Chicano culture. This facility is scheduled to close in late 2000 prior to the museum's move in early 2001 to a building adjacent to Yerba Buena Gardens. La Tienda, the museum shop, stocks colorful Mexican folk art, posters, books, and catalogs from museum exhibitions.

Two interesting small museums are in Building C. The **Museo Italo-Americano** (☎ 415/673–2200) mounts impressive exhibits of the works of Italian and Italian-American artists—paintings, sculpture, etchings, and photographs. The exhibits at the **San Francisco African-American Historical and Cultural Society** (☎ 415/441–0640) document past and contemporary black arts and culture. In Building A is the **San Francisco**

Craft and Folk Art Museum (☎ 415/775–0990), an airy space with exhibits of American folk art, tribal art, and contemporary crafts. The museum shop is a sure bet for whimsical gifts from around the world. Next door to the Craft and Folk Art Museum is the **SFMOMA Rental Gallery** (☎ 415/441–4777), where the art is available for sale or rent. Most of the museums and shops at Fort Mason close by 6 or 7. The museum admission fees range from pay-what-you-wish to $3. ⊠ *Buchanan St. and Marina Blvd.,* ☎ *415/979–3010 for event information.*

NEED A **Greens to Go** (⊠ Fort Mason, Bldg. A, ☎ 415/771–6222), the take-out
BREAK? wing of the famous Greens restaurant carries mouthwatering breads and pastries.

⑫ Fort Point. Designed to mount 126 cannons with a range of up to 2 mi, Fort Point was constructed between 1853 and 1861 to protect San Francisco from sea attack during the Civil War—but it was never used for that purpose. It was, however, used as a coastal defense fortification post during World War II, when soldiers stood watch here. This National Historic Site is a museum filled with military memorabilia. The building has a gloomy air and is suitably atmospheric. On days when Fort Point is staffed, guided group tours and cannon drills take place. The top floor affords a unique angle on the bay. Take care when walking along the front side of the building as it's slippery, and the waves have a dizzying effect. Just north of this structure is the cluster of buildings known as **Fort Point Mine Depot,** an army facility that functioned as the headquarters for underwater mining operations throughout World War II. ⊠ *Marine Dr. off Lincoln Blvd.,* ☎ *415/556–1693.* 🖅 *Free.* ⊙ *Wed.–Sun. 10–5.*

★ **⑬ Golden Gate Bridge.** The suspension bridge that connects San Francisco with Marin County has long wowed sightseers with its rust-color beauty, 750-ft towers, and simple but powerful Art Deco design. At nearly 2 mi, the Golden Gate, completed in 1937 after four years of construction, was built to withstand winds of more than 100 mph. Though frequently gusty and misty (walkers should wear warm clothing), the bridge offers unparalleled views of the Bay Area. The east walkway yields a glimpse of the San Francisco skyline as well as the islands of the bay. The view west takes in the wild hills of the Marin Headlands, the curving coast south to Land's End, and the majestic Pacific Ocean. A vista point on the Marin side affords a spectacular view of the city. On sunny days sailboats dot the water, and brave windsurfers test the often-treacherous tides beneath the bridge. Muni Buses 28 and 29 make stops at the Golden Gate Bridge toll plaza, on the San Francisco side. ⊠ *Lincoln Blvd. near Doyle Dr. and Fort Point,* ☎ *415/921–5858.* ⊙ *Open daily, 24 hrs for cars and bikes, 5 AM–9 PM for pedestrians.*

★ **⑧ Palace of Fine Arts.** San Francisco's rosy rococo Palace of Fine Arts is at the western end of the Marina. The palace is the sole survivor of the many tinted plaster buildings (a temporary classical city of sorts) built for the 1915 Panama-Pacific International Exposition, the world's fair that celebrated San Francisco's recovery from the 1906 earthquake and fire. The expo lasted for 288 days and the buildings extended about a mile along the shore. Bernard Maybeck designed this faux Roman Classic beauty, which was reconstructed in concrete and reopened in 1967. The massive columns, great rotunda (dedicated to the glory of Greek culture), and swan-filled lagoon have been used in countless fashion layouts and films. ⊠ *Baker and Beach Sts.,* ☎ *415/561–0364 for palace tours.*

⑨ **Presidio.** Part of the Golden Gate National Recreation Area, the Presidio was a military post for more than 200 years. Don Juan Bautista de Anza and a band of Spanish settlers first claimed the area in 1776. It became a Mexican garrison in 1822 when Mexico gained its independence from Spain; U.S. troops forcibly occupied the Presidio in 1846. The U.S. Sixth Army was stationed here until October 1994, when the coveted space was transferred into civilian hands. The more than 1,400 acres of rolling hills, majestic woods, and redbrick army barracks present an air of serenity on the edge of the city. There are two beaches, a golf course, a visitor center (☞ *below*), and picnic sites, and the views of the bay, the Golden Gate Bridge, and Marin County are sublime. ⊠ *Between the Marina and Lincoln Park.*

⑩ **Presidio Museum.** This is one of the oldest buildings on the base put up by the U.S. Army. These days, the museum focuses on the role played by the military in San Francisco's development. Behind the museum are two cabins that housed refugees from the 1906 earthquake and fire. Photos on the wall of one depict rows and rows of temporary shelters at the Presidio and in Golden Gate Park following the disaster. The Presidio Museum plans to move into the visitor center by 2000. ⊠ *Lincoln Blvd. and Funston Ave.,* ☎ *415/561–4331.* ☜ *Free.* ⊙ *Wed.–Sun. noon–4.*

⑪ **Presidio Visitor Center.** National Park Service employees at what's officially the William P. Mott Jr. Visitor Center dispense maps, brochures, and schedules for guided walking and bicycle tours, along with information about the Presidio's past, present, and future. ⊠ *Montgomery St. between Lincoln Blvd. and Sheridan Ave.,* ☎ *415/561–4323.* ☜ *Free.* ⊙ *Daily 9–5.*

OFF THE BEATEN PATH	**WAVE ORGAN** – Fashioned by stonecutters George Gonzales and Thomas Lipps, this unusual instrument gives off harmonic sounds produced by the seawater that passes through its three stone chambers. ⊠ *North of the Marina Green at the end of the jetty by Yacht Rd. (Park in lot north of Marina Blvd. at Lyon St.).*

GOLDEN GATE PARK

William Hammond Hall conceived one of the nation's great city parks and began in 1870 to put into action his plan for a natural reserve with no reminders of urban life. Hammond began work in the Panhandle and eastern portions of Golden Gate Park, but it took John McLaren the length of his tenure as park superintendent, from 1890 to 1943, to complete the transformation of 1,000 desolate brush- and sand-covered acres into a rolling, landscaped oasis. Urban reality now encroaches on all sides, but the park remains a great getaway. On Sunday John F. Kennedy Drive is closed to cars and comes alive with joggers, bicyclists, and in-line skaters. In addition to cultural and other attractions there are public tennis courts, baseball diamonds, soccer fields, and trails for horseback riding. From May to October, **Friends of Recreation and Parks** (☎ 415/263–0991) conducts weekend walking tours. The fog can sweep into the park with amazing speed; always bring a sweatshirt or jacket.

The **Golden Gate Park Explorer Pass** ($14) grants admission to the M. H. de Young and Asian Art museums, plus the California Academy of Sciences and the Japanese Tea Garden. The passes, which are good for up to six months (the length depends on what time of year you buy the pass), can be purchased at the above sights except for the tea garden, or at TIX Bay Area in Union Square (☞ Union Square, *above*).

Because the park is so large, a car will come in handy if you're going to tour it from one end to the other—though you'll still do a fair amount of walking. You can make the jump between the attractions on the eastern edge of the park and the ones near the ocean on public transportation.

On weekends you can park all day for $3 at the University of California at San Francisco garage (enter at Irving Street and 2nd Avenue south of the park); from there a free shuttle leaves every 10 minutes for the park's museums. Muni also serves the park. Bus 5-Fulton stops along its northern edge, and the N-Judah light-rail car stops a block south of the park until 9th Avenue, two blocks the rest of the way west.

Numbers in the text correspond to numbers in the margin and on the Golden Gate Park map.

A Good Walk

Begin on the park's north side at Fulton Street and 6th Avenue, where the Bus 5-Fulton and Bus 21-Hayes from downtown stop. Walk south into the park at 6th Avenue. The road you'll come to is John F. Kennedy Drive. Turn left on the blacktop sidewalk and head east. Across the drive on your right is the Rhododendron Dell. (If it's springtime and the rhododendrons are in bloom, detour into the dell and return to Kennedy Drive heading east.) Past the first stop sign you'll see the exterior gardens of the **Conservatory of Flowers** ① on your left. Explore the gardens, then walk south (back toward Kennedy Drive) from the conservatory entrance. Continue east on Kennedy Drive a short way to the three-way intersection and turn right (south) at Middle Drive East.

Less than a block away at the intersection of Middle Drive and Bowling Green drives you'll see a sign for the National AIDS Memorial Grove. Before you enter the grove, follow the curve of Bowling Green Drive to the left, past the **Bowling Green** ② to the **Children's Playground** ③. If you've got kids in tow, you'll probably be spending time here. If not, still take a peek at the vintage Herschell-Spillman Carousel.

Reverse direction on Bowling Green Drive and enter the **National AIDS Memorial Grove** ④, a sunken meadow that stretches west along Middle Drive East. At the end of the wheelchair-access ramp make a left to view the Circle of Friends, then continue west along the graded paths (ignore the staircase on the right halfway through the grove) to another circle with a poem by Thom Gunn. Exit north from this circle. As you're standing in the circle looking at the poem, the staircase to take is on your left. At the top of the staircase make a left and continue west on Middle Drive East. You'll come to the back entrance of the **California Academy of Sciences** ⑤.

At the end of Middle Drive East, turn right and follow the signs leading to the **Shakespeare Garden** ⑥. After touring the garden, exit via the path on which you entered and turn left (to the south). A hundred feet shy of the Ninth Avenue and Lincoln Way entrance to Golden Gate Park is the main entrance to **Strybing Arboretum and Botanical Gardens** ⑦. You could spend an afternoon here, but to sample just a bit of this fine facility take the first right after the bookstore. Follow the path as it winds north and west. Take your second right and you'll see signs for the fragrance and Biblical gardens.

Backtrack from the gardens to the path you started on and make a right. As the path continues to wind north and west, you'll see a large fountain off to the left. Just before you get to the fountain, make a right and head toward the duck pond. A wooden footbridge on the pond's left side crosses the water. Signs on the other side identify the mallards, geese, American coots, mews, and other fowl in the pond. Stay to the right on the path, heading toward the exit gate. Just before the gate, continue to the right to the Primitive Garden. Take the looped board-walk past ferns, gingko, cycads, conifers, moss, and other plants. At the end of the loop, make a left and then a right, exiting via the Eugene L. Friend gate. Go straight ahead on the crosswalk to the black-top path on the other side. Make a right, walk about 100 ft, and make a left on Tea Garden Drive. A few hundred feet east of here is the entrance to the **Japanese Tea Garden** ⑧.

Tour the Japanese Tea Garden, exiting near the gate you entered. Make a left, and you'll soon pass the **Asian Art Museum** ⑨ and **M. H. de Young Memorial Museum** ⑩. Near the main entrance to the de Young is a crosswalk that leads south to the Music Concourse, with its gnarled trees, century-old fountains and sculptures, and the Golden Gate Bandshell. Turn left at the closest of the fountains and head east toward the bronze sculpture of Francis Scott Key.

Turn left at the statue and proceed north through two underpasses. At the end of the second underpass, you'll have traveled about 2 mi. If you're ready to leave the park, take the short staircase to the left of the blue and green playground equipment. At the top of the staircase is the 10th Avenue and Fulton Street stop for the Bus 5-Fulton heading back downtown. If you're game for walking ½ mi more, make an immediate left as you exit the second underpass, cross 10th Avenue, and make a right on John F. Kennedy Drive. After ⁷⁄₁₀ mi you'll see the Rose Garden on your right. Continue west to the first stop sign. To the left is a sign for **Stow Lake** ⑪. Follow the road past the log cabin to the boathouse.

From Stow Lake it's the equivalent of 30 long blocks on John F. Kennedy Drive to the western end of the park and the ocean. If you walk, you'll pass meadows, the Portals of the Past, the buffalo paddock, and a nine-hole golf course. You can skip most of this walk by proceeding west on John F. Kennedy Drive from the stop sign mentioned above, making the first right after you walk underneath Cross-Over Drive, and following the road as it winds left toward 25th Avenue and Fulton. On the northwest corner of Fulton Street and 25th Avenue, catch the Bus 5-Fulton heading west, get off at 46th Avenue, walk one block west to 47th Avenue, and make a left. Make a right on John F. Kennedy Drive.

By foot or vehicle, your goal is the **Dutch Windmill** ⑫ and adjoining garden. A block to the south is the **Beach Chalet** ⑬.

TIMING

You can easily spend a whole day in Golden Gate Park, especially if you walk the whole distance. Set aside at least an hour each for the Academy of Sciences, the Asian Art Museum, and the de Young Museum. Even if you plan to explore just the eastern end of the park (up to Stow Lake), allot at least four hours.

Sights to See

★ ⑨ **Asian Art Museum.** The museum's collection includes more than 12,000 sculptures, paintings, and ceramics from 40 countries, illustrating major periods of Asian art. The bulk of the art and artifacts, though, come from China. On the first floor are special exhibitions as well as galleries dedicated to works from Korea and China. On the second floor are treasures from Iran, Turkey, Syria, India, Tibet, Nepal, Pakistan, India, Japan, Afghanistan, and Southeast Asia. This facility will close prior to the museum's move to the Civic Center in 2002. ⊠ *Tea Garden Dr. off John F. Kennedy Dr., near 10th Ave. and Fulton St.,* ☎ *415/668–8921 or 415/379–8801.* ⌫ *$7 ($2 off with Muni transfer), good also for same-day admission to the M. H. de Young Museum and the Legion of Honor Museum in Lincoln Park; free 1st Wed. of month.* ⊙ *Tues.–Sun. 9:30–5, 1st Wed. of month until 8:45.*

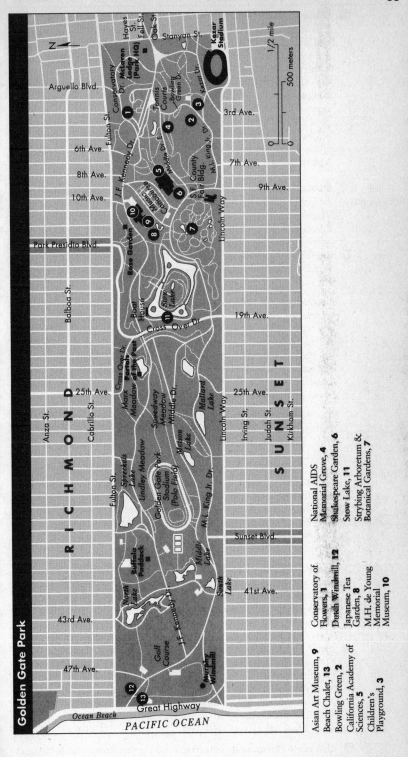

Golden Gate Park

1/2 mile

500 meters

Hayes St.

Fell St.

Oak St.

Stanyan St.

Kezar Stadium

Arguello Blvd.

Conservatory Dr.

McLaren Lodge (Park HQ)

Kezar Dr.

Bowling Green Dr.

3rd Ave.

Tennis Courts

Fulton St.

6th Ave.

8th Ave.

10th Ave.

J.F. Kennedy Dr.

Middle Dr.

Nancy Pelosi Dr.

7th Ave.

9th Ave.

M.L. King Jr. Dr.

S.F. County Fair Bldg.

Lincoln Way

Rose Garden

Park Presidio Blvd.

Balboa St.

Anza St.

Cabrillo St.

25th Ave.

Boat House

Stow Lake

Cross-Over Dr.

19th Ave.

Marx Meadow

John F Kennedy Dr.

Martin Luther King Jr. Dr.

Speedway Meadow

Middle Dr.

Mallard Lake

Metson Lake

25th Ave.

Irving St.

Judah St.

Kirkham St.

Lincoln Way

R I C H M O N D

S U N S E T

Fulton St.

Spreckels Lake

Lindley Meadow

Golden Gate Park Stadium (Polo Field)

M.L. King Jr. Dr.

Sunset Blvd.

Buffalo Paddock

Middle Lake

North Lake

South Lake

43rd Ave.

47th Ave.

J.F. Kennedy Dr.

Golf Course

Murphy Windmill

41st Ave.

Great Highway

Ocean Beach

PACIFIC OCEAN

Asian Art Museum, **9**
Beach Chalet, **13**
Bowling Green, **2**
California Academy of Sciences, **5**
Children's Playground, **3**

Conservatory of Flowers, **1**
Dutch Windmill, **12**
Japanese Tea Garden, **8**
M.H. de Young Memorial Museum, **10**

National AIDS Memorial Grove, **4**
Shakespeare Garden, **6**
Stow Lake, **11**
Strybing Arboretum & Botanical Gardens, **7**

⑬ **Beach Chalet.** This Spanish Colonial–style structure, architect Willis Polk's last design, was built in 1925 after his death. A wraparound federal works project mural by Lucien Labaudt depicts San Francisco in the 1930s; the labels describing the various panels add up to a mini-history of Depression-era life in the city. A three-dimensional model of Golden Gate Park, artifacts from the 1894 Mid-Winter Exposition and other park events, a visitor center, and a gift shop that sells street signs and other city paraphernalia are on the first floor as well. On a clear day, the brew pub–restaurant upstairs (notice the carved bannister on the way up) has views past Ocean Beach to the Farallon Islands, about 30 mi offshore. ⊠ *1000 Great Hwy., at west end of John F. Kennedy Dr.*

OFF THE BEATEN PATH **BUFFALO PADDOCK** – The original denizens of the paddock arrived at the park in 1894 for the Mid-Winter Exposition. The present herd, from Wyoming, was acquired in 1984. ⊠ *John F. Kennedy Dr. west of Spreckels Lake.*

★ ☘ ⑤ **California Academy of Sciences.** A three-in-one attraction, the nationally renowned academy houses an aquarium, numerous science and natural-history exhibits, and a planetarium.

Leopard sharks, silver salmon, sea bass, and other fish loop around the mesmerizing Fish Roundabout, the big draw at **Steinhart Aquarium.** Feeding time is 2 PM. At the Touch Tide Pool, you can cozy up to starfish, hermit crabs, and other critters. Elsewhere at Steinhart swim dolphins, sea turtles, piranhas, manatees, and other sea life. There are also reptile and amphibian displays and an alligator pond. Vibrantly colored fish vie for attention with iridescent coral at the tropical coral reef. Always amusing to watch, the penguins dine at 11:30 AM and 4 PM.

The multimedia earthquake exhibit in the Earth and Space Hall at the **Natural History Museum** simulates quakes, complete with special effects. Videos and displays in the Wild California Hall describe the state's wildlife, and there's a re-creation of the environment of the rocky Farallon Islands. Dinosaur bones and a Brontosaurus skull draw dinophiles to the Hall of Fossils. African Hall contains animals (real but stuffed) specific to Africa in their native vegetation; don't miss the sights and sounds of the African watering hole at the end of the room. The natural-history wing's other attractions include the gem and mineral hall, an insect room, Far Side of Science cartoons by Gary Larson, and an open play and learning space for small children.

There is an additional charge (up to $2.50) for **Morrison Planetarium** shows (☎ 415/750–7141 for schedule), which you enter through the Natural History Museum. Daily multimedia shows present the night sky through the ages under a 55-ft dome, complete with special effects and music. The **Laserium** presents evening laser-light shows (☎ 415/750–7138 for schedule and fees) at Morrison Planetarium, accompanied by rock, classical, and other types of music; educational shows outline laser technology. A cafeteria is open daily until one hour before the museum closes. ⊠ *Music Concourse Dr. off South Dr., across from Asian Art and de Young museums,* ☎ *415/750–7145.* ⊡ *$8.50; $1 discount with Muni transfer; free 1st Wed. of month.* ☉ *Memorial Day–Labor Day, daily 9–6; Labor Day–Memorial Day, daily 10–5; 1st Wed. of month closes at 8:45 PM.*

☘ ③ **Children's Playground.** Kids have been coming here to cut loose since the 1880s. The equipment has changed over the years, but the squeals and howls remain the same. A menagerie of handcrafted horses and other animals—among them cats, frogs, roosters, and a tiger—twirl on the 1912 Herschell-Spillman Carousel, inside a many-windowed circular structure. The Romanesque-style Sharon Building looms over the playground. The 1887 structure has been rebuilt twice, following the earthquake of 1906 and a 1980 fire. ⊠ *Bowling Green Dr., off Martin Luther King Jr. Dr.,* ☎ *415/831–2700.* ☺ *Playground free, carousel $1.* ☺ *Playground open daily dawn–midnight; carousel June–Sept., daily 10–5, Oct.–May, Fri.–Sun. 10–4:30 (carousel hrs vary).*

❶ Conservatory of Flowers. The oldest building in the park and the last remaining wood-frame Victorian conservatory in the country, the Conservatory, which was built in the late 1870s, is a copy of the one in the Royal Botanical Gardens in Kew, England. Heavily damaged during a 1995 storm, the whitewashed facility is closed indefinitely but its architecture and gardens make it a worthy stop nonetheless. The gardens in front of the Conservatory are planted seasonally, with the flowers often fashioned like billboards—trumpeting a Super Bowl victory by the 49ers football team or depicting the Golden Gate Bridge or other city sights. On the east side of the Conservatory (to the right as you face the building), cypress, pine, and redwood trees surround the **Fuchsia Garden**, which blooms in summer and fall. To the west several hundred feet on John F. Kennedy Drive is the **Rhododendron Dell**. The dell contains the most varieties—850 in all—of any garden in the country. It's especially beautiful in March when many of the flowers bloom and is a favorite spot of locals for Mother's Day picnics. ⊠ *John F. Kennedy Dr. at Conservatory Dr.*

⓬ Dutch Windmill. Two windmills anchor the western end of the park. The restored 1902 Dutch Windmill once pumped 20,000 gallons of well water per hour to the reservoir on Strawberry Hill (☞ Stow Lake, *below*). With its heavy cement bottom and wood-shingled arms and upper section the windmill cuts quite the sturdy figure. The structure overlooks the equally photogenic **Queen Wilhelmina Tulip Garden**, which bursts into full bloom in early spring and late summer. The **Murphy Windmill**, on Martin Luther King Jr. Drive near the Great Highway, was the world's largest windmill when it was built in 1905. Now in disrepair, its wings clipped, the Murphy Windmill also pumped water to the Strawberry Hill reservoir. ⊠ *Between 47th Ave. and the Great Hwy.*

★ ❽ Japanese Tea Garden. A serene 4-acre landscape of small ponds, streams, waterfalls, stone bridges, Japanese sculptures, *mumsai* (planted bonsai) trees, perfect miniature pagodas, and some nearly vertical wooden "humpback" bridges, the tea garden was created for the 1894 Mid-Winter Exposition. Go in the spring if you can (March is particularly beautiful), when the cherry blossoms are in bloom. ⊠ *Tea Garden Dr. off John F. Kennedy Dr.,* ☎ *415/752–4227 or 415/752–1171.* ☺ *$3.50.* ☺ *Mar.–Sept., daily 9–6:30; Oct.–Feb., daily 8:30–6.*

NEED A BREAK?	Rest your feet and take in the soothing sights of the Japanese Tea Garden from a seat in the covered-roof, open-air **Tea House**, a low-lit space with hanging lanterns and long wooden benches. Tea and cookies are served.

❿ M. H. de Young Memorial Museum. Works on display at the de Young include American paintings, sculpture, textiles, and decorative arts from Colonial times through the 20th century. The John D. Rockefeller III Collection of American Paintings is especially noteworthy, with more than 200 paintings of American masters like John Singleton Copley, Thomas Eakins, George Caleb Bingham, and John Singer Sargent. Frederic Church's moody, almost psychedelic *Rainy Season in the Trop-*

ics dominates the room of landscapes. Within the gallery of American still lifes are the trompe l'oeil paintings of William Harnett. The de Young also has collections of African and Native American art, including sculpture, baskets, and ceramics. Ongoing textile installations showcase everything from tribal clothing to couture. The museum hosts traveling exhibitions that sometimes involve extra admission charges and extended hours. The **Café de Young** has outdoor seating in the lovely Oakes Garden. ⊠ *Tea Garden Dr. off John F. Kennedy Dr., near 10th Ave. and Fulton St.,* ☏ *415/863–3330.* ☏ *$7 ($2 off with Muni transfer), good also for same-day admission to the Asian Art Museum and the Legion of Honor Museum in Lincoln Park; free 1st Wed. of month until 5.* ⊙ *Tues.–Sun. 9:30–5, 1st Wed. of month until 8:45.*

❹ National AIDS Memorial Grove. San Francisco has lost many residents, gay and straight, to AIDS. This 15-acre grove, started in the early 1990s by people with AIDS and their families and friends, was conceived as a living memorial to those the disease has claimed. Hundreds of volunteers toiled long and hard raising funds and clearing this patch of green, also known as De Laveaga Dell. In 1996 Congress passed a bill granting the grove status as a national memorial. Coast live oaks, Monterey pines, coast redwoods, and other trees flank the grove, which is anchored at its east end by the stone Circle of Friends (of donors, people who have died of AIDS, and those who loved them). A 1996 poem by San Franciscan Thom Gunn in the tan fieldstone circle at the west end of the grove reads: WALKER WITHIN THIS CIRCLE PAUSE/ALTHOUGH THEY DIED OF ONE CAUSE/REMEMBER HOW THEIR LIVES WERE DENSE/WITH FINE COMPACTED DIFFERENCE. ⊠ *Middle Dr. E, west of tennis courts.*

OFF THE
BEATEN PATH

PORTALS OF THE PAST – An evocative relic of a Nob Hill mansion that was wrecked by the 1906 earthquake and fire, the Ionic columns that once framed the mansion's entryway now stand in solitude on the edge of Lloyd Lake. ⊠ *Beside Lloyd Lake off John F. Kennedy Dr., south of 25th Ave.*

❻ Shakespeare Garden. Two hundred flowers and herbs mentioned in the Bard's plays grow here. Bronze-engraved passages contain relevant floral quotations. ⊠ *Middle Dr. E at southwest corner of California Academy of Sciences.*

⓫ Stow Lake. One of the most picturesque spots in Golden Gate Park, this placid body of water surrounds Strawberry Hill. A couple of bridges allow you to cross over and ascend the hill (the old 19th-century stone bridge on the southwest side of the lake is especially quaint). A waterfall cascades down from the top of the hill, and panoramic views make it worth the short hike up here. Down below, rent a boat, surrey, or bicycle or stroll around the perimeter. Just to the left of the waterfall sits the elaborate Chinese Pavilion, a gift from the city of Taipei. It was shipped in 6,000 pieces and assembled on the shore of Strawberry Hill Island in 1981. ⊠ *Off John F. Kennedy Dr. ½ mi west of 10th Ave.,* ☏ *415/752–0347.*

❼ Strybing Arboretum & Botanical Gardens. The 55-acre arboretum specializes in plants from areas with climates similar to that of the Bay Area, such as the west coast of Australia, South Africa, and the Mediterranean; more than 8,000 plant and tree varieties bloom in gardens throughout the grounds. Among the highlights are the Biblical, fragrance, California native plants, succulents, and primitive gardens, the new and old world cloud forests, and the duck pond. The exhaustive reference library holds approximately 18,000 volumes, and the bookstore is a great resource. Maps are available at the main and Eugene L. Friend entrances. ⊠ *9th Ave. at Lincoln Way,* ☎ *415/661–1316.* 🎫 *Free.* 🕐 *Weekdays 8–4:30, weekends and holidays 10–5. Tours leave the bookstore weekdays at 1:30, weekends at 10:30.*

LINCOLN PARK AND THE WESTERN SHORELINE

Few other American cities provide a close-up view of the power and fury of the surf attacking the shore. A different breed of San Franciscan chooses to live in this area: surfers who brave the heaviest fog to ride the waves; writers who seek solace and inspiration in this city outpost; dog lovers committed to giving their pets a good workout each day.

From Land's End in Lincoln Park you'll have some of the best views of the Golden Gate (the name was originally given to the opening of San Francisco Bay long before the bridge was built) and the Marin Headlands. From the historic Cliff House south to the sprawling San Francisco Zoo, the Great Highway and Ocean Beach run along the western edge of the city. The wind is often strong along the shoreline, summer fog can blanket the ocean beaches, and the water is cold and usually too rough for swimming. Carry a jacket and bring binoculars.

Numbers in the text correspond to numbers in the margin and on the Lincoln Park and the Western Shoreline map.

A Good Drive

A car is useful out here. There are plenty of hiking trails, and buses travel to all the sights mentioned, but the sights are far apart. Start at **Lincoln Park** ①. The park entrance is at 34th Avenue and Clement Street. Those without a car can take Bus 38-Geary—get off at 33rd Avenue and walk north (to the right) one block on 34th Avenue to the entrance. At the end of 34th Avenue (labeled on some maps as Legion of Honor Drive within Lincoln Park) is the **California Palace of the Legion of Honor** ②, a splendid art museum. From the museum, head back out to Clement Street and follow it west. At 45th Avenue Clement turns into Seal Rock Drive. When Seal Rock dead-ends at 48th Avenue, turn left on El Camino del Mar and right on Point Lobos Avenue. After a few hundred yards, you'll see parking lots for **Sutro Heights Park** ③ and the **Cliff House** ④. (To get from the Legion of Honor to Point Lobos Avenue by public transit, take Bus 18 from the Legion of Honor parking lot west to the corner of 48th and Point Lobos avenues.) Two large concrete lions near the southeast corner of 48th and Point Lobos guard the entrance to Sutro Heights Park. After taking a quick spin through the park, exit past the lions, cross Point Lobos, make a left, and walk down to the Cliff House. From the Cliff House it's a short walk farther downhill to **Ocean Beach** ⑤.

The **San Francisco Zoo** ⑥ is a couple of miles south, at the intersection of the Great Highway and Sloat Boulevard. If you're driving, follow the Great Highway (heading south from the Cliff House, Point Lobos Avenue becomes the Great Highway), turn left on Sloat Boulevard, and park in the zoo's lot on Sloat. The hike along Ocean Beach from the Cliff House to the zoo is a flat but scenic 3 mi. To take public transportation from the Cliff House, reboard Bus 18, which continues south to the zoo.

TIMING

Set aside at least three hours for this tour—more if you don't have a car. An hour can easily be spent in the Palace of the Legion of Honor and 1½ hours at the zoo.

Sights to See

★ ❷   **California Palace of the Legion of Honor.** Spectacularly situated on cliffs overlooking the ocean, the Golden Gate Bridge, and the Marin Headlands, this landmark building is a fine repository of European art. A pyramidal glass skylight in the entrance court illuminates the lower-level galleries, which exhibit prints and drawings, English and European porcelain, and ancient Assyrian, Greek, Roman, and Egyptian art. The 20-plus galleries on the upper level are devoted to the permanent collection of European art (paintings, sculpture, decorative arts, tapestries) from the 14th to the 20th century. The noteworthy Rodin collection includes two galleries devoted to the master and a third with works by Rodin and other 19th-century sculptors. An original cast of Rodin's *The Thinker* welcomes you as you walk through the courtyard.

The **Legion Café,** on the lower level, has a garden terrace and a view of the Golden Gate Bridge. North of the museum (across Camino del Mar) is George Segal's *The Holocaust,* a sculpture that evokes life in concentration camps during World War II. It is hauntingly eloquent at night, when backlit by lights in the Legion's parking lot. ⊠ *34th Ave. at Clement St.,* ☎ *415/863–3330 for 24-hr information.* ⊇ *$7 ($2 off with Muni transfer), good also for same-day admission to Asian Art and M. H. de Young museums; free 2nd Wed. of month.* ☉ *Tues.–Sun. 9:30–5; 1st Sat. of month until 8:45.*

❹   **Cliff House.** Three buildings have occupied this site since 1863. The original Cliff House hosted several U.S. presidents and wealthy locals who would drive their carriages out to Ocean Beach; it was destroyed by fire on Christmas Day 1894. The second Cliff House, the most beloved and resplendent of the three, was built in 1896; it rose eight stories with an observation tower 200 ft above sea level. The current building dates from 1909. The complex, which includes restaurants, a pub, and a gift shop, will remain open in 2000 while undergoing a gradual renovation to restore its early 20th-century look.

The upstairs brunch at the Cliff House is standard—eggs any style, good omelets, and the like—but the views enhance the experience. Lunch and dinner are nothing to write home about, but there are those vistas, which can be 30 mi or more on a clear day. The dining areas overlook Seal Rock (the barking marine mammals sunning themselves are actually sea lions).

Below the Cliff House is the splendid **Musée Mécanique** (☎ 415/386–1170), a time-warped arcade with antique mechanical contrivances, including peep shows and nickelodeons. Some favorites are the giant, rather creepy "Laughing Sal," an arm-wrestling machine, and mechanical fortune-telling figures who speak from their curtained boxes. A disturbing display is the "Opium-Den," a tiny diorama with Chinese figures clearly depicting the effects of heavy drug use. The museum stays opens daily from Memorial Day to Labor Day between 10 and 8 and the rest of the year on weekdays between 11 and 7 and on weekends between 10 and 7. Admission is free, but you may want to bring change to play the games.

The Musée Mécanique looks out on a fine observation deck and the **Golden Gate National Recreation Area Visitors' Center** (☎ 415/556–8642), which contains fascinating historical photographs of the Cliff House and the glass-roof Sutro Baths. The Sutro complex, which comprised six enormous baths, 500 dressing rooms, and several restaurants, covered 3 acres north of the Cliff House. The baths were closed in 1952 and burned down in 1966. You can explore the ruins on your own (they

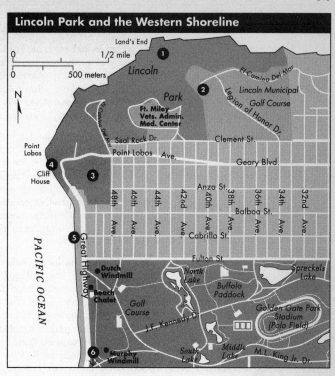

Lincoln Park and the Western Shoreline

look a bit like water-storage receptacles) or take ranger-led walks on weekends. The visitor center, open daily from 10 to 5 except major holidays, provides information about these and other trails. ⊠ *1090 Point Lobos Ave.,* ☎ *415/386–3330.* ⊙ *Weekdays 8 AM–10:30 PM, weekends 8 AM–11 PM; cocktails served nightly until 2 AM.*

❶ Lincoln Park. At one time most of the city's cemeteries were here, segregated by nationality. In 1900, the Board of Supervisors voted to ban burials within city limits (two exceptions are the cemetery at Mission Dolores and the one in the Presidio). Large Monterey cypresses line the fairways at Lincoln Park's 18-hole golf course. There are scenic walks throughout the 275-acre park, with postcard-perfect views from many spots. The trail out to **Land's End** starts outside the Palace of the Legion of Honor, at the end of El Camino del Mar. Be careful if you hike here; landslides are frequent. ⊠ *Entrance at 34th Ave. at Clement St.*

❺ Ocean Beach. Stretching 3 mi along the western side of the city, this is a good beach for walking, running, or lying in the sun—but not for swimming. Surfers here wear wet suits year-round as the water is extremely cold. Riptides are also very dangerous here. Paths on both sides of the Great Highway lead from Lincoln Way to Sloat Boulevard (near the zoo); the beachside path winds through landscaped sand dunes, and the paved path across the highway is good for biking and in-line skating. The **Beach Chalet** (☞ Golden Gate Park, *above*) restaurant and brew pub are across the Great Highway from Ocean Beach, about five blocks south of the Cliff House. ⊠ *Along the Great Hwy. from the Cliff House to Sloat Blvd. and beyond.*

❻ San Francisco Zoo. More than 1,000 birds and animals—220 species altogether—reside at the zoo. Among the more than 130 endangered species are the snow leopard, Sumatran tiger, jaguar, and Asian elephant. A favorite attraction is the greater one-horned rhinoceros, next to the

African elephants. Another popular resident is Prince Charles, a rare white tiger and the first of its kind to be exhibited in the West.

African Kikuyu grass carpets the circular outer area of **Gorilla World,** one of the largest and most natural gorilla habitats of any zoo in the world. Trees and shrubs create communal play areas. Fifteen species of rare monkeys—including colobus monkeys, white ruffed lemurs, and macaques—live and play at the two-tier **Primate Discovery Center,** which contains 23 interactive learning exhibits on the ground level.

Magellanic penguins waddle about **Penguin Island,** splashing and frolicking in its 200-ft pool. Feeding time is 3 PM. Koalas peer out from among the trees in **Koala Crossing,** and kangaroos and wallabies headline the **Walkabout** exhibit. The 7-acre **South American Gateway** recreates habitats on that continent, replete with howler monkeys, tapirs, and a cloud forest. The **Feline Conservation Center,** a natural setting for rare cats, plays a key role in the zoo's efforts to encourage breeding among endangered felines. Don't miss the big cat feeding—they love their horse meat—Tuesday through Sunday at 2.

There are about four dozen information kiosks called story boxes throughout the zoo. When turned on with blue and red keys ($2), each box will recite animal facts and basic zoological concepts in four languages—English, Spanish, Cantonese, and Tagalog. The **children's zoo** has a population of about 300 mammals, birds, and reptiles, plus an insect zoo, a baby-animal nursery, a deer park, a nature trail, a nature theater, and a restored 1921 Dentzel carousel. A ride astride one of the 52 hand-carved menagerie animals costs $1. ✉ *Sloat Blvd. and the Great Hwy. (Muni L-Taraval streetcar from downtown),* ☎ *415/753-7080.* ✎ *$9 ($1 off with Muni transfer); free 1st Wed. of month.* ☉ *Daily 10–5; children's zoo weekdays 11–4, weekends 10:30–4:30.*

❸ Sutro Heights Park. Crows and other large birds battle the heady breezes at this clifftop park on what were the grounds of the home of mining engineer and former San Francisco mayor Adolph Sutro. Monterey cypresses and Canary Island palms dot the park, and photos on placards depict what you would have seen before the house burned down in 1896. All that remains of the main house is its foundation. Climb up for a sweeping view of the Pacific Ocean and the Cliff House below, and try to imagine what the perspective might have been like from one of the upper floors. ✉ *Point Lobos and 48th Aves.*

MISSION DISTRICT

The sunny Mission district wins out in San Francisco's system of microclimates—it's always the last to succumb to fog. Home to Italian and Irish communities in the early 20th century, the Mission has been heavily Latino since the late 1960s, when immigrants from Mexico and Central America began arriving. Despite its distinctive Latino flavor, the Mission has in recent years seen an influx of Chinese, Vietnamese, Arabic, and other immigrants, along with a young bohemian crowd enticed by cheap rents and the burgeoning arts and entertainment scene. The district is yet again in transition, as gentrification is leading to higher rents, forcing some longtime residents to move. The Mission, still a bit scruffy in patches, lacks some of the glamour of other neighborhoods, but a walk through it provides the opportunity to mix with a heady cross-section of San Franciscans.

The eight blocks of Valencia Street between 16th and 24th streets—what's come to be known as the Valencia Corridor—typifies the neighborhood's diversity. Businesses on the block between 16th and 17th streets, for instance, include an upscale Vietnamese restaurant, a Lebanese restaurant where in the evening belly dancers writhe gracefully, the Bombay Ice Cream parlor (try a scoop of the zesty cardamom ice cream) and adjacent Indian grocery and sundries store, a tattoo parlor, the yuppie-chic Blondie's bar, pizzerias and taquerias, a Turkish restaurant, a sushi bar, bargain and pricey thrift shops, a cyber café, and the Puerto Allegre restaurant (a hole-in-the-wall whose pack-a-punch margaritas locals revere).

Cinco de Mayo is an important event in the Mission: Music, dance, and parades commemorates the victory, on May 5, 1862, of Mexicans over French troops that had invaded their country. On Memorial Day weekend, the revelers come out in earnest, when **Carnaval** transforms the neighborhood into a northern Rio de Janeiro for three days. Festivities close down several blocks (usually of Harrison Street), where musicians and dancers perform and crafts and food booths are set up. The Grand Carnaval Parade, along 24th and Mission streets, caps the celebration.

Numbers in the text correspond to numbers in the margin and on the Mission District/Noe Valley map.

A Good Walk

The spiritual heart of the old Mission lies within the thick, white adobe walls of **Mission Dolores** ①, where Dolores Street intersects with 16th Street. From the mission, cross Dolores Street and head east on 16th Street. Tattooed and pierced hipsters abound a block from Mission Dolores, but the eclectic area still has room for a place like **Creativity Explored** ②, where people with developmental disabilities work on art and other projects. Cafés and bookstores tumble willy-nilly into each other in the next block, between Guerrero and Valencia streets, which contains the idiosyncratic Roxie Cinema (☞ Film *in* Chapter 4), a great venue for art and independent films. At the intersection of 16th and Valencia streets, head south (to the right), poking your head into any shops that intrigue you. At 18th Street walk a half block west (right) to view the mural adorning the **Women's Building** ③.

Head back to Valencia Street and make a right to check out the shops and cafés on the next several blocks. A few businesses the likes of which—depending on where you live—you might not see back home include Leather Tongue Video at Number 714, the leftist Modern Times Bookstore (☞ Booksellers *in* Chapter 6) at Number 888, and Good Vibrations, a tastefully jolly women-run erotica emporium at Number 1210.

By the time you reach 24th Street and head east (left off Valencia), the atmosphere becomes distinctly Latin American. Record stores such as Discolandia, at Number 2964, sell the latest Spanish-language hits, family groceries sell Latin-American ingredients and delicacies, shops proffer religious goods, and restaurants serve authentic dishes from several nations.

A half block east of Folsom Street, mural-lined **Balmy Alley** ④ runs south from 24th Street to 25th Street. View the murals then head back up Balmy to 24th and continue east a few steps to the **Precita Eyes Mural Arts and Visitors Center** ⑤. From the center continue east past St. Peter's Church, where Isías Mata's mural *500 Years of Resistance,* on the exterior of the rectory, reflects on the struggles and survival of Latin-American cultures. At 24th and Bryant streets is the **Galeria de la Raza/Studio 24** ⑥ art space.

Diagonally across from the Galería, on Bryant at the northeast corner near 24th Street, you can catch the Bus 27-Bryant to downtown. If you want to combine tours of the Mission District and Noe Valley (☞ *below*) but save yourself a little walking, take a Muni Bus 48–Quintara/24th Street heading west (board directly across from the Galería on 24th Street) and get off at Church Street, where the Noe Valley tour begins.

TIMING

The above walk takes about two hours, including brief stops at the various sights listed. If you plan to go on a mural walk with Precita Eyes, add at least another hour.

Sights to See

❹ Balmy Alley. Mission District artists have transformed the walls of their neighborhood with paintings. Balmy Alley is one of the best-executed examples. The entire one-block alley is filled with murals. Local children working with adults started the project in 1971. Since then dozens of artists have steadily added to it, with the aim of promoting peace in Central America, as well as community spirit and AIDS awareness. (Be careful in this area. The other end of the street adjoins the back of a somewhat dangerous housing project.) ⊠ *24th St. between and parallel to Harrison and Treat Sts. (alley runs south to 25th St.).*

❷ Creativity Explored. An atmosphere of joyous, if chaotic, creativity pervades the workshops of Creativity Explored, an art education center and gallery for developmentally disabled adults. Several dozen adults work at the center each day—guided by a staff of 13 working artists—painting, working in the darkroom, producing videos, and crafting prints, textiles, and ceramics. On weekdays, you can drop by and see the artists at work. Five blocks east is **Creativity Explored II** (⊠ 2795 16th St., ☎ 415/863–2946), the work space for the center's more severely developmentally disabled adults; the gallery next door to it, open from 8:30 to 3, displays works from both centers. ⊠ *3245 16th St.,* ☎ *415/863–2108.* ☉ *Weekdays 8:30–3:30.*

❻ Galería de la Raza/Studio 24. San Francisco's premiere showcase for Latino art, the gallery exhibits the works of local and international artists. Next door is the nonprofit Studio 24, which sells prints and paintings by Chicano artists, as well as folk art, mainly from Mexico. In early November the studio brims with art objects paying tribute to *Dia de los Muertos* (Day of the Dead). In Mexican tradition death is not feared but seen as a part of life—thus the many colorful skeleton figurines doing everyday things like housework or playing sports. ⊠ *2857 24th St., at Bryant St.,* ☎ *415/826–8009.* ☉ *Tues.–Sat. noon–6.*

NEED A BREAK?

If you've worked up an appetite walking the Mission, consider a *panadería* (bakery) stop at **Dominguez** (⊠ 2951 24th St., at Alabama St., ☎ 415/821–1717) or **La Victoria** (⊠ 2937 24th St., at Alabama St., ☎ 415/550–9292). The shops sell Latin-American pastries and plenty of atmosphere. For an old-fashioned soda or some homemade ice cream or candy, stop into the **Saint Francis Fountain and Candy Store** (⊠ 2801 24th St., at York St., ☎ 415/826–4200), in business since 1918.

❶ Mission Dolores. Mission Dolores encompasses two churches standing side by side. Completed in 1791, the small adobe building known as Mission San Francisco de Asís is the oldest standing structure in San Francisco and the sixth of the 21 California missions founded by Father Junípero Serra in the 18th and early 19th centuries. Its ceiling depicts original Ohlone Indian basket designs, executed in vegetable dyes. Frescoes and a hand-painted wooden altar decorate the tiny chapel; some artifacts were brought from Mexico by mule in the late 18th century. There is a small museum, and the pretty little mission cemetery (made famous by a scene in Alfred Hitchcock's *Vertigo*)

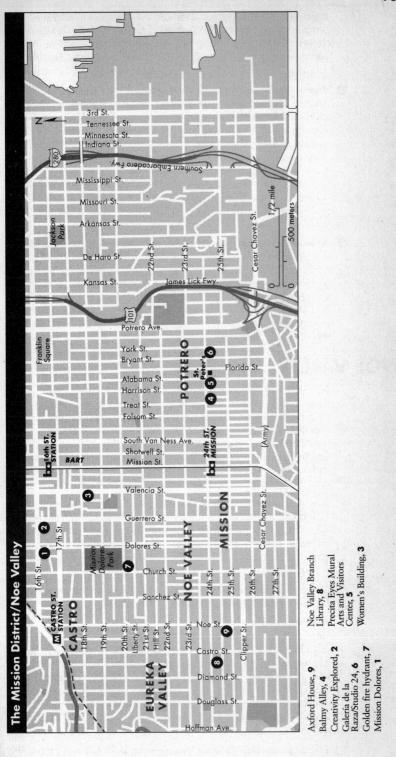

The Mission District/Noe Valley

Axford House, **9**
Balmy Alley, **4**
Creativity Explored, **2**
Galería de la
Raza/Studio 24, **6**
Golden fire hydrant, **7**
Mission Dolores, **1**

Noe Valley Branch
Library, **8**
Precita Eyes Mural
Arts and Visitors
Center, **5**
Women's Building, **3**

maintains the graves of mid-19th-century European immigrants. (The remains of an estimated 5,000 Native Americans lie in unmarked graves.) Services are held in both the Mission San Francisco de Asís and next door in the handsome multidome Basilica. ⊠ *Dolores and 16th Sts.,* ☎ *415/621–8203.* 🎦 *$2 (audio tour $5).* ☉ *Daily 9–4.*

❺ **Precita Eyes Mural Arts and Visitors Center.** This nonprofit arts organization sponsors guided walks of the Mission District's murals. Most tours start with a 45-minute slide presentation. The bus, bike, and walking trips, which take between one and three hours, pass by several dozen murals. May is Mural Awareness Month, with visits to murals-in-progress and presentations by artists. You can pick up a map of 24th Street's murals at the center and buy art supplies, T-shirts, postcards, and other mural-related items. ⊠ *2981 24th St.,* ☎ *415/285–2287.* 🎦 *Free to center, $5–$10 for tours.* ☉ *Center weekdays 10–5, weekends 10–4; walks Sat. at 11 and 1:30 or by appointment, bus tours 2nd Sun. of month, bike tours 3rd Sun. of month.*

❸ **Women's Building.** The cornerstone of the female-owned and -run businesses in the neighborhood is the Women's Building, which since 1979 has held workshops and conferences of particular interest to women. It houses offices for many social and political organizations and sponsors talks and readings by writers like Alice Walker and Angela Davis. The building's two-sided exterior mural depicts women's peacekeeping efforts over the centuries. ⊠ *3543 18th St.,* ☎ *415/431–1180.* ☉ *Weekdays 9–5.*

NOE VALLEY

Noe Valley and adjacent Twin Peaks were once known as Rancho San Miguel, a parcel of land given to the last Mexican mayor of San Francisco (then known as Yerba Buena) in 1845. Mayor Don José de Jesús Noe built his ranch house at 22nd and Eureka streets, and the area continued as a bucolic farming community until 1906. Because Noe Valley was so little affected by the quake, many of the displaced headed here and decided to stay. It was predominantly working class and largely Irish until the 1970s, when it saw an influx of well-heeled liberals.

Noe Valley storefronts are modest looking, everyone seems to know each other, and the pace is fairly slow. Crowds slump in front of 24th Street's bagel shop and nearby coffee shops, and strollers clog the sidewalk. Resident and *Zippy the Pinhead* cartoonist Bill Griffith describes the street as "primarily an urban mall for caffeine addicts and people who have jobs that don't require them to go to an office."

Numbers in the text correspond to numbers in the margin and on the Mission District/Noe Valley map.

A Good Walk

Start at Church and 24 streets (the J-Church streetcar from downtown stops here). Walk north (back toward downtown) on Church Street. At Number 1079—between 23rd and 22nd streets—you'll see a house with a large mural of a rain forest painted on it. To the right at Numbers 1081–1089 are three Queen Anne bungalows with lacy wedding-cake trim. Continue north to the southeast corner of 20th and Church streets, where a **golden fire hydrant** ⑦ figured in the 1906 earthquake and fire.

Take a gander at 20th Street heading west. If the hill looks too steep, head back to 24th Street and have a cappuccino. Otherwise, proceed up 20th past Victorian houses of various vintages and make a left at Sanchez. As you make the turn, you'll see the meticulously maintained

Spanish Mission–style residence at 701 Sanchez. Continue south on Sanchez one block to Liberty Street. Across Sanchez at this intersection a staircase leads to the upper level of Liberty Street. Walk up it, enjoy the views of Pacific Heights north from the top, then look south across Liberty Street, where you'll see another set of stairs. Take them (from the landing on a sunny day you'll take in views of the Bay Bridge and Oakland) and continue south. On the northeast corner of Sanchez and 21st streets is a Tudor-style mansion; the garden was designed by John McLaren, responsible for much of Golden Gate Park. This hill is the site of a former resort spot where Californians came to soak in the healing waters of the area's many springs. The Native Americans who lived near Mission Dolores came up here for water from those springs. The same source helped extinguish fires after the 1906 quake. The dried-up springs left shaky soil that made some structures here vulnerable during the Loma Prieta quake of 1989.

It isn't hard to figure out how Hill Street, parallel to and between 21st and 22nd streets, got its name. The street was once known as Nanny Goat Hill for the goats that grazed there. Proceed downhill on Sanchez Street. Make a right at 22nd Street, where Victorian houses line both sides of the street. Make a left at Noe, walk south to 24th Street, and make a right. Continue west on 24th to Castro Street and turn left. Walk the short block to Jersey Street and head west (right). Halfway down the block is the **Noe Valley Branch Library** ⑧. From the library, backtrack east on Jersey, make a right, walk a half block to 25th Street, and make a left. As you walk down 25th Street you'll see the side of the Art Deco James Lick Middle School. On the northwest corner of 25th and Noe streets is the **Axford House** ⑨, a private home. Walk north from the Axford House to 24th Street; Church Street, where your walk began, is two blocks east (to the right). If you stop into the Just for Fun & Scribbledoodles card and gift shop at Number 3982, you can make photo stickers to commemorate your Noe Valley tour.

TIMING

This loop through Noe Valley takes about an hour, not counting stops to shop or sip tea or coffee.

Sights to See

⑨ **Axford House.** This mauve house was built in 1877, when the Mission was still a rural area, as evidenced by the hayloft in the gable of the adjacent carriage house. The house is perched several feet above the sidewalk. Several types of roses grow in the well-maintained garden that surrounds the house. ⊠ *1190 Noe St., at 25th St.*

NEED A
BREAK?

A subdued atmosphere prevails at **Lovejoy's Antiques & Tea Room** (⊠ 1195 Church St., at 24th St., ☎ 415/648–5895), whose name was inspired by the British series about a fictional antiques dealer with a penchant for mysteries. The room is homey yet stylish, its tables and couches mixing in nicely with the antiques for sale. High tea and cream tea are served, along with traditional English-tearoom "fayre," such as the Ploughman's lunch and sandwiches (oak-smoked finnan haddock is a favorite) served on soft, white, crustless triangles.

⑦ **Golden fire hydrant.** When all the other fire hydrants went dry during the fire that followed the 1906 earthquake, this one kept pumping. Noe Valley and the Mission District were thus spared the devastation wrought elsewhere in the city, which explains the goodly number of prequake homes here. ⊠ *Church and 20th Sts., southeast corner, across from Mission Dolores Park.*

8   **Noe Valley Branch Library.** In the early 20th century philanthropist Andrew Carnegie told Americans he would build them elegant libraries if they would fill them with books. A community garden flanks part of the yellow-brick library Carnegie financed, and there's a deck (accessed through the children's book room) with picnic tables where you can relax and admire Carnegie's inspired structure. ⊠ *451 Jersey St.,* ☎ *415/695–5095.* ☉ *Tues. 10–9, Wed. 1–9, Thurs. 10–6, Fri. 1–6, Sat. noon–6.*

THE CASTRO

Historians are still trying to discover what drew tens of thousands of gays and lesbians to the San Francisco area during the second half of the 20th century. Some point to the libertarian tradition rooted in Barbary Coast piracy, prostitution, and gambling. Others note that as a huge military embarkation point during World War II, the city was occupied by many single men. Whatever the cause, San Francisco became the city of choice for lesbians and gay men, and in the 1970s Castro Street—nestled at the base of Twin Peaks and just over Buena Vista hill from Haight Street—became its social, cultural, and political center.

The Castro district is one of the liveliest and most welcoming neighborhoods in the city, especially on weekends. Come Saturday and Sunday, the streets teem with folks out shopping, pushing political causes, heading to art films, and lingering in bars and cafés. Cutting-edge clothing stores and gift shops predominate, and pretty young pairs of all genders and sexual persuasions (even heterosexual) hold hands.

Numbers in the text correspond to numbers in the margin and on the Castro and the Haight map.

A Good Walk

Begin at **Harvey Milk Plaza** ① on the southwest corner of 17th and Market streets; it's outside the south entrance to the Castro Street Muni station (K, L, and M streetcars stop here). Across Castro Street from the plaza is the neighborhood's landmark, the **Castro Theatre** ②. Many shops line Castro Street between 17th and 19th streets, 18th between Sanchez and Eureka streets, and Market Street heading east toward downtown. Several doors south of the Castro Theatre at Number 489 is A Different Light Bookstore (☞ Booksellers *in* Chapter 6), which operates as an unofficial community center.

After exploring the shops on 18th and Castro streets, head west up 19th Street to Douglass Street and turn left. On the corner of Douglass and Caselli streets sprawls **Clarke's Mansion** ③. Continue north on Douglass Street to 18th Street and make a right. Cross Castro Street and make a left on Noe Street. Stay on the left (west) side of Noe. At the intersection of 16th, Market, and Noe streets, cross Market Street and turn left on the north side of the Market. At Number 2362 is the **Names Project** ④, the birthplace and continuing workshop for the AIDS Memorial Quilt.

The rest of this walk is strenuous. If you're not up for it, backtrack east on Market one block to Café Flore (☞ *below*). For an unforgettable vista, continue west on Market Street. Make a right at Castro Street, walk one block to 16th Street, turn left, and head up the steep hill to Flint Street. Turn right on Flint and follow the trail on the left (just past the tennis courts) up the hill. The beige buildings on the left contain the **Randall Museum** ⑤ for children. Turn right up the dirt path, which soon loops back up Corona Heights. At the top you'll be treated to an all-encompassing view of the city. To the east is downtown.

SWEET PAINTED LADIES

BRIGHT, CHEERFUL, AND STURDILY proud, San Francisco's Painted Ladies are wooden (mostly redwood) Victorian homes built in the 19th and early 20th century. They provide the perfect grace notes of exuberance for a metropolis that burst onto the scene as capriciously as did the City by the Bay. Though viewed as picturesque antiques these days, the homes, about 15,000 of which survive today, represented the height of modernity in their time.

Made possible by the newly created streetcar and cable car lines—not to mention sewer systems and money from the gold and silver rushes of the 1800s—the Painted Ladies had indoor plumbing (the later ones electricity, too) and other modern touches like porcelain bathroom and kitchen fixtures and machine-tooled wood detailing. The older Victorians downtown perished in the 1906 earthquake and fire. But west of Van Ness Avenue, where grand mansions were dynamited to halt the fire's spread, and in the Haight, the outer Mission District, and Noe Valley, sterling examples remain.

Were the Painted Ladies always as brilliantly hued as they are today? Apparently so: Various accounts in the late 1800s mention bright, even "garish" colors. Some writers attributed this to the city's carefree attitudes, others to the desire of San Franciscans to create a visual reality as different as possible from that of the more conservative East Coast cities from which many of them had come.

Three main Victorian styles emerged in San Francisco. The architecture of Renaissance Italy's palaces informed the Italianate style, characterized by Corinthian porch columns, tall and narrow doorways, and slanted bay windows. (The bay window was invented in San Francisco, where the standard lot is only 25 ft wide, to take advantage of water views.) The Stick style employs wood strips as ornamentation—as opposed to floral and other patterns—and squared-off bay windows, which let in even more light than slanted bays. The Stick style evolved into what came to be known as the Stick-Eastlake style, with faux gables, mini-mansards, and other embellishments adding a playful quality to the basic Stick look. If you see a home with a rounded turret or other curvy elements, it's probably a Queen Anne, the third major San Francisco style. Angled roofs, lacy detailing, and jolly bits of frou-frou—arching portals, wedding-cake trim, rounded shingling—enliven Queen Anne homes.

THERE'S PLENTY OF OVERLAPPING of these styles. Many Italianate houses built in the 1870s but remodeled in the 1890s, for example, acquired Queen Anne touches. The Atherton House (☞ A Good Walk in Pacific Heights, *above*) daffily combines the Stick-Eastlake and Queen Anne styles. And you'll find Gothic, Tudor, and Greek Revival Victorians in much smaller numbers.

To view the quintessential strip of Victorians, head to Alamo Square and look east toward downtown. The Queen Anne homes—710–720 Steiner Street—in the foreground, which have been painted and photographed numerous times, are known as Postcard Row.

— Daniel Mangin

Among the rows of homes on the hills and valleys to the south are many Victorians.

You can retrace your steps back to Castro Street. To continue north and walk the Haight Street tour (☞ *below*), follow the trail down the other side of Corona Heights to a grassy field. The gate to the field is at the intersection of Roosevelt Way and Museum Way. Turn right on Roosevelt (head down the hill) and cross Roosevelt at Park Hill Terrace. Walk up Park Hill to Buena Vista Avenue, turn left, and follow the road as it loops west and south around Buena Vista Park to the Spreckels Mansion.

TIMING

Allot an hour to an hour and a half to visit the Castro district. Set aside an extra hour to hike Corona Heights and visit the Randall Museum.

Sights to See

★ ➋ **Castro Theatre.** The neon marquee is the neighborhood's great landmark, and the 1,500-seat theater, which opened in 1922, is the grandest of San Francisco's few remaining movie palaces. Janet Gaynor, who in 1927 won the first Oscar for best actress, worked as an usher here. The Castro's elaborate Spanish baroque interior is fairly well preserved. Before many shows the theater's pipe organ rises from the orchestra pit and an organist plays pop and movie tunes, usually ending with the Jeanette McDonald standard "San Francisco" (go ahead, sing along). The crowd can be enthusiastic and vocal, talking back to the screen as loudly as it talks to them. Classics like *Who's Afraid of Virginia Woolf?* take on a whole new life, with the assembled beating the actors to the punch and fashioning even snappier comebacks for Elizabeth Taylor. Catch classics, a Fellini film retrospective, or the latest take on same-sex love here. The **Gay and Lesbian Film Festival** (☎ 415/703–8650) takes place in June at the Castro and other venues. ✉ *429 Castro St.,* ☎ *415/621–6120.*

➌ **Clarke's Mansion.** Built for attorney Alfred "Nobby" Clarke, this off-white Baroque Queen Anne home completed in 1892 was dubbed Clarke's Folly when his wife refused to inhabit it because it was in an unfashionable part of town—at the time, everyone who was anyone lived on Nob Hill. The greenery-shrouded house is a beauty, with dormers, cupolas, rounded bay windows, and huge turrets topped by gold-leaf spheres. ✉ *250 Douglass St., between 18th and 19th Sts.*

➊ **Harvey Milk Plaza.** An 18-ft-long rainbow flag, a gay icon, flies above this plaza named for the man who electrified the city in 1977 by being elected to its Board of Supervisors as an openly gay candidate. In the early 1970s, Milk had opened a camera store on the block of Castro Street between 18th and 19th streets. The store became ground zero for his campaign to gain thorough inclusion for gays in the city's social and political life. The liberal Milk hadn't served a full year of his term before he and Mayor George Moscone, also a liberal, were shot in November 1978 at City Hall. The murderer was a conservative ex-supervisor named Dan White, who had recently resigned his post and then become enraged when Moscone wouldn't reinstate him. Milk and White had often been at odds on the board, and White felt that Milk had been part of a cabal to keep him from returning to his post. Milk's assassination shocked the gay community, which became enraged when the famous "Twinkie defense"—that junk food had led to diminished mental capacity—resulted in a manslaughter verdict for White. During the so-called White Night Riot of May 21, 1979, gays and their sympathizers stormed City Hall, torching its lobby and several police cars. Milk, who had feared assassination, had left behind

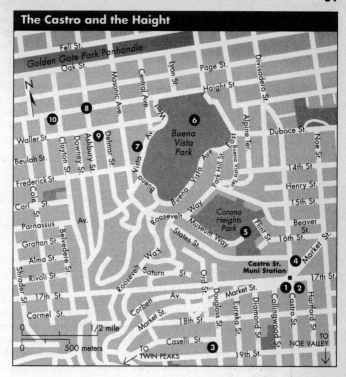

The Castro and the Haight

a videotape in which he urged the community to continue the work he began. His legacy is the high visibility of gay people throughout city government. A plaque at the base of the flagpole lists the names of 17 past and present openly gay and lesbian state and local officials. ⊠ *Southwest corner of Castro and Market Sts.*

❹ **Names Project.** Open to anyone who wishes to work on a panel or view the work of those who have, the Names Project has created a gigantic quilt made of more than 42,000 hand-sewn and -decorated panels, pieced together by loved ones to serve as a memorial to those who have died of AIDS. People come from all over the country to this storefront as a labor of love and grief; others have sent panels here by mail. New additions to the quilt are always on display. Next door to the Project is Under One Roof, a gift shop that funnels its profits to area AIDS organizations. ⊠ *2362 Market St.,* ☎ *415/863–1966.* ⏰ *Mon.–Sat. noon–7, Sun. noon–6; quilting bee Wed. 7 PM–10 PM and 2nd Sat. of month 1–5.*

NEED A BREAK? Sometimes referred to as "Café Hairdo" for its proliferation of extremely well coiffed young gay men, **Café Flore** (⊠ 2298 Market St., ☎ 415/ 621–8579) serves coffee drinks, beer, and light meals. It's a good place to catch the latest Castro gossip.

☝ ❺ **Randall Museum.** The highlight of this facility is the educational animal room, popular with children, where you can observe birds, lizards, snakes, spiders, and other creatures that cannot be released to the wild because of injury or other problems. Also here are a greenhouse, woodworking and ceramics studios, and a theater. The Randall sits on 16 acres of public land; the hill that overlooks the museum is variously known as Red Rock, Museum Hill, and, correctly, Corona Heights. ⊠ *199 Museum Way, off Roosevelt Way,* ☎ *415/554–9600.* 🎫 *Free.* ⏰ *Tues.–Sat. 10–5; animal room 10–1 and 2–5.*

OFF THE
BEATEN PATH

TWIN PEAKS – Windswept and desolate Twin Peaks yields sweeping vistas of San Francisco and the neighboring east and north bay counties. You can get a real feel for the city's layout here; arrive before the late-afternoon fog turns the view into pea soup during the summer. To drive, head west from Castro Street up Market Street, which becomes Portola Drive past Corbett Street. Turn right (north) at the intersection of Portola Drive and Twin Peaks Boulevard and follow the signs to the top. Muni Bus 37-Corbett heads west to Twin Peaks from Market Street. Catch this bus above the Castro Street Muni light-rail station on the island west of Castro at Market Street.

THE HAIGHT

East of Golden Gate Park is the neighborhood known as "the Haight." Despite a fair amount of gentrification, this is still home to a wandering tribe of Deadheads, with anarchist book collectives and shops selling incense and tie-dye T-shirts.

Once an enclave of large middle-class families of European immigrants, the Haight began to change during the late 1950s and early 1960s. Families were fleeing to the suburbs, and the big old Victorians were deteriorating or being chopped up into cheap housing. Young people found the neighborhood an affordable spot in which they could live according to new precepts. By 1966 the Haight had become a hot spot for rock bands like the Grateful Dead—whose members moved into a big Victorian near the corner of Haight and Ashbury streets—and Jefferson Airplane, whose grand mansion was north of the district at 2400 Fulton Street.

Back in 1967 Gray Lines instituted their "Hippie-Hop," advertising it as "the only foreign tour within the continental limits of the United States," piloted by a driver "especially trained in the sociological significance of the Haight." Sharing the continuing fascination with events of the 1960s, many visitors to San Francisco still want to see the setting of the Summer of Love.

The Haight's famous political spirit—it was the first neighborhood in the nation to lead a freeway revolt, and it continues to host regular boycotts against chain stores—exists alongside some of the finest Victorian-lined streets in the city. The area is also known for its vintage merchandise, including clothes, records, and books, and miscellany like crystals, jewelry, and candles.

Numbers in the text correspond to numbers in the margin and on the Castro and the Haight map.

A Good Walk

Start your visit on the western edge of **Buena Vista Park** ⑥, at Haight Street and Buena Vista Avenue West. The avenue, which becomes Buena Vista Avenue East before returning to Haight Street, loops around the park. If you're up for a climb, walk a few blocks south on Buena Vista Avenue West along the edge of the park to **Spreckels Mansion** ⑦. From the mansion, backtrack on its side of the street to Central Avenue. Head down Central two blocks to Haight Street, and make a left.

The avowedly radical Bound Together Anarchist Book Collective at 1369 Haight Street has been "fighting the good fight" against capitalism for decades. Whatever your political persuasion, you may find the collection of political literature intriguing. For a 1960s flashback, head across the street to Pipedreams, at Number 1376. This head shop keeps the hippie era alive with merchandise like hookahs, bongs, and water pipes.

The flashbacks continue as you cross Masonic Avenue. You can't miss the brightly colored building on the southwest corner of Haight and Masonic that houses Positively Haight Street. Here you can purchase tie-dye T-shirts, dresses, and scarves, along with Grateful Dead paraphernalia.

Continue west to the fabled **Haight-Ashbury intersection** ⑧. Despite the franchise operations, you won't need to close your eyes to conjure the 1960s. A motley contingent of folks attired in retro fashions and often sporting hippie-long hair hangs here. Most of the assembled are either under 25 or over 50; many are homeless. Consider yourself hopelessly square if by now someone hasn't sidled up to you to proffer "buds" or perhaps something stronger than marijuana. One block south of Haight and Ashbury is the **Grateful Dead house** ⑨, the pad that Jerry Garcia and band inhabited in the 1960s.

The stores along Haight Street up to Shrader Street are worth checking out. You will encounter many panhandlers along this walk. At Clayton Street, you can stop in at the meditative Peace Arts Center on the ground floor of the **Red Victorian Bed & Breakfast** ⑩.

TIMING

The distance covered here is only several blocks, and although there are shops aplenty and other amusements, an hour or so should be enough.

Sights to See

❻ **Buena Vista Park.** Great city views can be had from this eucalyptus-filled park. Although it's not exactly sedate (drug deals are common), it's a very pretty park, especially on a sunny day. Don't wander here after dark. ⊠ *Haight St. between Lyon St. and Buena Vista Ave. W.*

❾ **Grateful Dead house.** Nothing unusual marks the house of legend. On the outside, it's just one more well-kept Victorian on a street that's full of them—but true fans of the Dead may find some inspiration here. The three-story house (closed to the public) is tastefully painted in sedate mauves, tans, and teals (no bright tie-dye colors). ⊠ *710 Ashbury St., just past Waller St.*

❽ **Haight/Ashbury intersection.** On October 6, 1967, hippies took over the intersection of Haight and Ashbury streets to proclaim the "Death of Hip." If they thought hip was dead then, they'd find absolute confirmation of it today, what with the Gap holding court on one quadrant of the famed corner. (There's a Ben and Jerry's, too, an environmentally conscious enterprise whose ethos some might say shows traces of the hippie philosophy.)

Everyone knows the Summer of Love had something to do with free love and LSD, but the drug and other excesses of the Summer of Love have tended to obscure the residents' serious attempts to create an America more spiritually oriented, more environmentally aware, and less caught up in commercialism. The Diggers, a radical group of actors and populist agitators, for example, operated a free shop a few blocks off Haight Street. Everything really was free at the free shop; people brought in things they didn't need and took things they did. The Diggers also distributed free food in Golden Gate Park every day.

Among the folks who hung out in or near the Haight during the late 1960s were writers Richard Brautigan, Allen Ginsberg, Ken Kesey, and Gary Snyder; anarchist Abbie Hoffman; rock performers Marty Balin, Jerry Garcia, Janis Joplin, and Grace Slick; LSD champion Timothy Leary; and filmmaker Kenneth Anger.

⑩ Red Victorian Peace Center Bed & Breakfast. By even the most generous accounts the Summer of Love quickly crashed and burned, and the Haight veered sharply away from the higher goals that inspired the fabled summer. In 1977 Sami Sunchild acquired the Red Vic, built as a hotel in 1904, with the aim of preserving the best of 1960s ideals. She decorated her rooms with 1960s themes—one chamber is called the Flower Child Room—and on the ground floor opened the Peace Art Center. Here you can buy her paintings, T-shirts, and "meditative art," along with books about the Haight and prayer flags. There's also a meditation room. ⊠ *1665 Haight St.*, ☎ *415/864–1978.*

NEED A BREAK?   Boisterous **Cha Cha Cha** (⊠ 1801 Haight St., at Shrader St., ☎ 415/386–5758) serves island cuisine, a mix of Cajun, southwestern, and Caribbean influences. The decor is Technicolor tropical plastic, and the food is hot and spicy. Try the fried calamari or chili-spiked shrimp. Reservations are not accepted. Expect a wait for dinner.

⑦ Spreckels Mansion. Not to be confused with the Spreckels Mansion of Pacific Heights, this house was built for sugar baron Richard Spreckels in 1887. Later tenants included Jack London and Ambrose Bierce. The boxy, putty-color Victorian is in mint condition. ⊠ *737 Buena Vista Ave. W.*

2 DINING

San Francisco, one of the world's great dining cities, is the culinary stomping grounds of such nationally celebrated chefs as Jeremiah Tower, Traci Des Jardins, Nancy Oakes, and Mark Franz. San Francisco is also the West Coast's capital of ethnic eating and home to a growing number of restaurants whose cooks mastered their craft in Bangkok's noodle shops or in the dim sum kitchens of Hong Kong. Diversity is the key to the city's culinary richness, and it has absolutely spoiled the locals. Whether it's the best *taco de carne asada* this side of Guadalajara or the finest seared foie gras this side of Paris, San Francisco has it all—most often within convenient walking distance.

By Sharon
Silva

SAN FRANCISCO HAS MORE RESTAURANTS per capita than any other city in the United States, and nearly every ethnic cuisine is represented, from Afghan to Indian to Vietnamese. Selecting some 120 recommended restaurants is a next-to-impossible task. We have chosen several restaurants to represent each popular style of dining in various price ranges, in most cases because of the superiority of the food but in some instances because of the view or ambience.

The areas of town most frequented by visitors have received the greatest attention. This has meant leaving out some great places in the more distant districts, such as the Mission, Haight-Ashbury, the Sunset, and the Richmond. The outlying restaurants that are recommended were chosen because they offer an experience not available elsewhere. All listed restaurants serve lunch and dinner unless otherwise specified. The restaurants here are organized by neighborhood, which are listed alphabetically.

Most upper-end restaurants offer valet parking—worth considering in crowded neighborhoods such as North Beach, Union Square, and the Civic Center. There is often a nominal charge and a time-length restriction on validated parking.

Smoking is banned in all Bay Area workplaces, including restaurants, bars, and supper clubs.

Restaurants do change their policies about hours, credit cards, and the like. Many restaurants close for Thanksgiving and Christmas. It is always best to call in advance.

A significant trend among more expensive restaurants is the bar menu, which provides light snacks—fried calamari, crab cakes, oysters on the half shell, tempura-style vegetables, pizza and other flat breads—often for as little as $25 for two. The price ranges listed below are for an average three-course meal.

Fodor's Choice

One of the city's most talked-about restaurants, **Jardinière** is a serious pre-theater event, thanks in large part to the incredible cooking of chef-owner Traci Des Jardins. *$$$*

Stars, a must for visiting gourmets, is run by world-renowned chef Jeremiah Tower, who many believe invented California cuisine. *$$$*

A touch of France in South of Market, **Fringale** offers Gallic classics at neighborhood prices. *$$–$$$*

The large, lively **Rose Pistola,** with its mix of Ligurian and neighborhood specialties, is a magnet for North Beach residents and visitors alike. *$$–$$$*

Vineria, an out-of-the-way Italian spot in the Mission District, serves delicious pastas at distinctly palatable prices, and is definitely worth a visit. *$–$$*

CATEGORY	COST*
$$$$	over $50
$$$	$30–$50
$$	$20–$30
$	under $20

per person for a three-course meal, excluding drinks, service, and 8.5% sales tax

The Castro

Contemporary

$$$ ✕ **Mecca.** This sleek bar and restaurant on the edge of the Castro is a mecca for both local Armani-clad cocktailers and Bay Area foodies. If clubbing is not your thing, reserve a seat in the dining area, away from the always crowded, velvet-curtained circular bar that anchors the cavernous space. In late 1998, Mike Fennelly took over the kitchen, delivering an American menu with strong Cajun and Asian accents. Choices include an iced shellfish platter, curried potato samosas with pineapple salsa, shrimp dumplings with a spicy tahini sauce, roast chicken, and lemon-mascarpone cheesecake. ⊠ *2029 Market St.,* ☎ *415/621–7000. AE, DC, MC, V. No lunch.*

$$–$$$ ✕ **2223.** Opened in the mid-1990s, when the Castro was a dining-out wasteland, the smart, sophisticated 2223—the address became the name when the principals couldn't come up with a better one—was an instant success and has continued to attract a loyal clientele. That means you'll need a strong pair of lungs, however, as the restaurant's popularity and absence of sound buffers make conversation difficult. Thin-crust pizzas, earthy seasonal soups, chicken with garlic-mashed potatoes, pork loin with wilted escarole, and duck confit salad are among the kitchen's best dishes. For Saturday and Sunday brunch there might be French toast or eggs Benedict on a tasty herb scone. ⊠ *2223 Market St.,* ☎ *415/431–0692. MC, V. No lunch weekdays.*

Chinatown

Chinese

$–$$ ✕ **Great Eastern.** Cantonese chefs are known for their expertise with seafood, and the kitchen at Great Eastern lives up to that venerable tradition. In the busy dining room, large tanks are filled with Dungeness crabs, black bass, abalone, catfish, shrimp, rock cod, and other creatures of the sea, and a wall-hung menu in both Chinese and English specifies the cost of selecting what can be pricey indulgences. Sea conch stir-fried with yellow chives, crab with vermicelli in a clay pot, and steamed fresh scallops with garlic sauce are among the chef's many specialties. In the wee hours Chinese night owls often drop in for a plate of noodles or a bowl of *congee* (rice gruel). ⊠ *649 Jackson St.,* ☎ *415/986–2550. AE, MC, V.*

$–$$ ✕ **R&G Lounge.** The name conjures up an image of a dark bar with a cigarette-smoking piano player, but the restaurant, on two floors, is actually as bright as a new penny. Downstairs (entrance on Kearny Street) is a no-tablecloth dining room that is always packed at lunch and dinner. The classier upstairs space (entrance on Commercial Street), complete with shoji-lined private rooms, is a favorite stop for Chinese businessmen on expense accounts and anyone seeking exceptional Cantonese banquet fare. A menu with photographs helps diners decide among the many exotic dishes, from dried scallops with seasonal vegetables to steamed clams with eggs to deep-fried salt-and-pepper Dungeness crab. ⊠ *631 Kearny St.,* ☎ *415/982–7877 or 415/982–3811. AE, DC, MC, V.*

Civic Center

Contemporary

$$$ ✕ **Jardinière.** One of the city's most talked-about restaurants since its
★ opening in late 1997, Jardinière continues to be *the* place to dine before a performance at the nearby Opera House and Davies Symphony Hall. The chef-owner is Traci Des Jardins, who made her name at the fashionable Rubicon. The sophisticated interior, with its eye-catching

88

Downtown San Francisco Dining

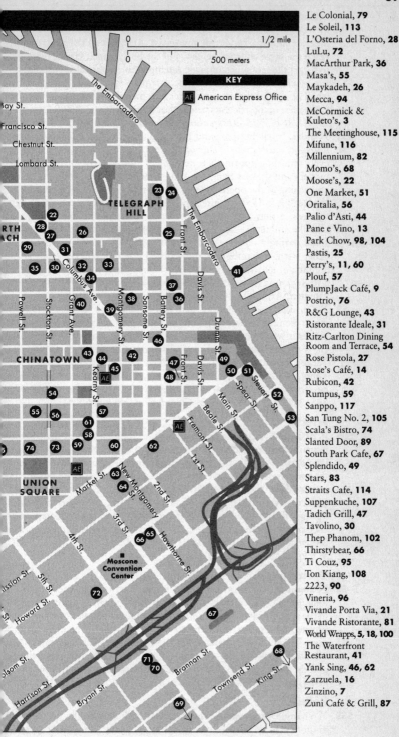

KEY

AE American Express Office

oval atrium and curving staircase, is the work of designer Pat Kuleto. First courses of rabbit rillettes, duck confit, and foie gras are pricey but memorable ways to launch any repast. Alas, not all the main courses reach the same culinary heights, but the finely honed service helps you to forget the few shortcomings. A temperature-controlled cheese room lets you trade in a wedge of chocolate torte for a more European finish. The special three-course "staccato menu" puts music-loving diners in their orchestra seats before the curtain goes up. ⊠ *300 Grove St.,* ☎ *415/861–5555. Reservations essential. AE, DC, MC, V. No lunch.*

$$$ ✕ **Stars.** It has been around for more than decade, but this culinary
★   hot spot, the domain of superchef Jeremiah Tower, remains a must on every traveling gourmet's itinerary. It's also where many of the local movers and shakers hang out and is a popular place for dining before an evening at the opera or symphony. Although it underwent a pleasing face-lift in 1998—white slipcovered chairs, striking star-shape light fixtures, a new star-patterned carpet—Stars didn't lose its famous clublike ambience. The food ranges from grills to ragouts to sautés—some daringly creative and some classical. Those on a budget can order a stylish hamburger, thin-crusted pizza, or chicken tacos at the counter, or slowly enjoy a flute of champagne at the mile-long bar. ⊠ *150 Redwood Alley, at Van Ness Ave.,* ☎ *415/861–7827. Reservations essential. AE, DC, MC, V. No lunch.*

$$ ✕ **Carta.** The defining idea here is a difficult one to carry off: a different menu from a different country or region every month. Yet Carta makes it work beautifully. The talented chefs, alums of some of the city's toniest spots, travel to an assortment of destinations: Oaxaca, Turkey, Dordogne, Morocco, and New England, to name just a few. There are usually about 10 small plates, three main courses, and three desserts. Sunday brunch is a highlight. ⊠ *1772 Market St.,* ☎ *415/863–3516. AE, DC, MC, V. Closed Mon. No lunch Sat.*

Eclectic

$$$ ✕ **Absinthe.** Despite the restaurant's name, the long-banned cloudy green liqueur is not served here. But a number of house-created cocktails are, including Death in the Afternoon, a mixture of Pernod and champagne that was reputedly a favorite of Ernest Hemingway. The plush banquettes draw the city's social set for cold seafood platters, Madeira-doused sweetbreads, imported French cheeses, and other delicacies. Though the burgundy walls, yards of wood, and sophisticated ambience recall a French brasserie, the menu shows Italian and American influences as well. ⊠ *398 Hayes St.,* ☎ *415/551–1590. AE, DC, MC, V. Closed Mon. No lunch.*

German

$–$$ ✕ **Suppenkuche.** Bratwurst and braised red cabbage accompany a long list of German beers at this lively, hip outpost of German cuisine in the trendy Hayes Valley corridor. Strangers sit down together at unfinished pine tables when the room gets crowded, which it regularly does. The food—homemade soups, sauerbraten, smoked pork chops, schnitzel, apple strudel—is simple, tasty, and easy on the pocketbook, and the brews are first-rate. There's also a good weekend brunch. ⊠ *601 Hayes St.,* ☎ *415/252–9289. AE, MC, V. No lunch.*

Italian

$$$ ✕ **Vivande Ristorante.** Owner-chef Carlo Middione, a highly regarded authority on the food of southern Italy, has long run a smart take-out shop and casual dining room in Lower Pacific Heights (☞ Vivande Porta Via, *below*). His larger *ristorante,* within walking distance of the Opera House and Symphony Hall, features the same rustic fare found at the original location, like stuffed calamari, risotto laced with seafood, pasta tossed with a tangle of mushrooms, and a hearty osso buco. The spacious room is welcoming, and a late-supper menu lets music lovers grab a bite after performances. ✉ *670 Golden Gate Ave.,* ☎ *415/673–9245. AE, MC, V.*

Mediterranean

$$$ ✕ **Zuni Café & Grill.** Zuni's Italian-Mediterranean menu and its un-
★ pretentious atmosphere pack in an eclectic crowd from early morning to late evening. A spacious, window-filled balcony dining area over-looks the large bar, where shellfish, one of the best oyster selections in town, and drinks are dispensed. A whole roast chicken and Tuscan bread salad for two is a popular order here, as are the grilled meats and veg-etables. Even the hamburgers have an Italian accent—they're topped with Gorgonzola and served on herbed focaccia. Don't miss the kitchen's addictive shoestring potatoes. ✉ *1658 Market St.,* ☎ *415/552–2522. Reservations essential. AE, MC, V. Closed Mon.*

Seafood

$$–$$$ ✕ **Hayes Street Grill.** Up to 15 different kinds of seafood are chalked on the blackboard each night at this extremely popular restaurant. The fish is simply grilled, with a choice of sauces ranging from tomato salsa to a spicy Sichuan peanut concoction to beurre blanc. Fresh crab slaw and superb crab cakes are regular appetizers, and for dessert, the crème brûlée is legendary. ✉ *320 Hayes St.,* ☎ *415/863–5545. Reser-vations essential. AE, D, DC, MC, V. No lunch weekends.*

Vegetarian

$$ ✕ **Millennium.** Tucked into the former carriage house of the venera-ble Abigail Hotel, Millennium offers what it describes as "organic cui-sine." That label translates to a menu of low-fat, dairy-free dishes made with organic ingredients that keep vegans and their carnivore friends equally satisfied. The kitchen looks to the Mediterranean, with pastas and polenta among its most successful dishes. For true believers, there is seitan (a whole wheat meat substitute) steak in marsala sauce, a choco-late mousse cake made from tofu, and organic wines and beers. ✉ *246 McAllister St.,* ☎ *415/487–9800. MC, V.*

Cow Hollow/Marina

American

$–$$ ✕ **Perry's.** This popular watering hole and meeting place for the but-ton-down singles set and inveterate sports enthusiast serves good, hon-est saloon food—London broil, corned beef hash, calves' liver, one of the best hamburgers in town, and a great breakfast. Brunch is served on weekends. A second location, **Perry's Downtown,** serves the same sig-nature burgers and other Perry's standards in a clubby, mahogany-lined space although the kitchen is generally less reliable. ✉ *1944 Union St.,* ☎ *415/922–9022;* ✉ *185 Sutter St.,* ☎ *415/989–6895. AE, MC, V.*

Contemporary

$ ✕ **World Wrapps.** Ground zero of the late-'90s wrap rage, this utterly hip human fueling station knows no geographical boundaries and sells what are essentially global burritos. Fillings range from Peking duck to Thai chicken, from roasted vegetables to couscous and cucumber. A wide selection of healthful smoothies—papaya, blackberry, and the like—matches up surprisingly well with the hearty wraps. Under-standably, the crowd here is mostly young and athletic. There are two additional locations, on Polk Street and on Market Street, and plenty more are popping up around the Bay Area and beyond. ✉ *2257 Chest-nut St.,* ☎ *415/563–9727;* ✉ *2227 Polk St.,* ☎ *415/931–9727;* ✉ *2012 Market St.,* ☎ *415/487–7300. No credit cards.*

French

$–$$ ✕ **Bistro Aix.** This lively bistro is a comfortable space composed of light wood banquettes, paper-top tablecloths, and a heated patio. The friendly service and attractive prices draw diners from the surrounding neighborhood and beyond. On weekdays, an early bird two-course prix fixe dinner is available for not much more than the price of a movie ticket. Addictive cracker crust pizzas, superb steamed mussels, crisp-skinned roast chicken, and *steak frites* are additional draws. ⊠ *3340 Steiner St.,* ☏ *415/202–0100. MC, V. No lunch.*

$–$$ ✕ **Cassis Bistro.** Take a seat at the tiny bar and enjoy a glass of wine while you wait for a free table in this sunny yellow, postage stamp–size operation that recalls the small bistros tucked away on side streets in French seaside towns. The servers have solid Gallic accents; the food—onion tart, veal ragout, braised rabbit, tarte Tatin—is comfortingly home style; and the prices are geared toward the penurious. Bare hardwood floors make conversations a challenge on busy nights. ⊠ *2120 Greenwich St.,* ☏ *415/292–0770. No credit cards. Closed Sun.–Mon. No lunch.*

Italian

$$–$$$ ✕ **Pane e Vino.** A long table topped with prosciutto, a wheel of Parmigiano-Reggiano, and various antipasti seduces everyone who enters this highly popular trattoria. Polenta with mushrooms, gnocchi with rabbit, and thick veal chops are among the dishes regulars can't resist. The Italian-born owner-chef concentrates on specialties from Tuscany and the north, dishing them up in a charming room decorated with rustic wooden furniture and bright white walls punctuated with colorful pottery. ⊠ *3011 Steiner St.,* ☏ *415/346–2111. MC, V. No lunch Sun.*

$$–$$$ ✕ **Zinzino.** The long, narrow dining space—a study in industrial-chic—at this animated *ristorante* ends in a heated patio that fills up on all but the chilliest nights. The menu is irresistible. Thin pizzas are topped with prosciutto and arugula, eggplant and bread crumbs, or fennel sausage and caramelized onions; a mound of lump-free mashed potatoes imaginatively flavored with Chianti accompanies a thick beef tenderloin; and a roast half chicken is paired with a salad of frisée, warm potatoes, and goat cheese. For dessert, try the roasted apple with vanilla-bean ice cream and caramel sauce. ⊠ *2355 Chestnut St.,* ☏ *415/346–6623. MC, V. No lunch.*

$–$$ ✕ **Rose's Café.** Chef Reed Hearon opened this more casual kin of Rose Pistola (☞ North Beach *below*) in 1997. Breakfast, lunch, and dinner can be taken in the dining room or outside on a heater-equipped patio. In the morning, folks line up for seductive breads and frittatas. Midday is the time for a hot hero sandwich, a grilled chicken salad, or a pizza topped with arugula and prosciutto. Evening hours find customers working their way through a grilled hangar steak or roast chicken with mashed potatoes and vegetables. For dessert try the memorable *affogato* (vanilla and chocolate ice cream doused with chocolate sauce and served with piping-hot espresso for pouring over the top). ⊠ *2298 Union St.,* ☏ *415/775–2200. AE, MC, V.*

Mediterranean

$$–$$$ ✕ **PlumpJack Café.** This clubby dining room, with its smartly attired
★   clientele of bankers and brokers, socialites and society scions, takes its name from an opera composed by famed oil tycoon and music lover Gordon Getty, whose sons are two of the partners here. The regularly changing menu spans the Mediterranean, with creamy risottos, an herbed chicken flanked by polenta, and crispy duck confit among the possibilities. The café is an offshoot of the nearby highly regarded wine shop of the same name, which stocks the racks that line the dining room with some of the most reasonably priced vintages in town. ⊠ *3127 Fillmore St.,* ☏ *415/463–4755. AE, MC, V. Closed Sun. No lunch Sat.*

Mexican

$–$$ ✕ **Café Marimba.** Fanciful folk art adorns the walls of this colorful Mexican café, where an open kitchen turns out contemporary renditions of regional specialties: silken *mole negro* (sauce of chilies and chocolate) from Oaxaca, served in tamales and other dishes; shrimp prepared with roasted onions and tomatoes in the style of Zihuatanejo; and chicken with a marinade from Yucatán stuffed into an excellent taco. Although the food is treated to many innovative touches, authenticity plays a strong role—even the guacamole is made to order in a *molcajete*, the three-legged lava-rock version of a mortar. Fresh fruit drinks and tangy margaritas are good thirst quenchers. A young, lively crowd shows up in force, which makes quiet conversation nearly impossible. ✉ *2317 Chestnut St.,* ☎ *415/776–1506. AE, MC, V. No lunch Mon.*

Pan-Asian

$–$$ ✕ **Betelnut.** A pan-Asian menu and an adventurous drinks list—with everything from house-brewed rice beer to martinis—draw a steady stream of hip diners to this Union Street landmark. Richly lacquered walls, bamboo ceiling fans, and hand-painted posters create a comfortably exotic mood in keeping with the unusual but accessible food. Not everything that comes from the kitchen is wildly successful, but don't pass up a plate of the tasty stir-fried dried anchovies, chilies, peanuts, garlic, and green onions. Sadly, service is often amateurish. ✉ *2030 Union St.,* ☎ *415/929–8855. D, DC, MC, V.*

Steak

$$–$$$ ✕ **Izzy's Steak & Chop House.** Izzy Gomez was a legendary San Francisco saloon keeper, and his namesake eatery carries on the tradition. Here you'll find terrific steaks, chops, and seafood plus all the trimmings, from cheesy scalloped potatoes to creamed spinach. A collection of Izzy memorabilia and antique advertising art covers almost every inch of wall space. There's validated parking at the Lombard garage. ✉ *3345 Steiner St.,* ☎ *415/563–0487. AE, DC, MC, V. No lunch.*

Vegetarian

$$ ✕ **Greens.** Long popular with vegetarians and carnivores alike, this beau-
★ tiful restaurant with expansive bay views is owned and operated by the Green Gulch Zen Buddhist Center of Marin County. The dining room offers a wide, eclectic, and creative spectrum of meatless cooking—corn fritters, black bean soup, thin-crust pizzas, Southwestern-inspired savory tarts. The on-site bakery is an irresistible stop on your way out. Dinners are à la carte on weeknights, but only a five-course prix fixe dinner is served on Saturday. Sunday brunch is a good time to watch local sailboat owners take out their crafts. There's public parking at Fort Mason Center. ✉ *Bldg. A, Fort Mason (enter across Marina Blvd. from Safeway),* ☎ *415/771–6222. MC, V. No lunch Mon., no dinner Sun.*

Embarcadero North

American

$$ ✕ **Fog City Diner.** The diner is an American institution, and Fog City Diner is arguably among the sleekest examples of that beloved national tradition. The long, narrow dining room emulates a luxurious railroad car, with dark wood paneling, huge windows, shiny chrome fixtures, and comfortable booths. The menu is both classic and contemporary, from burgers and fries, chili dogs and hot fudge sundaes to crab cakes and salads of baby lettuce with candied walnuts. The shareable "small plates" are a fun way to go. Grumblers have complained of inconsistent service, but the booths remain full at lunch and dinner. ✉ *1300 Battery St.,* ☎ *415/982–2000. D, DC, MC, V.*

\$\$ ✕ **MacArthur Park.** At happy hour, a sea of suits fills this handsomely renovated pre-earthquake brick warehouse. Much of the crowd stays on for the legendary baby back ribs, but the oak-wood smoker and mesquite grill also turn out a wide variety of other all-American dishes, from steaks to hamburgers to seafood. Coleslaw aficionados will appreciate the horseradish-spiked dressing that coats their favorite salad. Takeout is also available. ✉ *607 Front St.,* ☎ *415/398–5700. AE, DC, MC, V. No lunch weekends.*

Chinese

\$\$–\$\$\$ ✕ **Harbor Village.** At lunchtime, businesspeople looking to impress their clients fill the dining room of this outpost of upmarket Cantonese cooking, all of them enjoying the extraordinary array of dim sum offerings. At dinnertime, fresh seafood from the restaurant's own tanks, crisp Peking duck, and various exotica—bird's nest in supreme broth, shark fin, and crab roe—are among the most popular requests from the loyal customers who regularly fill this 400-seat branch of a Hong Kong establishment. The setting is opulent, with Chinese antiques and teak furnishings; a gallery of private rooms harbors large banquet tables perfect for celebrating any special occasion. There's validated parking at the Embarcadero Center Garage. ✉ *4 Embarcadero Center,* ☎ *415/781–8833. AE, DC, MC, V.*

French

\$\$ ✕ **Pastis.** At lunchtime the sunny cement bar and sleek wooden banquettes in this exposed brick dining room are crowded with workers from nearby offices; they come to fuel up on steamed salmon with celery root or grilled prawns marinated in pastis (anise-flavored liqueur). The evening menu may include a dreamy seared foie gras with *verjuice* (sour grape juice) or lamb medallions on herby white beans. Pastis is chef-owner Gerald Hirigoyen's popular successor to his SoMa bistro Fringale (☞ South of Market, *below*), and a worthy addition to the city's Gallic restaurant roster. ✉ *1015 Battery St.,* ☎ *415/391–2555. AE, MC, V. Closed Sun. No lunch Sat.*

Italian

\$\$–\$\$\$ ✕ **Il Fornaio.** An offshoot of the Il Fornaio bakeries, this handsome tile-floored, wood-paneled complex combines a café, bakery, and upscale trattoria with outdoor seating. The Tuscan cooking, laid out in a sizable menu, features crisp, thin pizzas from a wood-burning oven, house-made pastas and gnocchi, grilled poultry like duck with a balsamic vinegar sauce, and meats like a veal chop with sage and rosemary. Anticipate a wait for a table. Il Fornaio has become as comfortable as an old shoe, which means the kitchen has a tendency to rest on past laurels. ✉ *Levi's Plaza, 1265 Battery St.,* ☎ *415/986–0100. AE, DC, MC, V.*

\$\$–\$\$\$ ✕ **Splendido.** The stunning view of the Ferry Building and the bay, the spectacular lighting, the limestone pillars, and the open kitchen combine to make this restaurant a southern European oasis on the Embarcadero. In the past, the food has been a mix of Mediterranean cuisines. But chef Giovanni Perticone has moved it more firmly into the Italian camp with his silky spinach and ricotta ravioli with brown butter and sage, gnocchi with seafood and peas in a light tomato sauce, thin, crisp pizzas, and simply grilled meats and fish. Validated parking is available at the Embarcadero Center garage. ✉ *Embarcadero 4,* ☎ *415/ 986–3222. AE, DC, MC, V. No lunch weekends.*

Seafood

\$\$\$ ✕ **The Waterfront Restaurant.** A two-story restaurant has occupied this space for more than three decades, but only in the past few years could it claim a kitchen of such high caliber. On the top floor try the exquisite—and pricey—East-West menu with such exotic pairings as Maine lobster and Japanese shiso leaves, monkfish stew in lotus leaves, and grilled sea bass flavored with Thai kaffir lime. In the more casual downstairs, where both indoor and outdoor seating is available, the menu offers simpler seafood at lower prices. ⊠ *Pier 7*, ☎ *415/391–2696. Reservations essential for upstairs. AE, D, DC, MC, V. No lunch weekends.*

Embarcadero South

American

$$ ✕ **Harry Denton's.** Every night's a party at this madcap waterfront hangout, where singles congregate in a Barbary Coast–style bar, and the rugs are rolled up at 10:30 on Thursday, Friday, and Saturday nights for dancing in the dining room. At lunchtime the place is quieter, attracting diners with its fine bay view and earthy menu that offers everything from pasta to old-fashioned pot roast with mashed potatoes. Wise regulars don't challenge the kitchen, sticking mostly to burgers and pizzas from the wood-fired oven. ⊠ *161 Steuart St.*, ☎ *415/882–1333. AE, DC, MC, V. No lunch weekends.*

Contemporary

$$$ ✕ **Boulevard.** Two of San Francisco's top restaurant talents—chef Nancy Oakes and designer Pat Kuleto—are responsible for this highly successful eatery in one of the city's most magnificent buildings. The setting is the 1889 Audiffred Building, a Parisian look-alike that was one of the few downtown buildings to survive the 1906 earthquake and fire. Oakes's menu is seasonally in flux, but you can always count on her signature juxtaposition of delicacies such as foie gras with homey comfort foods like maple-cured pork loin and roasted chicken. For those who can't find or afford a table during regular hours, Boulevard offers a less formal weekday afternoon bistro service. Portions are generous in either case, so come with an appetite. ⊠ *1 Mission St.*, ☎ *415/543–6084. Reservations essential. AE, D, DC, MC, V. No lunch weekends.*

$$$ ✕ **One Market.** A giant among American chefs, Bradley Ogden gained fame at Campton Place and later at his Lark Creek Inn in Marin County. In 1993 he and partner Michael Dellar opened this huge, bustling brasserie across from the Ferry Building. The handsome two-tier dining room, done in mustard tones, seats 170, and a spacious bar-café serves snacks, including addictive wire-thin onion rings and oysters on the half shell, beginning at noon. The kitchen has had its ups and downs, however, due to a serious spate of executive chef turnover. ⊠ *1 Market St.*, ☎ *415/777–5577. Reservations essential. AE, DC, MC, V. Closed Sun. No lunch Sat.*

Financial District

American

$$–$$$ ✕ **Garden Court.** The Palace Hotel is the setting of this quintessential Old San Francisco restaurant. From breakfast until the early dinner hours, light splashes through the stunningly beautiful stained-glass ceiling and against the towering Ionic columns and crystal chandeliers. The menu includes some famous dishes devised by Palace chefs early in this century—Green Goddess salad, for example—but dinner here is not the strong suit. It is the extravagant Sunday buffet brunch, one of the city's great traditions, that draws accolades. ⊠ *Market and New Montgomery Sts.*, ☎ *415/546–5011. Reservations essential. Jacket required. AE, DC, MC, V. No dinner Sun.*

Chinese

$ ✕ **Yank Sing.** The city's oldest teahouse, Yank Sing began in China-
★ town but moved to the Financial District several years ago. The kitchen
offers five dozen or so varieties of dim sum on a rotating basis. The
Battery Street location seats 300, while the older Stevenson Street site
is far smaller, a cozy refuge for Market Street office workers who fuel
up on steamed buns and parchment chicken at lunchtime. Take-out coun-
ters in both establishments make a meal-on-the-run a delicious com-
promise. ⊠ *427 Battery St.,* ☎ *415/362–1640;* ⊠ *49 Stevenson St.,
at Market St.,* ☎ *415/541–4949. AE, DC, MC, V. Stevenson branch
closed weekends. No dinner.*

Contemporary

$$$ ✕ **Cypress Club.** Although restaurateur John Cunin calls his fashion-
able spot a "San Francisco brasserie," the term is more descriptive of
the food than the ambience. The contemporary American cooking—
roasted pumpkin soup, braised veal cheeks, salmon Rossini, hangar
steak with bacon-potato tart—draws a loyal crowd, but the decor de-
fies categorizing. It could be interpreted as anything from a parody of
an ancient temple to a futuristic space bar, with stone mosaic floors,
hammered copper arches, wall murals depicting scenes of northern Cal-
ifornia, yards of curved wood, imposing pillars, and overstuffed vel-
vet upholstery. ⊠ *500 Jackson St.,* ☎ *415/296–8555. AE, DC, MC,
V. No lunch.*

$$$ ✕ **Rubicon.** With investors like Robin Williams, Robert Dé Niro, and
Francis Ford Coppola, this sleek, cherry wood–lined restaurant, an off-
shoot of New York's famed Drew Nierporent restaurant empire, was
destined to be famous. Set in a stately stone building dating from 1908,
Rubicon has the dignified air of a men's club in the downstairs dining
room and a somewhat less appealing atmosphere in the more ascetic
upstairs space. The excellent fare, primarily sophisticated renditions of
seafood, meats, and poultry such as sea bass with leeks, lobster-crowned
gnocchi, and grilled quail, is served on both floors to Hollywood big
shots and San Francisco's glamorous set. ⊠ *558 Sacramento St.,* ☎ *415/
434–4100. AE, DC, MC, V. Closed Sun. No lunch Sat.*

$$–$$$ ✕ **Globe.** This smart spot with brick walls, slip-covered chairs, and terra-
cotta floors seats less than four dozen diners and never lacks for eager
customers, so book ahead. The sophisticated fare, which delivers a Californian punch with a thick Mediterranean accent, includes salad of
frisée and lardoons of pancetta topped with a poached egg, sea-fresh
grilled sardines, and a lavish T-bone steak with all the trimmings. The
building, a former livery stable completed in 1911, is a historic gem
that makes eating here all the more enjoyable. The doors stay open until
after midnight. ⊠ *290 Pacific Ave.,* ☎ *415/391–4132. Reservations
essential. AE, DC, MC, V. Closed Sun. No lunch Sat.*

$$–$$$ ✕ **Jack's.** Founded in 1864, Jack's, allegedly named for the jackrab-
bits that resided in the vicinity, is the oldest San Francisco restaurant
still in its original location. It was closed in early 1997 for retrofitting,
and then reopened in late 1998, following a renovation that brought
old-fashioned 22-karat gilding and a brand-new elevator to the four-
floor building. The menu harkens back to the restaurant's early days,
with lamb chops, mock turtle soup, and celery Victor, but also looks
ahead with gnocchi with a rabbit sauce and other contemporary plates.
Long a haven for the city's male movers and shakers, women are now
warmly welcomed. ⊠ *615 Sacramento St.,* ☎ *415/421–7355. Reservations essential. AE, DC, MC, V. No lunch weekends.*

French

$$–$$$ ✕ **Le Central.** This venerable institution is the quintessential French
brasserie: noisy and crowded, with tasty but not-so-subtly cooked

classics, such as garlicky pâtés, leeks vinaigrette, steak with Roquefort sauce, cassoulet, and grilled blood sausage with crisp french fries. Local power brokers, even an occasional rock star such as Mick Jagger, snag noontime tables. Staff from the nearby French consulate dine here as well, giving the place an air of authenticity. A traditional zinc bar provides a good perch for people-watching. ⊠ *453 Bush St.,* ☎ *415/391–2233. AE, DC, MC, V. Closed Sun.*

$–$$ ✕ **Plouf.** This sleek spot, handsomely turned out in chrome and the color of the sea, is a gold mine for mussel lovers, with seven generously portioned, reasonably priced preparations from which to choose. Among them are *marinière* (garlic and parsley), apple cider, leeks and cream, and crayfish and tomato. Plouf means "splash," and the appetizers maintain the seaside theme, with plenty of raw oysters on the half shell and a seafood salad of rock shrimp, mussels, and octopus among the offerings. Main courses run the gamut from *steak frites* to steamed sea bass. French vintages are well represented on the carefully selected wine list. ⊠ *40 Belden Pl.,* ☎ *415/986–6491. MC, V. Closed Sun. No lunch Sat.*

$ ✕ **Café Claude.** This standout French bistro is on an alley near the Notre Dame des Victoires Catholic church and the French consulate. The interior design is comfortably French, with a zinc bar, old-fashioned banquettes, and cinema posters that once actually outfitted a bar in the City of Light's 11th arrondissement. Order a salade niçoise or simple daube from the French-speaking staff, and you might forget what country you're in. On weekends the boisterous crowds regularly spill out into the alleyway. ⊠ *7 Claude La.,* ☎ *415/392–3505. AE, DC, MC, V. Closed Sun.*

Italian

$$–$$$ ✕ **Palio d'Asti.** Restaurateur Gianni Fassio draws a lively crowd to this authentic Northern Italian spot. The kitchen's freshly baked breads, exquisite pastas, and carefully constructed sauces are legendary. An open kitchen and visible pizza oven let you watch your meal as it is expertly assembled. Colorful flags decorate the restaurant, each representing a neighborhood that participates in the famed Palio, a horse race that's been held every year since medieval times in Fassio's hometown of Asti. The small wine bar is a wonderful place to sit and enjoy a few small plates and a memorable Italian wine. Nearby, **Paninoteca Palio d'Asti** (⊠ 505 Montgomery St.) offers stylish takeout or eat-in lunchtime *panini* (Italian sandwiches) served on house-made bread with such fillings as prosciutto and smoked salmon. ⊠ *640 Sacramento St.,* ☎ *415/395–9800. AE, D, DC, MC, V. Closed weekends.*

Japanese

$$–$$$$ ✕ **Kyo-ya.** Rarely replicated outside Japan, the refined experience of ★ dining in a fine Japanese restaurant has been introduced with extraordinary authenticity at this showplace within the Palace Hotel. In Japan a "kyo-ya" is a nonspecialized restaurant that serves a wide range of food. Here, the range is spectacular, encompassing tempuras, one-pot dishes, deep-fried and grilled meats, and three dozen sushi selections. The lunch menu is more limited than dinner but does include a *shokado,* a sampler of four dishes encased in a lacquered box. *Kaiseki* meals, multicourse seasonal dinners, are also offered, priced for an emperor. ⊠ *Palace Hotel, 2 New Montgomery St., at Market St.,* ☎ *415/546–5000. AE, D, DC, MC, V. Closed Sun. No lunch Mon. and Sat.*

Seafood

$$$–$$$$ ✕ **Aqua.** This quietly elegant and ultrafashionable spot, heavily mirrored and populated by a society crowd, is among the city's most lauded seafood restaurants—and among the most expensive. Chef-owner

Michael Mina creates contemporary versions of French, Italian, and American classics. Mussel, crab, or lobster soufflé; chunks of lobster alongside lobster-stuffed ravioli; and the signature ultrarare ahi tuna paired with foie gras are especially good. Desserts are miniature museum pieces—try the warm chocolate tart—and the wine list is superb. ⊠ *252 California St.,* ☎ *415/956–9662. Reservations essential. Jacket and tie. AE, DC, MC, V. Closed Sun. No lunch Sat.*

$$ ✕ **Tadich Grill.** Owners and locations have changed many times since this old-timer opened during the Gold Rush era, but the 19th-century atmosphere remains. Simple sautés are the best choices, or cioppino during crab season, and an old-fashioned house-made tartar sauce accompanies deep-fried items. There is seating at the counter as well as in private booths, but expect long lines for a table at lunchtime on weekdays. The utterly professional white-coated waiters are a reminder of good old-fashioned service. ⊠ *240 California St.,* ☎ *415/391–2373. Reservations not accepted. MC, V. Closed Sun.*

The Haight

Contemporary

$$$ ✕ **Eos Restaurant & Wine Bar.** The culinary marriage of California cuisine and the Asian pantry is the specialty of chef-owner Arnold Wong, who serves an impressive East-West menu at this popular spot. Grilled skirt steak is marinated in a Thai red curry and served with mashed potatoes and bok choy; rock shrimp cakes arrive with a gingery mayonnaise; and blackened catfish is paired with lemongrass risotto. Sometimes diners may find the competing flavors dizzying, but Wong's faithful following keeps his innovative kitchen in motion. The wine bar next door shelves some 400 vintages, any of which is available at your table. ⊠ *901 Cole St.,* ☎ *415/566–3063. Reservations essential. AE, MC, V. No lunch.*

Indian

$$–$$$ ✕ **Indian Oven.** One of the Lower Haight's most popular restaurants, this handsome, cozy Victorian storefront never lacks for customers. Many of these lovers of subcontinental food come here to order the tandoori specialties—chicken, lamb, breads—but the *sag paneer* (spinach with Indian cheese) and *aloo gobhi* (potatoes and cauliflower with black mustard seeds and other spices) are also excellent. You can start your meal with crisp vegetable *pakoras* (fritters), served with a sprightly tamarind chutney, chased with an Indian beer or a tall, cool glass of fresh lemonade. A complete meal, called a *thali* for the metal plate on which it is served, includes a choice of entrée, plus soup, a curried vegetable, cardamom-scented basmati rice, nan, and chutney. ⊠ *223 Fillmore St.,* ☎ *415/626–1628. AE, D, DC, MC, V. No lunch.*

Thai

$–$$ ✕ **Thep Phanom.** The fine Thai food and the lovely interior at this lower Haight institution keep local food critics and restaurant goers singing its praises. Duck is deliciously prepared in a variety of ways—in a fragrant curry, minced for salad, resting atop a bed of spinach. Other specialties are seafood in various guises, stuffed chicken wings, and fried quail. A number of daily specials supplement the regular menu, and a wonderful mango sorbet is sometimes offered for dessert. ⊠ *400 Waller St.,* ☎ *415/431–2526. AE, D, DC, MC, V. No lunch.*

Japantown

Japanese

$–$$ ✕ **Sanppo.** This modestly priced, casual spot has an enormous selection of almost every type of Japanese food: yakis, nabemono dishes, donburi, udon, and soba, not to mention featherlight tempura and sushi. Grilled eel on rice in a lacquered box and a tempting array of small dishes for snacking make Sanppo a favorite of locals and visitors alike. Seating is Western style. Ask for validated parking at the Japan Center garage. ⊠ *1702 Post St.,* ☎ *415/346–3486. Reservations not accepted. MC, V.*

$ ✕ **Mifune.** Thin, brown soba and thick, white udon are the specialties at this North American outpost of an Osaka-based noodle empire. A line often snakes out the door, but the house-made noodles, served both hot and cold and with more than a score of toppings, are worth the wait. Seating is at rustic wooden tables, where diners can be heard slurping down big bowls of such traditional Japanese combinations as fish cake–crowned udon and *tenzaru* (cold noodles and hot tempura with a gingery dipping sauce) served on lacquered trays. Validated parking is available at the Japan Center garage. ⊠ *Japan Center, Kintetsu Bldg., 1737 Post St.,* ☎ *415/922–0337. Reservations not accepted. AE, D, DC, MC, V.*

Lower Pacific Heights

Contemporary

$$–$$$ ✕ **The Meetinghouse.** A small, regularly changing menu of modernized American dishes is served in this appealing room of creamy yellow walls, broad plank floors, and Shaker furniture. Among the most popular first courses are johnnycakes filled with rock shrimp and oyster stew with celery root; hominy-crusted catfish and roasted chicken on a savory bread pudding and greens are satisfying entrées. Partner Joanna Karlinsky, the house bread baker and pastry chef, turns out homemade biscuits, habit-forming Meyer lemon meringue pie, and wonderful berry shortcakes. ⊠ *1701 Octavia St.,* ☎ *415/922–6733. AE, MC, V. Closed Sun.–Mon. No lunch.*

Italian

$$–$$$ ✕ **Laghi.** For many years, Laghi was a much-loved trattoria in the Richmond District, where it was housed in a small storefront with little available parking. In late 1998, chef-owner Gino Laghi moved his estimable operation to this much larger space, complete with open kitchen, big banquettes, and a sleek wine bar. Old customers and new fans quickly flocked here to enjoy the pastas, including pumpkin-filled ravioli with butter and sage; creamy risottos with everything from fiddlehead ferns to porcini mushrooms to truffles; and roasted rabbit and other game. The wine list of Italian labels is reasonably priced, and the service is friendly and helpful. ⊠ *2101 Sutter St.,* ☎ *415/931–3774. AE, DC, MC, V.*

$$–$$$ ✕ **Vivande Porta Via.** Tucked in among the boutiques on upper Fillmore Street, this pricey Italian delicatessen-restaurant, operated by well-known chef and cookbook author Carlo Middione, draws a crowd at lunch and dinner for both its take-out and sit-down fare. Glass cases holding prosciutto di Parma, creamy balls of mozzarella, sweet-and-sour *caponatina* (eggplant antipasto), mile-high *torta rustica* (savory cheese pie), and dozens of other delicacies span one wall. The rest of the room is given over to seating and shelves laden with wines, olives, oils, vinegars, dried pastas, and other Italian gourmet goods. The regularly changing menu includes half a dozen pastas and risottos, including such satisfying southern Italian plates as classic Sicilian pasta *alla Norma* (with eggplant) or spaghetti with fresh tuna and olives, and such northern specialties as risotto with radicchio, pancetta, and pine nuts. Cap off your meal with a lemon tartlet. ⊠ *2125 Fillmore St.,* ☎ *415/ 346–4430. MC, V.*

The Mission District

Cambodian

$ ✕ **Angkor Borei.** This Cambodian restaurant deep in the Mission is a modest yet handsome space decorated with lovely Khmer objects. The menu offers a wonderful array of curries, plump spring rolls, and delicate crepes stuffed with vegetables and a smattering of meat and seafood. Chicken threaded onto skewers, grilled, and served with mildly pickled vegetables is a house specialty. Aromatic Thai basil, lemongrass, and softly sizzling chilies lace many of the dishes at this true neighborhood restaurant. ⊠ 3471 Mission St., ☎ 415/550–8417. AE, D, MC, V. No lunch Sun.

Contemporary

$$–$$$ ✕ **42 Degrees.** Chef Jim Moffat is the culinary brains behind this sleek, industrial-style space with a curving metal staircase and a seductive view of the bay. The name refers to the latitude on which Provence, Tuscany, and northern Spain lie. The California menu, infused with Mediterranean touches, changes weekly and ranges from creamy bone marrow on toast to duck breast with fiddlehead ferns. Small appetites can graze on a selection of tapas-size plates from the chalkboard menu. Nightly jazz keeps late-night patrons—mostly a younger crowd with bucks to spend—tapping their toes. ⊠ 235 16th St., ☎ 415/777–5558. MC, V. Closed Sun. No dinner Mon. and Tues.

French

$ ✕ **Ti Couz.** Big, thin crêpes just like you find in Brittany are the specialty here, filled with everything from savory ham and Gruyère cheese to bittersweet chocolate. The blue-and-white dining room is always crowded. Rounding out the menu at this Gallic spot are traditional, buttery buckwheat cakes and French hard cider served in classic pottery bowls. ⊠ 3108 16th St., ☎ 415/252–7373. MC, V.

Italian

$–$$ ✕ **Vineria.** The North Mission is home to a continually expanding pop-
★   ulation of eateries, but this is arguably the finest kitchen in the neighborhood. The talented duo behind Vineria are the same women who run the highly successful L'Osteria del Forno in North Beach (☞ below), and many of the offerings are identical, including a full list of wonderful panini. There are, however, more pastas at this slightly larger space. The all-Italian wine list is small but superb. ⊠ 3228 16th St., ☎ 415/552–3889. MC, V. Closed Mon.–Tues. No lunch.

Latin

$–$$ ✕ **Charanga.** Cozy and lively, this neighborhood tapas restaurant, named for a Cuban salsa style that relies on flute and violins, serves an eclectic mix of small plates, from mushrooms cooked with garlic and sherry to *patatas a la brava,* twice-fried potatoes with a roasted-tomato sauce. Asian influences show up on this Latin table as well, in such dishes as shrimp and calamari with coconut rice and ginger sauce. The small dining room, with its walls of exposed brick and soothing green, is a friendly, fun place to eat and socialize. Order a pitcher of sangria and enjoy yourself. ⊠ 2351 Mission St., ☎ 415/282–1813. Reservations not accepted. MC, V. Closed Sun.–Mon. No lunch.

$ ✕ **La Santaneca.** El Salvadorans live in the Mission in large numbers, and they dream of the food they grew up with, especially the *pupusa,* a stuffed cornmeal round that is more or less the hamburger of their homeland. It usually comes filled with cheese, meat, or both, and is eaten along with seasoned shredded cabbage. The cooks turn out pupusas in great numbers, as well as fried plantains, tamales filled with pork and potatoes, *chicharrones* (fried pork skins) and yucca, and other plates that Central Americans crave. ✉ *3781 Mission St.,* ☎ *415/648–1034. No credit cards.*

Mexican

$ ✕ **La Taqueria.** Although there are a number of taquerias in the Mission, this attractive spot, with its arched exterior and modest interior, is one of the oldest and finest. The tacos are superb: a pair of warm corn tortillas topped with your choice of meat—*carne asada* (grilled steak) and *carnitas* (slowly cooked pork) are favorites—and a spoonful of perfectly fresh salsa. Big appetites may want to try one of the burritos, a large flour tortilla wrapped around hearty spoonfuls of meat, rice, beans, and salsa. Chase your chili-laced meal with a cooling *agua fresca* (fresh fruit cooler) of watermelon or pineapple. ✉ *2889 Mission St.,* ☎ *415/285–7117. No credit cards.*

Vietnamese

$$ ✕ **Slanted Door.** Behind the canted facade of this trendy north Mission restaurant, you'll find what owner Charles Phan describes as "real Vietnamese home cooking." There are fresh spring rolls packed with rice noodles, pork, shrimp, and pungent mint leaves, and fried vegetarian imperial rolls concealing bean thread noodles, cabbage, and taro. Five-spice chicken, green papaya salad, and a special of steamed sea bass fillet are among the best dishes. The kitchen, alas, falters more than the crowded tables would have you believe. The menu changes every two weeks or so, but popular dishes are never abandoned. ✉ *584 Valencia St.,* ☎ *415/861–8032. MC, V. Closed Mon.*

Nob Hill

French

$$$–$$$$ ✕ **Ritz-Carlton Dining Room and Terrace.** There are two distinctly dif-
★ ferent places to eat in this neoclassic Nob Hill showplace. The Dining Room is formal and elegant and has a harpist playing. It serves only three- to five-course dinners, priced by the course, not by the item. The Terrace, a cheerful, informal spot with a large garden patio for outdoor dining, serves breakfast, lunch, dinner, and a Sunday jazz brunch, with piano music at lunchtime and a jazz trio at weekend dinners. In the Dining Room executive chef Sylvain Portay, who was previously chef de cuisine at New York's Le Cirque, turns out an urbane seasonal French menu—squab with foie gras, lobster salad with caviar cream, a dreamy chocolate soufflé. ✉ *600 Stockton St.,* ☎ *415/296–7465. AE, D, DC, MC, V. Closed Sun. No lunch.*

Noe Valley

Middle Eastern

$$ ✕ **Fattoush.** Blue tile floors, comfortable banquettes, and bright white walls contribute to the inviting character of this restaurant. Lamb shanks paired with pureed spinach-chickpea sauce and a Palestinian dish of lamb chunks cooked in yogurt with rice and pine nuts are just two of the half dozen fine lamb dishes available. *Sambusak,* phyllo pastry filled with spinach, mushrooms, and nuts served with tahini, is a perfect vegetarian main course. A selection of hot and cold appetizers are offered, including the familiar baba ghanoush and a rich hummus strewn with sumac-dusted onions. Brunch is offered on weekends, and outdoor tables are available on sunny days. ✉ *1361 Church St.,* ☎ *415/641–0678. MC, V. No lunch Mon.*

North Beach

Afghan

$–$$ ✕ **Helmand.** Don't be put off by its location on a rather scruffy block of Broadway—inside you'll find authentic Afghani cooking, elegant surroundings with white table linens and rich Afghan carpets, and amazingly low prices. Highlights include *aushak* (leek-filled ravioli served with yogurt and ground beef), pumpkin served with yogurt and garlic sauce, and any of the tender lamb dishes, in particular the kabob strewn with yellow split peas and served on Afghani flat bread. There's free nighttime validated parking at 468 Broadway. ✉ *430 Broadway,* ☎ *415/362–0641. AE, MC, V. No lunch.*

American

$$$ ✕ **Bix.** In a historic building that was an assay office in Gold Rush days, this old-fashioned supper club was the brainchild of the owners of Fog City Diner. Bix is reminiscent of a theater, with a bustling bar—memorable martinis and generous gin fizzes—and dining tables downstairs and banquettes on the balcony. Opt for the lower level; the acoustics upstairs are dreadful. The menu offers contemporary renditions of classic American fare, from Waldorf salad to bananas Foster. There's piano music in the evening. ✉ *56 Gold St.,* ☎ *415/433–6300. AE, D, DC, MC, V. No lunch weekends.*

Contemporary

$$–$$$ ✕ **Black Cat.** The menu at this combination restaurant and jazz lounge, the latter called the Blue Bar, is made up of dishes that reflect the city's ethnic diversity. You'll find the Wharf's shellfish soups and sand dabs with tartar sauce, North Beach's pastas, Chinatown's roast duck and chow mein, and the Barbary Coast's chops and grills here. The name is taken from a famous San Francisco café-bar, a bohemian hangout for everyone from artists to trade unionists from the 1930s to the 1960s. The ambience is a spirited one, with live jazz and a tempting bar menu—barbecued salmon spring rolls, terrine of foie gras—served up until the wee hours in the seriously blue lounge. ✉ *501 Broadway,* ☎ *415/981–2233. Reservations essential. AE, DC, MC, V.*

$$ ✕ **Enrico's Sidewalk Café.** For years this historic North Beach hangout was more a drinking spot than a dining destination, but a reliable kitchen has changed all that. Diners regularly tuck into the Caesar salad, thin-crust pizzas, grilled fish, and nicely done pastas, while gently swaying to first-rate live music. Grazers will be happy to find a slew of eclectic tapas, from smoked salmon bruschetta to fried oysters. The crowd includes local power brokers, struggling writers, twentysomethings, and out-of-towners—all of them hooked on the freewheeling atmosphere. An outdoor patio is outfitted with heat lamps to keep the serious people-watchers warm until closing. ✉ *504 Broadway,* ☎ *415/982–6223. AE, DC, MC, V.*

French

$ ✕ **Des Alpes.** Opened in 1908, this spot has long been where the savvy diner finds a Basque meal at a rock-bottom price: soup, salad, two entrées—sweetbreads on puff pastry and rare roast beef are a typical pair—and ice cream are included in the budget tariff. It's a haven for ravenous souls, with wood-paneled walls and bright checkered cloths on the tables. Service is family style, and the *intime* bar that fronts the dining room is a delightful step back in time. ✉ *732 Broadway,* ☎ *415/788–9900. D, DC, MC, V. Closed Mon. No lunch.*

Italian

$$–$$$ ✕ **Rose Pistola.** Chef-owner Reed Hearon's popular 130-seat spot draws
★   huge crowds. The name honors one of North Beach's most revered bar-

keeps, and the food celebrates the neighborhood's Ligurian roots. A wide assortment of small cold and hot antipasti—roasted peppers, house-cured fish, fava beans and pecorino cheese, crostini topped with cheese, arugula, and figs—and pizzas from the wood-burning oven are favorites, as is the classic San Francisco seafood stew called cioppino. A large and inviting bar area opens onto the sidewalk, and an immense exhibition kitchen lets customers keep an eye on their orders. ⊠ *532 Columbus Ave.,* ☎ *415/399–0499. Reservations essential. AE, MC, V.*

$$ ✕ **Ristorante Ideale.** The food here is what you might sit down to in a Roman trattoria—grilled vegetables, pasta with greens and pine nuts, ravioli filled with ricotta and spinach, a rosemary-laced *arrosto misto* (mixed grill), and coffee granita. The red tile floors, rows of wine racks, and friendly, although sometimes frazzled, staff make this one of the nicest spots in the neighborhood, a place where you appreciate just how *simpatico* North Beach can be. On weekends, expect a wait for a table. ⊠ *1309 Grant Ave.,* ☎ *415/391–4129. DC, MC, V. Closed Mon. No lunch.*

$–$$ ✕ **Tavolino.** A snacker's paradise, this light, airy space celebrates the Venetian tradition of *cicchetti,* small plates usually consumed in a neighborhood bar with a glass of local wine. Some of the offerings fit right in with the classics, such as deep-fried anchovy-stuffed olives, *tramezzini* (triangular sandwiches) filled with mozzarella and sliced tomatoes, fried calamari, and green beans dressed with olive oil. Other dishes are just shrunken versions of Italian *primi* or main dishes, such as squid ink risotto, house-made sausage with polenta, and a hearty lasagna. Tavolino is a nice place to stop for an afternoon sandwich and a glass of wine, or later in the evening for a serious cocktail and an order of sea bass marinated in vinegar with onions. ⊠ *401 Columbus Ave.,* ☎ *415/392–1472. AE, DC, MC, V.*

$ ✕ **Capp's Corner.** This is one of North Beach's last family-style trattorias, a pleasantly down-home spot where the men at the bar still roll dice for drinks and diners sit elbow to elbow at long oilcloth-covered tables. The fare is bountiful, well-prepared five-course dinners—not award winning, but a meal here will mean you'll still be able to send your children to college. For calorie counters or the budget-minded, a simpler option includes a tureen of minestrone, salad, and pasta. ⊠ *1600 Powell St.,* ☎ *415/989–2589. AE, D, DC, MC, V.*

$ ✕ **L'Osteria del Forno.** An Italian-speaking staff, a small, unpretentious dining area, and irresistible aromas drifting from the open kitchen make customers who pass through the door of this modest storefront operation feel as if they've just stumbled into Italy. The kitchen produces small plates of simply cooked vegetables, a few baked pastas, a roast of the day, creamy polenta, and wonderful thin-crust pizzas—including a memorable "white" pie topped with porcini mushrooms and mozzarella. At lunch try one of the delectable focaccia sandwiches. ⊠ *519 Columbus Ave.,* ☎ *415/982–1124. Reservations not accepted. No credit cards. Closed Tues.*

Mediterranean

$$–$$$ ✕ **Moose's.** Restaurateur Ed Moose's latest venture was destined to become a celebrity hangout from the moment it opened in 1992, with politicians and media types following him from his former digs at Washington Square Bar & Grill. In 1997, Brian Whitmer, who has done stints at Montrachet in New York and Montrio in Carmel, joined Moose's as executive chef and managing partner, introducing a Mediterranean menu with heavy French, Italian, and Californian accents. Among his popular creations are the warm shiitake and buffalo mozzarella salad, risotto with wild mushrooms, and sturgeon wrapped in pancetta. The surroundings are classic and comfortable, with views of Washington

Square and Russian Hill from a front café area. Counter seats have a view of the open kitchen. There's live music at night and a fine Sunday brunch. ⊠ *1652 Stockton St.,* ☎ *415/989–7800. Reservations essential. AE, DC, MC, V. No lunch Mon.–Wed.*

Middle Eastern

$$ ✕ **Maykadeh.** Although it sits in the middle of a decidedly Italian neighborhood, this authentic Persian restaurant serves a large following of faithful customers. Lamb dishes with rice are the specialties, served in a setting so elegant that the modest check comes as a surprise. The chicken, lamb, and beef kabobs and the *chelo* (Persian pilaf) are popular choices. Carnivores will appreciate first courses of lamb tongue in a sour cream-and-lime sauce and grilled lamb brains with saffron. ⊠ *470 Green St.,* ☎ *415/362–8286. MC, V.*

Northern Waterfront

Indian

$$–$$$ ✕ **Gaylord's.** You'll find a vast selection of mildly spiced northern Indian food here, along with meats and breads from the tandoor ovens and a wide range of vegetarian dishes. Although the kitchen sometimes stumbles, the elegantly appointed dining room goes a long way in soothing disappointments. So do the prime bay views. Validated parking is offered at the Ghirardelli Square garage. ⊠ *Ghirardelli Sq.,* ☎ *415/771–8822. AE, D, DC, MC, V.*

Seafood

$$ ✕ **McCormick & Kuleto's.** This seafood emporium in Ghirardelli Square is a visitor's dream come true: a fabulous view of the bay from every seat in the house; an Old San Francisco atmosphere; and dozens of varieties of fish and shellfish prepared in scores of globe-circling ways, from tacos, pot stickers, and fish cakes to grills, pastas, and stew. The food has its ups and downs—stick with the simplest preparations, such as oysters on the half shell and grilled fish—but even on foggy days you can count on the view. Validated parking is available in the Ghirardelli Square garage. ⊠ *Ghirardelli Sq. at Beach and Larkin Sts.,* ☎ *415/929–1730. AE, D, DC, MC, V.*

Richmond District

Chinese

$$ ✕ **Hong Kong Flower Lounge.** This upmarket Cantonese restaurant was one of the first to serve San Franciscans the same plates that rich Hong Kong residents have long enjoyed. The kitchen is celebrated for its seafood which is plucked straight from tanks. Chefs here keep up with whatever is hot in Hong Kong eateries, so check with the generally genial waiters to find out what's new on the menu. Be sure to ask about the prices before you order, as current trends can be costly. Midday dim sum is available. ⊠ *5322 Geary Blvd.,* ☎ *415/668–8998. AE, D, DC, MC, V.*

$–$$ ✕ **Ton Kiang.** The lightly seasoned Hakka cuisine of southern China, rarely found in this country, was introduced to San Francisco at this restaurant, with such regional specialties as salt-baked chicken, braised stuffed bean curd, delicate fish and beef balls, and casseroles of meat and seafood cooked in clay pots. Don't overlook the seafood offerings here—salt-and-pepper squid or shrimp, braised catfish, or stir-fried crab, for example. The dim sum is some of the finest in the city; especially noteworthy are the dumplings stuffed with shark's fin. ⊠ *5821 Geary Blvd.,* ☎ *415/387–8273. MC, V.*

$ ✕ **San Tung No. 2.** History records that many of the best chefs at Beijing's imperial kitchens hailed from China's northeastern province of

Shandong. This modest but bright Shandong restaurant is a good introduction to the region's cuisine—specialties include steamed dumplings and hand-pulled noodles either in soup or stir-fried. Typical accompaniments include a salad of jellyfish, seaweed, or cucumber and a plate of cold poached chicken marinated in Shaoxing wine. ⊠ *1031 Irving St.,* ☎ *415/242–0828. MC, V.*

Japanese

$$–$$$ ✕ **Kabuto Sushi.** For one of the most spectacular acts in town, head out Geary Boulevard past Japantown to tiny Kabuto. Here, behind the sushi counter, master chef Sachio Kojima has been flashing his knives for nearly two decades, serving up everything from buttery yellow fin tuna to perfectly fresh raw shrimp to golden sea urchin on pads of pearly rice. In addition to exceptional sushi and sashimi, traditional Japanese dinners are served in the adjoining dining room. For an authentic experience, request tatami seating in the shoji-screened area. Be sure to consider the excellent selection of sakes, each one rated for dryness and labeled with its place of origin. ⊠ *5116 Geary Blvd.,* ☎ *415/752–5652. MC, V. Closed Mon. No lunch.*

Russian

$–$$ ✕ **Katia's.** This bright Richmond District gem offers Russian food with considerable flair at remarkably reasonable prices. Try the borscht, a dollop of sour cream topping a mélange of beets, cabbage, and other vegetables. Small plates of smoked salmon and blini, marinated mushrooms, and meat- or vegetable-filled piroshki are also wonderful ways to start a meal, and light chicken or potato cutlets or delicate *pelmeni* (small meat-filled dumplings in broth) are fine main courses. Save room for a meringue drizzled with berry sauce or a flaky napoleon. There is live Russian music on most evenings. The slow service may occasionally try your patience. ⊠ *600 5th Ave.,* ☎ *415/668–9292. AE, DC, MC, V. Closed Mon.*

Singaporean

$–$$ ✕ **Straits Café.** This highly popular restaurant serves the unique fare of Singapore, a cuisine that combines the culinary traditions of China, India, and the Malay archipelago. That exotic mix translates into complex curries, rice cooked in coconut milk, fragrant satays, and seafood noodle soups. The handsome dining room includes one wall that re-creates the old shop-house fronts of Singapore. ⊠ *3300 Geary Blvd.,* ☎ *415/668–1783. AE, MC, V.*

Vietnamese

$–$$ ✕ **La Vie.** This small Vietnamese restaurant caters to a mostly neighborhood clientele with such traditional dishes as *nep chien* (deep-fried balls of sticky rice stuffed with a mixture of finely cut pork, shrimp, and mushrooms). One fun-to-eat entrée consists of small cakes made from shrimp, rice flour, and yellow mung beans: You wrap up the cakes in crisp lettuce leaves and dip them in a spicy fish sauce. The *beef la lot* (minced beef wrapped in a tropical leaf) and eggplant with garlic sauce are also recommended. The attentive staff is always happy to answer questions about the food. ⊠ *5380 Geary Blvd.,* ☎ *415/668–8080. AE, MC, V.*

$–$$ ✕ **Le Soleil.** The food of Vietnam is the specialty of this pastel, light-filled restaurant in the heart of Inner Richmond. An eye-catching painting of Saigon hangs on one wall, and a large aquarium of tropical fish adds to the tranquil mood. The kitchen prepares traditional dishes from every part of the country. Try the excellent raw-beef salad; crisp, flavorful spring rolls; a simple stir-fry of chicken and aromatic fresh basil leaves; or large prawns simmered in a clay pot. ⊠ *133 Clement St.,* ☎ *415/668–4848. MC, V.*

Russian Hill

French

$$$$ ✕ **La Folie.** Long a favorite of dedicated Francophiles, this small, ter-
★ ribly Parisian establishment underwent a refurbishing in 1998, making the storefront café even lovelier. But the food is the true star here,
especially the five-course discovery menu that allows a sample of such
rarified mouthfuls as lobster salad with a mango vinaigrette and quail
with white truffles. Much of the food is edible art—whimsical presentations in the form of savory terrines, *galettes* (flat, round cakes),
and napoleons—or such elegant accompaniments as bone-marrow
flan. The exquisite food and professional service come at a hefty price,
so save this special place for a very special occasion. ⊠ *2316 Polk St.,*
☎ *415/776–5577. Reservations essential. AE, D, DC, MC, V. Closed
Sun. No lunch.*

Italian

$$$ ✕ **Acquerello.** This elegant restaurant—white tablecloths, fresh flowers,
exquisite china—is one of the most romantic spots in town. Both the ser-
vice and the food are exemplary, and the menu covers the full range of
Italian cuisine. The gnocchi and tortellini are memorable, as are the fish
dishes. Chef Suzette Gresham's fine creations include a first course of
squab paired with greens and pine nuts, and a main of beef fillet stuffed
with prosciutto and Parmesan cheese. ⊠ *1722 Sacramento St.,* ☎ *415/
567–5432. AE, D, DC, MC, V. Closed Sun.–Mon. No lunch.*

$$ ✕ **Antica Trattoria.** The dining room is stark, with off-white walls, dark
wood, a partial view of the kitchen, and a strong sense of restraint.
The food is characterized by the same no-nonsense quality. A small menu
delivers classic plates such as fennel with blood oranges and red onions;
whole wheat pasta tossed with Bolognese sauce; and venison medallions matched with wilted greens. The Italian wine list is fairly priced,
and the genial service is polished but not overly formal. ⊠ *2400 Polk
St.,* ☎ *415/928–5797. MC, V. Closed Mon. No lunch.*

Spanish

$$ ✕ **Zarzuela.** Until the mid-'90s San Francisco lacked a great tapas restau-
rant—but Spanish-born chef Lucas Gasco changed all that when he and
partner Andy Debanne opened their charming Zarzuela. The small,
crowded storefront serves nearly 40 different hot and cold tapas plus
some dozen main courses. There is a tapa to suit every palate, from poached
octopus atop new potatoes and hot garlic-flecked shrimp to slabs of
Manchego cheese with paper-thin slices of serrano ham. ⊠ *2000 Hyde
St.,* ☎ *415/346–0800. Reservations not accepted. D, MC, V. Closed Sun.*

Steak

$$$ ✕ **Harris'.** Ann Harris knows her beef. She grew up on a Texas cattle
★ ranch and was married to the late Jack Harris of Harris Ranch fame.
In her own large, New York–style restaurant she serves some of the best
dry-aged steaks in town, but don't overlook the starter of spinach salad
or the entrée of calves' liver with onions and bacon. Be sure to include
a side of the fine creamed spinach. If you're a martini drinker, don't pass
up the opportunity to enjoy a superb example of the art form. ⊠ *2100
Van Ness Ave.,* ☎ *415/673–1888. AE, D, DC, MC, V. No lunch.*

South of Market

American

$$$ ✕ **Momo's.** Baseball fans spilling out of the new San Francisco Giants
ballpark slated to open in April 2000 will want to stop at this former
printing plant, now serious drinking and dining hangout. A shiny
stainless steel exhibition kitchen delivers smoky-sweet baby back ribs,

crisp onion rings, chopped salad, thick steaks, and thin pizzas to crowds in the Craftsman-appointed dining room with its big banquettes and high ceilings. The large patio and long, wood-lined bar are gathering places for everyone from sports enthusiasts to groups of young women out for a night on the town to businesspeople shaking hands on a deal. ⊠ *760 Second St.,* ☎ *415/227–8660, AE, MC, V.*

Contemporary

$$$ ✕ **Hawthorne Lane.** In 1995 Anne and David Gingrass, of Postrio fame
★ (☞ Union Square, *below*), joined the booming bevy of SoMa eateries with this instantly popular establishment on a quiet alley a block or so from the Moscone Center and the Museum of Modern Art. In the large, high-ceiling bar there's a selection of irresistible small plates— Thai-style squid, skewers of grilled chicken, and tempura-battered green beans with mustard sauce. Patrons in the light-flooded dining room engage in more serious eating, from perfectly seared foie gras to grilled quail on scalloped potatoes, all turned out with Mediterranean and Asian touches. The breadbasket is full of house-made delights, including biscuits, bread sticks, rye, and rolls. The desserts are suitably decadent. ⊠ *22 Hawthorne St.,* ☎ *415/777–9779. Reservations essential. D, DC, MC, V. No lunch weekends.*

French

$$–$$$ ✕ **Bizou.** Chef Loretta Keller, who once cooked alongside Jeremiah Tower at Stars, has developed her own distinctive French country menu here. Partisans of her rustic cooking cite the thin, crisp pizza topped with caramelized onions, fried snap beans with aioli or fig sauce, and pan-fried skate in brown butter as evidence of her talents. The space itself is small and unpretentious. Outsized windows means it's also sunny and bright. Although service can sometimes be uneven, Keller's faithful following doesn't seem to mind. ⊠ *598 4th St.,* ☎ *415/543–2222. AE, MC, V. Closed Sun. No lunch Sat.*

$$–$$$ ✕ **Fringale.** The bright yellow paint on this dazzling bistro stands out
★ like a beacon on an otherwise bleak industrial street, attracting a well-dressed clientele. They come for the reasonably priced French Basque–inspired creations of Biarritz-born chef Gerald Hirigoyen, whose classic *frisée aux lardoons* (curly salad greens with crisp bacon cubes and a poached egg), *steak frites,* steamed mussels, and flaky apple tart are hallmarks. Small tables covered with cloths and white paper, a sensible wine list, and a crew of waiters sporting Gallic accents will have you practicing your French. ⊠ *570 4th St.,* ☎ *415/543–0573. Reservations essential. AE, MC, V. Closed Sun. No lunch Sat.*

$–$$ ✕ **South Park Café.** This utterly Parisian spot is open from early morning for your caffe latte to late at night for a wedge of fruit tart or a flute of champagne. No place in the City of Light itself serves a more authentic *steak frites* than this warm, sometimes clamorous spot overlooking a grassy square. A notable first-course is the salad greens with baked goat cheese. For an entrée try the *boudin noir* (black sausage) with sautéed apples. ⊠ *108 South Park, at Bryant St.,* ☎ *415/495–7275. MC, V. Closed Sun. No lunch Sat.*

Latin

$$ ✕ **Thirstybear.** Just around the corner from the cathedral-like San Francisco Museum of Modern Art, Thirstybear is a combination brew pub and tapas outpost. The cavernous interior of concrete floors, rustic brick walls, and shiny tanks holding homemade brews is cool and utilitarian, but the small plates of garlic-and-sherry-infused fish cheeks, steamed mussels, grilled garlic-studded shrimp, and white beans with sausage and aioli will warm you right up. Bigger appetites can dig into paella Valenciana. ⊠ *661 Howard St.,* ☎ *415/974–0905. MC, V. No lunch Sun.*

Mediterranean

$$–$$$ **✕ LuLu.** Since its opening day in 1993, a seat at this boisterous restau-
★ rant has been one of the hottest tickets in town, although the throngs
have faded somewhat since founding chef Reed Hearon divorced himself from the operation in 1996. The food, under the watchful eye of
executive chef Jody Denton, has remained satisfyingly uncomplicated
and delectable. Under the high barrel-vaulted ceiling, beside a large open
kitchen, diners feast on sizzling mussels roasted in an iron skillet, plus
pizzas, pastas, and wood-roasted poultry, meats, and shellfish. Sharing dishes is the custom here. A smaller, quieter room off to one side
makes conversation easier. The café on the opposite side serves food
from morning until late at night. ⊠ *816 Folsom St.,* ☎ *415/495–
5775. Reservations essential. AE, DC, MC, V.*

Sunset District

Contemporary

$$ **✕ Beach Chalet.** In a historic colonnaded building with handsome
Works Project Administration–produced murals depicting San Fran-
cisco in the mid-'30s, the Beach Chalet is the place to watch the sun
set over the Pacific. The microbrewery beers run the gamut from a light
pilsner to Playland pale ale, named for a now-gone nearby amusement
park that entertained generations of San Franciscans. The food is an
eclectic mix of steamed mussels and pizzette, buttermilk-dipped onion
rings and house-made chorizo, thick burgers, and seafood gumbo. It's
a 40-minute ride on the N Judah streetcar from downtown—and well
worth the trip. ⊠ *1000 Great Hwy.,* ☎ *415/386–8439. MC, V.*

$ **✕ Park Chow.** After a morning or afternoon in Golden Gate Park, this
contemporary, yet homey, spot is just what your appetite ordered. In
the mood for spaghetti and meatballs? That's here. Prefer Thai noodles
with rock shrimp and chicken? That's also here. Or what about a big
American burger, a lamb and goat cheese pizza straight from the wood-
burning oven, or an order of iron-skillet mussels? They are all here, too,
along with Sicilian cannoli and Southern pecan pie. There's another branch
on the distant reaches of the Castro. ⊠ *1240 Ninth Ave.,* ☎ *415/665–
9912;* ⊠ *215 Church St.,* ☎ *415/552–2469. MC, V.*

Union Square

Contemporary

$$$$ **✕ Campton Place.** This elegant, ultrasophisticated small hotel put new
★ American cooking on the local culinary map with famed opening chef
Bradley Ogden, who was followed by the nearly equally celebrated Jan
Birnbaum, and later by yet another favorite, Todd Humphries, who
left in early 1999. The kitchen continues to offer a refined American
table that relies on the freshest local ingredients and handsome pre-
sentation. A small side bar is a comfortable spot for sipping a martini
while waiting for a table in the subtly appointed dining room. Brunch
and breakfast are major events. ⊠ *340 Stockton St.,* ☎ *415/955–5555.
Reservations essential. AE, D, DC, MC, V.*

$$$–$$$$ **✕ Postrio.** There's always a chance to catch a glimpse of some celebrity
here, including Postrio's owner, superchef Wolfgang Puck, who peri-
odically commutes from Los Angeles to make an appearance in the
restaurant's open kitchen. A stunning three-level bar and dining area
is highlighted by palm trees and museum-quality contemporary paint-
ings. Attire is formal. The food is Puckish Californian with Mediter-
ranean and Asian overtones: Chinese roast duck with mango sauce,
house-cured salmon on a giant blini, and irresistible pastries. Sub-
stantial breakfast and bar menus (with great pizza) can be found here

as well. Although ripples of dissatisfaction with the fare have been heard from some quarters, reservations are still tough to come by. ✉ *545 Post St.*, ☎ *415/776–7825. Reservations essential. AE, D, DC, MC, V.*

$$$ ✕ **Oritalia.** For many years, Oritalia—the name is a blend of the Orient and Italy—was a small, highly regarded restaurant in Lower Pacific Heights. In 1998 it moved downtown, to a much larger space in the Juliana Hotel. The burnt orange dining room, with silk-clad chandeliers, ample booths, and carefully chosen Asian artifacts, is a handsome site for the menu of unusual dishes. Steamed chicken, sticky rice, and vegetables in a black bean sauce arrive hidden in a blanket of gold foil, while beef cheek *agnolotti* (small stuffed pasta) are served in a tomato broth. Shrimp and fresh water chestnuts wrapped in bacon and crab cakes swaddled in seaweed are just two of the intriguing starters. Desserts are equally imaginative, including an addictive passion fruit cheesecake. ✉ *586 Bush St.*, ☎ *415/782–8122. AE, DC, MC, V. No lunch.*

$$–$$$ ✕ **Grand Café.** In the heart of the theater district, this inviting combination dining room and bar is a magnet for folks seeking everything from an early morning breakfast to a late-night snack. The Californian-French menu includes rack of lamb, banana cream pie, pizzas, and charcuterie plates. The dramatic and somewhat imposing dining room, formerly a hotel ballroom, is decorated with fanciful sculptures of stylized human figures, chandeliers, and eight murals that evoke such early 20th-century styles as expressionism and fauvism. The smaller bar area has a wood-burning oven and dozens of pen-and-ink cartoons to keep you amused. ✉ *Hotel Monaco, 501 Geary St.*, ☎ *415/292–0101. AE, D, DC, MC, V.*

$$–$$$ ✕ **Rumpus.** With Caesar salad, burgers, and club sandwiches at lunchtime, this casual bistro has a true American menu with a pocketbook-friendly price list. But there is also a handful of wonderful Mediterranean-inspired dishes, such as the onion tart with black olives and ravioli plump with crabmeat. The out-of-the-way location, tucked at the end of an old-time alley in the heart of downtown, gives this convivial eatery a San Francisco insider's feel. ✉ *1 Tillman Pl., at Grant Ave.*, ☎ *415/421–2300. AE, MC, V. No lunch Sun.*

French

$$$$ ✕ **Fleur de Lys.** The creative cooking of French chef-partner Hubert Keller has brought every conceivable culinary award to this romantic spot, which some consider the best French restaurant in town. The menu changes constantly, but such dishes as seared foie gras, truffled vichyssoise, and venison medallions with tender braised greens are Keller hallmarks. Perfectly smooth service adds to the overall enjoyment of eating here. There are tasting menus for both omnivores and vegetarians, and the elaborately canopied dining room is reminiscent of a sheikh's tent. ✉ *777 Sutter St.*, ☎ *415/673–7779. Reservations essential. Jacket required. AE, DC, MC, V. Closed Sun. No lunch.*

$$$$ ✕ **Masa's.** Julian Serrano headed up the kitchen at this pretty, flower-filled dining spot in the Vintage Court hotel for more than a dozen years, ★ carrying on the tradition of the restaurant's late founder, Masa Kobayashi. In 1998, the torch was passed to Chad Callahan, who had served as the number two chef for several years. Time will tell if Callahan can develop his own style in this celebrated food temple, but regulars have generally been pleased with the silky smooth transition. Dinners are prix fixe, with two menus offered, a four-course menu du jour and a five-course menu, both laced with truffles and foie gras and both priced at a king's ransom. ✉ *648 Bush St.*, ☎ *415/989–7154. Reservations essential. Jacket and tie required. AE, D, DC, MC, V. Closed Sun.–Mon. and 1st 2 wks of Jan. No lunch.*

$$–$$$ ✕ **Brasserie Savoy.** This big-city dining room, with its traditional cane chairs and high ceiling, is located in the small, comfortable Hotel Savoy. Here, Francophiles know they can enjoy a classic bouillabaisse, a hearty pot-au-feu, or a crisp-skinned roast chicken. The small bar is just the place to polish off half a dozen raw oysters or sip a celebratory kir. ⊠ *Hotel Savoy, 580 Geary St.,* ☎ *415/441–8080. AE, MC, V. No lunch.*

Italian

$$–$$$ ✕ **Scala's Bistro.** Smart leather-and-wood booths, an extravagant mural along one wall, and an appealing menu of Italian plates make this one of downtown's most attractive destinations. A large open kitchen stands at the rear of the fashionable dining room, where regulars and out-of-town visitors alike sit down to breakfast, lunch, and dinner. Grilled Portobello mushrooms and a tower of fried calamari or zucchini are among the favorite antipasti, and the pastas and grilled meats are satisfying. ⊠ *432 Powell St.,* ☎ *415/395–8555. AE, D, DC, MC, V.*

Seafood

$$$ ✕ **Farallon.** Outfitted with sculpted purple-and-pink jellyfish lamps, ★   kelp-covered columns, sea urchin chandeliers, and seashell covered walls, this swanky Pat Kuleto–designed restaurant is loaded with style *and* customers. Chef Mark Franz, who gained his fame at Stars, cooks up exquisite seafood that draws serious diners from coast to coast. Such showy concoctions as spot prawns, scallops, and lobster suspended in a pyramid of aspic, and truffled mashed potatoes doused with a sauce of crab and sea urchin are regular fare here. The desserts, including a very adult peppermint patty, are by former Stars whiz Emily Luchetti. ⊠ *450 Post St.,* ☎ *415/956–6969. AE, DC, MC, V. No lunch Sun.*

Vietnamese

$$–$$$ ✕ **Le Colonial.** Until the mid-'90s, Trader Vic's, a well-known Polynesian-inspired haunt of the city's social elite, occupied this restaurant. In 1998, Le Colonial refurbished the space—stamped tin ceiling, period photographs, slow-moving fans, tropical plants—creating a 1920s French colonial setting in which to serve its upscale Vietnamese food. The space still draws the local blue bloods, this time for its spring rolls, creamy coconut soup, steamed sea bass, coconut curry prawns, and sticky rice in a lotus leaf. Upstairs, a suave lounge with couches is the ideal place to sip a cocktail before dinner or polish off a nightcap at the end of the evening. ⊠ *20 Cosmo Pl.,* ☎ *415/931–3600. AE, MC, V. Closed Sun. No lunch Sat.*

3 LODGING

Like its neighborhoods and its population, San Francisco's accommodations come in shapes and sizes to satisfy every whim. There are luxury hotels, bed-and-breakfasts housed in Victorian mansions, and stylish motels with offbeat attitudes. Hotels here are more than hotels: They are part of the scenery, as old as the city itself, beloved by loyal customers who return year after year.

Updated by
Andy Moore

FEW CITIES IN THE UNITED STATES can rival San Francisco's variety in lodging. There are plush hotels ranked among the finest in the world, renovated older buildings with a European flair, and the popular chain hotels found in most American cities. One of the brightest spots in the lodging picture is the proliferation of small bed-and-breakfasts housed in elegant Victorian edifices, where evening hors d'oeuvres and wine service are common practice. Another encouraging trend is the growing number of ultra-deluxe modern hotels, such as the Radisson Miyako and the Mandarin Oriental, which specialize in attentive Asian-style hospitality.

The **San Francisco Convention and Visitors Bureau** (☏ 415/391–2000) publishes a free lodging guide with a map and listings of San Francisco and Bay Area hotels; or call 888/782–9673 to reserve a room at over 60 visitors bureau–recommended hotels in the city or near the airport. **San Francisco Reservations** (☏ 800/677–1500) handles advance reservations at over 250 Bay Area hotels, often at special discount rates. Although there are more than 30,500 hotel rooms available on any given day, San Francisco is one of the top destinations in the United States for tourists as well as business travelers and convention goers. Reservations are always advised, especially during the peak seasons (May–October and December).

San Francisco's geography makes it conveniently compact. No matter what their location, the hotels listed below are on or close to public transportation lines. A few properties on Lombard Street and in the Civic Center area have free parking, while hotels in the Union Square and Nob Hill areas almost invariably charge $17–$26 a day for a spot in their garage.

San Francisco hotel prices may come as a not-so-pleasant surprise. Weekend rates for double rooms downtown and at the wharf start at about $130 and average over $100 per night city-wide (slightly less on weekdays and off-season). Adding to the expense is the city's 14% transient occupancy tax, which can significantly boost the cost of a lengthy stay. The good news is that because of the hotel building boom of the late 1980s, there is now an oversupply of rooms, which has led to frequent discounts. Check for special rates and packages when making reservations. For those in search of true budget accommodations (under $60), try the **Adelaide Inn** (☞ Union Square/Downtown, *below*) or the **YMCA Central Branch** (⊠ 220 Golden Gate Ave., ☏ 415/885–0460).

An alternative to hotels and motels is staying in private homes and apartments, available through **American Family Inn/Bed & Breakfast San Francisco** (⊠ Box 420009, San Francisco 94142, ☏ 415/931–3083, FAX 415/921–2273), **Bed & Breakfast California** (⊠ 205 Park Rd., Suite 209, Burlingame 94010, ☏ 650/696–1690 or 800/872–4500, FAX 650/696–1699), and **American Property Exchange** (⊠ 2800 Van Ness Ave., San Francisco 94109, ☏ 415/447–2040, FAX 415/447–2058).

Fodor's Choice

The opulent lobby and elegant rooms at the **Ritz-Carlton, San Francisco** have earned it its rating as one of the top hotels in the world. *$$$$*

Sherman House, a landmark mansion in Pacific Heights, is San Francisco's most luxurious small hotel. *$$$$*

The **Hotel Monaco,** with its whimsical, steamship-style decor and devotion to pampering guests, has been a hit since its opening in late 1995. *$$$–$$$$*

In case you want to see the world.

At American Express, we're here to make your journey a smooth one. So we have over 1,700 travel service locations in over 130 countries ready to help. What else would you expect from the world's largest travel agency?

do more

Travel

**Call 1 800 AXP-3429 or visit
www.americanexpress.com/travel**

In case you want to be welcomed there.

We're here to see that you're always welcomed at establishments everywhere. That's why millions of people carry the American Express® Card – for peace of mind, confidence, and security, around the world or just around the corner.

do more

AMERICAN EXPRESS

Cards

To apply, call 1 800 THE-CARD
or visit www.americanexpress.com

In case you're running low.

We're here to help with more than 190,000 Express Cash locations around the world. In order to enroll, just call American Express at 1 800 CASH-NOW before you start your vacation.

do more **AMERICAN EXPRESS**

Express Cash

And in case you'd rather be safe than sorry.

We're here with American Express® Travelers Cheques. They're the safe way to carry money on your vacation, because if they're ever lost or stolen you can get a refund, practically anywhere or anytime. To find the nearest place to buy Travelers Cheques, call 1 800 495-1153. Another way we help you do more.

do more

Travelers Cheques

The **Hotel Rex** evokes the spirit of San Francisco in the 1920s, with richly decorated rooms and literary soirées. *$$$–$$$$*

An old-fashioned English garden, wonderful complimentary breakfast, and personable owners make the tiny **Union Street Inn** a prime spot for a romantic getaway. *$$$–$$$$*

CATEGORY	COST*
$$$$	over $200
$$$	$120–$200
$$	$80–$120
$	under $80

All prices are for a standard double room, excluding 14% tax.

Union Square/Downtown

The largest variety and greatest concentration of hotels is in the city's downtown hub, Union Square, where you can find the best shopping, the theater district, and convenient transportation to every spot in San Francisco. If the grand hotels right on Union Square are beyond your budget, consider the more modest establishments a few blocks to the west, between Mason and Jones streets—but be careful when walking there late at night.

$$$$
★ **Campton Place.** Behind a simple brownstone facade with a white awning, quiet reigns. Highly attentive personal service—from unpacking assistance to nightly turndown—begins the moment uniformed doormen greet guests outside the marble-floor lobby. Rooms, though a little smaller than those at other luxury hotels, are supremely elegant, decorated with Asian touches in light, subtle tones. They overlook an atrium, which lends a cozy, residential feel. The Campton Place Restaurant, listed as one of San Francisco's best by Gourmet magazine in 1998, is famed for its breakfasts. ⌷ *340 Stockton St., 94108,* ☎ *415/781–5555 or 800/235–4300,* ⅢX *415/955–5536. 107 rooms, 10 suites. Restaurant, bar, in-room safes, minibars, no-smoking rooms, room service, dry cleaning, concierge, meeting rooms, parking (fee). AE, DC, MC, V.*

$$$$ **The Clift.** Towering over San Francisco's theater district is the venerable Clift. Its crisp, forest-green awnings and formal door service provide subtle hints of the elegance within. In the lobby, dark paneling and enormous chandeliers lend a note of grandeur. Rooms—some rich with dark woods and burgundies, others refreshingly pastel—all have large writing desks. Be sure to sample a cocktail in the dramatic art deco Redwood Room lounge, complete with chandeliers and a sweeping redwood bar. ⌷ *495 Geary St., 94102,* ☎ *415/775–4700 or 800/ 652–5438,* ⅢX *415/441–4621. 218 rooms, 108 suites. Restaurant, bar, in-room data ports, minibars, no-smoking floor, room service, exercise room, laundry service and dry cleaning, concierge, meeting rooms, parking (fee). AE, DC, MC, V.*

$$$$
★ **Hotel Monaco.** The hottest hotel in town, with its yellow beaux-arts facade, stands in stark contrast to its more stately neighbor, the Clift. The contrast continues inside, where a French inglenook fireplace climbs almost two stories above the lobby toward the three huge domes of a vaulted ceiling, which is hand-painted with hot-air balloons, World War I–era planes, and miles of blue sky. Though small, the rooms are comfortable and inviting, with Chinese-inspired armoires and highback upholstered chairs; in the outer rooms, bay window seats overlook the theater district. Though the riot of stripes and colors may strike some guests as a bit outré, it's all been done so tastefully you can't help but appreciate the flair. The Grand Café and Bar, in which hotel guests get preferred seating, features a French-California menu. ⌷ *501 Geary*

114

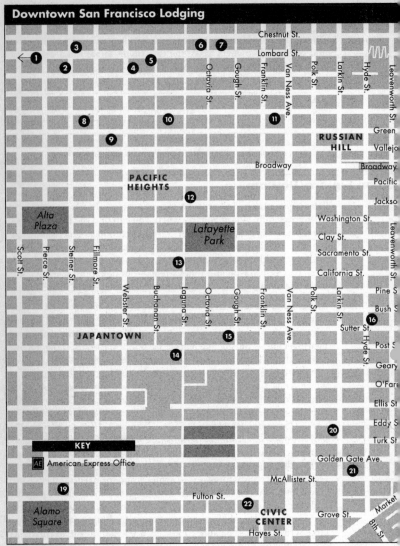

Downtown San Francisco Lodging

La Quinta Motor Inn, **70**
Mandarin Oriental, **39**
The Mansions, **13**
Marina Inn, **6**
Mark Hopkins
Inter–Continental, **31**
Marriott at
Fisherman's Wharf, **23**
The Maxwell, **58**
Nob Hill Lambourne, **36**
Pacific Heights Inn, **11**

Palace Hotel, **60**
Pan Pacific Hotel, **50**
Park Hyatt, **29**
Petite Auberge, **43**
Phoenix Hotel, **20**
Prescott Hotel, **49**
Presidio Travelodge, **1**
Radisson Miyako
Hotel, **14**
Red Roof Inn, **67**

Renaissance Stanford
Court, **32**
The Ritz–Carlton, San
Francisco, **34**
San Francisco
Residence Club, **33**
San Remo, **27**
Shannon Court
Hotel, **47**
Sherman House, **9**
Sir Francis Drake
Hotel, **52**

Town House Motel, **7**
Travelodge Hotel at
Fisherman's Wharf, **26**
Tuscan Inn, **25**
Union Street Inn, **8**
Vintage Court, **35**
W San Francisco, **71**
The Westin, **68**
Westin St. Francis, **61**
White Swan Inn, **44**
York Hotel, **16**

St., 94102, ☎ 415/292–0100 or 800/214–4220, FAX 415/292–0111. 177 rooms, 24 suites. Restaurant, bar, in-room data ports, in-room safes, minibars, no-smoking rooms, room service, spa, laundry service and dry cleaning, business services, parking (fee). AE, D, DC, MC, V.

$$$$ 🏨 **Pan Pacific Hotel.** Exotic flower arrangements and elegant Asian touches set this business hotel apart from others. A graceful sculpture, *Joie de Dance*, encircles the fountain in the lobby, where two fireplaces add to the refined atmosphere. Guest rooms feature such business amenities as in-room fax machines and modem lines, not to mention elegant bathrooms lined with terra-cotta Portuguese marble. Complimentary personal valet service and the hotel's fleet of luxury cars serving as shuttles for guests add to a pampering experience. The hotel's restaurant, Pacific, is well regarded for its California cuisine. ⊠ *500 Post St., 94102, ☎ 415/771–8600 or 800/327–8585, FAX 415/398–0267. 311 rooms, 19 suites. Restaurant, bar, lobby lounge, in-room data ports, in-room safes, minibars, no-smoking floors, refrigerators, room service, exercise room, piano, laundry service and dry cleaning, concierge, business services, meeting rooms, parking (fee). AE, D, DC, MC, V.*

$$$$ 🏨 **Prescott Hotel.** A gourmet's delight might be the best way to describe
★ this plush hotel, thanks to its partnership with Wolfgang Puck's Postrio, one of San Francisco's best restaurants. Cuisine-conscious guests can order room service from the restaurant or dine at tables reserved for hotel guests—no small perk considering it can otherwise take months to get a reservation at Postrio. The Prescott's rooms, which vary only in size and shape, are traditional in style and decorated in a rich hunter green; bathrooms have marble-top sinks and gold fixtures. There's a brick-and-wood fireplace in the hunting-lodge-style living room—a perfect setting for the complimentary coffee and tea services and evening wine and cheese receptions. ⊠ *545 Post St., 94102, ☎ 415/563–0303 or 800/283–7322, FAX 415/563–6831. 134 rooms, 30 suites. Restaurant, bar, lobby lounge, in-room data ports, minibars, no-smoking floors, room service, concierge, business services, meeting rooms, parking (fee). AE, D, DC, MC, V.*

$$$$ 🏨 **Westin St. Francis.** Guests as illustrious as Emperor Hirohito, Queen Elizabeth II, and many presidents have stayed here since it opened in 1904. No wonder; with an imposing facade, black marble lobby, and gold-top columns, the St. Francis looks more like a great public building than a hotel. The effect is softened by the columns and exquisite woodwork of the Compass Rose bar and restaurant, a romantic retreat from the bustle of Union Square. Many rooms in the original building are small by modern standards, but all retain their original Victorian-style moldings and are decorated with Empire-style furnishings. Rooms in the modern tower are larger, with Oriental-style lacquered furniture. Ask for a room above the 15th floor for a spectacular view of the city. ⊠ *335 Powell St., 94102, ☎ 415/397–7000, FAX 415/774–0124. 1,108 rooms, 84 suites. 3 restaurants, 2 bars, in-room data ports, in-room safes, no-smoking floors, room service, exercise room, nightclub, laundry service and dry cleaning, concierge, business services, meeting rooms, travel services, parking (fee). AE, D, DC, MC, V.*

$$$–$$$$ 🏨 **Galleria Park.** A few blocks east of Union Square, this hotel with
★ a black marble facade is close to the Chinatown Gate and Crocker Galleria, one of San Francisco's most elegant shopping areas. The staff is remarkably pleasant and helpful. The comfortable rooms all have floral bedspreads, stylish striped wallpaper, and white furniture that includes a writing desk. In the lobby, dominated by a massive fireplace, complimentary coffee and tea are served in the mornings, wine in the evenings. The third-floor rooftop Cityscape Park features an outdoor jogging track. Adjoining the hotel is Perry's Downtown, a casual steak-and-burger eatery where singles like to congregate. ⊠ *191 Sutter St.,*

94104, ☎ 415/781–3060 or 800/792–9639, 800/792–9855 in CA, FAX 415/433–4409. 162 rooms, 15 suites. 2 restaurants, in-room data ports, minibars, no-smoking floors, room service, exercise room, jogging, laundry and dry cleaning, concierge, business services, meeting rooms, parking (fee). AE, D, DC, MC, V.

$$$–$$$$
★
🏨 **Hotel Rex.** Literary and artistic creativity are celebrated at the stylish Hotel Rex, where thousands of books, largely antiquarian, line the 1920s-style lobby. Original artwork adorns the walls, and the proprietors even host book readings and roundtable discussions in the common areas, which are decorated in warm, rich tones. Upstairs, quotations from works by California writers are painted on the terra-cotta-color walls near the elevator landings. Rooms have writing desks and lamps with whimsically hand-painted shades. Striped bedspreads and carpets and restored period furnishings evoke the spirit of 1920s salon society, but rooms also have modern amenities like voice mail and CD players. ✉ 562 Sutter St., 94102, ☎ 415/433–4434 or 800/433–4434, FAX 415/433–3695. 92 rooms, 2 suites. Bar, lobby lounge, in-room data ports, minibars, no-smoking rooms, laundry service and dry cleaning, concierge, parking (fee). AE, D, DC, MC, V.

$$$–$$$$
🏨 **Hotel Triton.** This just may be the zaniest place to stay in town. Guests enter via a whimsical lobby of three-leg furniture, star-pattern carpeting, and inverted gilt pillars—stylized spoofs of upside-down Roman columns. The hotel caters to fashion, entertainment, music, and film-industry types, who seem to appreciate the iridescent multi-color rooms with S-curve chairs, curly-neck lamps, and oddball light fixtures. On the downside, rooms are uncommonly small. If you care about space, try a king room or junior suite. Twenty-four rooms have been designated environmentally sensitive. They feature extra air and water filtration, biodegradable toiletries, and all-natural linens. The trendy newsstand–coffeehouse–dining room Café de la Presse, which serves as a gathering place for foreign visitors to the city, is attached to the hotel. ✉ 342 Grant Ave., 94108, ☎ 415/394–0500 or 888/364–2622, FAX 415/394–0555. 133 rooms, 7 suites. In-room data ports, minibars, no-smoking floors, exercise room, laundry service and dry cleaning, business services, meeting rooms, parking (fee). AE, D, MC, V.

$$$–$$$$
🏨 **Inn at Union Square.** With its tiny but captivating lobby with trompe l'oeil bookshelves painted on the walls, this inn feels like someone's home. Comfortable rooms with sumptuous goose-down pillows promote indolence. Brass lion's-head door knockers are a unique touch. Guests like to lounge in front of the wood-burning fireplaces found in each floor's tiny sitting area, and with good reason: By the time the staff clears away the afternoon tea and pastries, they're already setting out the complimentary evening wine and hors d'oeuvres. Tips are not accepted, and the hotel is completely no-smoking. ✉ 440 Post St., 94102, ☎ 415/397–3510 or 800/288–4346, FAX 415/989–0529. 30 rooms. In-room data ports, parking (fee). AE, DC, MC, V.

$$$–$$$$
🏨 **Sir Francis Drake Hotel.** Beefeater-costumed doormen (including the internationally renowned Tom Sweeney) welcome you into the regal lobby, which has wrought-iron balustrades, chandeliers, and Italian marble. The guest rooms have a simpler decor with California-style furnishings and floral-print fabrics. On the top floor, Harry Denton's Starlight Room has been all the rage since its opening in 1995. The hotel's surprisingly affordable restaurant, Scala's Bistro, serves excellent food in its dramatic though somewhat noisy dining room. ✉ 450 Powell St., 94102, ☎ 415/392–7755 or 800/227–5480, FAX 415/395–8559. 394 rooms, 23 suites. 2 restaurants, in-room data ports, minibars, no-smoking rooms, exercise room, nightclub, concierge, meeting rooms, parking (fee). AE, D, DC, MC, V.

$$$-$$$$ 🏨 **York Hotel.** Hitchcock fans may recognize the exterior of this reasonably priced, family-owned hotel four blocks west of Union Square. It's the building where Kim Novak as Judy Barton stayed in *Vertigo*. Inside, the peach-stone facade and ornate, high-ceiling lobby give the hotel a touch of elegance. The moderate-size rooms—all with huge closets—are a tasteful mix of Mediterranean styles, with a terra-cotta, burgundy, and forest green color scheme. The Plush Room cabaret, where well-known entertainers perform four to five times a week, is the York's drawing card. This is perhaps the most gay-friendly of San Francisco's high-end hotels. Continental breakfast is included. ⊠ *940 Sutter St., 94109,* ☎ *415/885–6800 or 800/808–9675,* 🖷 *415/885–2115. 91 rooms, 5 suites. Bar, in-room data ports, in-room safes, minibars, no-smoking floors, exercise room, nightclub, laundry service, concierge, business services, parking (fee). AE, D, DC, MC, V.*

$$$ 🏨 **Chancellor Hotel.** Built for the 1915 Panama Pacific International Exposition, the Chancellor was the tallest building in San Francisco when it opened. Although not as grand now as some of its neighbors, this busy hotel is one of the best buys on Union Square for visitors wanting comfort without extravagance. Floor-to-ceiling windows in the modest lobby overlook cable cars on Powell Street en route to nearby Union Square or Fisherman's Wharf. The moderate-size Edwardian-style rooms have high ceilings and peach and green color schemes; deep bathtubs are a treat. Connecting rooms are available for families, and the Chancellor Café is a handy place for meals. ⊠ *433 Powell St., 94102,* ☎ *415/362–2004 or 800/428–4748,* 🖷 *415/362–1403. 135 rooms, 2 suites. Restaurant, bar, no-smoking floors, room service, laundry service, concierge, car rental, parking (fee). AE, D, DC, MC, V.*

$$$ 🏨 **Hotel Diva.** A gray awning and burnished silver facade give this reasonably priced hotel a slick, high-tech look that sets it apart from others in San Francisco. Fresh from a 1998 renovation, the futuristic decor extends to the somewhat small rooms, which have angular sofas, wireframe chairs, and black-lacquer furniture. Although the Diva's proximity to the Curran Theater attracts actors, musicians, and others of an artistic bent, the hotel is also popular with business travelers, who have free access to the tiny business center, and families, who entertain themselves with the in-room Nintendo and VCRs. A complimentary Continental breakfast is delivered to guests' rooms. ⊠ *440 Geary St., 94102,* ☎ *415/885–0200 or 800/553–1900,* 🖷 *415/346–6613. 79 rooms, 32 suites. Restaurant, in-room data ports, in-room safes, minibars, no-smoking floors, room service, in-room VCRs, exercise room, laundry service and dry cleaning, concierge, business services, meeting room, parking (fee). AE, D, DC, MC, V.*

$$$ 🏨 **The Maxwell.** Behind dramatic black and red curtains, the Maxwell's lobby makes an impression with boldly patterned furniture in rich velvets and brocades. The Maxwell is simple but very stylish and just a block from Union Square. Rooms have a clubby, retro feel and deep jewel tones, with classic Edward Hopper prints on the walls. Max's On The Square serves American breakfast, lunch, and dinner as well as after-theater drinks. ⊠ *386 Geary St., 94102,* ☎ *415/986–2000 or 888/734–6299,* 🖷 *415/397–2447. 151 rooms, 2 suites. Restaurant, bar, in-room data ports, no-smoking rooms, room service, laundry service, concierge, parking (fee). AE, D, DC, MC, V.*

$$$ 🏨 **Shannon Court Hotel.** Passing through the elaborate wrought-iron and glass entrance into the marble-tiled lobby of the Shannon Court evokes the old world charm of turn-of-the-century San Francisco. This hotel has some of the most spacious standard rooms in the Union Square area; many have sofa beds for families. Two of the luxury suites on the 16th floor have rooftop terraces with lofty city views. Complimentary morning coffee and afternoon tea and cookies are served in the lobby

area. The hotel's restaurant, City of Paris, is open all day until midnight and serves California French cuisine in a casual atmosphere, with good live jazz on weekends. ⊠ *550 Geary St., 94102,* ☎ *415/775–5000 or 800/228–8830,* FAX *415/928–6813. 172 rooms, 4 suites. Restaurant, bar, lobby lounge, no-smoking floor, refrigerators, laundry service and dry cleaning, concierge, parking (fee). AE, D, DC, MC, V.*

$$$ 🏨 **Vintage Court.** This bit of the Napa Valley just off Union Square has inviting rooms—some with sunny window seats—decorated with jade and rose floral fabrics. Complimentary wine served nightly in front of the lobby fireplace and a deluxe Continental breakfast have created a congenial atmosphere without driving prices up. For fine food guests need go no farther than the lobby, home to Masa's, one of the city's most celebrated French restaurants. Guests have access to an affiliated health club one block away. Security is one potential drawback, as some room doors have only flimsy push-button locks. Secure your valuables in the front desk safe. ⊠ *650 Bush St., 94108,* ☎ *415/392–4666 or 800/654–1100,* FAX *415/433–4065. 107 rooms, 2 suites. Restaurant, bar, minibars, no-smoking floors, refrigerators, parking (fee). AE, D, DC, MC, V.*

$$$ 🏨 **White Swan Inn.** The White Swan has all the comforts of home—personal front-door keys, complimentary soft drinks, and free copies of the *San Francisco Chronicle*. Rooms are large, with dark wood furniture and an English country theme. Each room has a fireplace (there are 26 guest rooms and 30 fireplaces on the property). Afternoon tea, appetizers, and wine are served in the lounge, where comfortable chairs and sofas invite lingering. The breakfasts (included in the room rate) here are famous, and guests can purchase the inn's cookbook to try to duplicate their crab and cheese souffle toasts, chocolate scones, or artichoke pesto puffs at home. The entire inn is no-smoking. ⊠ *845 Bush St., 94108,* ☎ *415/775–1755 or 800/999–9570,* FAX *415/775–5717. 23 rooms, 3 suites. Breakfast room, in-room data ports, no-smoking floors, concierge, meeting rooms, parking (fee). AE, MC, V.*

$$–$$$ 🏨 **The Andrews.** Two blocks west of Union Square, this Queen Anne–style abode with a gold and buff facade began its life in 1905 as the Sultan Turkish Baths. Today Victorian antique reproductions, old-fashioned flower curtains with lace sheers, iron bedsteads, and large closets more than make up for the diminutive size of guest rooms (the scrupulously clean bathrooms are even smaller). The buffet-style Continental breakfast is complimentary. Fino, the hotel restaurant, has been praised for its pizza and carbonaras, and guests enjoy complimentary wine nightly. ⊠ *624 Post St., 94109,* ☎ *415/563–6877 or 800/926–3739,* FAX *415/928–6919. 48 rooms. Restaurant, no-smoking floors, concierge, parking (fee). AE, DC, MC, V.*

$$–$$$ 🏨 **Bijou.** With plush velvet upholstery and rich detailing, this hotel is decorated as a nostalgic tribute to 1930s cinema. The mini lobby theater, Le Petit Theatre Bijou, shows movies from the hotel's collection of 65 San Francisco–themed films to guests. The smallish rooms are named after these films and decorated with black-and-white prints from them. The staff is friendly, but the service is definitely no-frills. The handcrafted chrome ticket booth in the lobby offers a hot line to current San Francisco film shoots and casting calls for extras. ⊠ *111 Mason St., at Eddy St., 94102,* ☎ *415/771–1200 or 800/771–1022,* FAX *415/346–3196. 65 rooms. No-smoking rooms, laundry service, concierge, parking (fee). AE, D, DC, MC, V.*

$$–$$$ 🏨 **Clarion Bedford Hotel.** Guests pass under art nouveau arches to enter the bright yellow lobby of this handsome 1929 building. Avant garde film posters from 1920s Russia adorn the walls. The light and airy rooms are decorated in yellow and peach with white furniture, canopied beds, and vibrant floral bedspreads. Most rooms in this 17-story property (it's the tallest on the block) have gorgeous bay and city views, but the baths are small. Business class guest rooms feature special desk lighting and an ergonomic chair. There is an evening wine reception in the lobby. ⊠ *761 Post St., 94109,* ☎ *415/673–6040 or 800/227–5642,* 𝔽𝔸𝕏 *415/563–6739. 137 rooms, 7 suites. Restaurant, bar, lobby lounge, in-room data ports, minibars, room service, laundry service and dry cleaning, parking (fee). AE, D, DC, MC, V.*

$$–$$$ 🏨 **Commodore International.** Entering the lobby is like stepping onto the main deck of an ocean liner of yore: Neodeco chairs look like the backdrop for a film about transatlantic crossings; and steps away is the Titanic Café, where goldfish bowls and bathysphere-inspired lights add to the sea-cruise mood. The fairly large rooms with monster closets are painted in soft yellows and golds and decorated with photographs of San Francisco landmarks. If red is your color, you may find yourself glued to a seat in the hotel's Red Room, a startlingly scarlet cocktail lounge. ⊠ *825 Sutter St., 94109,* ☎ *415/923–6800 or 800/338–6848,* 𝔽𝔸𝕏 *415/923–6804. 113 rooms. Restaurant, in-room data ports, no-smoking rooms, nightclub, laundry service and dry cleaning, concierge, parking (fee). AE, D, MC, V.*

$$–$$$ 🏨 **King George.** The staff at the King George has prided itself on service and hospitality since the hotel's opening in 1914, when guest rooms started at $1 a night. Prices have remained relatively low compared to other hotels in the neighborhood since. The front desk and concierge staff are adept at catering to their guests' every whim: They'll book anything from a Fisherman's Wharf tour to a dinner reservation. Behind the green and white Victorian facade, rooms are compact but nicely furnished in classic English style, with walnut furniture and a red and green color scheme. High tea at the Windsor Tearoom is an authentic English treat. ⊠ *334 Mason St., 94102,* ☎ *415/781–5050 or 800/288–6005,* 𝔽𝔸𝕏 *415/391–6976. 141 rooms, 2 suites. Tea shop, in-room data ports, in-room safes, no-smoking floors, laundry service and dry cleaning, concierge, business services, meeting rooms, parking (fee). AE, D, DC, MC, V.*

$$–$$$ 🏨 **Petite Auberge.** The dozens of teddy bears in the reception area may seem a bit precious, but the rooms in this re-creation of a French country inn never stray past the mark. Rooms are small, but each has a teddy bear, bright flowered wallpaper, an old-fashioned writing desk, and a much-needed armoire—there's little or no closet space. Most rooms have working fireplaces; the suite has a whirlpool tub. Afternoon tea, wine, and hors d'oeuvres are served in the lobby by the fire, and a full breakfast is included. The entire inn is no-smoking. ⊠ *863 Bush St., 94108,* ☎ *415/928–6000 or 800/365–3004,* 𝔽𝔸𝕏 *415/775–5717. 25 rooms, 1 suite. Breakfast room, parking (fee). AE, DC, MC, V.*

$–$$ 🏨 **Golden Gate Hotel.** Captain Nemo, a 25-pound black and white cat who must live very well indeed, serves as the unofficial doorman for this homey, family-run B&B three blocks northwest of Union Square. Built in 1913 as a hotel, the four-story Edwardian has a yellow and cream facade with black trim, and bay windows front and back. The original "birdcage" elevator lifts guests to hallways lined with historical photographs and guest rooms individually decorated with antiques, wicker pieces, and Laura Ashley bedding and curtains. Fourteen rooms have private baths, some with claw-foot tubs. Continental breakfast and afternoon tea and cookies, included in the room rate, are served in the cozy parlor by a fire. ⊠ *775 Bush St., 94108,* ☎ *415/392–3702 or 800/835–1118,* 𝔽𝔸𝕏 *415/392–6202. 25 rooms. Lobby lounge, no-smoking floor, parking (fee). AE, DC, MC, V.*

$–$$ 🏨 **Grant Plaza Hotel.** One block in from the Chinatown Gate guarded by its famous stone lions, this hotel may seem worlds away from Union Square, yet it and the Financial District are only a stone's throw away. Amazingly low room rates for this part of town make the Grant

Plaza a find for budget travelers wanting to look out their window at the exotic architecture and fascinating street life of Chinatown. The smallish rooms, all with private baths, are very clean and modern. All rooms have electronic locks, voice mail, and satellite TV. The two large, beautiful stained-glass windows near the top floor elevator area are worth a look. ⊠ *465 Grant Ave., 94108,* ☎ *415/434–3883 or 800/ 472–6899,* FAX *415/434–3886. 72 rooms, 1 suite. Concierge, parking (fee). AE, DC, MC, V.*

$ 🏨 **Adelaide Inn.** The bedspreads at this quiet retreat may not match the drapes or carpets, and the floors may creak, but the rooms are sunny, clean, and remarkably cheap. Tucked away in an alley, the funky European-style pension hosts many guests from Germany, France, and Italy, making it fun to chat over complimentary coffee and rolls downstairs in the mornings. Baths are shared. ⊠ *5 Isadora Duncan Ct., at Taylor St. between Geary and Post Sts., 94102,* ☎ *415/441–2474 or 415/441–2261,* FAX *415/441–0161. 18 rooms. Breakfast room, refrigerators. AE, MC, V.*

Financial District

High-rise growth in San Francisco's Financial District has turned it into a mini-Manhattan and a spectacular sight by night. Shoppers and sightseers enjoy easy access to nearby Union Square, the Embarcadero, Pier 39 at Fisherman's Wharf, Market Street's shops, and the burgeoning South of Market (SoMa) area with its many restaurants and nightclubs. Don't expect much nightlife in the Financial District itself, though. Many restaurants and bars in the neighborhood close soon after the last commuters catch their BART train home.

$$$$ 🏨 **Hyatt Regency.** The gray bunkerlike exterior of the Hyatt Regency, at the foot of Market Street, is an unlikely introduction to the spectacular 17-story atrium lobby within. In addition to a plethora of meeting spaces, it has the Embarcadero Center, with more than 125 shops and restaurants, as its neighbor. The Equinox, San Francisco's only revolving rooftop restaurant, sits atop the hotel like a crown jewel. Some rooms have bay-view balconies. ⊠ *5 Embarcadero Center, 94111,* ☎ *415/788–1234 or 800/233–1234,* FAX *415/398–2567. 745 rooms, 60 suites. 2 restaurants, bar, lobby lounge, no-smoking floors, room service, exercise room, concierge, parking (fee). AE, D, DC, MC, V.*

$$$$ 🏨 **Mandarin Oriental.** Since the Mandarin comprises the top 11 floors
★ (38 to 48) of San Francisco's third-tallest building—the First California Center—all rooms provide panoramic vistas of the city and beyond. The glass-enclosed sky bridges that connect the front and back towers of the hotel are almost as striking as the views. Rooms are decorated in light creamy yellow with black accents; those in the front tower fill up quickly because of their dramatic ocean views. The Mandarin Rooms in each tower have bathtubs flanked by windows; enjoy a decadent bathing experience with loofah sponges, plush robes, and silk slippers. The second-floor restaurant, Silks, earns rave reviews for its innovative California cuisine with Asian touches. ⊠ *222 Sansome St., 94104,* ☎ *415/276–9888 or 800/622–0404,* FAX *415/433–0289. 154 rooms, 4 suites. Lobby lounge, in-room data ports, minibars, no-smoking floors, room service, health club, laundry service and dry cleaning, concierge, business services, meeting rooms, parking (fee). AE, D, DC, MC, V.*

$$$$ 🏨 **Palace Hotel.** This landmark hotel—with a guest list that has included Enrico Caruso, Woodrow Wilson, and Amelia Earhart—was the epitome of luxury when it opened in 1875. Today its historic splendor is best seen in the stunning entryway and the belle epoque Garden Court restaurant, with its graceful chandeliers and lead-glass ceiling. After

the lavish public spaces, the rooms seem uninspired, although modern conveniences, like TVs inside mahogany armoires, are well integrated into the decor. Though service is sometimes disappointing, the hotel is a logical choice for business travelers, with a prime location near the Financial District, a business center, a health club, and an indoor lap pool. One of the restaurants, Maxfield's, is named for the Maxfield Parrish Pied Piper mural hanging over the bar. The modern Kyoya restaurant is to the immediate right of the hotel entrance. ⊠ *2 New Montgomery St., 94105, ☎ 415/512–1111, FAX 415/543–0671. 517 rooms, 33 suites. 3 restaurants, bar, room service, health club, laundry service, parking (fee). AE, D, DC, MC, V.*

$$$$ 🏨 **Park Hyatt.** Contemporary in design but with a touch of old world style, the Park Hyatt is a well-managed property across Battery Street from the Embarcadero Center. Convenient to the waterfront, downtown, and the South of Market area, the hotel's public areas feature large floral displays and fine artworks on the walls. The good-size rooms are decorated with Australian lacewood, polished granite, stylish furniture, and fresh flowers. Amenities include voice mail and Neutrogena toiletries. The Park Grill restaurant serves upscale California cuisine, and an elegant afternoon tea is served in the Lounge. Complimentary car service is offered within downtown San Francisco. ⊠ *333 Battery St., 94111, ☎ 415/392–1234 or 800/492–8822, FAX 415/421–2433. 322 rooms, 38 suites. Restaurant, 2 bars, in-room data ports, minibars, room service, laundry service and dry cleaning, business services, parking (fee). AE, D, DC, MC, V.*

$$$–$$$$ 🏨 **Harbor Court.** Within shouting distance of the Bay Bridge and the
★ hot South of Market area with its plentiful nightclubs and restaurants, this cozy hotel, formerly an Army/Navy YMCA, is noted for the exemplary service of its warm, friendly staff. Some guest rooms, with double sets of soundproof windows, overlook the bay; others face a dressed-up rooftop. In the evening complimentary wine is served in the cozy lounge, sometimes accompanied by live guitar. Guests have free access to YMCA facilities (including a 150-ft heated indoor pool), on one side of the hotel, and a convenient entrance to Harry Denton's Bar and Grill, with its turn-of-the-century mahogany bar and plush saloon atmosphere, on the other. There's also a complimentary limousine service to the Financial District. ⊠ *165 Steuart St., 94105, ☎ 415/882–1300 or 800/346–0555, FAX 415/882–1313. 136 rooms. In-room data ports, minibars, no-smoking floors, room service, laundry service and dry cleaning, business services, parking (fee). AE, D, DC, MC, V.*

South of Market (SoMa)

This up and coming area is a convenient spot for leisure and business travelers to bed down. The San Francisco Museum of Modern Art and the Yerba Buena Gardens are nearby, among other attractions.

$$$$ 🏨 **W San Francisco.** The city's first newly built hotel in 10 years, the W San Francisco's 31-story tower opened in May 1999, nodding architecturally to two of its neighbors, the landmark Pacific Telephone Building and SFMOMA. Across the street from the Yerba Buena Center for the Arts and Moscone Convention Center, the W's gray facade is trimmed with black granite piping, and its octagonal 3-story glass entrance leads into a lobby decorated—like the entire hotel—in modern high-style. Stone, corrugated metal, frosted glass, and other urban-industrial elements are offset by accents of polished mahogany, floor-to-ceiling yellow-green mohair drapes, and broad-striped carpeting. Each guest room has either a cozy corner sitting area or a padded window seat perch overlooking the city. The snugly beds have pillow-top mattresses, goose-down comforters and pillows, and 250-thread count linens. Cordless phones

and Aveda bath products are added bonuses. ⊠ *181 Third St., 94103,* ☎ *415/626–0777,* FAX *415/817–7848. 418 rooms, 5 suites. Restaurant, bar, café, in-room data ports, in-room safes, minibars, no-smoking floor, refrigerators, room service, in-room VCRs, indoor pool, hot tub, massage, exercise room, laundry service and dry cleaning, concierge, business services, meeting rooms, parking (fee). AE, D, DC, MC, V.*

\$\$\$ ⊞ **The Argent.** Rising 36 stories over one of the busiest intersections in the city, the Argent has a luxuriously appointed lobby. The bar and adjacent restaurant overlook a sunny outdoor garden. The guest rooms all feature floor-to-ceiling picture windows with dramatic views of the city. About half of the larger-than-average rooms face south and are especially sunny. They overlook the nearby Yerba Buena Center For The Arts, the Moscone Convention Center, the southeastern part of the city, and the Bay and hills in the distance. The equally scenic rooms on the north side peer through the various tall buildings of the Financial District, old and new, with some glimpsing fragments of the Bay and Alcatraz. ⊠ *50 Third St., 94103,* ☎ *415/974–6400 or 877/222–6699,* FAX *415/543–8268. 643 rooms, 24 suites. Restaurant, bar, lobby lounge, in-room data ports, in-room safes, minibars, no-smoking floor, refrigerators, room service, massage, exercise room, piano, laundry service and dry cleaning, concierge, business services, meeting rooms, parking (fee). AE, D, DC, MC, V.*

Nob Hill

Synonymous with San Francisco's high society, Nob Hill contains some of the city's best-known luxury hotels. All have spectacular views and noted restaurants. Cable car lines that cross Nob Hill should help you avoid the short but very steep trek from Union Square.

\$\$\$\$ ⊞ **The Huntington.** The family-owned Huntington provides an oasis of gracious personal service in an atmosphere of understated luxury. The privacy of the hotel's many celebrated guests, from Bogart and Bacall to Picasso and Pavarotti, has always been impeccably preserved. Rooms and suites, many of which have great views of Grace Cathedral, the bay, or the city skyline, are large because they used to be residential apartments. Most rooms have wet bars, all have large antique desks, and some suites have kitchens. The hotel's famous Big Four Restaurant, named after railroad magnates Charles Crocker, Leland Stanford, Mark Hopkins, and C. P. Huntington, serves contemporary American cuisine in an elegant clublike setting filled with San Francisco and Western memorabilia. ⊠ *1075 California St., 94108,* ☎ *415/474–5400; 800/227–4683; 800/652–1539 in CA;* FAX *415/474–6227. 101 rooms, 36 suites. Restaurant, bar, in-room data ports, in-room safes, no-smoking rooms, room service, laundry service and dry cleaning, concierge, meeting rooms, parking (fee). AE, D, DC, MC, V.*

\$\$\$\$ ⊞ **Mark Hopkins Inter-Continental.** The circular drive to this regal Nob Hill landmark leads to a lobby with floor-to-ceiling mirrors and marble floors. The rooms, with dramatic neoclassic furnishings of gray, silver, and khaki and bold leaf-print bedspreads, lead into bathrooms lined with Italian marble (at press time, a renovation of rooms is scheduled which will include changes in decor). Rooms on high floors have views of either the Golden Gate Bridge or the downtown cityscape. No visit would be complete without a visit to the vibrant Top of the Mark, *the* rooftop cocktail lounge in San Francisco since 1939, featuring panoramic views with live bands and dancing in the evenings. ⊠ *999 California St., 94108,* ☎ *415/392–3434 or 800/662–4455,* FAX *415/421–3302. 361 rooms, 30 suites. Restaurant, 2 bars, room service, exercise room, laundry service and dry cleaning, concierge, business services, meeting rooms, car rental, parking (fee). AE, D, DC, MC, V.*

$$$$ 🏨 **Renaissance Stanford Court.** Despite its relatively large size, the Stanford Court has a distinctly residential feeling. The lobby is dominated by a stained-glass dome, a dramatic mural depicting scenes of early San Francisco, and high-quality arts and antiques—notably the Maxfield Parrish painting *Old White Birch*. Rooms are decorated in a variety of styles but invariably achieve understated elegance with a mix of English country manor–style furnishings accented with Asian artwork and accessories. The hotel's restaurant, Fournou's Ovens—famed for its Provençal decor, 54-square-ft roasting oven, Mediterranean-influenced cuisine, and world-class wine cellar—is usually packed. ✉ *905 California St., 94108,* ☎ *415/989–3500; 800/227–4736; 800/622–0957 in CA;* FAX *415/986–8195. 384 rooms, 9 suites. Restaurant, bar, lobby lounge, in-room data ports, no-smoking floors, room service, exercise room, piano, laundry service and dry cleaning, concierge, business services, meeting rooms, parking (fee). AE, DC, MC, V.*

$$$$ 🏨 **The Ritz-Carlton, San Francisco.** Consistently rated one of the top
★   hotels in the world by *Condé Nast Traveler,* the Ritz-Carlton is a stunning tribute to beauty, splendor, and warm, sincere service. Beyond the neoclassic facade, crystal chandeliers illuminate an opulent lobby adorned with Georgian antiques and a collection of museum-quality 18th- and 19th-century paintings. The hotel's fitness center is a destination in its own right, with an indoor swimming pool, saunas, and a whirlpool; you can even get an in-room massage. The renowned Dining Room features a three-, four-, or five-course seasonal menu with modern French accents by celebrated chef Sylvain Portay, originally from New York's beloved Le Cirque. Afternoon tea in the Lobby Lounge—which overlooks the hotel's beautifully landscaped garden courtyard—is a San Francisco institution. ✉ *600 Stockton St., at California St., 94108,* ☎ *415/296–7465 or 800/241–3333,* FAX *415/296–8261. 276 rooms, 60 suites. 2 restaurants, bar, lobby lounge, health club, laundry service and dry cleaning, concierge, business services, meeting rooms, parking (fee). AE, D, DC, MC, V.*

$$$ 🏨 **Nob Hill Lambourne.** This urban retreat, designed with the travel-
★   ing executive in mind, takes pride in pampering business travelers with personal computers, fax machines, and personalized voice mail; an on-site spa with massages, body scrubs, manicures, and pedicures helps them relax. If that's not enough, videos on such topics as stress reduction and yoga are available on request. Rooms have queen-size beds with hand-sewn mattresses, silk-damask bedding, and contemporary furnishings in muted colors. All rooms have modern kitchenettes and stereos. A deluxe Continental breakfast and evening wine service are complimentary. ✉ *725 Pine St., at Stockton St., 94108,* ☎ *415/ 433–2287 or 800/274–8466,* FAX *415/433–0975. 14 rooms, 6 suites. Lobby lounge, in-room data ports, no-smoking floors, in-room VCRs, spa, business services, parking (fee). AE, D, DC, MC, V.*

$–$$$ 🏨 **San Francisco Residence Club.** In contrast to the neighboring showplace hotels, the Residence Club, once an apartment building, is a humble guest house with million-dollar views and a money-saving meal plan. Though it has a fancy Nob Hill address, the building has seen better days and most of the very modest rooms share baths. Many of the rooms, however, have sweeping views of the city and the bay; some have TVs and refrigerators. The club's dedicated international clientele ranges from leisure travelers and business professionals to longer-term residents who enjoy the full American breakfast *and* dinner included in the daily, weekly, or monthly room rate. The dining room is a great place to meet interesting people, and the garden patio is a pleasant place to relax. ✉ *851 Powell St., 94108,* ☎ *415/421–2220,* FAX *415/421–2335. 84 rooms. Dining room, lobby lounge, coin laundry. No credit cards; $100 advance deposit via check required.*

Fisherman's Wharf/North Beach

All accommodations in Fisherman's Wharf are within a few blocks of restaurants, shops, and cable car lines. Because of city ordinances, no hotel exceeds four stories, so this is not the area for fantastic views of the city or the bay. Reservations are always necessary, sometimes weeks in advance during peak summer months when rates rise by as much as 30%. Some street-side rooms can be noisy. Nearby North Beach has surprisingly few lodgings. A few small B&Bs, however, hide in unassuming Victorians on the neighborhood's side streets.

$$$–$$$$ ▥ **Hyatt at Fisherman's Wharf.** Location is the key to this hotel's popularity: It's within walking distance of Ghirardelli Square, the Cannery, Pier 39, Aquatic Park, and docks for Alcatraz ferries and bay cruises. It's also across the street from a cable car turnaround. The moderate-size guest rooms, a medley of greens and burgundies, have double-pane windows to keep out the often considerable street noise. Each floor has a laundry room. In the North Point Lounge, part of the hotel's conference center, a domed Tiffany skylight crowns a large, comfy meeting area with a fireplace and fountain. ⊠ *555 N. Point St., 94133,* ☎ *415/563–1234 or 800/233–1234,* ℻ *415/563–2218. 305 rooms, 8 suites. Restaurant, sports bar, in-room data ports, no-smoking floors, room service, outdoor pool, outdoor hot tub, health club, coin laundry, meeting rooms, parking (fee). AE, D, DC, MC, V.*

$$$–$$$$ ▥ **Marriott at Fisherman's Wharf.** Behind an unremarkable sand-color facade, the Marriott strikes a grand note in its lavish, low-ceiling lobby, with marble floors and English club–style furniture. With the Transamerica Pyramid downtown to its left and the Cannery nearby on its right, the hotel is well situated for business and pleasure. Rooms, all with forest green, burgundy, and cream color schemes, were renovated in 1998 and have either a king-size bed or two double beds. ⊠ *1250 Columbus Ave., 94133,* ☎ *415/775–7555 or 800/228–9290,* ℻ *415/474–2099. 273 rooms, 12 suites. Restaurant, bar, no-smoking floors, health club, meeting rooms, parking (fee). AE, D, DC, MC, V.*

$$$–$$$$ ▥ **Tuscan Inn.** The major attraction here is the friendly, attentive staff, which provides such services as a complimentary limousine to the Financial District. The condolike exterior of the inn—reddish brick with white concrete—gives little indication of the charm of the relatively small, Italian-influenced guest rooms, with their white-pine furniture and floral bedspreads and curtains. Room service is provided by Cafe Pescatore, the Italian seafood restaurant off the lobby. Morning coffee, tea, and biscotti are complimentary, and wine is served in the early evening. ⊠ *425 N. Point St., at Mason St., 94133,* ☎ *415/561–1100 or 800/648–4626,* ℻ *415/561–1199. 208 rooms, 12 suites. Restaurant, minibars, no-smoking rooms, room service, laundry service and dry cleaning, meeting rooms, parking (fee). AE, D, DC, MC, V.*

$$$ ▥ **Travelodge Hotel at Fisherman's Wharf.** Occupying an entire city block, this is the only bay-front hotel at Fisherman's Wharf and is known for its reasonable rates: as low as $89 in the off-season. The higher-price rooms on the third and fourth floors have balconies that provide unobstructed views of Alcatraz and overlook a landscaped courtyard and pool. Rooms are simply decorated with rosewood furniture and drapes and bedspreads in taupe and rust tones. (At press time an extensive renovation is being undertaken; call hotel for updates on construction schedule.) ⊠ *250 Beach St., 94133,* ☎ *415/392–6700 or 800/ 578–7878,* ℻ *415/986–7853. 242 rooms, 8 suites. 3 restaurants, no-smoking rooms, outdoor pool, parking (fee). AE, D, DC, MC, V.*

$$–$$$ ▥ **Hotel Bohème.** In the middle of historic North Beach, this little bargain gives guests a taste of the area's historical bohemian flair. The small rooms, decorated with European armoires, bistro tables, and memo-

rabilia from the 1950s and '60s, recall the beat generation; rumor has it that the late poet Allen Ginsberg used to stay here. Coral-color walls and handmade lampshades complete the nostalgic mood. Enjoy complimentary sherry in the lobby while you decide which of the many nearby Italian restaurants and cafés to visit. ⊠ *444 Columbus Ave., 94133,* ☎ *415/433–9111,* ⅋ *415/362–6292. 15 rooms. In-room data ports. AE, D, MC, V.*

$ 🏨 **San Remo.** This three-story, blue-and-white Italianate Victorian
★ just a few blocks from Fisherman's Wharf has reasonably priced rooms and a down-home, slightly faded elegance. The smallish rooms are crowded with furniture: vanities; rag rugs; pedestal sinks; ceiling fans; antique armoires; and brass, iron, or wooden beds. Guests share six black-and-white-tile shower rooms, one bathtub chamber, and six scrupulously clean toilets with brass pull chains and oak tanks. The penthouse has a wonderful 360-degree view of the city and a private bath and is often requested by honeymooners and other romantics. ⊠ *2237 Mason St., 94133,* ☎ *415/776–8688 or 800/352–7366,* ⅋ *415/ 776–2811. 61 rooms, 1 suite. No-smoking rooms, coin laundry, parking (fee). AE, DC, MC, V.*

Pacific Heights, Cow Hollow, and the Marina

Lombard Street, a major traffic corridor leading to the Golden Gate Bridge, stretches past San Francisco's poshest neighborhoods: Pacific Heights, Cow Hollow, and the Marina. The cheapest accommodations are along Lombard Street. If you prefer to be out of the hustle and bustle, opt for lodgings on smaller side streets. Wherever you stay in this area, it's a short walk to the Marina, where sailboats bob on the bay and park goers fly kites.

$$$$ 🏨 **Sherman House.** This magnificent Italianate mansion at the foot of
★ residential Pacific Heights is San Francisco's most luxurious small hotel. Rooms are individually decorated with Biedermeier, English Jacobean, or French Second Empire antiques. The decadent mood is enhanced by tapestry-like canopies over four-poster featherbeds, wood-burning fireplaces with marble mantels, and sumptuous bathrooms, some with whirlpool baths. The six romantic suites attract honeymooners from around the world, and the elegant in-house dining room serves superb French-inspired cuisine. Room rates include a full breakfast, as well as evening wine and hors d'oeuvres in the Gallery, an upstairs sitting room. ⊠ *2160 Green St., 94123,* ☎ *415/563–3600 or 800/424–5777,* ⅋ *415/563–1882. 8 rooms, 6 suites. Dining room, room service, in-room VCRs, piano, concierge, airport shuttle. AE, DC, MC, V.*

$$$–$$$$ 🏨 **Union Street Inn.** Innkeeper David Coyle was a chef for the Duke and
★ Duchess of Bedford, England, and his partner Jane Bertorelli has been innkeeping for 15 years. With the help of her many family heirlooms, they've made this ivy-draped 1902 Edwardian a delightful B&B inn filled with antiques and unique artwork. Equipped with candles, fresh flowers, and wine glasses, rooms are very popular with honeymooners. The private Carriage House, which has its own whirlpool tub, is separated from the main house by an old-fashioned English garden complete with lemon trees. An elaborate complimentary breakfast is served to guests in the parlor, in the garden, or in their rooms. Afternoon tea and evening hors d'oeuvres are also complimentary. Late sleepers should avoid the English Garden room, which can be noisy mornings. ⊠ *2229 Union St., 94123,* ☎ *415/346–0424,* ⅋ *415/922–8046. 6 rooms. Breakfast room, no-smoking rooms, parking (fee). AE, MC, V.*

$$$ 🏨 **Jackson Court.** On a quiet residential block in tony Pacific Heights, Jackson Court is a converted brownstone mansion built in 1900. Now it's a B&B and time-share—and a truly serene oasis within this busy

city. The light, spacious decor features a mixture of antique and contemporary furnishings amid fresh flowers. The centerpiece of the parlor is an unusual hand-carved fireplace with gentle spiritlike faces said to be the original owners'. Afternoon tea and cookies are served here. The adjacent wood-paneled Game Room is a resource center for local information, books, and games. Some guest rooms have fireplaces and window seats. A generous Continental breakfast is served in the upstairs kitchen each morning and can be taken to guests' rooms on trays. ⊠ *2198 Jackson St., 94115,* ☎ *415/929–7670,* ℻ *415/929–1405. 8 rooms, 2 suites. No-smoking floor, recreation room. AE, MC, V.*

$$–$$$ 🏨 **Bed and Breakfast Inn.** Hidden in an alleyway off Union Street, between Buchanan and Laguna, this ivy-covered Victorian contains English country–style rooms full of antiques, plants, and floral paintings. Though the rooms with shared baths are quite small, they are inexpensive at $80 a night. The Mayfair, a private apartment above the main house, comes complete with a living room, kitchenette, and spiral staircase leading to a sleeping loft. The Garden Suite, a larger, more deluxe apartment, has a cozy country kitchen, whirlpool bath, and plenty of room for four guests. ⊠ *4 Charlton Ct., at Union St., 94123,* ☎ *415/921–9784. 9 rooms, 5 with bath, 2 apartments. Breakfast room, parking (fee). No credit cards.*

$$–$$$ 🏨 **Hotel Del Sol.** Once a typical '50s-style motor court, the Hotel Del Sol has been converted into an anything-but-typical artistic statement playfully celebrating California's vibrant (some might say wacky) culture. The sunny courtyard and yellow and blue three-story building are candy for the eyes. Rooms face boldly striped patios, citrus trees, and a heated swimming pool and hammock under towering palm trees. Even the carports have striped dividing drapes. Rooms evoke a beach house feeling with plantation shutters, tropical-stripe bedspreads, and rattan chairs. Some rooms have brick fireplaces, and one named "The Sandbox" features bunk beds, child-friendly furnishings, toys, and games. There are even free kites for kids. ⊠ *3100 Webster St., 94123,* ☎ *415/921–5520 or 877/433–5765,* ℻ *415/931–4137. 47 rooms, 10 suites. In-room data ports, in-room safes, no-smoking rooms, pool, sauna, laundry service, concierge, free parking. AE, D, DC, MC, V.*

$$ 🏨 **Bel-Aire Travelodge.** This cute motel is a block away from busy Lombard Street and therefore much quieter than many on the main drag. It is made up of twin white and blue L-shape buildings facing each other on the northwest and northeast corners of Steiner and Greenwich streets, with exterior corridors and outside parking. The rooms are furnished with contemporary motel-style blond wood furniture, with beige walls, blue carpeting, and pastel leaf-patterned bedspreads. Bathrooms have showers only, and there is a mirrored vanity table in each room. Other amenities include coffeemakers, cable TV, and free local calls. ⊠ *3201 Steiner St., 94123,* ☎ *415/921–5162 or 800/280–3242,* ℻ *415/921–3602. 32 rooms. No-smoking rooms, airport shuttle, free parking. AE, D, DC, MC, V.*

$$ 🏨 **Coventry Motor Inn.** Among the many motels on busy Lombard Street, this is one of the better-built and one of the quietest, especially in the rooms not facing Lombard. Its handsome oak-paneled lobby has leather furniture and photographs of historic San Francisco. The unusually spacious rooms—decorated with floral wallpaper and plaid bedspreads—all have well-lit dining/working areas. Many rooms have bay windows; some on the upper floors have partial views of the Golden Gate Bridge. Covered parking is available. ⊠ *1901 Lombard St., 94123,* ☎ *415/567–1200,* ℻ *415/921–8745. 69 rooms. No-smoking floor, free parking. AE, DC, MC, V.*

$$ 🏨 **Cow Hollow Motor Inn and Suites.** Solidly built by the same family that runs it, this large, modern hotel has interior corridors and rooms that are more spacious than average, with sitting/dining areas. Decorated with blue carpeting and bedspreads and floral wallpaper, the rooms have dark wood traditional furniture of good quality. Some rooms have views of the Golden Gate Bridge. The large suites here ($195–$245) seem very much like typical San Francisco apartments with their hardwood floors, Oriental carpets, antique furnishings, fireplaces, and fully equipped kitchens. Covered parking is available. ⊠ *2190 Lombard St., 94123,* ☎ *415/921–5800,* ℻ *415/922–8515. 117 rooms, 12 suites. Restaurant, no-smoking floor, meeting room, free parking. AE, DC, MC, V.*

$–$$ 🏨 **Marina Inn.** This inn five blocks from the Marina offers small hotel-style accommodations at motel prices. English country–style rooms are simply appointed, with a queen-size two-poster bed, private bath, small pine-wood writing desks, nightstands, and armoires; the wallpaper and bedspreads are vividly floral. Some rooms facing Octavia and Lombard streets have bay windows with window seats, but they are noisier than the inside rooms. A simple complimentary Continental breakfast and afternoon sherry are served in the central sitting room. ⊠ *3110 Octavia St., at Lombard St., 94123,* ☎ *415/928–1000 or 800/274–1420,* ℻ *415/928–5909. 40 rooms. Lobby lounge, no-smoking floor, barbershop, beauty salon. AE, MC, V.*

$–$$ 🏨 **Pacific Heights Inn.** One of the most genteel-looking motels in town, this two-story motor court near the busy intersection of Union and Van Ness is dressed up with wrought-iron railings and benches, hanging plants, and pebbled exterior walkways facing onto the parking lot. Rooms are on the small side, with floral bedspreads and brass beds. About half of the rooms have kitchenettes or small extra bedrooms. Morning pastries and coffee are served in the lobby. ⊠ *1555 Union St., 94123,* ☎ *415/ 776–3310 or 800/523–1801,* ℻ *415/776–8176. 23 rooms, 17 suites. Kitchenettes, no-smoking rooms, free parking. AE, DC, MC, V.*

$–$$ 🏨 **Presidio Travelodge.** After most of the west-bound traffic on Lombard Street veers off onto the Golden Gate Bridge approach, the street continues for two much quieter blocks leading up to one of the entrance gates of the Presidio, a former army base, now woodsy national parkland. It's a terrific location for this gray and blue three-story motel. The clean, comfortable rooms have blond wood furniture and standard motel amenities such as coffeemakers and cable TV. One room, the Bear's Den, has a VCR and library of children's videos. Another has a special shower designed for people in wheelchairs. ⊠ *2755 Lombard St., 94123,* ☎ *415/931–8581,* ℻ *415/776–0904. 27 rooms. No-smoking rooms, refrigerators, free parking. AE, D, DC, MC, V.*

$–$$ 🏨 **Town House Motel.** What this family-oriented motel lacks in luxury and ambience, it makes up for in value: The simple rooms, most with refrigerators, are nicely furnished with a southwestern pastel color scheme and lacquered-wood furnishings. Continental breakfast in the lobby is complimentary. ⊠ *1650 Lombard St., 94123,* ☎ *415/ 885–5163 or 800/255–1516,* ℻ *415/771–9889. 24 rooms. No-smoking rooms, airport shuttle, free parking. AE, D, DC, MC, V.*

Civic Center/Van Ness

Though the city's government buildings here have been hidden under scaffolding for the last few years, major projects like the construction of the San Francisco Public Library and the renovation of the War Memorial Opera House have been completed, and the neighborhood is experiencing a renaissance of sorts. Fine restaurants, including Jeremiah Tower's famous Stars, flank Van Ness Avenue, and smaller, hipper places have opened west of Van Ness Avenue on Hayes Street.

$$$–$$$$ 🏨 **The Archbishop's Mansion.** Everything at the Archbishop's Mansion
   ★   is extravagantly romantic, starting with the cavernous common areas,

where a chandelier used in the movie *Gone With the Wind* hangs above a 1904 Bechstein grand piano once owned by Noël Coward. The 15 guest rooms, each named for a famous opera, are individually decorated with intricately carved antiques; many have Jacuzzi tubs or fireplaces. Though not within easy walking distance of many restaurants or attractions, its perch on the corner of Alamo Square near the Painted Ladies—San Francisco's famous Victorian homes—makes for a scenic, relaxed stay. Enjoy the complimentary Continental breakfast in the ornate dining room or in the privacy of your own suite. There's also an afternoon wine service. ⊠ *1000 Fulton St., 94117,* ☎ *415/563–7872 or 800/543–5820,* FAX *415/885–3193. 10 rooms, 5 suites. Breakfast room, lobby lounge, no-smoking rooms, in-room VCRs, piano, meeting room, limited free parking. AE, MC, V.*

$$$–$$$$ 🏨 **The Mansions.** An arresting combination of funky elegance and eccentricity, the Mansions is a lavish place that will delight some, but possibly annoy others with its gimmickry. Fresh flowers and antique furniture decorate the rooms, which vary in theme from the supposedly haunted Coit to the grander Presidential and Josephine suites (the latter a favorite of Barbra Streisand). Housed in a twin-turret 1887 Queen Anne, the hotel's minimuseums display historic documents and—as an indulgence to resident ghost Claudia's predilection for pigs—various "porkabilia." Rates include a full breakfast and a campy magic show. Dinner in the dining room, heavily endowed with colorful stained glass, features desserts dusted with 24-karat gold flakes. This is a pet-friendly hotel. ⊠ *2220 Sacramento St., 94115,* ☎ *415/929–9444,* FAX *415/567–9391. 15 rooms, 6 suites. Breakfast room, dining room, billiards, laundry service, parking (fee). AE, DC, MC, V.*

$$$–$$$$ 🏨 **Radisson Miyako Hotel.** Near the Japantown complex and not far from Fillmore Street and Pacific Heights, this pagoda-style hotel is popular with business travelers. Some guest rooms are in the tower building; others are in the garden wing, which has a traditional Japanese garden with a waterfall. Japanese-style rooms have futon beds with tatami mats, while Western rooms have traditional beds with mattresses—but all feature gorgeous Asian furniture and original artwork. Most have their own soaking rooms with a bucket and stool and a Japanese tub (1 ft deeper than Western tubs), and in-room shiatsu massages are available. The hotel's award-winning Yoyo Tsunami Bistro specializes in Asian fusion cuisine. ⊠ *1625 Post St., at Laguna St., 94115,* ☎ *415/ 922–3200 or 800/533–4567,* FAX *415/921–0417. 209 rooms, 9 suites. Restaurant, bar, in-room data ports, minibars, exercise room, laundry service and dry cleaning, business services. AE, D, DC, MC, V.*

$$$ 🏨 **Hotel Majestic.** One of San Francisco's original grand hotels, and once the decade-long residence of screen stars Joan Fontaine and Olivia de Havilland, this five-story white 1902 Edwardian surrounds you with elegance. Most of the romantic guest rooms have gas fireplaces, a mix of French and English antiques, and either a large, hand-painted, four-poster canopied bed or two-poster bonnet twin beds; some have original claw-foot bathtubs. Afternoons bring complimentary sherry and homemade biscotti to the exquisite lobby, replete with black-marble stairs, antique chandeliers, plush Victorian chairs, and a white-marble fireplace. The hotel's Café Majestic has a turn-of-the-century San Francisco mood and an innovative menu of California cuisine with an Asian touch. Glass cases in the bar house a large collection of rare butterflies from Africa and New Guinea. ⊠ *1500 Sutter St., 94109,* ☎ *415/441–1100 or 800/869–8966,* FAX *415/673–7331. 51 rooms, 9 suites. Restaurant, bar, laundry service and dry cleaning, parking (fee). AE, DC, MC, V.*

$$$ 🏨 **Inn at the Opera.** This seven-story hotel a block or so from city hall, ★   Davies Hall, and the War Memorial Opera House has hosted the likes

of Pavarotti and Baryshnikov, as well as lesser lights of the music, dance, and opera worlds. Behind the marble-floor lobby are rooms of various sizes, decorated with creamy pastels and dark wood furnishings. The bureau drawers are lined with sheet music, and every room is outfitted with terry robes, a microwave oven, a minibar, and a basket of apples. All rooms have queen-size beds, though the standard rooms are a bit cramped; larger rooms are more expensive. Continental breakfast is included in the room rate. A major attraction is the sumptuous, dimly lighted Ovation restaurant. Stars congregate in its mahogany and green-velvet interior before and after performances. ⊠ *333 Fulton St., 94102,* ☎ *415/863–8400; 800/325–2708; 800/423–9610 in CA;* FAX *415/861–0821. 30 rooms. Restaurant, lobby lounge, room service, concierge, parking (fee). AE, DC, MC, V.*

$$ 🏨 **The Abigail.** This hotel, a former B&B, retains its distinctive atmosphere with an eclectic mix of faux-stone walls, a faux-marble front desk, and an old-fashioned telephone booth in the lobby. Hissing steam radiators, down comforters, and antiques complete the mood. Room 211—the hotel's only suite—is the most elegant and spacious. The hotel caters to artists performing at nearby theaters. Complimentary Continental breakfast is served. Millennium Restaurant, right off the lobby, serves food so delicious it's hard to believe it's vegan (no meat or dairy). ⊠ *246 McAllister St., 94102,* ☎ *415/861–9728 or 800/ 243–6510,* FAX *415/861–5848. 60 rooms, 1 suite. Restaurant, laundry service and dry cleaning, parking (fee). AE, D, DC, MC, V.*

$$ 🏨 **Phoenix Hotel.** From the piped-in, poolside jungle music to the aquatic-themed ultrahip Backflip restaurant and lounge immersed in shimmering hues of blue and green, the Phoenix evokes the tropics— or at least a fun, kitschy version of it. Although probably not the place for a traveling executive seeking peace and quiet—or anyone put off by its location on the fringes of the seedy Tenderloin District—the Phoenix does boast a list of celebrity guests, including such big-name bands as R.E.M. and Pearl Jam. Rooms are simple, with handmade bamboo furniture, tropical-print bedspreads, and original art by local artists. All rooms face the courtyard pool (with a mural by Francis Forlenza on its bottom) and sculpture garden. A rock and roll hairstylist is on call. ⊠ *601 Eddy St., 94109,* ☎ *415/776–1380 or 800/248–9466,* FAX *415/885–3109. 41 rooms, 3 suites. Restaurant, bar, room service, outdoor pool, massage, nightclub, laundry service, free parking. AE, D, DC, MC, V.*

The Airport

A construction boom near San Francisco International Airport during the mid-'80s brought several new luxury-class hotels to this rather bleak-looking area, where rates are about 20% less than those at in-town counterparts. Airport shuttle buses are provided by all of the following hotels. Because they cater primarily to midweek business travelers, airport hotels often cut weekend prices; be sure to inquire.

$$$$ 🏨 **Hotel Sofitel–San Francisco Bay.** Parisian boulevard lampposts, a Métro sign, and a kiosk covered with posters bring an unexpected bit of Paris to this bay-side hotel. The French-theme public spaces—the Gigi Brasserie, Baccarat Restaurant, and La Terrasse Bar—have a light, open, airy feeling that extends to the rooms, each of which has a minibar and writing desk. ⊠ *223 Twin Dolphin Dr., Redwood City 94065,* ☎ *650/598–9000 or 800/763–4835,* FAX *650/598–0459. 377 rooms, 42 suites. 2 restaurants, bar, lobby lounge, health club, laundry service, concierge, meeting rooms, free parking. AE, DC, MC, V.*

$$$$ 🏨 **The Westin.** This bay-front hotel, with an elegant, palm-tree-lined entrance and a sparkling fountain, is geared toward business travelers and conventioneers. The medium-size guest rooms have cherry wood furnishings with Asian touches and gold, green, and rose colors. The rich, dark paneled restaurant, Alfiere, is in the lobby and has a Mediterranean-influenced menu. ✉ *1 Old Bayshore Hwy., Millbrae 94030,* ☎ *650/692–3500 or 800/228–3000,* 𝐅𝐀𝐗 *650/872–8111. 387 rooms, 3 suites. Restaurant, lobby lounge, in-room data ports, no-smoking floors, room service, indoor pool, exercise room, business services, free parking. AE, DC, MC, V.*

$$$–$$$$ 🏨 **Embassy Suites San Francisco Airport–Burlingame.** With excellent
★   service and facilities, this California mission–style hostelry is arguably the most lavish in the airport area. Set on the bay with up-close views of planes taking off and landing, it consists entirely of suites that open onto a nine-story atrium and tropical garden replete with ducks, parrots, fish, and a waterfall. Living rooms all have a work area, sleeper sofa, wet bar, television, microwave, and refrigerator. Rates include a full breakfast and evening cocktail. ✉ *150 Anza Blvd., Burlingame 94010,* ☎ *650/342–4600 or 800/362–2779,* 𝐅𝐀𝐗 *650/343–8137. 340 suites. Restaurant, bar, no-smoking rooms, room service, indoor pool, sauna, exercise room, concierge, business services, free parking. AE, DC, MC, V.*

$$–$$$$ 🏨 **Hyatt Regency San Francisco Airport.** The spectacular 29,000-square-ft, eight-story lobby atrium of this dramatic Hyatt Regency 2 mi south of the airport encloses a world of water, light, and air. You'll feel like you're outdoors and the weather is always perfect. This is the largest airport convention hotel in Northern California, boasting a high level of personal service for business and leisure travelers alike. Almost every service and amenity one could think of is here, including several dining options, athletic facilities, and entertainment options. Rooms are modern and well-equipped. Scalini serves upscale northern Italian fare. ✉ *1333 Bayshore Hwy., Burlingame 94010,* ☎ *650/347–1234,* 𝐅𝐀𝐗 *650/696–2669. 793 rooms, 42 suites. Restaurant, café, deli, lobby lounge, piano bar, sports bar, in-room data ports, no-smoking floor, room service, pool, outdoor hot tub, exercise room, jogging, laundry service and dry cleaning, concierge, business services, convention center, meeting rooms, airport shuttle, car rental, free parking. AE, D, DC, MC, V.*

$$–$$$ 🏨 **The Clarion.** This busy hotel 1 mi south of the airport is frequented by airline personnel. Respite from the bustle in the gigantic, glass-front lobby can be found in an adjoining garden area, where wrought-iron benches, a heated pool, and a whirlpool tub are set among pine trees. ✉ *401 E. Millbrae Ave., Millbrae 94030,* ☎ *650/692–6363 or 800/223–7111,* 𝐅𝐀𝐗 *650/697–8556. 440 rooms, 6 suites. Restaurant, bar, in-room data ports, no-smoking floors, room service, outdoor pool, outdoor hot tub, exercise room, jogging, meeting rooms, airport shuttle, parking (fee). AE, DC, MC, V.*

$$–$$$ 🏨 **La Quinta Motor Inn.** Literally a stone's throw from Highway 101, this inn with weathered wood balconies and a red-tile roof provides quiet, well-insulated accommodations for the tired visitor. A complimentary Continental breakfast with a juice bar is served in the lobby until 10 daily; there's also a restaurant next door. ✉ *20 Airport Blvd., South San Francisco 94080,* ☎ *650/583–2223 or 800/531–5900,* 𝐅𝐀𝐗 *650/589–6770. 171 rooms, 3 suites. In-room data ports, no-smoking rooms, outdoor pool, hot tub, exercise room, coin laundry, laundry service and dry cleaning, airport shuttle. AE, D, DC, MC, V.*

$–$$ ⊞ **Red Roof Inn.** This five-story hotel, which attracts families and business travelers, underwent an extensive renovation in 1998. The reasonably priced rooms are plain but very clean, with light wood furnishings. Upper floors facing the airport and San Francisco have better views but are noisier when planes start flying early in the morning. ⊠ *777 Airport Blvd., Burlingame 94010,* ☎ *650/342–7772 or 800/843–7663,* 𝔽𝔸𝕏 *650/342–2635. 212 rooms. Restaurant, no-smoking rooms, outdoor pool, free parking. AE, DC, MC, V.*

4 NIGHTLIFE AND THE ARTS

A spirit of playfulness has pervaded San Francisco's arts, entertainment, and nightlife scenes ever since its days as a rowdy sailors' port. Perhaps nothing is more purely San Franciscan than *Beach Blanket Babylon* at Club Fugazi, a hilarious cabaret that parodies local moods and mores. In addition, the San Francisco Opera, the San Francisco Symphony, and the San Francisco Ballet are all nationally renowned, while dozens of alternative groups represent everything from gay and lesbian performance art to family circus and mime.

NIGHTLIFE

Updated by
Denise M. Leto

SAN FRANCISCO HAS A TREMENDOUS POTPOURRI of evening entertainment, from ultrasophisticated cabarets to bawdy bistros that reflect the city's Gold Rush past. Although it's a compact city with the prevailing influences of some neighborhoods spilling into others, the following generalizations should help you find the kind of entertainment you're looking for. **Nob Hill** is noted for its plush piano bars and panoramic skyline lounges. **North Beach,** infamous for its topless and bottomless "dance clubs," has cleaned up its image considerably and yet still maintains a sense of its beatnik past in atmospheric bars and coffeehouses. **Fisherman's Wharf,** although touristy, is great for people-watching and attracts plenty of street performers. Tony **Union Street** is home away from home for singles in search of company. South of Market—**SoMa,** for short—has become a hub of nightlife, with a bevy of popular nightclubs, bars, and lounges in renovated warehouses and auto shops. The gay and lesbian scenes center around the **Castro District** and the clubs and bars along **Polk Street.** Twentysomethings and alternative types should check out the ever-funky **Mission District** and **Haight Street** scenes.

For information on who is performing where, check out the *San Francisco Chronicle*'s pink "Datebook" insert—or consult the *San Francisco Bay Guardian,* free and available in racks around the city, listing neighborhood, avant-garde, and budget-priced events. The *S.F. Weekly* is also free and packed with information on arts events around town. Another handy reference is the weekly magazine *Key,* offered free in most major hotel lobbies and at Hallidie Plaza (Market and Powell streets). For a phone update on musical and cultural events, call the **Convention and Visitors Bureau's Events Hotline** (☎ 415/391–2001).

With the exception of the hotel lounges and discos noted below, casual dress is the norm. A 1998 state law banned smoking in any indoor place of work—including all bars and clubs. In San Francisco, fines have been given out to people caught lighting up. Bars generally close between midnight and 2 AM. Bands and other performers usually begin between 8 PM and 11 PM. The cover charge at smaller clubs ranges from $3 to $10, and credit cards are rarely accepted. At the larger venues the cover may go up to $30, and tickets can often be purchased through **BASS** (☎ 415/776–1999 or 510/762–2277).

No-Fault Nightspots

Detailed descriptions of the following clubs can be found within listings for each category.

Rock/Pop/Folk/Blues: Slim's, which books the top artists in each of these areas, is almost risk-free. For more cutting-edge rock, Bottom of the Hill is a popular spot in Potrero Hill, while the Fillmore and Warfield grab the lion's share of touring national acts.

Jazz: Jazz at Pearl's books sophisticated acts in a romantic atmosphere, while the small, always crowded Up and Down Club highlights up-and-coming artists.

Cabaret: Club Fugazi's *Beach Blanket Babylon* revue has been going strong for more than 20 years. Judging by the sellout crowds nearly every night, they must be doing something right.

Comedy: Go where your favorite comics are. Cobb's Comedy Club is a good bet.

Dancing Emporiums: El Rio offers live salsa on Sunday and other genres throughout the week. The hot 1930s swing scene finds cool cats and kittens cutting a rug at Cafe Du Nord and the Hi-Ball Lounge.

Piano Bars: The Redwood Room is plush and utterly romantic. Showcasing top talents, Grand Views is an entertainment bargain—with a view.

Singles Bars: Gordon Biersch is the spot for a beer and a flirt.

Skyline Bars: Harry Denton's Starlight Room is *the* romantic room with a view.

Rock, Pop, Folk, and Blues

In the hip SoMa neighborhood and elsewhere, musical offerings range from straight-up rock to retro jazz to utter cacophony.

Bimbo's 365 Club (⊠ 1025 Columbus Ave., at Chestnut St., ☎ 415/474–0365) has a plush main room and an adjacent lounge that retain a retro ambience perfect for the "Cocktail Nation" programming that keeps the crowds hopping.

Bottom of the Hill (⊠ 1233 17th St., at Texas St., ☎ 415/621–4455), in Potrero Hill, showcases some of the city's best local alternative rock. The atmosphere is ultra low-key, although the occasional blockbuster act—Alanis Morissette, Pearl Jam—has been known to hop on stage.

The Fillmore (⊠ 1805 Geary Blvd., at Fillmore St., ☎ 415/346–6000), San Francisco's most famous rock music hall, serves up a varied menu of national and local acts: rock, reggae, grunge, jazz, folk, acid house, and more. Ticket prices range from $10 to $27.50 and shows are all-ages. Avoid steep service charges by buying tickets at the Fillmore box office on Sunday between 10 and 4.

Freight and Salvage Coffee House (⊠ 1111 Addison St., Berkeley, ☎ 510/548–1761), one of the finest folk houses in the country, is worth a trip across the bay. Some of the most talented practitioners of folk, blues, Cajun, and bluegrass perform in this alcohol-free space, where tickets range from $10 to $15.

Great American Music Hall (⊠ 859 O'Farrell St., between Polk and Larkin Sts., ☎ 415/885–0750) is a great eclectic nightclub. Here you can find top-drawer entertainment, with acts running the gamut from the best in blues, folk, and jazz to alternative rock. The colorful marble-pillared emporium (built in 1907 as a bordello) also accommodates dancing at some shows. Pub grub is available most nights.

John Lee Hooker's Boom Boom Room (⊠ 1601 Fillmore St., at Geary Blvd., ☎ 415/673–8000) attracts old-timers and hipsters alike with top-notch blues acts and, occasionally, a show by the man himself. It's hard to go wrong no matter which night you go. Live bands play nightly.

Justice League (⊠ 628 Divisadero St., near Hayes St., ☎ 415/289–2038) offers live jazz, hip-hop, and world grooves, as well as DJ-driven dance nights. Hipsters of many ages relax in the decidedly urban setting. The funky interior was hand-painted by local graffiti artist Twist.

Last Day Saloon (⊠ 406 Clement St., between 5th and 6th Aves., ☎ 415/387–6343) hosts major entertainers and rising local bands with a varied schedule of blues, Cajun, rock, and jazz.

Lou's Pier 47 (⊠ 300 Jefferson St., Fisherman's Wharf, ☎ 415/771–0377) is the place for cool music and hot Cajun seafood on the waterfront nightly.

Paradise Lounge (⊠ 1501 Folsom St., at 11th St., ☎ 415/861–6906), a quirky lounge with three stages for eclectic live music and dancing, also has spoken-word shows on Sunday and beyond-the-fringe performances at the adjoining Transmission Theatre. It's a long-favored hangout for San Francisco's alternative scenesters, 21 and over only.

Pier 23 (⊠ Pier 23, on the Embarcadero, ☎ 415/362–5125), a waterfront restaurant by day, turns into a packed club by night, with a musical spectrum ranging from Caribbean and salsa to Motown and reggae.

Red Devil Lounge (⊠ 1695 Polk St., at Clay St., ☎ 415/921–1695) is a lush, trendy supper club featuring local and up-and-coming live funk, rock, and jazz acts, along with the occasional DJ dance night. Intimate tables line the narrow balcony overlooking the dance floor.

The Saloon (⊠ 1232 Grant Ave., near Columbus Ave., ☎ 415/989–7666) is a favorite blues and rock spot among North Beach locals in the know.

Slim's (⊠ 333 11th St., near Folsom St., ☎ 415/522–0333), one of SoMa's most popular nightclubs, specializes in national touring acts— mostly classic rock, blues, and jazz. Co-owner Boz Scaggs helps bring in the crowds and famous headliners.

The Warfield (⊠ 982 Market St., at 6th St., ☎ 415/775–7722), once a movie palace, is one of the city's largest rock-and-roll venues. There are tables and chairs downstairs, and theater seating upstairs. Performers range from Porno for Pyros to Suzanne Vega to Harry Connick Jr.

Jazz

There's been a major revival in San Francisco's jazz scene, thanks largely to a new generation of local performers like the Broun Fellinis and Charlie Hunter, many of whom push the borders between jazz, hip-hop, funk, and reggae. Check the above-listed Rock, Pop, Folk, and Blues venues for special jazz events. More regular options run the gamut from mellow restaurant cocktail lounges to hip SoMa venues.

Blue Bar (⊠ 501 Broadway, ☎ 415/981–2233), tucked beneath the retro beat-generation restaurant Black Cat, finds thirty- and fortysomethings lounging in funky aqua armchairs around Formica tables. A blue light infuses the space with a dreamy feel. Live jazz bands play nightly in the intimate North Beach space, and a scaled-down version of Reed Hearon's "San Francisco cuisine" is available until 1 AM.

Bruno's (⊠ 2389 Mission St., at 19th St., ☎ 415/550–7455) is a slice of retro heaven in the Mission District. Huge red booths provide a comfy place to ogle the beautiful people ordering swanky cocktails. An excellent menu draws crowds, while two lounges attract rotating local jazz, swing, and retro bands. The surrounding neighborhood isn't the greatest. Take a taxi late at night.

Cafe du Nord (⊠ 2170 Market St., at Sanchez St., ☎ 415/861–5016) hosts some of the coolest jazz, blues, and alternative sounds in town. The atmosphere in this basement poolroom bar could be called "speakeasy hip." The music, provided mostly by local talent, is strictly top-notch. Adrian Bermudez offers free salsa lessons Tuesday at 9 PM, and the fabulous Juanda introduces beginners to swing at 8 PM on Sunday—followed by a chance to strut your steps to live music.

Elbo Room (⊠ 647 Valencia St., between 17th and 18th Sts., ☎ 415/ 552–7788) is a convivial spot to hear up-and-coming jazz acts upstairs, or to relax in the dark, moody bar downstairs. Thursday is dance night. Brazilian jazz, world music, and the occasional funk band round out the musical offerings.

Enrico's (⊠ 504 Broadway, at Kearny St., ☎ 415/982–6223) was the city's hippest North Beach hangout after its 1958 opening. Following the retirement of famed owner Enrico Banducci—who also brought Woody Allen, Barbra Streisand, and Lenny Bruce to his late, lamented "hungry i" in the early '60s—the luster faded. Today it's hip once again, with an indoor/outdoor café, a fine menu (tapas and Italian), and mellow nightly jazz combos.

Jazz at Pearl's (⊠ 256 Columbus Ave., near Broadway, ☎ 415/291–8255) is one of the few reminders of North Beach's heady beatnik days. With mostly straight-ahead jazz acts and dim lighting, this club has a mellow feel. The talent level is remarkably high, especially considering that there is rarely a cover.

Kimball's East (⊠ 5800 Shellmound St., Emeryville, ☎ 510/658–2555), in an East Bay shopping complex just off Highway 80, hosts such talents as Jeffrey Osborne, Tito Puente, and Mose Allison. This supper club features an elegant interior and fine food.

Moose's (⊠ 1652 Stockton St., near Union St., ☎ 415/989–7800), one of North Beach's most popular restaurants, also features great sounds in its small but stylish bar area. Combos play classic jazz nightly from 8.

Storyville (⊠ 1751 Fulton St., at Masonic St., ☎ 415/441–1751) is a dressy, classic jazz club featuring such performers as Elvin Jones, James Moody, and local favorite John Handy. Both the front and back rooms have live music four or five nights a week. The kitchen serves up New Orleans–inspired cuisine.

330 Ritch Street (⊠ 330 Ritch St., at Townsend St., ☎ 415/541–9574), a popular SoMa nightclub, blends stylish modern decor with an extensive tapas menu, a dance floor, and live jazz acts. The club is closed on Monday and Tuesday.

Up and Down Club (⊠ 1151 Folsom St., between 7th and 8th Sts., ☎ 415/626–2388), a hip restaurant–cum–club whose owners include supermodel Christy Turlington, books emerging jazz artists downstairs and offers dancing to a DJ upstairs every day except Sunday.

Yoshi's (⊠ 510 Embarcadero St., Oakland, ☎ 510/238–9200) is one of the area's best jazz venues. J. J. Johnson, Betty Carter, local favorite Kenny Burrell, Joshua Redman, and Cecil Taylor have played here, along with blues and Latin performers.

Cabarets

Traditional cabaret is no longer enjoying the strong comeback of recent years, but a few longtime favorites and alternative venues continue the tradition, and a new hot spot arrives occasionally to rejuvenate the San Francisco scene.

asiaSF (⊠ 201 9th St., at Howard St., ☎ 415/255–2742), an elegant and sophisticated SoMa bar and restaurant, is the hottest place in town for saucy, sexy fun. The entertainment, as well as gracious food service, is provided by "gender illusionists." These gorgeous men don daring dresses and strut in impossibly high heels on top of the bar, which serves as a catwalk, vamping to such tunes as *Cabaret* and *Big Spender.* The creative Asian-influenced cuisine is excellent.

Club Fugazi (⊠ 678 Green St., at Powell St., ☎ 415/421–4222) is most famous for *Beach Blanket Babylon,* a wacky musical revue that has become the longest-running show of its genre. A send-up of San Francisco moods and mores, *Beach Blanket* has run since 1974. Although the choreography is colorful, the singers brassy, and the songs witty, the real stars are the comically exotic costumes and famous ceiling-high "hats"—worth the price of admission in themselves. Order tickets as far in advance as possible. The revue has been sold out up to a month in advance. Those under 21 are admitted only to the Sunday matinee.

Finocchio's (✉ 506 Broadway, near Columbus Ave., ☎ 415/982–9388), an amiable, world-famous club, has been generating confusion with its female impersonators since 1936. The scene at Finocchio's (open from Thursday to Saturday) is decidedly retro, which for the most part only adds to its charm.

The Marsh (✉ 1062 Valencia St., near 22nd St., ☎ 415/826–5750), in the Mission District, books an eclectic mix of alternative and avant-garde theater, performance art, comedy, and the occasional musical act, with an emphasis on solo performances and seldom-staged plays. The room is homey and dimly lighted, and you can purchase freshly baked treats and excellent coffee at intermission.

New Orleans Room (✉ 950 Mason St., at California St., ☎ 415/772–5259), in the Fairmont Hotel, has a somewhat tacky 1960s hotel-bar ambience. Still, it's a low-key place to enjoy a cocktail along with show tunes by the pianist.

Plush Room (✉ 940 Sutter St., ☎ 415/885–2800), in the York Hotel, is an intimate cabaret space that began in the 1920s as a speakeasy. The luster may have faded a bit, but the 120-seat room still books some excellent talent, such as Bay Area favorite Welsa Whitfield. While the edges may be tattered and the neighborhood on the seedy side, the crowd that frequents the Plush Room likes to put on the Ritz and quaff a martini or two. There is a two-drink minimum.

Comedy Clubs

In the '80s it seemed as if every class clown or life-of-the-party type was cutting it up at a comedy club. The stand-up boom, like others from the decade, has gone bust, except for the two fine clubs listed below.

Cobb's Comedy Club (✉ 2801 Leavenworth St., at Beach St., ☎ 415/928–4320), in the Cannery, books such super stand-up comics as Jake Johannsen, Rick Overton, and Janeane Garofalo.

Punch Line (✉ 444 Battery St., between Clay and Washington Sts., ☎ 415/397–7573), a launching pad for the likes of Jay Leno and Whoopi Goldberg, features some of the area's top talents. Recent headliners have included Will Durst, Johnny Steele, and Dana Gould. Weekend shows often sell out. Buy tickets in advance at BASS outlets or from the club's charge line (☎ 415/397–4337). Eighteen and over only.

Dance Clubs

Some of the rock, blues, and jazz clubs listed above have active dance floors. Some also offer DJ dancing when live acts aren't on the stage. Below are several spots devoted solely to dancing.

DNA Lounge (✉ 375 11th St., near Harrison St., ☎ 415/626–1409), a longtime, two-floor SoMa haunt, headlines alternative rock, funk, and hip-hop, as well as weekly theme nights. On Wednesday the DJs spin industrial and alternative rock; on Friday look for '70s tunes; Saturdays bring '80s favorites and swing music in the VIP lounge.

El Rio (✉ 3158 Mission St., at Precita St., ☎ 415/282–3325) is a casual Mission District spot with salsa dancing on Sunday (from 4 PM), lounge music from around the world on Tuesday, Arab dance on

Thursday, a global dance party on Friday, and live rock starting at 9 PM on weekends.

Hi-Ball Lounge (⊠ 473 Broadway, ☎ 415/397–9464), a small, unpretentious North Beach club, is the place where the swing set gathers to jump and twist to live bands. Patrons sip swanky cocktails and swing until they sweat every night. Enthusiastic beginners are welcome. Even if you're not into wing tips and cocktail dresses, slip into one of the comfy red booths and enjoy the Sinatra grooves.

Metronome Ballroom (⊠ 1830 17th St., at De Haro St., ☎ 415/252–9000) is at its most lively on weekend nights, when ballroom, Latin, and swing dancers come for lessons and revelry. The ambience is lively but mellow at this alcohol-free spot.

Roccapulco (⊠ 3140 Mission St., near Cesar Chavez St., ☎ 415/296–8191), formerly Cesar's Latin Palace, got a face-lift and a spit-shine and is once again bringing in crowds. This cavernous Mission District dance hall and restaurant features Latin drag shows on Tuesday, salsa on Friday and Saturday, and mariachi music on Sunday. Occasionally major Latin acts such as Oscar de Leon take the stage.

Piano Bars

You only have eyes for her . . . or him. Six quiet spots provide the perfect atmosphere for holding hands and making plans.

Grand Views (⊠ 345 Stockton St., at Sutter St., ☎ 415/398–1234), on the top floor of the Grand Hyatt, offers piano music Monday through Saturday from 8 PM and a view of North Beach and the bay.

Masons (⊠ 650 Mason St., at California St., ☎ 415/772–5233), an elegant restaurant in the Fairmont Hotel, has fine jazz, show tunes, and standards by local and national talents.

Ovation (⊠ 333 Fulton St., near Franklin St., ☎ 415/553–8100), in the Inn at the Opera Hotel, is a popular spot for a romantic rendezvous. The focal point of this tastefully appointed, intimate restaurant-lounge is a crackling fireplace. A new menu features American grill specialties with an emphasis on seafood.

Redwood Room (⊠ 495 Geary St., near Taylor St., ☎ 415/775–4700), in the Clift Hotel, is an art deco lounge with a low-key but sensuous ambience. Klimt reproductions cover the walls, and mellow sounds fill the air.

Ritz-Carlton Hotel (⊠ 600 Stockton St., at Pine St., ☎ 415/296–7465) has a tastefully appointed lobby lounge where a harpist plays during high tea (weekdays 2:30–4:30, weekends 1–4:30). At 5:30, the lounge shifts to piano or a jazz trio for cocktails until 11 PM weeknights and 1 AM on weekends.

Washington Square Bar and Grill (⊠ 1707 Powell St., near Union St., ☎ 415/982–8123), affectionately known as the "Washbag" among San Francisco politicians and newspaper folk, hosts pianists performing jazz and popular standards nightly.

Skyline Bars

San Francisco is a city of spectacular vistas. Enjoy drinks, music, and sometimes dinner with 360-degree views at any of the bars below.

Carnelian Room (⊠ 555 California St., at Kearny St., ☎ 415/433–7500), on the 52nd floor of the Bank of America Building, has what is perhaps the loftiest view of San Francisco's magnificent skyline. Enjoy dinner or cocktails at 779 ft above the ground; reservations are a must for dinner. The dress code requires jackets, but ties are optional.

Cityscape (⊠ 333 O'Farrell St., at Mason St., ☎ 415/771–1400), in the tower of the Hilton Hotel, offers dancing to Top 40, rock, and pop nightly until 1 AM.

Crown Room (⊠ 650 Mason St., at California St., ☎ 415/772–5131), the aptly named lounge on the 23rd floor of the Fairmont Hotel, is one of the most luxurious of the city's skyline bars. Riding the glass-enclosed Skylift elevator is an experience in itself.

Equinox (⊠ 5 Embarcadero Center, ☎ 415/788–1234), on the 22nd floor of the Hyatt Regency, is known for its revolving 360-degree views of the city. You can sightsee, eat, and drink, all from the comfort of your own chair.

Grand Views (☞ Piano Bars, *above*).

Harry Denton's Starlight Room (⊠ 450 Powell St., ☎ 415/395–8595), on the 21st floor of the Sir Francis Drake Hotel, recreates the 1950s high life with rose-velvet booths, romantic lighting, and staff clad in tuxes or full-length gowns. Whenever live combos playing jazz and swing aren't holding court over the small dance floor, taped Sinatra rules.

Phineas T. Barnacle (⊠ 1090 Point Lobos Ave., at the western end of Geary Blvd., ☎ 415/666–4016), inside the Cliff House, provides a unique panorama of Seal Rock and the Pacific Ocean.

Top of the Mark (⊠ 999 California St., at Mason St., ☎ 415/392–3434), in the Mark Hopkins Hotel, was immortalized by a famous magazine photograph as a hot spot for World War II servicemen on leave or about to ship out. Now folks can dance to the sounds of that era on weekends—in a room with a view.

View Lounge (⊠ 55 4th St., at Market St., ☎ 415/896–1600), on the 39th floor of the San Francisco Marriott, is one of the loveliest of the city's skyline lounges. There's live piano music Monday–Wednesday beginning at 8:30 PM, and live R&B and blues Thursday–Saturday, from 9:30 PM to 1 AM.

Singles Bars

Ever notice how everyone looks so much better when you are visiting another town? Here's where the magic may happen for you.

Balboa Cafe (⊠ 3199 Fillmore St., at Greenwich St., ☎ 415/921–3944), a jam-packed hangout for the young and upwardly mobile crowd, is famous for its burgers and its single clientele.

Gordon Biersch Brewery and Restaurant (⊠ 2 Harrison St., at the Embarcadero, ☎ 415/243–8246) is a favorite of the swinging twentysomething set on Friday. The upstairs dining room and microbrewery beer is a nightly draw for adults of all ages.

Hard Rock Cafe (⊠ 1699 Van Ness Ave., at Sacramento St., ☎ 415/885–1699), part of the famous chain, is filled with a collection of rock-and-roll memorabilia that won't disappoint fans.

Harry Denton's (⊠ 161 Steuart St., near the Embarcadero, ☎ 415/882–1333), one of San Francisco's liveliest, most upscale saloons, is packed with well-dressed young professionals. When dinner service is through, there are live bands and dancing after 8 PM Sunday through Thursday, after 10 PM Friday and Saturday.

Holding Company (✉ 2 Embarcadero Center, at Front and Clay Sts., ☎ 415/986–0797), one of the most popular weeknight Financial District watering holes, is where scores of office workers gather to enjoy friendly libations. The Holding Company is open on weekdays only.

Perry's (✉ 1944 Union St., at Laguna St., ☎ 415/922–9022), the most famous of San Francisco's singles bars, is usually jam-packed. You can dine here on great hamburgers as well as more substantial fare.

Spoken Word

Nearly every night of the week, aspiring and established writers, poets, and performers step up to the mike and put their words and egos on the line. Check the listings section of the free alternative weekly papers and the *San Francisco Sunday Examiner and Chronicle* "Book Review" section for more exhaustive options.

Above Paradise (✉ 308 11th St., ☎ 415/861–6906), on the top floor of SoMa's Paradise Lounge, hosts spoken-word presentations every Sunday at 8. Two featured readers begin the evening. A sign-up sheet is available for the open-mike show that follows.

City Arts and Lectures (☎ 415/392–4400) hosts more than 50 fascinating conversations a year, mostly with literary artists. Events are usually held at the **Herbst Theatre** (✉ 401 Van Ness Ave.). Recent talks have included the words of Studs Terkel, Joan Didion, Bill Moyers, Alice Walker, and Joyce Carol Oates.

A Clean Well-Lighted Place for Books (✉ 601 Van Ness Ave., ☎ 415/567–6876) features free author readings and signings four to five times a week, ranging from strictly literary figures to such celebrities as Tony Bennett and luminaries like Jimmy Carter.

A Different Light (✉ 489 Castro St., ☎ 415/431–0891) is host to a multitude of literary offerings each month, including author readings and discussions. Much of the material is by and about the gay and lesbian community. All are welcome. Flyers at the store announce the occasional open-mike nights.

Luna Sea (✉ 2940 16th St., No. 216C, at S. Van Ness Ave., ☎ 415/863–2989), a gallery and theater space amid the burgeoning Mission District arts scene, has an ever-changing lineup of lesbian-themed women's projects, including visual arts displays, performance art, and readings. Some events are for women only. The space is smoke- and alcohol-free.

Modern Times (✉ 888 Valencia St., at 20th St., ☎ 415/282–9246), in the heart of the Mission District, hosts writers about six times a month for readings, question-and-answer sessions, and book signings.

West Coast Live (✉ 915 Cole St., ☎ 415/664–9500), billed as "San Francisco's Live Radio Show to the World," invites an audience to the weekly live broadcast at Fort Mason's Cowell Theater. The ever-changing guest list has such featured authors as Anne Lamott, improvisational theater sponsored by *True Fiction* magazine, and appearances from various celebs passing through town.

Wine Bars

Why not forgo that frothy pint of beer for the more sedate pleasures of the vine? These spots offer tasting "flights," wines grouped together by type for contrast and comparison.

Bubble Lounge (⊠ 714 Montgomery St., at Washington St., ☎ 415/434–4204), an upscale yet comfortable champagne bar, attracts a Financial District crowd. Upstairs, young executives nestle into wing chairs and overstuffed couches, while downstairs a lively atmosphere surrounds the pool table and another bar. Champagne is this lounge's raison d'être and the selection is excellent, with over 300 types to choose from. A full bar is also available, as are sushi and other delicate nibbles.

Eos Restaurant and Wine Bar (⊠ 901 Cole St., at Carl St., ☎ 415/566–3064) is a cozy space with hundreds of wines by the bottle and many by the glass. Tastings take place every Thursday at 6:30 PM. The wines from those tastings are available throughout the following week. The restaurant puts an emphasis on food and wine pairings.

Hayes and Vine (⊠ 377 Hayes St., at Gough St., ☎ 415/626–5301) provides a warm lounge, dominated by a stunning white-onyx bar, where patrons relax and taste a few of the 550 wines available by the bottle, or the 40 selections served by the glass. Cheeses, pâtés, and caviar are served.

London Wine Bar (⊠ 415 Sansome St., at Sacramento St., ☎ 415/788–4811), a warm Financial District spot open on weekdays only, pours 40 wines by the glass from a cellar of 8,000 bottles.

San Francisco's Favorite Bars

Locals patronize all the places listed above, but there are several joints they hold near and dear.

Backflip (⊠ 601 Eddy St., at Larkin St., ☎ 415/771–3547), in the hipster Phoenix Hotel in the sketchy Tenderloin, is a club house for a space age rat pack—a combination of aqua-tiled retro and Jetsons-attired waitresses and bartenders. The mixed crowd circling the round bar is definitely trendy, but the atmosphere remains friendly. Take in the funky details, such as the waterfall behind the glass wall in the restaurant and the pool and cabana on the patio.

Bix (⊠ 56 Gold St., off Montgomery St., ☎ 415/433–6300), a North Beach institution, is occasionally credited with the invention of the martini. It's just an urban legend, but you might believe it anyway at this lively, elegant bar and supper club.

Buena Vista Café (⊠ 2765 Hyde St., at Beach St., ☎ 415/474–5044), the wharf area's most popular bar, introduced Irish coffee to the New World—or so they say. Because it has a fine view of the waterfront, it's usually packed with tourists.

Cypress Club (⊠ 500 Jackson St., at Columbus Ave., ☎ 415/296–8555) is an eccentric restaurant-bar where sensual, '20s-style opulence clashes with Fellini/Dalì frivolity. The decor alone makes it worth a visit, but it's also a fine spot for a before-dinner or after-theater chat. Private dining rooms are available, and live jazz is played nightly.

Edinburgh Castle (⊠ 950 Geary St., near Polk St., ☎ 415/885–4074), cherished by Scots all over town, pours out happy and sometimes baleful Scottish folk tunes. You can work off your fish-and-chips and Scottish brews with a turn at the dart board or pool table. There's live music nightly from Wednesday to Saturday.

Harrington's (⊠ 245 Front St., near Sacramento St., ☎ 415/392–7595), a family-owned Irish saloon, is *the* place to be on St. Patrick's Day. The occasional Celtic rock group provides live music. The restaurant serves American fare except Sunday.

House of Shields (⌗ 39 New Montgomery St., at Market St., ☎ 415/ 392–7732), a saloon-style bar with a large wine cellar, attracts an older, Financial District crowd after work. Food is served until 8; the bar is closed on weekends.

Specs' (⌗ 12 Saroyan Pl., off Columbus Ave., ☎ 415/421–4112), a hidden hangout for artists and poets, is worth looking for. It's an old-fashioned watering hole, reflecting a sense of the North Beach of days gone by.

The Tonga Room (⌗ 950 Mason St., at California St., ☎ 415/772–5278), on the Fairmont Hotel's terrace level, has given San Francisco a beloved taste of high Polynesian kitsch for over 50 years. Fake palm trees, grass huts, a lake (three-piece combos play pop standards on a floating barge), and faux monsoons—courtesy of sprinkler-system rain and simulated thunder and lightning—create the ambience, which only grows more surreal as you quaff the selection of very potent cocktails. The weekday happy hour (5 PM–7 PM) features $6 Asian finger foods.

Tosca Café (⌗ 242 Columbus Ave., ☎ 415/391–1244), like Specs' and Vesuvio nearby, holds a special place in San Francisco lore. It has an Italian flavor, with opera, big band, and Italian standards on the jukebox, plus an antique espresso machine that's nothing less than a work of art. Known as a hangout for filmmaker Francis Ford Coppola and playwright and actor Sam Shepard (when they're in town), this place positively breathes a film noir atmosphere.

Vesuvio Café (⌗ 255 Columbus Ave., at Broadway, ☎ 415/362–3370), near the legendary City Lights Bookstore, is little altered since its 1960s heyday. The second-floor balcony is a fine vantage point for watching the colorful, slightly seedy Broadway–Columbus intersection.

Gay and Lesbian Nightlife

In the days before the gay liberation movement, bars were more than mere watering holes. They also served as community centers where members of a mostly undercover minority could network and socialize. In the 1960s they became hotbeds of political activity. The Tavern Guild of San Francisco, comprising the town's major gay establishments, achieved several of the community's first political victories, waging and winning a legal and public relations battle to end police harassment. Even teetotaling gays benefited from the confrontation. By the 1970s other social opportunities became available to gay men and lesbians, and the bars' importance as centers of activity decreased.

Old-timers may wax nostalgic about the vibrancy of pre-AIDS, '70s bar life, but you can still have plenty of fun today. The one difference is the one-night-a-week operation of some of the best clubs, which may cater to a different (sometimes straight) clientele on other nights. This type of club tends to come and go, so it's best to pick up one of the two main gay papers: the ***Bay Area Reporter*** (☎ 415/861–5019) or the ***San Francisco Bay Times*** (☎ 415/227–0800). Both, plus ***Frontiers,*** a club-info and gossip sheet, are usually available at the clubs listed below.

The papers reveal something else: There's more to gay nightlife than the bars. Most nights **Theatre Rhinoceros** (☎ 415/861–5079) has plays or solo shows on two stages. Check the gay papers for other cultural and miscellaneous activities, such as sports clubs, drop-in counseling groups, and readings.

Lesbian Bars

For a place known as a gay mecca, San Francisco has always suffered a surprising drought of seven-days-a-week women's bars. The meager selection is augmented by a few reliable one-nighters; call ahead to verify scheduling. Younger lesbians and gays don't segregate themselves quite as much as the older set. You'll find mixed crowds at a number of the bars listed under Gay Male Bars, *below*.

Blondies' Bar and No Grill (⊠ 540 Valencia St., near 16th St., ☎ 415/864–2052), a mixed bar most of the week, plays host to "Red," a diverse all-women's night every Sunday.

The Box (⊠ 628 Divisadero St., ☎ 415/647–8258), a long-running one-nighter, features "Mixtress" Paige Hodel, who keeps the dressed-to-sweat crowd in constant motion with house, hip-hop, and funk sounds. For your $7 expect to find a mixed, increasingly male crowd shaking their collective bootie every Thursday night to 4 AM.

Club Q (⊠ 177 Townsend St., at 3rd St., ☎ 415/647–8258), a monthly (first Friday of every month) dance party from Paige Hodel's One Groove Productions, is geared to "women and their friends" and is always packed. The cover charge is $7, and doors open at 9 PM.

CoCo Club (⊠ 139 8th St., entrance on Minna St., ☎ 415/626–2337) offers a variety of theme nights, including a drag cabaret, a coed erotic cabaret, and a woman's speakeasy. Every other Friday is "In Bed with Fairy Butch," an all-women's dance night.

G Spot (⊠ 401 6th St., at Harrison St., ☎ 415/337–4962), at SoMa's End Up club, features Top 40, house, and R&B every Saturday from 9 PM; several top San Francisco DJs keep the mix lively.

Hollywood Billiards (⊠ 61 Golden Gate Ave., near Taylor St., ☎ 415/252–2419), a macho pool hall six nights a week, has become the unlikely host of a smoldering lesbian scene every Wednesday during its ladies' night. For women, a table costs just $5 for three hours.

The Lexington Club (⊠ 3464 19th St., at Lexington St., ☎ 415/863–2052) is where, according to the slogan, "Every night is ladies' night." This all-girl club is geared toward the younger lesbian set.

Gay Male Bars

"A bar for every taste, that's the ticket," was how the curious "documentary" *Gay San Francisco* described late-'60s nightlife here. Leather bars, drag-queen hangouts, piano bars, and bohemian cafés were among the many options for gay men back then. The scene remains just as versatile today. Unless otherwise noted, there is no cover charge at the following establishments.

THE SOMA SCENE

SF-Eagle (⊠ 398 12th St., at Harrison St., ☎ 415/626–0880) is one of the few SoMa bars that remains from the days before AIDS and gentrification. International leather legend Mister Marcus often drops by to judge the Mr. SF Leather, Mr. Leather Calendar, and innumerable other contests, most of which are AIDS benefits. The Sunday afternoon "Beer Busts" (3 PM–6 PM) are a social high point.

The Stud (⊠ 399 9th St., at Harrison St., ☎ 415/252–7883) is still going strong after more than 30 years. Its DJs mix up-to-the-minute music with carefully chosen highlights from the glory days of gay disco. The ever-changing weekly schedule includes new wave, classic disco, funk, and rock. Tuesday is Trannyshack, a drag cabaret show.

IN THE CASTRO

The Café (✉ 2367 Market St., at 17th St., ☎ 415/861–3846) is in the heart of gay Castro. Always comfortable and often crowded with locals and visitors alike, it's a place where you can chat quietly or dance, as you please. The rare smoking deck means it's a favorite destination for friends of tobacco.

Café Flore (✉ 2298 Market St., at Noe St., ☎ 415/621–8579), more of a daytime destination, attracts a mixed crowd including poets, punks, and poseurs. You can mingle day and night at open-air tables or inside the glass walls over beer, wine, excellent coffee, or tea. A separate concessionaire serves surprisingly tasty food until 10 PM; breakfast is popular.

The Metro (✉ 3600 16th St., at Market St., ☎ 415/703–9750) is a semi-upscale bar with a balcony overlooking the intersection of Noe, 16th, and Market streets. Guppies (gay yuppies) love this place, especially since it has a fairly good restaurant adjoining the bar. Tuesday is Karaoke Night.

Midnight Sun (✉ 4067 18th St., at Castro St., ☎ 415/861–4186), one of the Castro's longest-standing and most popular bars, has riotously programmed giant video screens. Don't expect to be able to hear yourself think.

ON/NEAR POLK STREET

The Cinch (✉ 1723 Polk St., at Clay St., ☎ 415/776–4162), a neighborhood bar with pinball machines and pool tables, is one of several hosts of the gay San Francisco Pool Association's weekly matches.

Kimo's (✉ 1351 Polk St., at Pine St., ☎ 415/885–4535), a laid-back club, has floor-to-ceiling windows that provide a great view of hectic Polk Street. On Friday and Saturday nights drag, cabaret, and comedy shows take place upstairs.

Motherlode (✉ 1002 Post St., at Larkin St., ☎ 415/928–6006), around the corner from the Polk Street bars in the rough-and-tumble Tenderloin, is *the* place for transvestites, transsexuals, and their admirers, with frequent stage performances. If you're in town in December, be sure to check out the city's gaudiest Christmas display, right here.

N Touch (✉ 1548 Polk St., at Sacramento St., ☎ 415/441–8413), a tiny dance bar, has long been popular with Asian–Pacific Islander gay men. In addition to videos, there's dancing to '70s and '80s tunes Monday nights and karaoke Tuesday and Sunday nights; male strippers perform Thursday night. A monthly drag show and go-go dancers on weekends round out the entertainment.

The Swallow (✉ 1750 Polk St., at Clay St., ☎ 415/775–4152), for those tired of the young and the buff, is a quiet, posh bar that caters to an older gay male clientele. A pianist plays standards nightly beginning at 9 PM, and patrons are often welcome to croon along open-mike style.

AROUND TOWN

Alta Plaza Restaurant & Bar (✉ 2301 Fillmore St., at Clay St., ☎ 415/922–1444) is an upper Fillmore restaurant-bar that caters to nattily dressed guppies and their admirers. Jazz musicians perform from Sunday to Thursday; a DJ takes over on weekends.

Esta Noche (✉ 3079 16th St., near Valencia St., ☎ 415/861–5757), a longtime Mission District establishment, draws a steady crowd of Latino gays, including some of the city's wildest drag queens. The latter perform shows every Wednesday, Thursday, and Sunday night.

Lion Pub (⊠ 2062 Divisadero St., at Sacramento St., ☎ 415/241–0205), one of the community's more established enterprises, is a cozy neighborhood bar with an ever-changing array of antiques.

Martuni's (⊠ 4 Valencia St., at Market St., ☎ 415/567–6565), an elegant, low-key bar on the border between the Mission and Hayes Valley, draws a mixed crowd that enjoys cocktails in a refined environment without the brash glamour of the scene. In the back room, a pianist plays nightly; occasionally he's joined by cast members of musicals in town, who belt out favorites to an appreciative crowd in the intimate space.

THE ARTS

The best guide to arts and entertainment events in San Francisco is the "Datebook" section, printed on pink paper, in the *San Francisco Sunday Examiner and Chronicle*. Also consult any of the free alternative weeklies (☞ Nightlife, *above*). For up-to-date information about cultural and musical events, call the **Convention and Visitors Bureau's Events Hotline** (☎ 415/391–2001).

Half-price, same-day tickets to many local and touring stage shows go on sale (cash only) at 11 AM from Tuesday to Saturday at the **TIX Bay Area** (☎ 415/433–7827) booth, on the Stockton Street side of Union Square, between Geary and Post streets. TIX is also a full-service ticket agency for theater and music events around the Bay Area (open Tuesday, Wednesday, and Thursday from 11 AM until 6 PM and Friday and Saturday until 7 PM).

The city's charge-by-phone ticket service is **BASS** (☎ 415/776–1999 or 510/762–2277), with one of its centers in the TIX booth (☞ *above*) and another at Tower Records (⊠ Bay St. at Columbus Ave., ☎ 415/885–0500), near Fisherman's Wharf. **City Box Office** (⊠ 153 Kearny St., Suite 401, ☎ 415/392–4400) has a downtown charge-by-phone service for many concerts and lectures. The opera, symphony, the San Francisco Ballet's *Nutcracker,* and touring hit musicals are often sold out in advance. Tickets are usually available within a day of the performance for other shows.

Theater

San Francisco's theaters are concentrated on Geary Street west of Union Square, but a number of additional commercial theaters, as well as resident companies that enrich the city's theatrical scene, are within walking distance of this theater row. The three major commercial theaters are operated by the Shorenstein-Nederlander organization, which books touring plays and musicals, some before they open on Broadway.

The most venerable commercial theater is the **Curran** (⊠ 445 Geary St., ☎ 415/551–2000). The **Golden Gate** is a stylishly refurbished movie theater (⊠ Golden Gate Ave. at Taylor St., ☎ 415/551–2000), now primarily a musical house. The gorgeously restored 2,500-seat **Orpheum** (⊠ 1192 Market St., near the Civic Center, ☎ 415/551–2000) is used for the biggest touring shows.

The city's major nonprofit theater company is the **American Conservatory Theater (ACT),** which was founded in the mid-1960s and quickly became one of the nation's leading regional theaters. During its season from the early fall to the late spring, ACT presents approximately eight plays, from classics to contemporary works, often in rotating repertory. In December ACT stages a much-loved version of Charles Dickens's *A Christmas Carol.* The ACT ticket office is at 405 Geary Street (☎ 415/749–2228). Next door to ACT is its home, the **Geary Theater.**

The leading producer of new plays is the **Magic Theatre** (⌧ Bldg. D, Fort Mason Center, Laguna St. at Marina Blvd., ☎ 415/441–8822). Once Sam Shepard's favorite showcase, the Magic presents works by the latest rising American playwrights, such as Neena Beber, Karen Hartman, and Claire Chafee.

Marines Memorial Theatre (⌧ 609 Sutter St., at Mason St., ☎ 415/771–6900) offers touring shows plus some local performances. The **Stage Door Theater** (⌧ 420 Mason St., ☎ no phone) is small but dependable. **Theatre on the Square** (⌧ 450 Post St., ☎ 415/433–9500) is a popular smaller venue. For commercial and popular success, nothing beats *Beach Blanket Babylon,* the zany revue that has been running since 1974 at North Beach's **Club Fugazi** (☞ Cabarets *in* Nightlife, *above*). Conceived by the late San Francisco director Steve Silver, it is a hilarious mix of cabaret, show-biz parodies, and tributes to local landmarks.

The **Lorraine Hansberry Theatre** (⌧ 620 Sutter St., ☎ 415/474–8800) specializes in plays by black writers. The **Asian American Theatre Company** (⌧ 1840 Sutter St., ☎ 415/440–5545) is dedicated to working with local actors. **A Traveling Jewish Theatre** (⌧ 470 Florida St., ☎ 415/399–1809) stages various productions, often with Jewish themes. **Theatre Rhinoceros** (⌧ 2926 16th St., ☎ 415/861–5079) showcases gay and lesbian performers. The two-stage **New Conservatory Theatre** (⌧ 25 Van Ness Ave., ☎ 415/861–8972) hosts the annual Pride Season focusing on contemporary gay- and lesbian-themed works. The **San Francisco Shakespeare Festival** (☎ 415/422–2222) offers free weekend performances from Labor Day to October in Golden Gate Park. A uniquely Bay Area summertime freebie is the Tony Award–winning **San Francisco Mime Troupe** (☎ 415/285–1717), whose politically leftist, barbed satires are hardly mime in the Marcel Marceau sense; they perform afternoon shows at area parks from July 4 weekend through September.

Avant-garde theater, dance, opera, and performance art turn up in a variety of locations, not all of them theaters. Major presenting organizations include **Theatre Artaud** (⌧ 450 Florida St., in the Mission District, ☎ 415/621–7797), in a huge, converted machine shop, and the **Yerba Buena Center for the Arts** (⌧ 3rd and Howard Sts., ☎ 415/978–2787), which schedules contemporary theater events, in addition to dance and music.

Notable venues for small-scale plays and experimental works include **George Coates Performance Works** (⌧ 110 McAllister St., ☎ 415/863–4130), **Intersection for the Arts** (⌧ 446 Valencia St., ☎ 415/626–2787), **The Marsh** (⌧ 1062 Valencia St., ☎ 415/826–5750), and **Climate Theatre** (⌧ 285 9th St., ☎ 415/978–2345). Solo performers are a local staple and are annually spotlighted at the early fall **Solo Mio Festival,** which takes place at various venues (for information call Climate Theatre). Ground zero for absurdist theater is the **Exit Theatre** (⌧ 156 Eddy St., ☎ 415/673–3847), which also presents the annual **Fringe Festival** (☎ 415/931–1094) in September.

Berkeley Repertory Theatre (☎ 510/845–4700), across the bay, is the American Conservatory Theatre's major rival for leadership among the region's resident professional companies. It performs an adventurous mix of classics and new plays from fall to spring in a modern, intimate theater at 2025 Addison Street, near BART's downtown Berkeley station. Tickets are available at the TIX booth in San Francisco's Union Square. **California Shakespeare Festival** (☎ 510/548–9666), the Bay Area's largest outdoor summer theater event, performs in an amphitheater east of Oakland on Gateway Boulevard, just off state Highway 24.

Though San Francisco lacks an outstanding year-round source for live family entertainment, two animal-free, acrobatically inclined new-vaudeville-style groups offer excellent annual shows. **Make-A-Circus** (☎ 415/242–1414), which tours to parks and rec centers statewide in the summer, invites kids to learn circus skills at intermission, then join in during the second act. **The New Pickle Circus** (☎ 415/487–7940) generally performs at indoor locales around Christmastime.

Music

San Francisco's symphony, opera, and ballet are all based in the Civic Center. The symphony and other musical groups also perform in the smaller, 928-seat Herbst Theatre in the War Memorial Building, the Opera's "twin" at Van Ness Avenue and McAllister Street. Musical ensembles can be found all over the city: in churches and museums, in restaurants and parks, not to mention in Berkeley and on the peninsula. Each October, concert halls, clubs, and churches throughout the city host the acclaimed **San Francisco International Jazz Festival** (☎ 415/398–5655), featuring jazz legends alongside world-class up-and-comers.

San Francisco Symphony. The symphony performs from September to May. Michael Tilson Thomas, who is known for his innovative programming of 20th-century American works, is the musical director. Occasional guest conductors include Hugh Wolff and Roger Norrington, with featured soloists of the caliber of Andre Watts, Midori, and Frederica von Stade. Special events include a summer festival built around a particular composer, nation, or musical period, and summer Pops Concerts at various venues. Tickets run $12–$100. ⊠ *Davies Symphony Hall, 201 Van Ness Ave., at Grove St.,* ☎ *415/864–6000.*

Berkeley Symphony Orchestra. This East Bay ensemble has risen to considerable prominence under artistic director Kent Nagano's baton. The emphasis is on 20th-century composers from Messiaen to Zappa (including many world premieres), alongside more traditional pieces. The orchestra performs four concerts from August to June. ⊠ *Zellerbach Hall, Telegraph Ave. and Bancroft Way, UC Berkeley campus,* ☎ *510/841–2800.*

Cal Performances. This series, running from August to June at various UC Berkeley campus venues, offers the Bay Area's most varied bill of internationally acclaimed artists in all disciplines, from classical soloists to the latest jazz, world music, theater, and dance ensembles. ⊠ *Zellerbach Hall, Bancroft Way and Telegraph Ave., Berkeley,* ☎ *510/642–9988.*

San Francisco Performances. San Francisco's equivalent to Cal Performances brings an eclectic array of topflight global music and dance talents to various venues—mostly Civic Center's Herbst Theatre—from October to May. Recent guests have included Andre Watts, Wynton Marsalis, and John Williams. ☎ *415/398–6449.*

Philharmonia Baroque. This ensemble has been called a local baroque orchestra with a national reputation and the nation's preeminent group for performances of early music. Its season of concerts, from fall to spring, celebrates composers of the 17th and 18th centuries, including Handel, Vivaldi, and Mozart. ☎ *415/495–7445.*

Kronos Quartet. Twentieth-century works and a number of premieres make up the programs for this surprisingly avant-garde group, whose following includes both the young and mainstream, debunking all conceptions of string quartets as somber affairs. ☎ *415/731–3533.*

Chanticleer. This all-male a cappella ensemble is a Bay Area treasure. Lively and technically flawless performances show off a repertoire that ranges from sacred medieval music to contemporary avant-garde works. ☎ 415/896–5866.

Old First Concerts. This well-respected Friday evening and Sunday afternoon series offers chamber music, vocal soloists, new music, and jazz. Phone for tickets or visit the TIX booth in Union Square (☞ *above*). ✉ *Old First Presbyterian Church, 1751 Sacramento St., at Van Ness Ave.,* ☎ 415/474–1608.

Pops Concerts. Many members of the symphony perform in the summer Pops series in the 2,400-seat Davies Hall. The schedule includes light classics and Broadway, country, and movie music. Tickets cost as little as a few dollars. ✉ *Davies Symphony Hall, 201 Van Ness Ave., at Grove St.,* ☎ 415/864–6000.

Stern Grove. The nation's oldest continual free summer music festival hosts Sunday afternoon performances of symphony, opera, jazz, pop music, and dance. The amphitheater is in a eucalyptus grove below street level; dress for cool weather. ✉ *Sloat Blvd. at 19th Ave.,* ☎ 415/252–6252.

42nd Street Moon Productions. This group produces delightful "semi-staged" revivals of rare chestnuts from Broadway's musical comedy golden age at the New Conservatory Theatre Center in irregularly scheduled miniseasons throughout the year. ✉ *25 Van Ness Ave.,* ☎ 415/861–8972.

Opera

San Francisco Opera. Founded in 1923, this world-renowned company has resided in the Civic Center's War Memorial Opera House since it was built in 1932. Over its season, the opera presents approximately 70 performances of 10 operas from September to December and June to July. The opera uses supertitles: Translations are projected above the stage during almost all non-English operas. Long considered a major international company and the most important operatic organization in the United States outside New York, the opera frequently embarks on coproductions with European opera companies. ✉ *301 Van Ness Ave., at Grove St.,* ☎ 415/864–3330.

Ticket prices range from about $22 to $145. Standing-room tickets ($10) are always sold at 10 AM for same-day performances, and patrons often sell extra tickets on the Opera House steps just before curtain time at face value or less. The full-time box office is at 199 Grove Street, at Van Ness Avenue.

Pocket Opera. This lively, modestly priced alternative to grand opera aims to bring opera to a broad audience. The concert performances of popular and seldom-heard works are mostly in English. Offenbach's operettas are frequently on the bill during the February–June season. Concerts are held at various locations. ☎ 415/575–1102.

Lamplighters. This operatic alternative specializes in Gilbert and Sullivan but presents other light operas as well. The troupe performs at various venues including the Center for the Arts. ☎ 415/227–4797.

Dance

The **San Francisco Ballet** (✉ *301 Van Ness Ave.,* ☎ 415/865–2000) has regained much of its luster under artistic director Helgi Tomasson, and both classical and contemporary works have won admiring reviews. The company's primary season runs from February to May. Its repertoire includes such full-length ballets as *Swan Lake* and *Sleeping Beauty*; its annual December presentation of the *Nutcracker* is one of the most spectacular in the nation. The company also performs bold new dances from such star choreographers as William Forsythe and Mark Morris, alongside modern classics by George Balanchine and Jerome Robbins. Tickets and information are available at the Opera House (⊠ 301 Van Ness Ave., ☎ 415/865–2000).

Oakland Ballet. Founded in 1965, this company is not simply an imitation of the larger San Francisco Ballet across the bay. It has earned an outstanding reputation for reviving and preserving ballet masterworks from the early 20th century, by re-creating historic dances by such choreographers as Sergey Diaghilev and Bronisława Nijinska. The company's fall season ends with its own *Nutcracker* in December. All performances take place at Oakland's **Paramount Theatre** (⊠ 2025 Broadway, ☎ 510/465–6400), near the 19th Street BART station. ☎ *510/452–9288.*

Cal Performances and San Francisco Performances (☞ Music, *above*) are the area's leading importers of world-class dance troupes.

Approximately 30 of the Bay Area's estimated 200 ethnic dance companies and soloists perform at the **Ethnic Dance Festival** (⊠ Palace of Fine Arts Theatre, Bay and Lyon Sts., ☎ 415/474–3914), which takes place in June. Prices are modest.

The **Margaret Jenkins Dance Company** (☎ 415/826–8399) is a nationally acclaimed modern troupe. **Lines Contemporary Ballet** (☎ 415/863–3040) is a good bet for modern ballet. **Smuin Ballets/SF** (☎ 415/665–2222), led by former San Francisco Ballet Director Michael Smuin, is renowned for its fluidity and excitement. The company regularly integrates pop music into its performances. **Lawrence Pech Dance Company** (☎ 415/641–1423), formed in 1996, is considered a new gem in Bay Area dance. **ODC/San Francisco** (☎ 415/863–6606) mounts an annual Yuletide version of *The Velveteen Rabbit* at the Center for the Arts. The **Robert Henry Johnson Dance Company** (☎ 415/824–4782) mounts contemporary productions, usually at Yerba Buena Center for the Arts and Theatre Artaud. The **Dancers Group/Footwork** (☎ 415/824–5044) is a small but significant local company.

Film

The San Francisco Bay Area, including Berkeley and San Jose, is considered one of the nation's most important movie markets. Films of all sorts find an audience here. The area is also a filmmaking center: Documentaries and experimental works are produced on modest budgets, feature films and television programs are shot on location, and some of Hollywood's biggest directors (including George Lucas and Francis Ford Coppola) live in the city or, more often, in Marin County. In San Francisco about a third of the theaters regularly show foreign and independent films.

The **Castro Theatre** (⊠ 429 Castro St., near Market St., ☎ 415/621–6120), designed by Art Deco master Timothy Pfleuger, is worth visiting for its decor alone; it also offers revivals as well as foreign and independent engagements. Across the bay, the spectacular Art Deco **Paramount Theatre** (⊠ 2025 Broadway, Oakland, near 19th St. BART station, ☎ 510/465–6400) (☞ Oakland *in* Chapter 7) alternates between vintage flicks and live performances.

Foreign and Independent Films
Opera Plaza Cinemas (⊠ 601 Van Ness Ave., at Golden Gate Ave., ☎ 415/352–0810). **Lumière** (⊠ 1572 California St., near Polk St., ☎ 415/352–0810). **Clay** (⊠ 2261 Fillmore St., at Clay St., ☎ 415/352–0810). **Bridge** (⊠ 3010 Geary Blvd., near Masonic Ave., ☎ 415/352–0810).

Embarcadero Center Cinemas (⊠ 1 Embarcadero Center, Promenade level, ☎ 415/352–0810).

The **Roxie Cinema** (⊠ 3117 16th St., ☎ 415/863–1087) specializes in film noir and new foreign and indie features. The avant-garde **Red Vic Movie House** (⊠ 1727 Haight St., ☎ 415/668–3994) screens an adventurous lineup of contemporary and classic American and foreign titles in a funky setting. The **Cinematheque** (☎ 415/558–8129) splits its experimental film and video schedule between the San Francisco Art Institute (⊠ 800 Chestnut St., ☎ 415/558–8129) and the Yerba Buena Center for the Arts (⊠ 701 Mission St., between 3rd and Howard Sts., ☎ 415/978–2787).

The **Pacific Film Archive** (⊠ University Art Museum, 2625 Durant Ave., Berkeley, ☎ 510/642–1124) screens a comprehensive mix of old and new American and foreign films.

Festivals

The **San Francisco International Film Festival** (☎ 415/931–3456) takes over several theaters for two weeks in late April and early May, primarily the Castro Theatre (☞ *above*) and the AMC Kabuki complex at Post and Fillmore streets. The festival schedules about 150 films from around the globe, many of them American premieres. Marin County's **Mill Valley Film Festival** (☎ 415/383–5256), in early October, is also renowned.

The **Film Arts Festival of Independent Cinema** (☎ 415/552–8760), in November, showcases Bay Area documentary and independent film talent. The **San Francisco International Lesbian and Gay Film Festival** (☎ 415/703–8650), the world's oldest and largest of its kind, takes place in late June at various venues. The **San Francisco Jewish Film Festival** (☎ 415/621–0556) takes place in July. Look for the **Asian American Film Festival** (☎ 415/863–0814) in March, and the **Latino Film Festival** (☎ 415/553–8135) in September. The **American Indian Film Festival** (☎ 415/554–0525) takes place in November at the Palace of Fine Arts Theater.

5 OUTDOOR ACTIVITIES AND SPORTS

In San Francisco stockbrokers go surfing at noon, weathered old men brave chilling bay waters that not even Alcatraz prisoners could swim, and children flock to the Marina Green to fly kites against a backdrop of sailboats. The temperature rarely drops below 50°F, and parks, beaches, and open space are as plentiful as bay views and fresh air.

PARTICIPANT SPORTS AND THE OUTDOORS

Updated by
Denise M. Leto

PERHAPS MORE THAN ANYWHERE ELSE, physical fitness and outdoor activities are a way of life in the Bay Area. Joggers, bicyclists, and aficionados of virtually all sports can often find their favorite pastimes within walking distance of downtown hotels. Golden Gate Park has numerous paths for runners, strollers, in-line skaters, and cyclists. Hiking paths with incredible ocean and bay views are abundant throughout the **Golden Gate National Recreation Area** (☎ 415/556–0560), which encompasses the San Francisco coastline, the Marin Headlands, and Point Reyes National Seashore. Lake Merced in San Francisco and Lake Merritt in Oakland are among the most popular areas for joggers; and Berkeley's sprawling Tilden Park (☞ Berkeley *in* Chapter 7) is great for hiking and mountain biking.

For a listing of running races, tennis tournaments, bicycle races, and other participant sports, check the monthly issues of *City Sports* magazine, available free at sporting goods stores, tennis centers, and other recreational sites.

The most important running event of the year is the *San Francisco Examiner*'s **Bay-to-Breakers race** on the third Sunday in May. Up to 100,000 serious and not-so-serious runners dress up in crazy costumes—an adult version of Halloween, but twice the fun—and make their way from the Embarcadero to the Pacific Ocean. For race information and entry forms, call ☎ 415/512–5000 ext. 2222.

The **San Francisco Marathon & 5K** is held annually on the second Sunday in July. Beginning at the Golden Gate Bridge, the 26.2-mi marathon passes through downtown and up and over many of the city's steepest hills, drawing up to 7,000 runners. For entry forms and race information call ☎ 415/296–7111.

Bicycling

San Francisco has a number of scenic routes of varied terrain. With its legendary hills, the city offers countless cycling challenges—but also plenty of level ground. To avoid the former, look for a copy of the *San Francisco Biking/Walking Guide* ($3): Sold in select bookstores, the folding guide indicates street grades and delineates biking routes that avoid major hills and heavy traffic.

EMBARCADERO

A completely flat route, the Embarcadero gives you a clear view of open waters and the Bay Bridge on the pier side and sleek high-rises on the other. Rent a bike ($7 per hour) at **Start to Finish** (⊠ 599 2nd St., ☎ 415/243–8812) and ride downhill on Brannan Street to the Embarcadero. After crossing the Embarcadero, make a left and continue along the waterfront on the sidewalk, along with fellow bikers, joggers, and striders. After passing the Ferry Building, keep pedaling for about a mile to reach Pier 39. If you're not put off by crowds, continue through Fisherman's Wharf to Aquatic Park. On your return trip continue along the Embarcadero past Brannan Street for additional dockside views. Travel time can be anywhere from 30 minutes to an hour.

MARINA GREEN

The Marina Green is a popular patch of grass along Marina Boulevard adjacent to Fort Mason and the small craft marina. It's also the starting point of a well-trod route to the Golden Gate Bridge and beyond. Rent a bike ($7 per hour) at the Lombard branch of **Start to Finish** (⊠ 2530 Lombard St., at Divisadero St., ☎ 415/202–9830) and take Lombard Street west for three blocks until you reach the Presidio and hit Lincoln Boulevard. Lincoln Boulevard will eventually bring you to the base of the bridge, a 45-minute ride round-trip. If you're feeling ambitious, head across the bridge (signs indicate on which side cyclists must ride) and turn off on the first road leading northeast. After a 15-minute (downhill) ride, you'll arrive on Bridgeway in downtown Sausalito, where you can rest in a café. From there take your bike aboard the Blue and Gold Fleet's ferry (the ferry terminal is at the end of Bridgeway) for a half-hour ride back to San Francisco's Fisherman's Wharf.

GOLDEN GATE PARK

Golden Gate Park is a beautiful maze of roads and hidden bike paths, with rose gardens, lakes, waterfalls, museums, horse stables, bison, and ultimately, a spectacular view of the Pacific Ocean. On Sunday John F. Kennedy Drive is closed to motor vehicles, making it a popular and crowded route for those on people-powered wheels. Rent a bike for about $25 per day at **Park Cyclery** (⊠ 1749 Waller St., ☎ 415/751–7368) and take a 20- to 30-minute ride down John F. Kennedy Drive to the Great Highway, where land meets ocean. You may extend your ride another couple of miles by turning left, riding a few blocks, and hooking onto a raised bike path that runs parallel to the Pacific, winding through fields of emerald green ice plants and, after 2 mi, leading to Sloat Boulevard and the San Francisco Zoo.

Boat Cruises and Ferries

One of the best ways to experience San Francisco's natural beauty is by taking to the water. If sailing the bay and ocean kayaking aren't your speed, consider taking advantage of the city's numerous ferry and cruise lines. They're not just a mode of transportation; getting there is half the fun. Don't miss watching the sun set over the city from the deck of a ship.

Blue & Gold Fleet (☎ 415/705–5555) offers daily service from Pier 41 to Angel Island, the largest of the islands off San Francisco and a wildlife preserve. An easy path winds around the island's perimeter, ideal for a jaunt into nature. Bike rental is available on the island, or bring your own on the ferry. Other lines lead to infamous Alcatraz, the redwood haven of Muir Woods (via Tiburon and a van ride), and the sailing town of Sausalito, where the main activities include strolling, window-shopping, and dining on seafood. Boats leave frequently from Pier 41 on the 20-minute trips to Alcatraz and Tiburon and the 40-minute trip to Sausalito. If you'd just like a different perspective on San Francisco, you may opt for a cruise on the bay. Enjoy a cocktail and a stunning close-up view of the Golden Gate Bridge, Alcatraz, and Angel Island without having to leave the deck.

With the **Alameda/Oakland Ferry** (☎ 510/522–3300), you can sail from Pier 39 or the Ferry Building to Oakland's Jack London Square. The trip lasts 30 to 45 minutes, depending on your departure point, and leads to the gentrified heart of Oakland's shopping and restaurant district. The views sailing back to San Francisco may be more welcoming than those on the way into Oakland, but arriving in Oakland by boat conveys a historic sense of this East Bay city's heyday as a shipbuilding center in World War II.

Boating and Sailing

San Francisco Bay offers year-round sailing, but tricky currents and strong winds make the bay hazardous for inexperienced navigators.

Boat rentals and charters are available throughout the Bay Area and are listed under "Boat Renting" in the Yellow Pages.

A Day on the Bay (☎ 415/922–0227) is ideally located in San Francisco's small craft marina, just minutes from the Golden Gate Bridge and open waters. **Cass' Marina** (✉ 1702 Bridgeway, at Napa St., ☎ 415/332–6789), in Sausalito, has a variety of sailboats that can be rented as long as you have a qualified sailor in the group. The locals at the **Eagle Cafe** on Pier 39 can give you sailing tips.

Stow Lake (☎ 415/752–0347), in Golden Gate Park, has rowboat, pedal boat, and electric boat rentals. The lake is open daily for boating, but call for seasonal hours.

Fishing

Numerous fishing boats leave from San Francisco, Sausalito, Berkeley, Emeryville, and Point San Pablo. They go for salmon and halibut outside the bay or striped bass and giant sturgeon within the bay. In San Francisco lines can be cast from San Francisco Municipal Pier, Fisherman's Wharf, Baker Beach, or Aquatic Park. Trout fishing is possible at Lake Merced. You can rent rods and boats and buy bait at the **Lake Merced Boating and Fishing Company** (✉ 1 Harding Rd., ☎ 415/753–1101). One-day **licenses,** good for ocean fishing only, are available for around $10 on the charters. Some selected sportfishing charters are listed below. Most depart daily from Fisherman's Wharf during the salmon-fishing season, which is from March to October.

Lovely Martha's Sportfishing (✉ Fisherman's Wharf, Berth 3, ☎ 650/871–1691) offers salmon-fishing excursions as well as bay tours.

Wacky Jacky (✉ Fisherman's Wharf, Pier 45, ☎ 415/586–9800) will take you salmon fishing in a sleek, fast, and comfortable 50-ft boat.

Fitness

Thanks to the law of supply and demand, the number of fitness clubs in downtown San Francisco has soared. Although some clubs still retain private membership status, many facilities provide day passes for an average charge of $10 to $20. Several hotels have arrangements with neighborhood health clubs, and a number of hotels have health facilities of their own. The facilities at some hotels are open to nonguests for a fee: Try the swanky clubs at the **Hotel Nikko** (✉ 222 Mason St., ☎ 415/394–1153) or the **Fairmont's Club One** (✉ 950 Mason St., ☎ 415/834–1010), where the fees are $20 and $15, respectively.

The various branches of **24-Hour Fitness** (✉ 1200 Van Ness Ave., ☎ 415/776–2200; ✉ 350 Bay St., ☎ 415/395–9595; ✉ 3741 Buchanan St., ☎ 415/563–3535; ✉ 100 California St., ☎ 415/434–5080; ✉ 303 2nd St., at Folsom St., ☎ 415/543–7808) are open to the public for a $15 drop-in fee. Facilities and services vary, but most of the clubs have saunas, Jacuzzis, and steam rooms as well as aerobics classes and a complete line of fitness equipment. The **Embarcadero YMCA** (✉ 169 Steuart St., ☎ 415/957–9622), one of the finest facilities in San Francisco, has racquetball, a 25-m swimming pool, and aerobics classes. The $12 drop-in fee includes use of the sauna, steam room, and whirlpool plus a magnificent view of the bay. **Pinnacle Fitness** has two locations in the heart of the Financial District (✉ 61 New Montgomery St., ☎ 415/543–1110; ✉ 1 Post Plaza, at Market St., ☎ 415/781–6400). Both offer day passes for $15, which include use of the lap pool at the Post Plaza location and access to aerobics classes at both. The Post Plaza location offers boxing classes. The **World Gym** (✉ 260 De Haro St., at 16th St., ☎ 415/703–9650), though a bit off the beaten track, is a must-see for bodybuilding enthusiasts; a lack of extensive spa facilities is a fair trade-off for the extensive weight-training and aerobics equipment. The day rate of $10 includes aerobics classes.

Golf

Golfers can putt to their hearts' content in San Francisco. Call the **golf information line** (☎ 415/750–4653) to get detailed directions to the city's public golf courses or to reserve a tee time ($1 per player) up to seven days in advance. **Harding and Fleming parks** (⌂ Harding Rd. and Skyline Blvd., ☎ 415/664–4690) have an 18-hole, par-72 course and a 9-hole executive course, respectively. **Lincoln Park** (⌂ 34th Ave. and Clement St., ☎ 415/221–9911) has an 18-hole, par-68 course. **Golden Gate** (⌂ 47th Ave. between Fulton St. and John F. Kennedy Dr., ☎ 415/751–8987) is a 9-hole, par-27 course in Golden Gate Park just above Ocean Beach. **Sharp Park,** in Pacifica (⌂ Off Hwy. 1 at the Sharp Park Rd. exit, ☎ 650/359–3380), has 18 holes, par 72. **Glen Eagles Golf Course** (⌂ 2100 Sunnydale Ave., ☎ 415/587–2425) is a challenging 9-hole, par 36 course in McLaren Park. The **Presidio Golf Course** (⌂ 300 Finley Rd., near W. Pacific Ave. and Arguello Blvd., ☎ 415/561–4653) is an 18-hole, par-72 course managed by Arnold Palmer's company.

Horseback Riding

Along the coast, through the vineyards, and along dusty country roads, the Bay Area has miles of trails that are great for western-style horseback riding. In Half Moon Bay you can gallop along the beach with a horse from **Friendly Acres** (⌂ 2150 N. Cabrillo Hwy., ☎ 650/726–8550) or **Sea Horse Ranch** (⌂ 1828 N. Cabrillo Hwy., ☎ 650/726–8550). Olema, a small town near Point Reyes, has horses for rent at **Five Brooks** (⌂ 8001 Rte. 1, ☎ 415/663–1570). Trails lead through the Point Reyes National Park all the way to the sea. For a more sedate equestrian experience, consider taking a guided ride through **Golden Gate Park** (⌂ ☎ 415/668–7360). A guide will lead you and your steed through the park's vast woods and meadows for $25 per hour.

Ice-Skating

One of the best places from which to enjoy an impressive view of San Francisco's skyline is the skating rink at the **Rooftop@Yerba Buena Gardens** (⌂ 750 Folsom St., at 4th St., ☎ 415/777–3727), open year-round. Magnificent floor-to-ceiling windows border the NHL-regulation rink, distracting skaters with the city's twinkling lights by night and bathing the rink in natural light by day. Winter visitors can enjoy outdoor ice-skating at the **Kristi Yamaguchi Holiday Ice Rink** (⌂ Justin Herman Plaza, Embarcadero Center, ☎ 415/956–2688) from November through January and sometimes March, depending on weather. Most years, **Macy's** runs an outdoor rink at Union Square (☎ 415/397–3333) in November and December. **Berkeley Iceland** (⌂ 2727 Milvia St., 4 blocks from the Ashby BART station, ☎ 510/843–8800) provides year-round skating at an indoor rink.

In-Line Skating

Golden Gate Park is one of the country's best places for in-line skating, with smooth surfaces, manageable hills, and lush scenery. John F. Kennedy Drive, which extends almost to the ocean, is closed to cars on Sunday, when it seems that the city's entire population heads to the park with in-line skates. **Skates on Haight** (⌂ 1818 Haight St., ☎ 415/752–8376), near the Stanyan Street entrance to the park, offers free lessons (with a purchase) on Sunday morning and rents recreational and speed skates for $28 per day.

For beginners, the path along **the Marina** offers a 1½-mi (round-trip) easy route on a flat, well-paved surface, with glorious views of San Francisco Bay. **FTC Sports** (✉ 1586 Bush St., ☎ 415/673–8363) rents and sells in-line skates and protective gear. Advanced skaters may want to experience the challenge and take in the brilliant views of **Tilden Park** (☎ 510/843–2137 or 510/525–2233), in the Berkeley Hills (☞ Berkeley *in* Chapter 7). Follow signs to the parking lot at Inspiration Point. There you'll find the trailhead for Nimitz Way, a nicely paved 8-mi (round-trip) recreational path that stretches along a ridge overlooking San Francisco Bay and Mt. Diablo.

Skaters with a competitive edge can take part in the nightly pickup roller hockey games at **Bladium** (✉ 1050 3rd St., ☎ 415/442–5060), where a one-game pass costs $10 and gear can be rented for another $10. Reservations are required three days in advance.

Kayaking

Surrounded by water on three sides, San Francisco offers plenty of opportunities for all levels of kayaking enthusiasts and shops and organizations to equip and lead them. Specializing in sea kayaking, **Sea Trek** (✉ Schoonmaker Point Marina, Sausalito, ☎ 415/488–1000) offers guided trips to Angel Island for beginners; the evening trips are particularly popular. More advanced kayakers can head out to the Golden Gate and paddle to Muir Beach. If you'd like to rent a kayak and strike out on your own, the friendly and knowledgable folks at **Harbor Dive & Kayak Center** (✉ 200 Harbor Dr., Sausalito, ☎ 415/331–0904) will suit you up and recommend routes based on current conditions and your ability and interests.

Racquetball

Most racquetball clubs in San Francisco are private and require that drop-in guests be accompanied by a member. However, a few fitness centers offering day passes have racquetball courts on the premises. The **Embarcadero YMCA** (☞ Fitness, *above*) charges a $12 drop-in fee that includes use of their racquetball courts. At the University of San Francisco's **Koret Health and Recreation Center** (✉ Parker Ave. at Turk St., ☎ 415/422–6820), use of the courts is available to guests before 2 PM for $8. You can play squash at **Club One** (✉ The Fillmore Center, 1755 O'Farrell St., ☎ 415/776–2260) for $10. The **Northpoint Health Club** (✉ 2310 Powell St., at Bay St., ☎ 415/989–1449) has smaller-than-regulation courts for an entry fee of $7. The San Francisco Recreation and Park Department maintains two free racquetball courts at the **Mission Recreation Center** (✉ 2450 Harrison St., ☎ 415/695–5012).

Rock Climbing

Mission Cliffs Rock Climbing Center (✉ 2295 Harrison St., ☎ 415/550–0515) is one of the largest indoor climbing facilities in the country, with a 14,000-square-ft gym and a 4,000-square-ft bouldering area. Day passes cost $16; you can rent gear for $6. You can climb the outside bouldering wall at **Club One Citicorp** (✉ 1 Sansome St., ☎ 415/399–1010) for a $15 day fee. The wall may be closed during inclement weather, so call ahead. **City Rock** (✉ 1250 45th St., Suite 400, Emeryville, ☎ 510/654–2510) is a quick drive across the Bay Bridge. Classes are available for beginners for $25. Experienced climbers must pass a safety test before climbing. Day passes cost $14. An additional $6 rents shoes and a harness.

Swimming

The **San Francisco Recreation and Park Department** (☎ 415/252–7877) manages one outdoor swimming pool and eight indoor pools ($3 admission) throughout the city. The **Sava Pool** (✉ 19th Ave. and

Wawona St., ☎ 415/753–7000) is one of the more popular (and crowded) pools. **Hamilton Pool** (⊠ Geary Blvd. and Steiner St., ☎ 415/ 292–2001) is a favorite among swimmers. The **Embarcadero YMCA** (☞ Fitness, *above*) has a 25-m pool, gym, and spa facilities for a $12 day fee. The University of San Francisco's **Koret Health and Recreation Center** (☞ Racquetball, *above,* ☎ 415/422–6820), a few blocks from the Golden Gate Park Panhandle, has an especially well maintained Olympic-size pool as well as an exercise room. Visitors have access to the facilities before 2 PM daily for an $8 fee. The small pool at **Pinnacle Fitness** (☞ Fitness, *above*) is convenient to downtown.

Some hotels allow nonguests to use their swimming pools for a fee. Try the **Sheehan Hotel** (⊠ 620 Sutter St., ☎ 415/775–6500), a few blocks from Union Square: Its four-lane lap pool is open to the public for a $5 fee. **Hotel Nikko**'s (☞ Fitness, *above*) indoor pool is open to day users.

Tennis

San Francisco tennis clubs are private and require membership. However, the San Francisco Recreation and Park Department maintains 132 public tennis courts throughout the city. All courts are free except those in Golden Gate Park. The largest set of free courts is at **Mission Dolores Park** (⊠ 18th and Dolores Sts.), where six courts are available on a first-come, first-served basis. The 16 courts in **Golden Gate Park** (☎ 415/753–7001) are the only public ones for which you can make advance reservations. The fee for visitors is $6 for 90 minutes weekdays and $8 weekends; the resident fees are $4 and $6 respectively. For gorgeous views while you play, head up to the two **Buena Vista Park Courts** (⊠ Buena Vista and Duboce Aves., ☎ 415/753–7001). Popular with Marina locals, the four courts at the **George Moscone Recreation Center** (⊠ between Chestnut, Bay, Laguna, and Fillmore Sts., ☎ 415/753–7001) sometimes require a wait. Hidden among eucalyptus trees, the **Stern Grove Annex** (⊠ Sloat Blvd. at 19th Ave., ☎ 415/753–7001) only has two courts, but the park's beauty is a great distraction in case you have to wait.

Windsurfing and Gliding

In this city of brisk bay breezes and adventurous souls, windsurfing and gliding are popular pastimes throughout the year. The **San Francisco School of Windsurfing** (⊠ 1 Harding Rd., Lake Merced, ☎ 415/ 753–3235) offers rentals, lessons for beginners on mild Lake Merced, and lessons for more advanced surfers at Candlestick Point (where rentals are also available). Adventurous types should head to **Airtime** (⊠ 3620 Wawona St., ☎ 415/759–1177), near the San Francisco Zoo, which offers hang gliding and para-gliding instruction. Tandem gliding is also available for those who prefer to tag along for the ride.

SPECTATOR SPORTS

For a local perspective on Bay Area sports, look in sports bars and sporting goods stores for the *Bay Sports Review,* which lists game schedules and features interviews with sports luminaries.

Auto Racing

Sears Point International Raceway (⊠ Hwy. 121 at Hwy. 37, Sonoma, ☎ 707/938–8448 or 800/870–7223), at the southern edge of the Wine Country, hosts many motor-sports events.

Baseball

The **San Francisco Giants** play at 3Com Park at Candlestick Point (⊠ U.S. 101 at 3Com Park exit, 3 mi south of downtown, ☎ 415/467–

8000 or 800/734–4268). Pacific Bell Park, a new downtown bayfront stadium, is scheduled to open in 2000. Game-day tickets are usually available at 3Com. City shuttle buses marked BALLPARK EXPRESS run from numerous bus stops throughout San Francisco; call **Muni** (☎ 415/673–6864) for the stop nearest you. 3Com Park is often windy and cold, so take along extra layers of clothing. The **Oakland A's** play at the Oakland Coliseum (⊠ Coliseum Way off I–880, ☎ 510/638–0500 or 510/762–2255). Same-day tickets can usually be purchased at the stadium; on Wednesdays, tickets are often $1. To reach the Oakland Coliseum, take a BART train to the Coliseum stop.

Basketball

The **Golden State Warriors** play NBA basketball at the Oakland Coliseum Arena (⊠ Coliseum Way off I–880) from November to April. Tickets are available through **BASS** (☎ 510/762–2277). BART trains to the Coliseum stop are the easiest method of travel.

Football

The NFC West's **San Francisco 49ers** play at 3Com Park (⊠ U.S. 101 at 3Com Park exit, 3 mi south of downtown), but the games are almost always sold out far in advance (☎ 415/468–2249). The AFC West's **Oakland Raiders** play at the Oakland Coliseum (⊠ Coliseum Way off I–880). Except for high-profile games, tickets (☎ 510/762–2277) are usually available.

Hockey

Tickets for the NHL's **San Jose Sharks** are available from BASS (☎ 510/762–2277). Games are held at the San Jose Arena (☞ San Jose *in* Chapter 8).

Horse Racing

Depending on the season, horse racing takes place at the Golden Gate Fields or Bay Meadows tracks. Check local newspapers to find out which tracks are operating. The admission at **Golden Gate Fields** (⊠ 1100 Eastshore Hwy., off I–80, Albany, ☎ 510/559–7300), in the East Bay, is $2. **Bay Meadows** (⊠ 2600 Delaware Ave., off U.S. 101, San Mateo, ☎ 650/574–7223), on the Peninsula, charges $3.

Rodeo

San Francisco relives its western heritage every October with the **Grand National Rodeo, Horse, and Stock Show.** The Grand National is held at the **Cow Palace** (⊠ 2200 Geneva Ave., ☎ 415/469–6000), just south of the city limits in Daly City (from downtown take U.S. 101 south to Bayshore Boulevard south to Geneva Avenue west.)

Soccer

The **San Jose Clash** (☎ 408/985–4625) play Major League Soccer at Spartan Stadium (☞ San Jose *in* Chapter 8).

Tennis

In February, the stars of men's tennis square off at the **Sybase Classic** at the San Jose Arena (☞ San Jose *in* Chapter 8). For individual tickets, call **Ticketmaster** (☎ 415/421–8497); ticket packages are available by calling ☎ 408/223–2121. The **Bank of the West Women's Tennis Tour** visits Palo Alto in the summer. Tickets are available through BASS (☎ 510/762–2277).

BEACHES

San Francisco's beaches are perfect for romantic sunset strolls, but freezing-cold temperatures and treacherous currents make most waters dangerous for swimming. The beach areas are often either foggy or crowded on sunny days. On the positive side, San Francisco's beaches are quite clean and have dramatic natural settings.

Aquatic Park

Nestled in a quiet cove between the lush hills adjoining Fort Mason, the Municipal Pier, and the crowds at Fisherman's Wharf, Aquatic Park has a tiny but sandy beach with gentle water. The distant sound of bongo drums at Fisherman's Wharf adds to the peaceful mood. Keep an eye out for the swim-capped heads of members of the **Dolphin Club** (☎ 415/441–9329), who come every morning for a dip in these ice-cold waters. An especially large and raucous crowd jumps in on New Year's Day.

Baker Beach

Baker Beach is a local favorite, with gorgeous views of the Golden Gate Bridge, the Marin Headlands, and the bay. Its strong waves make swimming a dangerous prospect, but the mile-long shoreline is ideal for fishing, building sand castles, or watching sea lions play in the surf. On warm days the entire beach is packed with bodies (some nude) taking in the sun. Look for Baker Beach in the southwest corner of the Presidio, beginning at the end of Gibson Road, which turns off Bowley Street. The beach has picnic tables, grills, and trails that lead all the way to the Golden Gate Bridge.

China Beach

China Beach was named for the poor Chinese fishermen who once camped here (though it's sometimes marked on maps as James D. Phelan Beach). From April to October the tiny strip of sand offers swimmers gentle waters as well as changing rooms and showers. It's south of Baker Beach and bordered by the gleaming million-dollar homes of the Seacliff neighborhood.

Marin Beaches

The Marin headlands beaches are not safe for swimming. The cliffs are steep and unstable, making falls a constant danger. The Marin coast, however, offers two beaches for picnics and sunning: Muir and Stinson beaches. **Muir Beach** is in a rocky cove—a tiny, picturesque beach that's usually filled with the sounds of playful toddlers and family dogs. Swimming is recommended only at the wide, flat expanse of **Stinson Beach** and only from early May through September, when lifeguard services are provided. If possible, visit these areas during the week. Both beaches are crowded on weekends.

Ocean Beach

South of the Cliff House, Ocean Beach stretches along the western (ocean) side of San Francisco. Though certainly not the city's cleanest beach, it's wide and sandy, stretching for miles and perfect for a long walk or jog. It's popular with surfers, but swimming is not recommended. On summer evenings after sundown, numerous bonfires form a string of lights along the beach; permits are not necessary.

San Mateo County Coast

Less than an hour's drive south on scenic Highway 1 will bring you to the popular, 2-mi-long **Half Moon Bay State Beach** (☞ Half Moon Bay *in* Chapter 7), a picnicker's paradise. After lunch explore the tide pools of **James V. Fitzgerald Marine Reserve** (☎ 415/728–3584), near Montara, a few miles north of Half Moon Bay. Take Highway 92 east over the mountains to I–280 for a faster trip back to the city.

6 SHOPPING

From fringe fashions in the Haight to leather chaps in the Castro, San Francisco's many distinctive neighborhoods offer consumers a bit of everything. There are ginseng health potions in Chinatown, fine antiques and art in Jackson Square, handmade kites and kimonos in Japantown, and bookstores throughout the city specializing in everything from beat poetry to ecology. For those who prefer the mainstream, there are high-end boutiques on Union Street and fine department stores in Union Square.

SHOPPING IN SAN FRANCISCO means much more than driving to the local mall. Major department stores, swank fashion boutiques, discount outlets, art galleries, and specialty stores for crafts, vintage items, and more are scattered among the city's diverse neighborhoods. Most accept at least Visa and Master-Card, and many also accept American Express and Diners Club. Very few accept cash only, and policies vary on traveler's checks. The *San Francisco Chronicle* and *San Francisco Examiner* advertise sales. For smaller shops check the two free weeklies, the *San Francisco Bay Guardian* and *S.F. Weekly,* which can be found on street corners every Wednesday. Store hours vary slightly, but standard shopping times are between 10 and 5 or 6 on Monday, Tuesday, Wednesday, Friday, and Saturday; between 10 and 8 or 9 Thursday; and from noon to 5 on Sunday. Stores on and around Fisherman's Wharf often have longer hours in summer.

Updated by
Denise M. Leto

Major Shopping Districts

The Castro/Noe Valley

The Castro, often called the gay capital of the world, is also a major destination for nongay travelers. The Castro is filled with clothing boutiques, home accessory stores, and various specialty stores.

Especially notable is **A Different Light** (☞ Booksellers, *below*), one of the country's premier gay and lesbian bookstores. **Under One Roof** (⊠ 2362-B Market St., ☎ 415/252–9430), housed in the same building as the Names Project, donates the profits from its home and garden items, gourmet foods, bath products, books, frames, and cards to northern California AIDS organizations.

Just south of the Castro on 24th Street, largely residential Noe Valley is an enclave of gourmet food stores, used-record and -CD shops, clothing boutiques, and specialty gift stores. At **Panetti's** (⊠ 3927 24th St., ☎ 415/648–2414) you'll find offbeat novelty items, whimsical picture frames, journals, and more.

Chinatown

The intersection of Grant Avenue and Bush Street marks the gateway to Chinatown. Here, hordes of shoppers and tourists are introduced to 24 blocks of shops, restaurants, and markets—a nonstop tide of activity. Dominating the exotic cityscape are the sights and smells of food: crates of bok choy, tanks of live crabs, and hanging whole chickens. Racks of Chinese silks, toy trinkets, colorful pottery, baskets, and carved figurines are displayed chockablock on the sidewalks, alongside fragrant herb shops. The **Great China Herb Co.** (⊠ 857 Washington St., ☎ 415/982–2195), where they add up the bill on an abacus, is one of the biggest herb stores around.

Embarcadero Center

Five modern towers of shops, restaurants, offices, and a popular movie theater—plus the Hyatt Regency Hotel—make up the Embarcadero Center, downtown at the end of Market Street. It's one of the few major shopping centers with an underground parking garage.

Fisherman's Wharf

A constant throng of sightseers crowds Fisherman's Wharf, and with good reason: Pier 39, the Anchorage, Ghirardelli Square, and the Cannery are all here, each with shops and restaurants, as well as outdoor entertainment—musicians, mimes, and magicians. Best of all are the wharf's view of the bay and its proximity to cable car lines, which can shuttle shoppers directly to Union Square.

The Haight

Haight Street is a perennial attraction for visitors, if only to see the sign at Haight and Ashbury streets—the geographic center of the Flower Power movement during the 1960s. These days, in addition to ubiquitous tie-dyed shirts, you'll find high-quality vintage clothing, funky jewelry, folk art from around the world, and reproductions of art deco accessories (☞ Vintage Fashion, Furniture, and Accessories, *below*). Used-book stores and used-record stores are another specialty.

Hayes Valley

Hayes Valley, just west of the Civic Center, is packed with art galleries and such unusual stores as **Worldware** (☞ Clothing for Men and Women, *below*), where everything from clothing to furniture to candles is made of organic materials.

Jackson Square

Gentrified Jackson Square is home to a dozen or so of San Francisco's finest retail antiques dealers, many of which occupy elegant Victorian-era buildings (☞ Antique Furniture and Accessories, *below*).

Japantown

Unlike the other ethnic enclaves of Chinatown, North Beach, and the Mission, the 5-acre **Japan Center** (✉ between Laguna and Fillmore Sts. and Geary Blvd. and Post St.) is under one roof. The three-block complex includes an 800-car public garage and three shop-filled buildings. Especially worthwhile are the Kintetsu and Kinokuniya buildings, where shops and showrooms sell cameras, tapes and records, pearls, antique kimonos, *tansu* chests, paintings, and more.

The Marina District

Chestnut Street, one block north of Lombard Street and stretching from Fillmore to Broderick streets, caters to the shopping whims of Marina District residents, many of whom go for specialty foodstuffs.

The Mission

The diverse Mission District, home to large Latino and Asian populations, plus young artists and musicians of all nations, draws bargain hunters with its many used clothing, vintage furniture, and alternative book stores. Shoppers can unwind with a cup of *café con leche* at one of a dozen or so cafés.

North Beach

Sometimes compared to New York City's Greenwich Village, North Beach is only a fraction of the size, clustered tightly around Washington Square and Columbus Avenue. Most of its businesses are small eateries, cafés, and shops selling clothing, antiques, and vintage wares. Once the center of the beat movement, North Beach still has a bohemian spirit that's especially apparent at **City Lights** (☞ Booksellers, *below*), where the beat poets live on.

Pacific Heights

Pacific Heights residents seeking practical services head straight for Fillmore Street between Post Street and Pacific Avenue, and Sacramento Street between Lyon and Maple streets, where private residences alternate with good bookstores, fine clothing and gift shops, thrift stores, and art galleries. A local favorite is the **Sue Fisher King Company** (☞ Housewares and Accessories, *below*), whose quality home accessories fit right into this upscale neighborhood.

South of Market

The gritty warehouse and semi-industrial zone south of Market, often called SoMa, has the lowest prices. Dozens of **discount outlets,** most open daily, have sprung up along the streets and alleyways bordered by 2nd, Townsend, Howard, and 10th streets (☞ Outlets and Discount Stores, *below*). At the other end of the spectrum are the high-class gift shops of the **San Francisco Museum of Modern Art** and the **Center for the Arts Gift Shop** at Yerba Buena Gardens; both sell handmade jewelry and other great gift items (☞ Jewelry and Collectibles, *below*).

SoMa's South Park District, the so-called "Multimedia Gulch," is one of San Francisco's fastest-growing enclaves, home to much of the city's computer software industry, not to mention the 3rd Street offices of *Wired* magazine. Within the last few years the area has seen a proliferation of restaurants, designer boutiques, and specialty shops.

Union Square

Serious shoppers head straight to Union Square, San Francisco's main shopping area and the site of most department stores, including **Macy's, Neiman Marcus,** and **Saks Fifth Avenue** (☞ Department Stores, *below*). Also here are the **Virgin Megastore** (☞ Music, *below*), **F.A.O. Schwarz** and the **Disney Store** (☞ Toys and Gadgets, *below*), and **Borders Books and Music** (☞ Booksellers, *below*). Nearby are the pricey international boutiques of Emporio Armani, Versace, Hermès of Paris, Gucci, Alfred Dunhill, Louis Vuitton, and Cartier, plus a 50,000-square-ft Duty Free Shopping (DFS) Galleria. The streets around Union Square are currently enjoying a building boom, with such heavyweight retailers as Levi's, Old Navy, Prada, and Kenneth Cole scheduled to open soon.

The **San Francisco Shopping Centre** (⊠ 865 Market St., ☎ 415/495–5656), across from the cable car turnaround at Powell and Market streets, is distinguished by spiral escalators that wind up through the sunlit atrium. Inside are more than 35 retailers, including Nordstrom (☞ Department Stores, *below*), as well as a two-floor **Warner Bros.** store (☎ 415/974–5254), with T-shirts, posters, and other mementos of the studio's past and present. At Post and Kearny streets, the **Crocker Galleria** (⊠ 50 Post St., ☎ 415/393–1505) is a complex of 40 or so shops and restaurants that sit underneath a glass dome. The rooftop garden has dizzying views of the hectic streets and sidewalks below.

Union Street

Out-of-towners sometimes confuse Union Street—a popular stretch of shops and restaurants five blocks south of the Golden Gate National Recreation Area—with downtown's Union Square (☞ *above*). Union Street is a tiny, neighborhood version of Union Square. Nestled at the foot of a hill between Pacific Heights and the Marina District, the street is lined with high-end clothing, antiques, and jewelry shops, along with a few art galleries.

Department Stores

Since most of San Francisco's department stores cluster around Union Square and the San Francisco Shopping Centre, shoppers can hit all the major players without driving or walking from one end of town to the other.

Macy's (⊠ Stockton and O'Farrell Sts., ☎ 415/397–3333; ⊠ 835 Market St., ☎ 415/296–4061) two downtown locations are behemoths. One branch—with entrances on Geary, Stockton, and O'Farrell streets—houses the women's, children's, and housewares departments. The men's department occupies its own building across Stockton Street. A branch carrying mostly furniture is just a block away on Market Street, inside the San Francisco Shopping Centre.

Neiman Marcus (⊠ 150 Stockton St., ☎ 415/362–3900), with its Philip Johnson–designed checkerboard facade, gilded atrium, and stained-glass skylight, is one of the city's most luxurious shopping experiences. Although its high-end prices raise an eyebrow or two, its biannual "Last Call" sales—in January and July—draw a crowd.

Nordstrom (⌧ 865 Market St., ☎ 415/243–8500), the store that's known for service, is housed in a stunning building with spiral escalators circling a four-story atrium. Designer fashions, shoes, accessories, and cosmetics are specialties.

Saks Fifth Avenue (⌧ 384 Post St., ☎ 415/986–4300) feels like an exclusive, multilevel mall, with a central escalator ascending past a series of designer boutiques. With its extensive lines of cosmetics and jewelry, this branch of the New York–based store caters mostly to women, though there is a small men's department on the fifth floor. The restaurant, also on the fifth floor, overlooks Union Square.

Outlets and Discount Stores

Christine Foley (⌧ 430 9th St., ☎ 415/621–8126) offers discounts of up to 50% on sweaters for men, women, and children. In the small storefront showroom, pillows, stuffed animals, and assorted knickknacks sell at retail prices.

Cut Loose (⌧ 690 Third St., ☎ 415/495–4581) specializes in loose, flowing casual clothing for women at discounted prices. Cotton and washable wool separates are between 20% and 40% off retail prices. Pick up a free outlet map to SoMa while you're there.

Esprit (⌧ 499 Illinois St., at 16th St., south of China Basin, ☎ 415/957–2550), a San Francisco–based company, makes hip sportswear, shoes, and accessories, primarily for young women and children. Housed in a building as big as an airplane hangar, its bare-bones, glass-and-metallic interior feels somewhat sterile, but discounts of 30% to 70% keep customers happy.

Jeremy's New West (⌧ 2 South Park Rd., ☎ 415/882–4929), at a very fashionable SoMa address, specializes in top-notch merchandise for both men and women, including Prada and Jil Sander, at drastic discounts—sometimes up to 50%.

Loehmann's (⌧ 222 Sutter St., near Union Sq., ☎ 415/982–3215), with its drastically reduced designer labels, is for fashion-conscious bargain hunters. This is not the place to learn who's who in the design world, as labels are often removed, but savvy shoppers will find astounding bargains.

Tower Records Outlet (⌧ 660 3rd St., ☎ 415/957–9660), the city's most prolific record chain, has found a ready-made market in the burgeoning SoMa neighborhood. Always crowded, the outlet has new and used CDs (mostly remainders), videotapes, and magazines at discount prices.

Specialty Stores

Antique Furniture and Accessories

The most obvious place to look for antiques is Jackson Square. Another option is the Design Center in Lower Potrero Hill, where a few retail showrooms are mixed in with those open only to the trade.

Asakichi Japanese Antiques (⌧ 1730 Geary Blvd., ☎ 415/921–2147) carries antique blue-and-white Imari porcelains and handsome *tansu* chests. Upstairs, **Shige Antique Kimonos** (⌧ 1730 Geary Blvd., on Webster St. Bridge between Kinokuniya and Kintetsu Bldgs., ☎ 415/346–5567) has antique hand-painted, silk-embroidered kimonos as well as cotton *yukatas* (lightweight summer kimonos), *obis* (sashes worn with kimonos), and other kimono accessories.

Dragon House (⌧ 455 Grant Ave., ☎ 415/781–2351; ⌧ 315 Grant Ave., ☎ 415/421–3693), unlike many other Chinatown stores that peddle cheap reproductions of Chinese art, sells genuine antiques and Asian fine arts. Its collection of ivory carvings, ceramics, and jewelry dates back 2,000 years and beyond—a fact that's especially evident in their prices.

Hunt Antiques (⌧ 478 Jackson St., ☎ 415/989–9531) feels like an English town house, with fine 17th- to 19th-century period English furniture, porcelains, Staffordshire pottery, and paintings. In the heart of Jackson Square, Hunt is surrounded by other worthwhile shops.

Origins (⌧ 680 8th St., ☎ 415/252–7089), in SoMa's Baker Hamilton Square complex, imports unusual collector's items, Chinese furniture, porcelain, silk, and jade; antiques here are up to 400 years old.

Telegraph Hill Antiques (⌧ 580 Union St., ☎ 415/982–7055), a tiny North Beach shop, stocks paintings and diverse objets d'art, including crystal, cut glass, Victoriana, and bronzes. Among the store's collection of fine china is a nice selection of Wedgwood pieces.

A Touch of Asia (⌧ 1784 Union St., ☎ 415/474–3115) is full of high-end 19th- and 20th-century Asian antiques, mainly from Japan and Korea. Elm and cherrywood furniture, curio cabinets, and chests dominate. The store also carries Asian sculptures, prints and paintings, and antique vases.

Art Galleries

Art galleries are ubiquitous in San Francisco. While most surround Union Square, Hayes Valley near the Civic Center has become another gallery enclave. Pick up a copy of the free *San Francisco Arts Monthly* at the **TIX Bay Area** booth in Union Square (⌧ Stockton St., at Geary St., ☎ 415/433–7827) for listings of galleries throughout the city. For a quick overview, stop by **49 Geary Street,** which houses three of the city's best galleries. Most galleries are closed on Monday.

Art Options (⌧ 372 Hayes St., ☎ 415/252–8334) specializes in contemporary glass crafts and one-of-a-kind nonprecious jewelry from local and nationally known artists. A wide variety of affordable pieces are available.

Fraenkel Gallery (⌧ 49 Geary St., ☎ 415/981–2661), one of the city's preeminent photography galleries, shows 19th-century to contemporary works by local and international artists in exhibits that rotate about once a month.

Hespe Gallery (⌧ 1764 Union St., ☎ 415/776–5918) is filled with paintings and drawings by emerging Bay Area artists. Styles include figurative, abstract, and realist. Owner Charles Hespe is an instantly likable art enthusiast who equally delights buyers and browsers.

San Francisco Women Artists Gallery (⌧ 370 Hayes St., ☎ 415/552–7392), a nonprofit organization, is run and staffed by the women artists whose work is on display. In the tradition of the sketch clubs that began in the 1880s, in which groups of artists shared and critiqued each other's work, the SFWA displays sculptures, paintings, mixed-media pieces, and video installations. All works are juried, and prices are low.

Smile: A Gallery with Tongue in Chic (⌧ 500 Sutter St., ☎ 415/362–3436) has a colorful collection of urban folk art, jewelry, mobiles, contemporary crafts, and wearable art.

Vorpal Gallery (⊠ 393 Grove St., ☎ 415/397–9200), a nationally ac-claimed gallery with a sister store in New York, carries old and new masters (Rembrandt and Picasso, for example), as well as Latin-American art and works by emerging artists.

Beauty

The Beauty Store (⊠ 2124 Fillmore St., ☎ 415/346–2511; ⊠ 3600 16th St., ☎ 415/861–2019; ⊠ 2085 Chestnut St., ☎ 415/922–2526; ⊠ Four Embarcadero Center, ☎ 415/982–5599; ⊠ 1560 Haight St., ☎ 415/552–9696; ⊠ 756 Irving St., ☎ 415/255–8554; ⊠ Stonestown Galleria, ☎ 415/681–0779), a low-key beauty supply chain founded in San Francisco in 1980, carries a large selection of skin- and hair-care products ranging from such traditional names as Aveda and Paul Mitchell to such lesser known, diversity-minded brands as Image. The staff is interested in educating customers about the latest innovations in beauty and skin care and will patiently answer any questions.

Body Time (⊠ 2509 Telegraph Ave., Berkeley, ☎ 510/548–3686; ⊠ 2072 Union St., ☎ 415/922–4076; ⊠ 1932 Fillmore St., ☎ 415/771–2431; ⊠ 1465 Haight St., ☎ 415/551–1070) was founded in Berkeley in 1970 with a focus on premium-quality ingredients in natural perfumes, skin-care products, and aromatherapy products. This local minichain spe-cializes in sustainably harvested essential oils that customers can combine and dilute to create their own personal fragrances. The shop's practice of offering a discount to customers who bring back their empty bottles for a refill reflects its commitment to the environment.

Sephora (⊠ 1 Stockton St., ☎ 415/392–1545), the Paris-based inter-national chain, has brought its unique arrangement of beauty prod-ucts and perfumes to Union Square. Red carpet leads customers through the store's three categories: fragrance, color, and well-being. Sephora's philosophy of ease of use dictates that its products are grouped by func-tion instead of by brand. For example, lipstick is grouped with lipstick and arranged alphabetically by brand. Beyond its utility, the sleek, up-scale shop makes a fun browse.

Booksellers

All the major chains are represented in San Francisco. **Barnes & Noble** (⊠ 2550 Taylor St., ☎ 415/292–6762) is near Fisherman's Wharf. The Union Square branch of **Borders Books and Music** (⊠ 400 Post St., ☎ 415/399–1633) features four floors of books and magazines, topped off by a café where you can browse over a cappuccino. The **Virgin Mega-store** (⊠ 2 Stockton St., ☎ 415/397–4525) has a bookstore with a great selection of popular culture and travel books, as well as a large music department. Beyond the chains and blockbusters, countless small spe-cialty bookstores delight bibliophiles.

Alexander Book Co. (⊠ 50 2nd St., at Market St., ☎ 415/495–2992), with three floors of titles, is stocked with literature, poetry, and chil-dren's books, with a focus on hard-to-find works by men and women of color.

Booksmith (⊠ 1644 Haight St., at Clayton St., ☎ 415/863–8688) is the place to shop for current releases, children's titles, international news-papers, and offbeat periodicals.

Bound Together Anarchist Book Collective (⊠ 1369 Haight St., ☎ 415/431–8355), collectively run since 1976, is an old-school anarchist entity staffed entirely by volunteers, with profits contributed to anar-chist projects. Books and magazines are divided into sections with such headings as Conspiracies, Drugs, Film & Media, Magick & Spirit, and Syndicalist Periodicals. There's also a small Spanish-language section.

City Lights (⌂ 261 Columbus Ave., ☎ 415/362–8193), the city's most famous and historically interesting bookstore, is where the Beat renaissance of the 1950s was born, grew up, flourished, and then faltered. Poet Lawrence Ferlinghetti still remains active in the workings of his wooden three-story building in the heart of North Beach. Best known for poetry, contemporary literature and music, and translations of Third World literature, City Lights also carries books on nature, the outdoors, and travel.

A Clean Well-Lighted Place for Books (⌂ 601 Van Ness Ave., ☎ 415/441–6670), in Opera Plaza, is a great place to while away the hours before or after a performance. Paperback literature and books on opera and San Francisco history are particularly well stocked.

A Different Light (⌂ 489 Castro St., ☎ 415/431–0891), San Francisco's most extensive gay and lesbian bookstore, has books by, for, and about lesbians, gay men, bisexuals, and the transgendered. Subjects run the gamut from sci-fi and fantasy to religion and film criticism. There's also a large magazine section. A Different Light is the Castro's unofficial community center: Residents regularly phone for nonbook information, and a rack in front is chock-full of flyers for local events.

Green Apple Books (⌂ 506 Clement St., ☎ 415/387–2272), a local favorite since 1967, has one of the largest used-book departments in the city as well as new books in every field. Specialties are comic books, a history room, and a rare-books collection. Two doors down, at 520 Clement Street, you'll find a fiction annex which also sells CDs.

Kinokuniya Bookstore (⌂ Kinokuniya Bldg., 1581 Webster St., 2nd Floor, ☎ 415/567–7625), in the heart of the Japan Center, may have the nation's finest selection of English-language books on Japanese subjects. A major attraction is the collection of beautifully produced graphics and art books.

Modern Times Bookstore (⌂ 888 Valencia St., ☎ 415/282–9246), named after Charlie Chaplin's politically subversive film, carries quality literary fiction and nonfiction, much of it with a political bent. It also has a Spanish-language section and a wide variety of magazines. Author readings and public forums are held on a regular basis.

Rand McNally Map & Travel Store (⌂ 595 Market St., ☎ 415/777–3131) will help you get from Tiburon to Tanzania, with an array of travel books and accessories, maps, and gift items. This is a great place to browse for topographical maps of California's national parks.

Stacey's (⌂ 581 Market St., ☎ 415/421–4687) has evolved from purely a professional-books specialist to include a large selection of general-interest books.

Children's Clothing

Dottie Doolittle (⌂ 3680 Sacramento St., ☎ 415/563–3244) is where Pacific Heights mothers buy Florence Eiseman dresses for their little women. Less pricey clothes for boys and girls, from infants to age 14, is also offered.

Mudpie (⌂ 1694 Union St., ☎ 415/771–9262; ⌂ 2220 Chestnut St., ☎ 415/474–8395) is filled with children's special-occasion wear, such as velvet dresses and handmade booties. Quilts, toys, and overstuffed child-size furniture make this a fun store for browsing. The Chestnut Street branch is geared toward tots two years old and younger.

Small Frys (⌂ 4066 24th St., ☎ 415/648–3954), in the heart of Noe Valley, carries a complete range of colorful cottons, mainly for infants but also for older children, including Oshkosh and many California labels.

Yountville (⊠ 2416 Fillmore St., ☎ 415/922–5050), an upscale store for children up to age eight, carries California and European designs.

Clothing for Men and Women

True to its reputation as the most European of American cities, San Francisco is sprinkled liberally with stores that feature traditional and trendy clothes by local designers. Shoppers eager to roam off the beaten track will find plenty of options.

Bella Donna (⊠ 539 Hayes St., ☎ 415/861–7182) offers more than just owner Justine Kaltenbach's self-designed hats. The oversize designer creations of New York's J. Morgan Puett, Los Angeles's Kevin Simon, and other top designers make this shop one of Hayes Valley's treasures. Don't miss the upstairs loft, which stocks only bridal garments.

Designers Club (⊠ 3899 24th St., ☎ 415/648–1057), in Noe Valley, specializes in local and national designers who use natural fibers and luxurious fabrics. In addition to clothing, there's a wide selection of hats and handbags.

Haseena (⊠ 3024 Fillmore St., ☎ 415/775–6539; ⊠ 526 Hayes St., ☎ 415/252–1104) is a fashionable boutique geared toward the urban-chic set. Both outlets sell clothing and accessories for women.

North Beach Leather (⊠ 224 Grant Ave., ☎ 415/362–8300) is one of the city's best sources for high-quality leather garments—skirts, jackets, pants, dresses, and accessories.

Rolo (⊠ 2351 Market St., ☎ 415/431–4545; ⊠ 450 Castro St., ☎ 415/626–7171; ⊠ 1301 Howard St., ☎ 415/861–1999; ⊠ 25 Stockton St., ☎ 415/989–7656) is a San Francisco favorite, with men's and women's designer-brand denim, sportswear, shoes, and accessories that reveal a distinct European influence. The Howard Street location is Rolo's discount outlet.

Solo (⊠ 1599 Haight St., ☎ 415/621–0342) is an opulent space with luxurious women's clothing, much of it designed in-house. One-of-a-kind pieces, custom work, and hard-to-fit sizes are offered along with jewelry, hats, and scarves.

Worldware (⊠ 336 Hayes St., at Franklin St., ☎ 415/487–9030) is San Francisco's most ecologically correct store, featuring men's, women's, and children's clothing made from organic hemp, wool, and cotton. It also carries a potpourri of essential oils, skin care products, and aromatherapy candles.

Gourmet Food

Joseph Schmidt Confections (⊠ 3489 16th St., ☎ 415/861–8682) may not be the city's most famous chocolatier (Ghirardelli wins that prize), but it *is* the classiest. Egg-shape truffles, which come in more than 30 flavors, are Schmidt's best-selling product. The store's real specialty is its stunning array of edible, often seasonal, sculptures—from chocolate windmills to life-size chocolate turkeys. Try the unique line of creme-filled chocolate rounds called slicks.

Just Desserts (⊠ 248 Church St., ☎ 415/626–5774; ⊠ 1000 Cole St., ☎ 415/664–8947; ⊠ 3 Embarcadero Center, ☎ 415/421–1609; ⊠ 836 Irving St., ☎ 415/681–1277; ⊠ 3735 Buchanan St., ☎ 415/922–8675), a Bay Area favorite, carries chocolate velvet mousse cake, almond-flavored chocolate-chip blondies, and other deadly sins.

Lucca Delicatessen (⊠ 2120 Chestnut St., ☎ 415/921–7873) is a bit of old Italy in the upscale Marina District. Take a number and wait your turn to choose from imported olive oils, homemade pastas and

Italian sausages, and a wide selection of imported cheeses and prepared salads.

Molinari Delicatessen (⌷ 373 Columbus Ave., ☎ 415/421–2337), billing itself as the oldest delicatessen west of the Rockies, has been making its own salami, sausages, and cold cuts since 1896. Other homemade specialties include meat and cheese ravioli, tortellini with prosciutto filling, tomato sauces, and fresh pastas.

Real Food Company (⌷ 2140 Polk St., ☎ 415/673–7420; ⌷ 1023 Stanyan St., ☎ 415/564–2800; ⌷ 3939 24th St., ☎ 415/282–9500; ⌷ 3060 Fillmore St., ☎ 415/567–6900), one of the city's most successful health food purveyors, offers some of the freshest produce outside the farmers' markets, as well as a full line of fresh fish, meat, and wines. The Polk Street branch has a small delicatessen.

Handicrafts and Folk Art

Small galleries throughout the city sell crafts, pottery, sculpture, and jewelry from countries around the world.

The Americas (⌷ 1100 Folsom St., ☎ 415/864–4692) is a colorful SoMa outlet featuring such treasures as Pueblo and Navajo pottery, Day of the Dead artifacts, Zuni fetishes, brightly painted furniture, and wood carvings from Oaxaca.

Anokhi (⌷ 1864 Union St., ☎ 415/922–4441), a small and inviting store, stocks clothing, home furnishings, and accessories from India, with fabrics block-printed by hand in Jaipur. You'll also find Indian tea caddies, scarves, and sarongs, as well as some locally made pottery.

Collage (⌷ 1345 18th St., ☎ 415/282–4401) is a Potrero Hill studio-gallery that showcases the work of 80 Bay Area artists, including such handmade crafts as mosaic mirrors, earthquake-proof paper vessels, handblown glass objects, jewelry, and more.

Evolution (⌷ 271 9th St., ☎ 415/861–6665; ⌷ 805 University Ave., Berkeley, ☎ 510/540–1296) carries an unusual selection of furniture from Indonesia and, at its 9th Street store, pillows from Turkey. A wide range of Amish, Shaker, and Arts and Crafts reproduction furnishings can be found in its Berkeley location.

F. Dorian (⌷ 388 Hayes St., ☎ 415/861–3191) has cards, jewelry, and crafts from Mexico, Japan, Italy, Peru, Indonesia, the Philippines, Africa, and Sri Lanka, as well as the glass and ceramic works of local craftspeople.

Folk Art International/Boretti Amber/Xanadu (⌷ 140 Maiden La., ☎ 415/392–9999), three collections in one alluring space, offers a dazzling selection of Baltic amber jewelry, Latin-American folk art, Oaxacan wood carvings, and tribal art from Africa, Oceania, and Indonesia. Carved wood statues preside over a selection of utilitarian and ritual objects, including masks, sculptures, woven baskets, tapestries and textiles, tribal jewelry, and books on art and culture.

Global Exchange (⌷ 4018 24th St., between Noe and Castro Sts., ☎ 415/648–8068; ⌷ 2840 College St., Berkeley, ☎ 510/548–0370), a branch of the well-known nonprofit organization, sells handcrafted items from more than 40 countries. The staff works directly with village cooperatives and workshops: When you buy a Nepalese sweater, a South African wood carving, or a Pakistani cap, employees will explain the origin of your purchase.

Japonesque (⌗ 824 Montgomery St., ☏ 415/391–8860), at Jackson Square, specializes in handcrafted wooden boxes, sculpture, paintings, and handmade glass from Japan and the United States.

Ma-Shi'-Ko Folk Craft (⌗ Kinokuniya Bldg., 1581 Webster St., 2nd Floor, ☏ 415/346–0748) carries handcrafted pottery from Japan, including *mashiko,* the style that has been in production longer than any other. There are also masks and other antique and handcrafted goods, all from Japan.

Polanco (⌗ 393 Hayes St., ☏ 415/252–5753), a gallery that's devoted to showcasing the arts of Mexico, sells everything from antiques to traditional folk crafts to fine contemporary works. Brightly painted animal figures and a virtual village of Day of the Dead figures share space with religious statues and modern linocuts and paintings.

Soko Hardware (⌗ 1698 Post St., ☏ 415/931–5510), run by the Ashizawa family in Japantown since 1925, still specializes in beautifully crafted Japanese tools for gardening and carpentry.

Virginia Breier (⌗ 3091 Sacramento St., ☏ 415/929–7173), a colorful gallery of contemporary and traditional North American crafts, represents mostly emerging artists. Every piece in the store is one-of-a-kind, from jewelry to light fixtures to Japanese *tansus.*

Xela Imports (⌗ 3925 24th St., ☏ 415/695–1323), pronounced "Shay-La," carries merchandise from Africa, central Asia, and Bali, including jewelry, religious masks, fertility statuary, and decorative wall hangings. There are also textiles and jewelry from India.

Housewares and Accessories

Abitare (⌗ 522 Columbus Ave., ☏ 415/392–5800), a popular North Beach shop, has an eclectic mix of goods—soaps and bath supplies, candleholders, artsy picture frames, lamps, and one-of-a-kind furniture.

Biordi (⌗ 412 Columbus Ave., ☏ 415/392–8096), a family-run business for 50 years, imports hand-painted pottery directly from Italy—mainly Tuscany and Umbria—and ships it worldwide. Dishware sets can be ordered in any combination.

de Vera (⌗ 580 Sutter St., ☏ 415/989–0988; ⌗ 29 Maiden La., ☏ 415/788–0828) carries sleek decorative wares by owner and designer Federico de Vera. Both locations are brimming with household accessories and ephemera. The Sutter Street store also carries a line of de Vera's own furniture.

Fillamento (⌗ 2185 Fillmore St., ☏ 415/931–2224), a Pacific Heights favorite, has three floors of home furnishings—from dinnerware to bedding to bath and baby accessories—in addition to home office products. The eclectic mix of styles ranges from classic to contemporary.

Gordon Bennett (⌗ 2102 Union St., ☏ 415/929–1172; ⌗ Ghirardelli Sq., 900 N. Point St., ☏ 415/351–1172) carries housewares and ceramics made by local artists. The artfully designed wrought-iron garden sculptures and furniture, garden tools, and whimsical topiaries will tempt any homemaker.

Gump's (⌗ 135 Post St., ☏ 415/982–1616), in business since 1861, is famous for its Christmas window displays and high-quality collectibles. One of the city's most popular stores for bridal registries, Gump's carries exclusive lines of dinnerware, flatware, and glassware, as well as Asian artifacts, antiques, and furniture.

Maison d'Etre (⌗ 92 South Park, ☎ 415/357–1747), an upscale shopping spot directly across from SoMa's popular Caffe Centro, carries eclectic luxury items for the home, including wrought-iron light fixtures, luxurious pillows, and ornate mirrors.

Only on Castro (⌗ 518-A Castro St., ☎ 415/522–0122) showcases fine furnishings—mostly large pieces—with an international bent, including armoires, chests, and wrought-iron furniture from Malaysia and Indonesia.

Rayon Vert (⌗ 3187 16th St., ☎ 415/861–3516), an artful boutique on the Mission's most stylish stretch of sidewalk, sells refurbished furniture and housewares with a unique rustic look. Items range from imposing armoires in metal and glass to such smaller items as antique candle holders and Christmas ornaments.

Scheuer Linen (⌗ 340 Sutter St., ☎ 415/392–2813), a Union Square fixture since 1953, draws designers and everyday shoppers with luxurious linens for the bed, the bath, and the dinner table.

Sue Fisher King Company (⌗ 3067 Sacramento St., ☎ 415/922–7276; ⌗ 375 Sutter St., ☎ 415/398–2894) offers an assortment of decorative pillows and luxurious throws, Italian dinnerware, fine linens for the bedroom and kitchen, books on gardening and home decoration, and an aromatic mix of soaps, perfumes, and candles. Out back at the Sacramento Street location is a small garden area chock-full of plants.

Terra Mia (⌗ 2122 Union St., ☎ 415/351–2529; ⌗ 4037 24th St., ☎ 415/642–9911) lets shoppers create ceramic pieces using their own designs and the store's art supplies and kiln. Teapots, mugs, goblets, and tiles are among the items that can be fired and ready to use within a week.

Used Rubber U.S.A. (⌗ 597 Haight St., ☎ 415/626–7855; ⌗ 2500 San Pablo Ave., Berkeley, ☎ 510/644–8339) uses recycled bicycle tubes to make handsome-looking handbags, wallets, and day planners. Other ecologically friendly wares include organic cotton clothing colored with natural dyes and housewares made from bicycle parts and computer circuit boards.

Z Gallerie (⌗ 2071 Union St., ☎ 415/346–9000; ⌗ 2154 Union St., ☎ 415/567–4891) carries modern home furnishings and trendy accessories: dinnerware, desks, chairs, lamps, and posters.

Jewelry and Collectibles

Center for the Arts Gift Shop (⌗ 701 Mission St., ☎ 415/978–2710 ext. 168), in Yerba Buena Gardens, carries an outstanding line of handmade jewelry, ceramics, and crafts from both regional and national artists, as well as an unusual selection of glass tableware. Art publications, children's books, T-shirts, and cards top off the inventory.

Enchanted Crystal (⌗ 1895 Union St., ☎ 415/885–1335) has a large collection of glass jewelry, ornaments, and other art pieces, many crafted by Bay Area artists. The store also has one of the largest natural quartz balls in the world—a full 12 inches in diameter.

Jade Empire (⌗ 832 Grant Ave., ☎ 415/982–4498), one of the many fine jewelry stores in Chinatown, has uncut and pre-set jade, diamonds, and other gems as well as freshwater pearls, beads, porcelain dolls, and lanterns.

San Francisco Museum of Modern Art Gift Shop (⌗ 151 3rd St., ☎ 415/357–4035) is famous for its exclusive line of watches and jewelry, as well as its artists' monographs, Picasso dishes, and other dinnerware.

Posters, calendars, children's art-making sets and books, and art books for adults round out the offerings.

Shreve & Co. (⊠ 200 Post St., at Grant Ave., ☎ 415/421–2600), near Union Square, is one of the city's most elegant jewelers and the oldest retail store in San Francisco. Along with gems in dazzling settings, the store carries Baccarat crystal and Limoges porcelain figurines.

Union Street Goldsmith (⊠ 1909 Union St., ☎ 415/776–8048), a local favorite since 1976, prides itself on its wide selection of such rare gemstones as golden sapphires and violet tanzanite. You'll also find black Tahitian South Seas pearls. Three local jewelers work on the premises.

Wholesale Jewelers Exchange (⊠ 121 O'Farrell St., ☎ 415/788–2365), with 28 independent jewelers displaying their own merchandise, is the place to find gems and finished jewelry at less-than-retail prices.

ANTIQUE JEWELRY

Brand X (⊠ 570 Castro St., ☎ 415/626–8908) has vintage jewelry from the early part of the century, including a wide selection of estate jewelry and objets d'art.

Lang Antiques and Estate Jewelry (⊠ 323 Sutter St., ☎ 415/982–2213) carries vintage jewelry and small antique objects, including fine glass, amber, and silver.

Old and New Estates (⊠ 2181-A Union St., ☎ 415/346–7525) has antique and estate jewelry, crystal, objets d'art, antiques, and silver.

BEADS

The Bead Store (⊠ 417 Castro St., ☎ 415/861–7332) has a daunting collection—more than a thousand kinds of strung and unstrung beads, including such stones as lapis and carnelian, Czech and Venetian glass, African trade beads, Buddhist and Muslim prayer beads, and Catholic rosaries. Premade silver jewelry is another specialty, along with religious masks, figurines, and statuary from India and Nepal.

Yone (⊠ 478 Union St., ☎ 415/986–1424), in business since 1965, carries so many types of beads that the owner has lost track—somewhere between 5,000 and 10,000, he thinks. Individual beads, made of glass, wood, plastic, bone, sterling silver, and countless other materials, cost up to $100.

Music

Amoeba (⊠ 1855 Haight St., ☎ 415/831–1200; ⊠ 2455 Telegraph Ave., Berkeley, ☎ 510/549–1125), a longtime Berkeley favorite for new and used CDs, records, and cassettes at truly bargain prices, opened its doors to music-rich Haight Street in 1997. Both locations stock thousands of titles from punk and hip-hop to jazz and classical.

Aquarius Records (⊠ 1055 Valencia St., ☎ 415/647–2272) began as *the* punk rock store in the 1970s. Owner Windy Chien carries on the tradition in the store's swank Mission District space, opened in 1996, which carries a large selection of dance music and experimental electronics.

Reckless Records (⊠ 1401 Haight St., ☎ 415/431–3434) buys and sells rock and indie recordings, with a large section devoted to vinyl. Music-related magazines, T-shirts, and videos are also on sale.

Recycled Records (⊠ 1377 Haight St., ☎ 415/626–4075), a Haight Street landmark, buys, sells, and trades a vast selection of used records, including obscure alternative bands and hard-to-find imports.

Streetlight Records (⊠ 3979 24th St., ☎ 415/282–3550; ⊠ 2350 Market St., ☎ 415/282–8000), a Noe Valley staple since 1973 with a branch on Market Street, buys and sells thousands of used CDs, with an emphasis on rock, jazz, soul, and R&B. There is plenty of vinyl for purists.

Virgin Megastore (⊠ 2 Stockton St., ☎ 415/397–4525), the behemoth of Union Square, has hundreds of listening stations, a separate classical music room, and an extensive laser disc department, as well as a bookstore and a café overlooking Market Street.

Paper and Postcards

FLAX (⊠ 1699 Market St., near Valencia St., ☎ 415/552–2355), an art supply giant in mid-Market, gets the creative juices flowing. In addition to cards and handmade paper, FLAX features one-of-a-kind photo albums and journals (and everything you'll need to create your own), artist-made ribbon and boxes, and inspiring doodads for kids.

Kozo (⊠ 1969 Union St., ☎ 415/351–2114) brings the art of papermaking to new levels. In addition to specialty papers made of materials like bark, papyrus, and bird's nest, Kozo imports hand-silk-screened papers directly from Japan, Korea, and Italy. Also for sale are handbound photo albums and journals.

Quantity Postcard (⊠ 1441 Grant Ave., ☎ 415/986–8866) has a formidable collection of about 15,000 postcards, as well as autographed rock-concert posters by famed local artist Frank Kozik.

Sporting Goods

G & M Sales (⊠ 1667 Market St., ☎ 415/863–2855), a local institution since 1948, has one of the city's best selections of camping gear, with dozens of pitched tents on display, not to mention outerwear, hiking boots, ski goods, and fishing gear.

Lombardi's (⊠ 1600 Jackson St., ☎ 415/771–0600) has been serving its devoted clientele since 1948, with sports clothes and equipment, outerwear, camping goods, fitness equipment, and athletic footwear. Merchandise is discounted on a regular basis. Ski rentals are also available.

Niketown (⊠ 278 Post St., at Stockton St., ☎ 415/392–6453) is more a glitzy multimedia extravaganza than a sporting goods store, but it's still the best place in town to find anything and everything with that famous swoosh.

North Face (⊠ 180 Post St., ☎ 415/433–3223; ⊠ 1325 Howard St., ☎ 415/626–6444), a Bay Area–based company, is famous for its top-of-the-line tents, sleeping bags, backpacks, and outdoor apparel, including stylish Gore-Tex jackets and pants. The Howard Street store, an outlet, sells overstocked and discontinued items along with occasional seconds.

Patagonia (⊠ 770 N. Point St., near Fisherman's Wharf, ☎ 415/771–2050) specializes in technical wear for serious outdoors enthusiasts. Along with sportswear and casual clothing, the store carries body wear for backpacking, fly-fishing, kayaking, and the like.

Toys and Gadgets

ATYS (⊠ 2149-B Union St., ☎ 415/441–9220), with its roly-poly vases and corkscrew people, adds humor and design savvy to practical tools. ATYS imports whimsical gadgets for the home and office from Scandinavia, Italy, Germany, and Japan.

The **Disney Store** (⊠ 400 Post St., ☎ 415/391–6866; ⊠ Pier 39, ☎ 415/391–4119), with its colorful walls and gargoyle-shape pillars, sells a potpourri of books, toys, clothing, and Disney collectibles. You'll also find Disney-oriented table- and glassware for sale.

F.A.O. Schwarz (✉ 48 Stockton St., ☎ 415/394–8700), the San Francisco branch of the famed American institution, is every child's dream, with games, stuffed toys, motorized cars, model trains, and more.

Imaginarium (✉ 3535 California St., ☎ 415/387–9885; ✉ 3251 20th Ave., at the Stonestown Galleria, ☎ 415/566–4111), a California-based company, manufactures its own learning-oriented games and gadgets and imports European brands rarely found in larger stores.

Kitty Katty's (✉ 3804 17th St., ☎ 415/864–6543) is where toy designer Flower Frankenstein works behind the counter to create wildly whimsical toys for "people old enough to know better." Thrill to the sight of an Elvis impersonator doll, squeeze a Squeaky Tiki Charm, and admire the changing displays of art and prints by local artists.

Sanrio (✉ 39 Stockton St., ☎ 415/981–5568) is devoted to pop icon Hello Kitty and all her friends. You'll find a plethora of items ranging from lunch boxes to huge plush toys here.

Sharper Image (✉ 532 Market St., ☎ 415/398–6472; ✉ 680 Davis St., at Broadway, ☎ 415/445–6100; ✉ Ghirardelli Sq., 900 N. Point St., ☎ 415/776–1443) carries high-end gadgets that bring out the child in everyone. Marvel over five-language translators, super-shock-absorbent tennis rackets, state-of-the-art speaker systems, Walkman-size computers, digital cameras, and more.

Uncle Mame (✉ 2241 Market St., ☎ 415/626–1953) is a shrine to late 20th-century American pop culture. From cereal boxes to action figures, there's a collectible here for the kid inside every shopper.

Vintage Fashion, Furniture, and Accessories

FASHION

American Rag (✉ 1305 Van Ness Ave., ☎ 415/474–5214) stocks a huge selection of new and used men's and women's clothes from the United States and Europe, all in excellent shape. They also carry shoes and such accessories as sunglasses, hats, belts, and scarves.

Buffalo Exchange (✉ 1555 Haight St., ☎ 415/431–7733; ✉ 1800 Polk St., ☎ 415/346–5726), part of a national chain, is one of the few stores where you can trade your used clothes for theirs. A wide selection of Levi's, leather jackets, sunglasses, and vintage lunch boxes are among the offerings. Some new clothes are available as well.

Crossroads Trading Company (✉ 1901 Fillmore St., ☎ 415/775–8885; ✉ 2231 Market St., ☎ 415/626–8989) buys, sells, and trades men's and women's new and used clothing, some of it vintage. Used contemporary sportswear is the specialty. Ties, belts, hats, and purses are also in stock.

Held Over (✉ 1543 Haight St., ☎ 415/864–0818) carries an extensive collection of clothing, accessories, shoes, handbags, and jewelry from the 1940s, '50s, and '60s.

Rosalie's New Look (✉ 782 Columbus Ave., ☎ 415/397–6246), in North Beach, has a huge selection of wigs and a full-service salon that specializes in '60s updos and extensions. The staff is friendly and happy to let shoppers try on as many wigs as they please.

FURNITURE AND ACCESSORIES

Another Time (✉ 1586 Market St., ☎ 415/553–8900), an art deco–lover's delight, carries furniture and accessories by Heywood Wakefield and others. It's conveniently close to a host of other stores that stock vintage collectibles.

Cinema Shop (⊠ 606 Geary St., ☎ 415/885–6785), a tiny storefront, is jammed with more than 250,000 original posters, stills, lobby cards, and rare videotapes of Hollywood classics and schlock films.

Revival of the Fittest (⊠ 1701 Haight St., ☎ 415/751–8857) carries reproductions of such antique collectibles as clocks and vases along with cards, calendars, clothing, and jewelry.

San Francisco Rock Art and Collectibles (⊠ 1851 Powell St., ☎ 415/956–6749) takes you back to the 1960s with a huge selection of rock-and-roll memorabilia, including posters, handbills, and original art. Also available are posters from more recent shows—many at the legendary Fillmore Auditorium—with such musicians as George Clinton, Porno for Pyros, and Johnny Cash.

The Schlep Sisters (⊠ 4327 18th St., near Castro St., ☎ 415/626–0581) stocks secondhand American dinnerware and glass, as well as such 1950s home accessories as cookie jars and salt-and-pepper shakers.

Zonal (⊠ 568 Hayes St., ☎ 415/255–9307; ⊠ 2139 Polk St., ☎ 415/563–2220), in the newly gentrified Hayes Valley, looks like an old garage, and the sign on the window reads ALWAYS REPAIR, NEVER RESTORE. The specialty here is Depression-era American country furniture—vintage porch gliders bump up against gardening equipment and old croquet sets. The Polk Street store specializes in larger furniture items, linens, and rugs.

Wine and Spirits

Ashbury Market (⊠ 205 Frederick St., at Ashbury St., ☎ 415/566–3134), a quirky neighborhood-market-gone-upscale, is a new entry in the address books of the city's serious wine lovers. Eos (☞ Wine Bars *in* Chapter 4) wine buyer, Debbie Zacharias, stocks the shelves with an eclectic variety of wines, emphasizing California's Rhône-style producers. Ashbury Market also offers fine foods.

K&L Wine Merchants (⊠ 766 Harrison St., ☎ 415/896–1734), a spacious, well-stocked, and reasonably priced showroom, has a friendly staff that promises not to sell what they don't taste themselves.

Mr. Liquor (⊠ 250 Taraval St., ☎ 415/731–6222), in the city's Sunset District, is the only place to find well-known Bay Area importer Kermit Lynch's line of wines. It also has afternoon tastings: A sample of six to eight wines costs around $10.

PlumpJack Wines (⊠ 3201 Fillmore St., ☎ 415/346–9870), a Marina favorite, has a well-priced, well-stocked array of hard-to-find California wines, along with a small selection of imported wines. You'll also find gift baskets here.

The **Wine Club** (⊠ 953 Harrison St., ☎ 415/512–9086) is nothing much to look at, but it makes up for its bare-bones feel with a huge selection of wines at some of the best discount prices in the city. There's also a wide variety of wine paraphernalia, including glasses, books, openers, and decanters, along with caviar and cigars.

Wine House Limited (⊠ 535 Bryant St., ☎ 415/495–8486) is a throwback to a different age: A highly informed and friendly sales staff is willing to help you find the perfect wine for any occasion. This SoMa store has especially good burgundy, Bordeaux, and Rhône selections and a small but well-chosen assortment of California wines, all at reasonable prices.

7 SIDE TRIPS FROM SAN FRANCISCO

One of San Francisco's best assets is its surroundings. To the north is idyllic Marin County, home to Mediterranean-style waterfronts, redwood-shaded communities, and vast parklands. To the east are Berkeley and Oakland—one a colorful university town and the other a multifaceted port. South of the city are Silicon Valley and the peninsula, where cattle ranches and California mission architecture coexist with modern industry. Point your car north, east, or south, and you're bound to discover what makes the Bay Area such a coveted place to live.

MARIN COUNTY

Sausalito

Updated by
Chris Baty and
Sharon Silva

SAUSALITO'S BOUGAINVILLEA-COVERED hillsides, expansive yacht harbor, and aura of an artists' colony makes it feel like a resort on the Adriatic. Luckily you don't need a passport or an airplane ticket to enjoy Sausalito's superb views and laid-back charm. The town rests on the bay less than 10 mi north of San Francisco and is easily accessible by ferry. Mild weather encourages strolling and outdoor dining, although morning fog and afternoon winds can roll over the hills from the ocean, funneling through the central part of town once known as Hurricane Gulch.

Like much of San Francisco, Sausalito had a raffish reputation before it went upscale. Discovered in 1775 by Spanish explorers and named Sausalito (Little Willow) for the trees growing around its springs, the town served as a port for whaling ships during the 19th century. By the mid-1800s wealthy San Franciscans were making Sausalito their getaway across the bay. They built lavish Victorian summer homes in the hills, many of which still stand today. In 1875 the railroad from the north connected with ferryboats to San Francisco, bringing the merchant and working classes with it. This influx of hard-working, funloving folk polarized the town into "wharf rats" and "hill snobs," and the waterfront area grew thick with saloons, gambling dens, and bordellos. Bootleggers flourished during Prohibition, and shipyard workers swelled the town's population during the 1940s.

Sausalito developed its bohemian flair in the 1950s and '60s, when a group of artists, led by a charismatic Greek portraitist named Varda, established an artists' colony and a houseboat community here. Since then Sausalito has also become a major yachting center, and restaurants attract visitors for fresh seafood as well as spectacular views. The town remains friendly and casual, although summer traffic jams can fray nerves. If possible, visit on a weekday—and take the ferry.

Snaking between the bay and the hills is **Bridgeway,** Sausalito's main thoroughfare, crowded with shops, restaurants, and people. South on Bridgeway, toward San Francisco, an esplanade along the water is lined with restaurants on piers, all with picture-perfect views of the bay. Stairs along the west side of Bridgeway climb the hill to wooded neighborhoods filled with both opulent and rustic homes.

NEED A
BREAK?

Judging by the crowds gathered outside **Hamburgers** (⊠ 737 Bridgeway, ☎ 415/332–9471), you'd think someone was juggling flaming torches out front. They're really gaping at the juicy hamburgers sizzling on a rotating grill. Brave the line (it moves fast), get your food to go, and head for the esplanade to enjoy the sweeping views and the tastiest burger this side of the Golden Gate Bridge.

The handkerchief-size park in the center of town is the landmark **Plaza Viña del Mar,** named for Sausalito's sister city in Chile. The park has a fountain and two somber 14-ft-tall elephant statues created for the 1915 Panama-Pacific International Exposition in San Francisco.

On the waterfront, between the Hotel Sausalito and the Sausalito Yacht Club, is an unusual historic landmark—a **drinking fountain** inscribed with HAVE A DRINK ON SALLY. It's in remembrance of Sally Stanford (no relation to the university), the former San Francisco madam who later became the town's mayor. Although, as suggested by a sidewalk-level bowl that reads, HAVE A DRINK ON LELAND, the fountain may actually be in remembrance of her dog.

The **Village Fair** (⊠ 777 Bridgeway, ☎ 415/332–1902) is a four-story former warehouse that's been converted into a warren of clothing, crafts, and gift boutiques. Crafts workers often demonstrate their talents in the shops, and a brick walkway lined with leafy plants connects various levels. On the top floor, **Café Sausalito** (☎ 415/332–6579) serves sandwiches and coffee to patrons enjoying the views of San Francisco and Angel Island. Next door to the café are the **visitor center** (☞ Marin County Essentials, *below*) and a pictorial display on Sausalito's colorful history.

The **Sausalito Art Festival** (☎ 415/332–3555), held during Labor Day weekend, attracts more than 50,000 visitors to the northern waterfront area; ferry service to Sausalito is extended during the festival.

The U.S. Army Corps of Engineers uses the **Bay Model,** a 400-square-ft replica of the entire San Francisco Bay and the San Joaquin–Sacramento River delta, to reproduce the rise and fall of tides, the flow of currents, and the other physical forces at work on the bay. The model is housed in a former World War II shipyard building, along with a display on shipbuilding history. At the same site is the *Wapama,* a hulking World War I–era steam freighter being restored by volunteers. ⊠ *2100 Bridgeway, at Marinship Way,* ☎ *415/332–3871.* ⊡ *Free.* ☉ *Labor Day–Memorial Day, Tues.–Sat. 9–4; Memorial Day–Labor Day, Tues.–Fri. 9–4 and weekends 10–6.*

Some of the 400 **houseboats** that make up Sausalito's floating homes community line the shore of Richardson Bay. The sight of these colorful, quirky abodes is one of Marin County's most famous views. For a close-up view of the houseboats, head north on Bridgeway from downtown, turn right on Gate 6 Road, and park where it dead-ends at the public shore.

☾ The **Bay Area Discovery Museum** fills five former military buildings with entertaining and enlightening hands-on exhibits. Kids and their families can fish from a boat at the indoor wharf, explore the skeleton of a house, and make multitrack recordings. From San Francisco take the Alexander Avenue exit from U.S. 101 and follow signs to East Fort Baker. ⊠ *557 McReynolds Rd., at East Fort Baker,* ☎ *415/487–4398.* ⊡ *$7.* ☉ *Summer, Tues.–Sun. 10–5; fall–spring, Tues.–Thurs. 9–4 and Fri.–Sun. 10–5.*

Dining and Lodging

$$$ ✕ **Mikayla at Casa Madrona.** Although the food at this longtime Sausalito hilltop dining room (reached by elevator and then a flower-decked walkway) has followed a rocky course, the view is superb. The California menu is based on grilled fish and meats treated simply but elegantly. Bamboo furniture and handsome animal designs on the walls give the space a tropical feel. The Sunday buffet brunch with champagne is popular. ⊠ *801 Bridgeway,* ☎ *415/331–5888. Reservations essential weekends. AE, D, DC, MC, V. No lunch.*

$$ ✕ **Alta Mira.** This Sausalito landmark, in a Spanish-style hotel a block above Bridgeway, has spectacular views of the bay from both the heated front terrace and the windowed dining room. It's a favored destination Bay Area–wide for Sunday brunch (try the famed eggs Benedict and Ramos Fizz), alfresco lunch, or cocktails at sunset. Though the California-Continental cuisine is forgettable, the view never fails. ⊠ *125 Bulkley Ave.,* ☎ *415/332–1350. AE, DC, MC, V.*

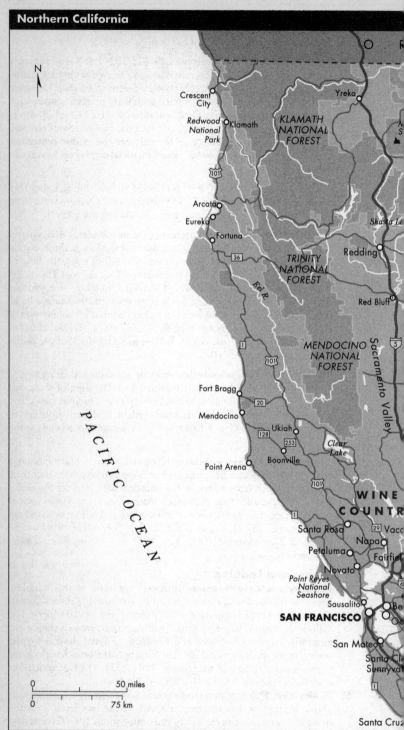

N

Crescent City

Redwood National Park

Klamath

KLAMATH NATIONAL FOREST

Yreka

Shasta L

Arcata

Eureka

Fortuna

Redding

Eel R.

TRINITY NATIONAL PARK

Red Bluff

Sacramento Valley

MENDOCINO NATIONAL FOREST

Fort Bragg

Mendocino

Ukiah

Clear Lake

Boonville

Point Arena

WINE COUNTR

PACIFIC OCEAN

Santa Rosa

Napa

Vac

Petaluma

Fairfie

Novato

Point Reyes National Seashore

Sausalito

Be

SAN FRANCISCO

O

San Mateo

Santa Cl

Sunnyva

50 miles

75 km

Santa Cruz

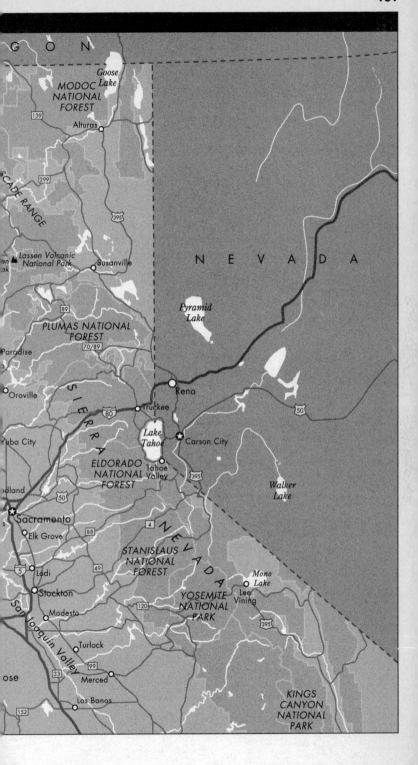

O R E G O N

Goose
Lake

MODOC
NATIONAL
FOREST

139

Alturas

SCADE RANGE

299

395

Lassen Volcanic
National Park

Susanville

N E V A D A

89

PLUMAS NATIONAL
FOREST

Paradise

70/89

Pyramid
Lake

Oroville

SIERRA

80

Truckee

Reno

50

Yuba City

Lake
Tahoe

Carson City

ELDORADO
NATIONAL
FOREST

Tahoe
Valley

395

odland

50

Walker
Lake

Sacramento

Elk Grove

88

4

NEVADA

5

Lodi

49

STANISLAUS
NATIONAL
FOREST

Stockton

Mono
Lake

Modesto

YOSEMITE
NATIONAL
PARK

Lee
Vining

120

395

Turlock

ose

33

99

Merced

152

Los Banos

San Joaquin Valley

KINGS
CANYON
NATIONAL
PARK

The Bay Area

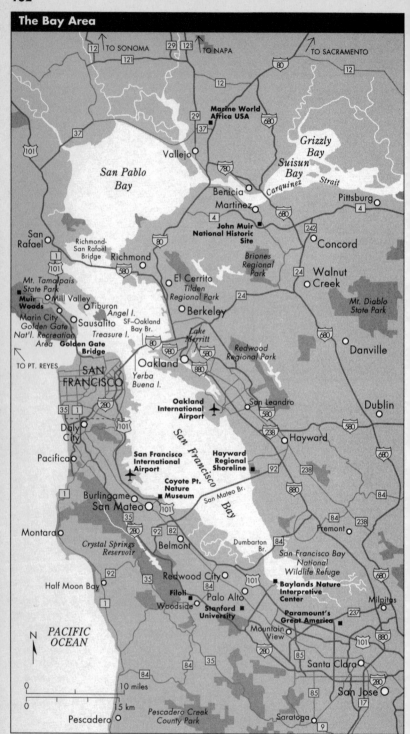

TO SONOMA
TO NAPA
TO SACRAMENTO

Marine World
Africa USA

Grizzly
Bay

Suisun
Bay

Vallejo

San Pablo
Bay

Benicia
Martinez
Carquinez Strait
Pittsburg

John Muir
National Historic
Site

Concord

San
Rafael

Richmond-
San Rafael
Bridge

Richmond

Briones
Regional
Park

Walnut
Creek

Mt. Tamalpais
State Park

El Cerrito
Tilden
Regional Park

Mt. Diablo
State Park

Muir
Woods

Mill Valley

Tiburon

Berkeley

Angel I.

Marin City
Golden Gate
Nat'l. Recreation
Area

Sausalito

SF–Oakland
Bay Br.

Treasure I.

Lake
Merritt

Redwood
Regional Park

Danville

Golden Gate
Bridge

TO PT. REYES

SAN
FRANCISCO

Oakland

Yerba
Buena I.

Dublin

Daly
City

Oakland
International
Airport

San Leandro

Hayward

Pacifica

San Francisco
International
Airport

San Francisco Bay

Hayward
Regional
Shoreline

Coyote Pt.
Nature
Museum

San Mateo Br.

Montara

Burlingame
San Mateo

Fremont

Crystal Springs
Reservoir

Belmont

Dumbarton
Br.

San Francisco Bay
National
Wildlife Refuge

Half Moon Bay

Redwood City

Baylands Nature
Interpretive
Center

PACIFIC
OCEAN

Filoli

Palo Alto

Milpitas

Woodside

Stanford
University

Paramount's
Great America

N

Mountain
View

10 miles

Santa Clara

15 km

San Jose

Pescadero

Pescadero Creek
County Park

Saratoga

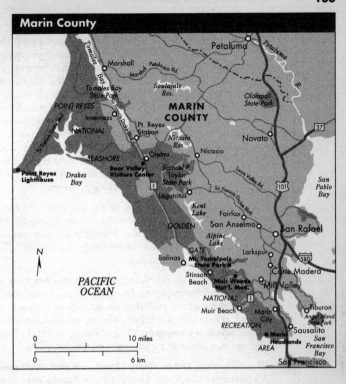

Marin County

$$ ✕ **Spinnaker.** Spectacular bay views are the prime attraction in this contemporary building on a point beyond the harbor near the yacht club—but diners can fuel up on a passable menu of homemade pastas and various seafood specialties as they gaze out at the remarkable scene. You might find a stately pelican perched on one of the pilings outside. ⊠ *100 Spinnaker Dr.,* ☎ *415/332–1500. AE, DC, MC, V.*

$–$$ ✕ **Christophe.** Small and very French, this charming dining room is one of the few bargains in town. The early bird dinners, which change seasonally, are a penny pincher's delight. A four-course meal costs no more than two admissions to a first-run movie, and the choices include such irresistible plates as duck confit, lamb fillet with port wine sauce, and chocolate profiteroles. Prices rise reasonably as the night goes on. ⊠ *1919 Bridgeway,* ☎ *415/332–9244. MC, V. Closed Mon. No lunch.*

$ ✕ **Lighthouse Café.** This inexpensive coffee shop serves breakfast and lunch—omelets, sandwiches, and burgers—every day from 6:30 (7 on weekends). Most find the down-to-earth atmosphere and simple fare—Danish meatballs, herring, and salmon open-face sandwiches—a welcome break from tourist traps and seafood extravaganzas. ⊠ *1311 Bridgeway,* ☎ *415/331–3034. Reservations not accepted. No credit cards.*

$$$ ⌂ **Hotel Sausalito.** Soft yellow, green, and orange tones create a warm, Mediterranean feel at this well-run inn decorated with handmade furniture and tasteful original art and reproductions. The rooms, some of which have harbor or park views, range from small ones that are good for budget-minded travelers to commodious suites. Continental breakfast is included. ⊠ *16 El Portal,* ☎ *415/332–0700 or 888/442–0700,* FAX *415/332–8788. 14 rooms, 2 suites. In-room data ports, no-smoking rooms, concierge. 2-night minimum on weekends. AE, DC, MC, V.*

Tiburon

Updated by
Chris Baty and
Sharon Silva

On a peninsula called Punta de Tiburon (Shark Point) by the Spanish explorers, this beautiful Marin County community maintains a villagelike atmosphere despite the ever-growing encroachment of commercial establishments concentrated in the downtown area. The harbor faces Angel Island across Raccoon Strait, and San Francisco is directly south, 6 mi across the bay—which makes the view from the decks of restaurants on the harbor a major attraction. Slightly more low-key than Sausalito, Tiburon has centered around the waterfront ever since the town's incarnation in 1884, when ferryboats from San Francisco connected here with a railroad to San Rafael. Whenever the weather is pleasant and particularly during the summer, the ferry is the most relaxing way to visit and avoid traffic and parking problems.

Tiburon's **Main Street** is lined on the bay side with restaurants with outdoor decks that jut out over the harbor, giving diners a bird's-eye view of San Francisco. Sunday brunch is popular here. On the other side of the narrow street are shops and galleries that sell casual clothing, jewelry, posters, and paintings.

At the end of the block, Main Street turns into **Ark Row,** a tree-shaded walk lined with antiques and specialty stores. Look closely, and you'll see that some of the buildings are actually old houseboats that once floated in Belvedere Cove before being beached and transformed into stores. **Windsor Vineyards** (⊠ 72 Main St., ☎ 415/435–3113) has free tastings in a converted 19th-century rooming house.

The stark-white **Old St. Hilary's Landmark and Wildflower Preserve,** a Victorian-era Carpenter Gothic church barged over from Strawbery Point in 1957, stands overlooking the town from its hillside perch. Operated by the Landmarks Society, the church is surrounded by a wildflower preserve that is spectacular in May and June, when the rare black jewel flower is in bloom. ⊠ *Esperanza St. off Mar West St.,* ☎ *415/435–2567.* ⌦ *Suggested $2 donation.* ⊙ *Apr.–Oct., Wed. and Sun. 1–4.*

In a wildlife sanctuary on the route into Tiburon is the 1876 **Lyford House,** a Victorian fantasy complete with period decor and furniture. Visitors to the house should make a point of sticking around for the Audubon Society's program on area birds, held on the grounds; call in advance for specific times. ⊠ *376 Greenwood Beach Rd., off Tiburon Blvd.,* ☎ *415/388–2524.* ⌦ *Suggested $2 donation.* ⊙ *Nov.–Apr., Sun. 1–4.*

Dining

$$–$$$ ✕ **Tutto Mare Ristorante.** With stunning views of the bay, Tutto Mare is a bustling outpost of Italian cuisine—more rustic than refined—with an emphasis on seafood. Downstairs, a wood-burning oven ensures crisp-crust pizzas, while upstairs an exhibition kitchen turns out grilled fish, meats, and fowl, and house-made pastas. The floor-to-ceiling windows on the second floor look out on a heated outdoor deck that is crowded with diners on mild days and evenings. Although the food and service can be inconsistent, the view is guaranteed to satisfy. ⊠ *9 Main St.,* ☎ *415/435–4747. AE, DC, MC, V.*

$$ ✕ **Guaymas.** This festive Mexican restaurant claims a knockout view of the bay, handsome whitewashed adobe walls, tile floors, and a heated terrace bar that serves a margarita to match the best Tijuana has to offer. The large open kitchen churns out a long list of such authentic Mexican dishes as seviche, *carnitas ropa* (slowly roasted pork with salsa and black beans), mesquite-grilled fish, and tamales. Sunday brunch is popular, so reserve in advance. ⊠ *5 Main St., at the ferry terminal,* ☎ *415/435–6300. DC, MC, V.*

$ ✕ **Sam's Anchor Cafe.** Sam's is a major draw for tourists and old salts who flock to its outside deck for bay views and beer. A college hangout since 1921, the informal restaurant has mahogany wainscoting and old photos on the walls. Crayons and a color-in menu cater to children. Burgers, sandwiches, soups, and salads are standards, but the food pales next to the atmosphere here. Stick to the simpler dishes. The pastas and seafood dishes are forgettable. Watch for the low-flying gulls. They know no restraint. ⊠ *27 Main St.,* ☎ *415/435–4527. AE, D, DC, MC, V.*

$ ✕ **Sweden House Bakery & Café.** This dollhouselike painted-wood café is a cozy place for pastries and coffee, breakfast, or sandwiches (chicken salad with walnuts and Swedish meat loaf are good choices). A morning order of the delicious Swedish pancakes with lingonberries may prompt you to book a flight to Stockholm. The secluded deck outside is nice on sunny days, although a sign warns, PLEASE WATCH YOUR FOOD OR THE BIRDS WILL EAT IT. ⊠ *35 Main St.,* ☎ *415/435–9767. Reservations not accepted. MC, V. No dinner.*

Mill Valley

Updated by
Chris Baty and
Sharon Silva

Shaded by dense redwood groves, Mill Valley has an idyllic, woodsy location and a friendly, neighborhood mood. Big-name attractions here are few. People come to enjoy the town's leisurely pace, to browse through the stores, or just to lose themselves in the misty confines of the surrounding forest. Lying at the base of Mt. Tamalpais, the Bay Area's tallest mountain, Mill Valley is virtually surrounded by parklands and traversed by creeks and streams. If it weren't for its very American coffee bars, organic food stores, and New Age establishments, this could be a village in Europe.

Mill Valley's rustic village flavor is no modern conceit but a holdover from the town's early days as a logging camp. In 1896 the Mill Valley and Mt. Tamalpais Scenic Railroad, "the crookedest railroad in the world," began transporting visitors from Mill Valley to the top of Mt. Tam and down to Muir Woods, and the town soon became a vacation retreat for joyriding city slickers. The trains stopped running in the 1940s, but you can still see the old railway depot, now transformed into the popular Depot Bookstore & Cafe.

The small **downtown area,** no more than five blocks square, is a collection of small, somewhat pricey boutiques selling everything from gourmet cookware to lacy pajamas. In the center of it all is Lytton Square, at the corner of Miller and Throckmorton avenues, where locals and visitors congregate on weekends to socialize in the many surrounding coffeehouses.

To see one of the many outdoor oases that make Mill Valley so appealing, follow Throckmorton Avenue a quarter mile south from Lytton Square to **Old Mill Park,** a shady patch of redwoods that shelters a playground, a reconstructed sawmill, and a replica passenger car from the Mt. Tam railway. From the park, Cascade Drive winds its way past creek-side homes to the trailheads of several forest paths.

NEED A
BREAK?

The central spot for people-watching, book browsing, and coffee sipping is the **Depot Bookstore & Cafe** (⊠ 87 Throckmorton Ave., ☎ 415/ 383–2665), in the center of Lytton Square. Built in 1924, the building originally served as the depot for the Mt. Tam railway, as evidenced by its tall arched windows and unique design.

Dining

$$ ✕ **Buckeye Roadhouse.** The atmosphere here is a blast from the past with a '90s twist: mahogany paneling, huge stone fireplace, hunting-lodge decor, and a view of Richardson Bay. Traditional American fare, prepared with a modern hand, includes crisp onion rings with house-made ketchup, baby back ribs with garlic mashed potatoes, and lemon pudding cake. Although the bar and dining room are usually jammed with diners, the service is generally first-rate. ⊠ *15 Shoreline Hwy., Mill Valley,* ☎ *415/331–2600. D, DC, MC, V.*

$$ ✕ **Frantoio.** Late fall into early winter—the time of the olive harvest—is just the time to visit this unique trattoria, whose dining room is dominated by an authentic olive oil mill. Here is the opportunity to taste freshly pressed olive oil in a salad, drizzled over pizza, or as a dip for bread. The sight of the great granite grinding stones at work is a marvel—and certainly worth a visit. ⊠ *152 Shoreline Hwy.,* ☎ *415/289–5777. AE, MC, V.*

$–$$ ✕ **Gira Polli.** Rosemary-laced roast chicken is the specialty here, slowly spun on a monumental Italian-imported rotisserie over an aromatic wood fire. The crisp-skinned birds come with herb-dusted roast potatoes and bread. Consider starting your meal with a salad of sliced tomatoes and milky fresh mozzarella, and capping if off with a wedge of lemony cheesecake. If the dining room is crowded, takeout is encouraged. ⊠ *590 E. Blithedale Ave.,* ☎ *415/383–6040. MC, V. No lunch.*

$–$$ ✕ **Thep Lela.** All the Thai classics are here—curries in a rainbow of colors; lemongrass-scented chicken soup; fish cakes dotted with green beans; and noodles tossed with bean sprouts. Be prepared for a wait. ⊠ *411 Strawberry Village,* ☎ *415/383–3444. MC, V. No lunch Sun.*

The Marin Headlands

Updated by
Chris Baty

The term "Golden Gate" may now be synonymous with the world-famous bridge, but it originally referred to the grassy, poppy-strewn hills flanking the passageway into San Francisco Bay. To the north side of the gate lie the Marin Headlands, part of the Golden Gate Recreation Area and home to the most dramatic scenery in the area. If you've just come from the enclosed silence of the nearby redwood groves, you'll be struck by the headlands' raw beauty. Windswept hills plunge down to the ocean, and creek-fed thickets shelter swaying wildflowers.

Photographers flock here for shots of the city, with the Golden Gate Bridge in the foreground and the city skyline on the horizon. Equally remarkable are the views north along the coast and out to sea, where the Farallon Islands are visible on clear days. The headlands are the only break in the Coast Range Mountains, providing access to the ocean for the rivers of California's 400-mi-long Central Valley.

The headlands' strategic position at the mouth of the bay made them a logical site for World War II military installations. Today you can explore the crumbling concrete batteries where naval guns once protected the approaches from the sea. For a look at a more recent episode in the area's military history, head to the now-defunct **Nike Missile Site** above Fort Barry, the only one remaining in the United States. The site is open on weekdays from 12:30 to 3:30, giving visitors a firsthand view of menacing Hercules missiles and missile-tracking radar. On the first Sunday of each month informative tours are conducted at both the missile site and the military barracks at Fort Cronkhite.

The headlands' main attractions are centered around Forts Barry and Cronkhite, which lie just across Rodeo Lagoon from each other. Fronting the lagoon is Rodeo Beach, a dark stretch of sand that attracts sand-castle builders and dog lovers. The **Marin Headlands Vis-**

itor Center (⊠ Fort Barry, Field and Bunker Rds., Bldg. 948, 94965, ☎ 415/331–1540) sells a useful guide to historic sites and wildlife and has exhibits on the area's history and ecology.

Most visitors only come for the day, but hearty types can take advantage of any of the 15 **campsites** (☎ 415/331–1540 for reservations) that dot the headlands. An alternative is the excellent **Marin Headlands Hostel** (☎ 415/331–2777), which houses visitors in the old military infirmary.

★ At the end of Conzelman Road is the **Point Bonita Lighthouse,** a recently restored beauty that is still guiding ships to safety with its original 1855 refractory lens. Half the fun of a visit is the half-mile walk from the parking area down to the lighthouse, which takes you through a rock tunnel and across a suspension bridge. Signposts along the way detail the bravado of surfmen, as the early lifeguards were called, and the tenacity of the "wickies," the first keepers of the light. ⊠ *End of Conzelman Rd.* ☜ *Free.* ⊗ *Weekends 12:30–3:30.*

The **California Marine Mammal Center** (☎ 415/289–7325) at Fort Cronkhite rehabilitates sick and injured seals and sea lions. You can visit the center and its very vocal patients daily from 10 to 4.

Craggy **Hawk Hill** is the best place on the West Coast to watch the migration of eagles, hawks, and falcons as they fly south for the winter. As many as a thousand have been sighted in a single day. The viewing area is about 2 mi up Conzelman Road from U.S. 101; look for a Hawk Hill sign. In September and October, on rain- and fog-free weekends at noon, you'll find the folks from the Golden Gate Raptor Observatory (☎ 415/331–0730) at the hill giving lectures about the birds.

Muir Woods

Updated by
Chris Baty and
Sharon Silva

One hundred and fifty million years ago ancestors of redwood and sequoia trees grew throughout the United States. Today the *Sequoia sempervirens* can be found only in a narrow, cool coastal belt from Monterey to Oregon. **Muir Woods National Monument,** 17 mi northwest of San Francisco, is a 550-acre park that contains one of the most majestic redwood groves in the world. Some redwoods in the park are nearly 250 ft tall and 1,000 years old. This grove was saved from destruction in 1905. Three years later it was named after naturalist John Muir, whose environmental campaigns helped to establish the National Park system. His response: "This is the best tree-lover's monument that could be found in all of the forests of the world. Saving these woods from the ax and saw is in many ways the most notable service to God and man I have heard of since my forest wandering began."

Muir Woods is a pedestrian's park; no cars are allowed in the redwood grove itself. Beginning from the park headquarters, a 2-mi, wheelchair-accessible **loop trail** crosses streams and passes ferns and azaleas, as well as magnificent stands of redwoods. Among the most famous are **Bohemian Grove** and the circular formation called **Cathedral Grove.** On summer weekends the trail is lined with visitors oohing and ahhing in a dozen languages about the trees. If you'd prefer a little more serenity, the challenging **Dipsea Trail** climbs west from the forest floor to soothing views of the ocean and the Golden Gate Bridge.

The weather in Muir Woods is usually cool and often wet, so dress warmly and wear shoes appropriate for damp trails. No picnicking or camping is allowed, and pets are not permitted. The park is open daily from 8 until sunset. Parking can be difficult here, so try to come early in the morning or late in the afternoon. The **Muir Woods Visitor Cen-**

ter has a wide selection of books and exhibits on redwood trees and the history of Muir Woods. ⊠ *Panoramic Hwy. off Hwy. 1,* ☏ *415/ 388–2595,* ✉ *$2.* ☉ *Daily 8 AM–sunset.*

Dining

$–$$ ✕ **Pelican Inn.** Hearty English fare—from fish-and-chips to prime rib and Yorkshire pudding—is served with a fine selection of imported beers and ales in this supremely inviting inn. Old farm tools hang above a large open hearth in the wood-paneled dining room, and the bar has the convivial ambience of a Tudor-style pub in the Cotswolds. Join in a game of darts to further the mood. ⊠ *10 Pacific Way, Muir Beach (off Hwy. 1),* ☏ *415/383–6000. MC, V. Closed Mon. except to guests at the inn.*

$ ✕ **Sand Dollar.** This is the only bar in town, so you're sure to meet lots of locals lingering inside by the fire on foggy days or out on the deck when the sun breaks through. It has an all-American menu: burgers and fries, salads, and sandwiches for lunch; fresh fish and pastas for dinner; and a dastardly mud pie for dessert. Sunny Sunday lunchtimes are like impromptu parties. ⊠ *3458 Hwy. 1, Stinson Beach,* ☏ *415/ 868–0434. MC, V.*

Mt. Tamalpais State Park

Updated by
Chris Baty

Although the summit of Mt. Tamalpais is less than ½ mi high, the mountain rises practically from sea level, dominating the topography of Marin County. About 18 mi northwest of San Francisco and adjacent to Muir Woods National Monument, Mt. Tamalpais affords views of the entire Bay Area and the Pacific Ocean to the west. For years this 6,300-acre park has been a favorite destination for hikers. There are more than 50 mi of trails, some rugged but many developed for easy walking through meadows, grasslands, and forests and along creeks. Mt. Tam, as it's called by locals, is also the reputed birthplace of mountain biking, as evidenced by the many Spandex-clad bikers whizzing down the park's winding roads.

The park's major thoroughfare, the **Panoramic Highway,** snakes its way up from U.S. 101 to the Pantoll Ranger Station (☞ Marin County Essentials, *below*) before dropping down to the town of Stinson Beach. Pantoll Road branches off the Panoramic Highway at the ranger station, connecting up with Ridgecrest Boulevard. Along these roads are numerous parking areas, picnic spots, scenic overlooks, and trailheads.

The **Mountain Theater,** also known as the Cushing Memorial Theater, is a natural amphitheater just off Ridgecrest Boulevard. Constructed in the 1930s, the theater has enough terraced stone seats for 3,750 people. Every May and June such popular plays as *The Music Man* and *My Fair Lady* attract hundreds of locals who tote overstuffed picnic baskets up the short trail to the theater.

The Rock Spring Trail starts at the Mountain Theater and gently climbs about 1¾ mi to the **West Point Inn,** once a stop on the Mt. Tam railroad route. Relax at a picnic table and stock up on water before forging ahead to Mt. Tam's Middle Peak, about 2 mi uphill.

Starting from the Pantoll Ranger Station, the precipitous **Steep Ravine Trail** brings you past stands of coastal redwoods and in the springtime, numerous small waterfalls. Take the connecting Dipsea Trail to reach the town of Stinson Beach and its swath of golden sand. If you're too weary to make the 2½-mi trek back up, Golden Gate Transit Bus 63 will carry you from Stinson Beach back to the ranger station.

Point Reyes National Seashore

Updated by
Chris Baty and
Sharon Silva

A triangular peninsula jutting out into the Pacific, **Point Reyes** is the only national seashore on the West Coast and one of the Bay Area's most spectacular treasures. When Francis Drake sailed down the California coast in 1579, he missed the Golden Gate and San Francisco Bay, but he did land at what he described as a convenient harbor, now thought to be Drake's Bay. Today Point Reyes's rolling hills and dramatic cliffs attract other kinds of explorers: hikers, whale-watchers, and solitude seekers.

The **Bear Valley Visitors Center** houses some fine exhibits on park wildlife and the evocative *Enchanted Shore* slide show. Rangers provide information on beaches, whale-watching, hiking trails, and backcountry camping. A ½-mi path from the visitors center leads to **Kule Loklo,** a brilliantly reconstructed Miwok Indian village that sheds light on the daily lives of the region's first inhabitants. ⊠ *Bear Valley Rd. west of Hwy. 1,* ☎ *415/663–1092.* ⊡ *Free.* ⊙ *Weekdays 9–5, weekends 8–5.*

You'll experience the diversity of Point Reyes's ecosystems on the scenic **Coast Trail,** which starts just outside the nearby town of Bolinas, at the Palomarin Trailhead. From here it's a 3-mi trek through eucalyptus groves and pine forests and along seaside cliffs to beautiful Bass Lake. On hot summer days you'll find locals from the nearby town of Bolinas making use of the *Tarzan*-esque rope swing. To reach the Palomarin Trailhead, take Bolinas–Olema Road toward Bolinas, follow signs to the Point Reyes Bird Observatory, and then continue until the road dead-ends.

The **Point Reyes Lighthouse,** in operation since December 1, 1870, is one of the park's premier attractions. The lighthouse originally cast a rotating beam lit by four wicks that burned lard oil. Keeping the wicks lit and the lens free of soot in Point Reyes's perpetually foggy climate was a constant struggle that reputedly drove the early attendants to alcoholism and insanity. On busy whale-watching weekends (late December–March), parking at the forged-iron-plate lighthouse may be restricted by park staff; on these days buses ($3) shuttle visitors to the lighthouse. If you don't want to walk down—and up—the 308 steps, you may want to skip the descent to the lighthouse itself (the whales are also visible from the cliffs above the lighthouse), but the view from the bottom is worth the effort. Wildlife enthusiasts should make a stop at Drake's Beach (watch for signs) on the way to the lighthouse. A colony of elephant seals established themselves here in 1997 and their numbers have been growing ever since. The lighthouse lies 22 mi from the Bear Valley Visitor Center at the end of the point, a scenic 45-minute drive over rolling hills dotted with old cattle ranches. ☎ *415/669–1534.* ⊡ *Free.* ⊙ *Thurs.–Mon. 10–4:30, except in very windy weather.*

Just off the southern end of Point Reyes, the tiny town of **Bolinas** wears its '60s idealism on its sleeve, attracting potters, poets, and peace lovers to its quiet streets. The main thoroughfare, Wharf Road, looks like a hippie-fied version of Main Street U.S.A. A funky gallery, a general store selling organic produce, a café, and an offbeat saloon line the street. Although privacy-seeking locals have torn down signs to the town, Bolinas isn't difficult to find: Heading north from Stinson Beach on Highway 1, make a left at the first road just past the Bolinas Lagoon (Bolinas–Olema Road) and then turn left at the stop sign.

OFF THE
BEATEN PATH

AUDUBON CANYON RANCH – Here budding ornithologists have the chance to view the nests of great blue herons and egrets. Five miles of hiking trails crisscross the 1,000-acre bird sanctuary off the marshy Bolinas Lagoon. There is also a small museum with displays on local geology and natural history. ⊠ *4900 Hwy. 1, north of Stinson Beach,* ☎ *415/868–9244.* ⊇ *$10 suggested donation.* ⊙ *Mid-Mar.–mid-July, weekends and holidays 10–4.*

Dining

$$–$$$ ✕ **Manka's.** Regional cuisine emphasizing fresh fish and game is served with style in this renovated 1917 hunting lodge. Candlelight, handsome wood-paneled walls, and a large fireplace provide a wonderful setting for dinner. In 1998 chef Derek Burns, late of San Francisco's celebrated (and now closed) Vertigo restaurant, took over the kitchen here, making a trip to West Marin an even more intriguing dining adventure. ⊠ *30 Callendar Way, at Argyll Way, Inverness,* ☎ *415/669–1034. AE, MC, V. Closed Tues.–Wed. (except Jan.–Feb., closed Sun.–Thurs.) No lunch.*

$–$$ ✕ **Station House Cafe.** In good weather hikers fresh from the park fill the adjoining garden to enjoy alfresco dining. Local ingredients dominate the menu. Steamed mussels, grilled salmon, and barbecued oysters are all predictable hits. ⊠ *11180 Hwy. 1, Point Reyes Station,* ☎ *415/663–1515. MC, V.*

Marin County Essentials

Arriving and Departing

BY BUS

Golden Gate Transit buses (☎ 415/923–2000) travel to Sausalito, Tiburon, and Mill Valley from 1st and Mission streets and from other points in San Francisco. For Mt. Tamalpais State Park, take Bus 20 to Marin City; in Marin City transfer to Golden Gate Transit Bus 63 (weekends and holidays only) to reach the park.

San Francisco Muni Bus 76 (☎ 415/673–6864) runs hourly from 4th and Townsend streets to the Marin Headlands Visitor Center on Sunday and holidays only. The trip takes 45 minutes one-way.

BY CAR

Take U.S. 101 north across the Golden Gate Bridge. For Sausalito, take the first exit, Alexander Avenue, just past Vista Point; follow signs to Sausalito and then go north on Bridgeway to the municipal parking lot near the center of town. For Tiburon, exit at Tiburon Boulevard. For Mill Valley, exit at East Blithedale, continue west on East Blithedale to Throckmorton Avenue, and turn left to reach Lytton Square. All three trips take from 30 to 45 minutes one-way, depending on traffic.

The Marin Headlands are a logical stop en route to Sausalito, but reaching them can be tricky. After exiting on Alexander Avenue, take the first left turn through a tunnel under the highway and look for signs to Fort Barry and Fort Cronkhite. Conzelman Road follows the cliffs that face the ocean; Bunker Road is a less spectacular inland route through Rodeo to Fort Barry and Fort Cronkhite.

For Muir Woods and Mt. Tamalpais, take the Highway 1–Stinson Beach exit off U.S. 101 and follow Highway 1 west and then north. Both trips may take from 45 minutes to over an hour, depending on traffic; allow plenty of extra time on summer weekends.

BY FERRY

Golden Gate Ferry (☎ 415/923–2000) crosses the bay to Sausalito from the south wing of the Ferry Building at Market Street and the Embarcadero; the trip takes 30 minutes. **Blue and Gold Fleet** ferries (☎ 415/705–5555) depart daily for Sausalito and Tiburon from Pier 41 at Fisherman's Wharf. Commuter ferries also depart to Tiburon weekdays only from the Ferry Building. The trip to Sausalito takes 30 minutes. Direct ferries travel to Tiburon in 20 minutes, but those making multiple stops can take up to an hour. The **Angel Island–Tiburon Ferry** (☎ 415/435–2131) sails from Tiburon across the strait to Angel Island, daily April–September and weekends October–March.

Guided Tours
Gray Line (☎ 415/558–9400), **Blue and Gold Fleet** (☎ 415/705–5555), and **Great Pacific Tour Co.** (☎ 415/626–4499) all offer excursions to Muir Woods, also stopping in Sausalito.

Visitor Information
Mill Valley Chamber of Commerce (✉ 85 Throckmorton Ave., 94941, ☎ 415/388–9700). **Sausalito Visitor Center** (✉ 777 Bridgeway, 94965, ☎ 415/332–0505). **Tiburon Peninsula Chamber of Commerce** (✉ 96-B Main St., 94920, ☎ 415/435–5633).

THE EAST BAY

Berkeley

Updated by
Chris Baty and
Sharon Silva

Although the **University of California** dominates Berkeley's history and contemporary life, the university and the town are not synonymous. The city of 100,000 facing San Francisco across the bay has other interesting attributes. Berkeley is culturally diverse and politically adventurous, a breeding ground for social trends, a continuing bastion of the counterculture, and an important center for Bay Area writers, artists, and musicians. Some longtime residents will point out that the city has lost its renegade '60s spirit, but most visitors will still be struck by Berkeley's liberal bent and the way it embraces all things offbeat.

Named for George Berkeley, an Irish philosopher and clergyman who crossed the Atlantic to convert Native Americans to Christianity, Berkeley grew with its university. The state legislature chartered the school in 1868 as the founding campus of the state university system and established it five years later on a rising plain of oak trees split by Strawberry Creek. Frederick Law Olmsted, who designed New York's Central Park, proposed the first campus plan. University architects over the years have included Bernard Maybeck as well as Julia Morgan, who designed Hearst Castle at San Simeon. The central campus occupies 178 acres, bound by Bancroft Way to the south, Hearst Avenue to the north, Oxford Street to the west, and Gayley Road to the east. With more than 30,000 students and a full-time faculty of 1,400, the University of California is one of the nation's leading intellectual centers and a major site for scientific research.

The **Berkeley Visitor Information Center** (✉ University Hall, Room 101, University Ave. and Oxford St., ☎ 510/642–5215) is the starting point for weekday 1½-hour student-guided tours of the campus. On weekends the tours leave from Sather Tower. More than 50 **cafés** surround the campus—without which the city might very well collapse. Students, faculty, and other Berkeley residents spend hours nursing coffee concoctions of various persuasions while they read, discuss, and debate—or eavesdrop on others doing the same. Northwest of campus, **Walnut Square** houses upscale boutiques and restaurants at Shattuck and Vine streets. Around the corner is Chez Panisse Café (☞ Dining, *below*), the culinary mecca at the heart of what is locally known as the Gourmet Ghetto, a three-block stretch of specialty shops and eateries. South of campus, along College Avenue near Ashby Avenue, the area known as **Elmwood** has many shops for browsing. Shingled houses line the tree-shaded streets near College and Ashby avenues. You can see hillside homes with spectacular views on the winding roads near the intersection of

Ashby and Claremont avenues. At the opposite side of the city, on **4th Street** north of University Avenue, an industrial area has been converted into a pleasant shopping street with a few popular eateries, several trendy home furnishings stores, and a couple of shops selling handcrafted and ecoconscious goods. Those looking for inexpensive lodging should investigate **University Avenue,** west of campus. The area is noisy, congested, and somewhat dilapidated, but rooms are plentiful.

Telegraph Avenue is Berkeley's student-oriented thoroughfare and the best place to get a dose of the city's famed counterculture. On any given day you might encounter a troop of chanting Hare Krishnas or a naked man walking down the street. Telegraph is first and foremost a place for shopping and socializing. Cafés, bookstores, poster shops, and street vendors line the avenue. T-shirt vendors and tarot card readers come and go on a whim, but a few establishments are neighborhood landmarks. **Cody's Books** (Number 2454) is one of the best bookstores in a city that reveres them. **Moe's Books** (Number 2476) carries a huge selection of used titles. **Amoeba Music** (Number 2455) has one of the Bay Area's largest and cheapest selections of new and used CDs and tapes. **Rasputin Music** (Number 2401) offers good prices on new CDs and a wide selection of used ones. Allen Ginsberg wrote his acclaimed poem *Howl* at **Caffe Mediterraneum** (Number 2475), a relic of '60s-era café culture.

Numbers in the text correspond to numbers in the margin and on the Berkeley map.

1 **Sproul Plaza,** just inside the U.C. Berkeley campus at Telegraph Avenue and Bancroft Way, was the site of several free speech and civil rights protests in the '60s. Today a lively panorama of political and social activists, musicians, and students show off Berkeley's flair for the bizarre. Preachers orate atop milk crates, amateur entertainers bang on makeshift drum sets, and protesters distribute leaflets on everything from marijuana to the Middle East.

2 **Sather Tower,** the campus landmark popularly known as the Campanile, can be seen for miles. The 307-ft structure was modeled on St. Mark's Tower in Venice and completed in 1914. The carillon is played weekdays at 7:50, noon, and 6, Saturday at noon and 6, and for an extended 45-minute concert Sunday at 2. Take the elevator 175 ft up to the observation deck for a view of the campus and a close-up look at the iron bells, which weigh up to 10,500 pounds. ☎ *$1.* ☉ *Mon.–Sat. 10–3:30, Sun. 10–1:45.*

3 The **Phoebe Hearst Museum of Anthropology,** in Kroeber Hall, has a collection of more than 4,000 artifacts, only a small fraction of which are on display at any time. Changing exhibits may cover the archaeology of ancient America or the crafts of Pacific Islanders. ☎ *510/642-3681.* ☎ *$2.* ☉ *Wed.–Sun. 10–4:30, Thurs. until 9.*

4 The **U.C. Berkeley Art Museum** houses a surprisingly interesting collection of works spanning five centuries, with an emphasis on contemporary art. Changing exhibits line the spiral ramps and balcony galleries. Don't miss the series of vibrant paintings by abstract expressionist Hans Hofmann. On the ground floor, the **Pacific Film Archive,** offers programs of historic and contemporary films. ☎ *2626 Bancroft Way,* ☎ *510/642–0808; 510/642–1124 for film-program information.* ☎ *$6.* ☉ *Wed. and Fri.–Sun. 11–5, Thurs. 11–9.*

5 More than 13,500 species of plants from all over the world flourish in the 34-acre **U.C. Botanical Garden**—thanks to Berkeley's temperate climate. Informative tours of the garden are given weekends at 1:30.

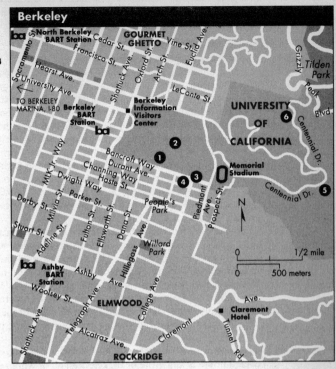

Benches and shady picnic tables make this a relaxing alternative to the busy main campus. ⊠ *Centennial Dr.,* ☎ *510/642–3343.* ⊠ *$3.* ☺ *Daily 9–4:45.*

☾ ➏ The fortresslike **Lawrence Hall of Science,** a dazzling hands-on science center, lets kids look at insects under microscopes, solve crimes using chemical forensics, and explore the physics of baseball. On weekends there are special lectures, demonstrations, and planetarium shows. On clear Saturday nights the museum sets up telescopes on its outdoor plaza for the popular Saturday Night Stargazing from 8 to 11. ⊠ *Centennial Dr.,* ☎ *510/642–5132.* ⊠ *$6.* ☺ *Daily 10–5.*

OFF THE BEATEN PATH	**INDIAN ROCK** – An outcropping of nature in a sea of north Berkeley homes, this is an unbeatable spot for a sunset picnic. Grab a take-out meal on nearby Solano Avenue, then pick up Indian Rock Path where Solano Avenue hits the Alameda. You'll know you've reached the rock when you see amateur rock climbers clinging precariously to its side. At the top you'll join after-work walkers and cuddling couples, all watching the sun sinking beneath the Golden Gate Bridge.

Tilden Park (☎ 510/562–7275), an oasis in the midst of the city, has a botanical garden, an 18-hole golf course, and an environmental education center. You'll find paths and picnic sites on its 2,000 acres. Both kids and kids at heart will love the park's miniature steam trains, pony rides, and the vintage menagerie-style carousel. Swimming is permitted at Lake Anza.

Outdoorsy types will enjoy the **Berkeley Marina,** with its spectacular views of San Francisco and Angel Island (from a ¾-mi wooden pier) and its picnic-friendly grassy expanses. At the northern tip of the marina, the 92-acre **Cesar E. Chavez Park** fills with kite fliers on sunny days. ⊠ *University Ave., ½ mi west of I–80.*

Dining and Lodging

$$–$$$$ ✕ **Chez Panisse Café & Restaurant.** The famed Alice Waters remains
★ the mastermind behind the culinary wizardry at this legendary eatery. In the downstairs restaurant, where formality and personal service create the ambience of a private club, the daily-changing menu is prix fixe and pricey—although the cost is lower on weekdays when four courses rather than five are the rule. Upstairs in the café the atmosphere is informal, the crowd livelier, the prices lower, and both an à la carte and a fixed menu are in force. The food is simpler, too: penne with new potatoes, arugula, and sheep's milk cheese; fresh figs with Parmigiano-Reggiano cheese and arugula; and grilled tuna with savoy cabbage. ⊠ *1517 Shattuck Ave., north of University Ave.,* ☎ *510/548–5525 for restaurant; 510/548–5049 for café. Reservations essential for restaurant. AE, D, DC, MC, V. Closed Sun.*

$$ ✕ **Café Rouge.** After you've finished shopping along upscale 4th Street, take a seat in this spacious two-story bistro, complete with zinc bar, skylights, and festive lanterns. The short, seasonal menu runs the gamut from the sophisticated—salmon with fennel-and-olive compote or oysters on the half shell—to the everyday—spit-roasted chicken or a hamburger topped with cheddar. Begin your meal with the smoked salmon, endive, and Meyer lemon salad or a plate of the house-made charcuterie, and cap it off with the ginger-poached Bosc pear. ⊠ *1782 4th St.,* ☎ *510/525–1440. MC, V. No dinner Mon.*

$$ ✕ **Lalime's.** The Mediterranean food served in this charming, flower-covered house is a favorite of Berkeleyites, all of whom are probably hoping to keep it a secret. Prix fixe and à la carte menus are offered, both of them in constant flux. Choices can range from grilled ahi tuna to creamy Italian risotto to seared duck foie gras. The dining room, on two levels, is done in light colors, creating a cheerful mood that makes this the perfect spot for any special occasion. Add your name to the mailing list and receive the restaurant newsletter, which includes upcoming menus. ⊠ *1329 Gilman St.,* ☎ *510/527–9838. Reservations essential. MC, V. No lunch.*

$$ ✕ **Rivoli.** Husband and wife team Wendy Rucker and Roscoe Skipper use indigenous California ingredients in French- and Italian-inspired dishes for a menu that changes weekly. Typical offerings include linguine with scallops, stuffed pork chops, and a ricotta tart. Desserts can range from a pear granita with gingersnaps to a refreshing Meyer lemon tart. Attentive service adds to the overall appeal, and the lovely garden adds a cheerful note. ⊠ *1539 Solano Ave.,* ☎ *510/526–2542. Reservations essential. AE, MC, V. No lunch.*

$–$$ ✕ **Mazzini.** Simple, unpretentious food is what you'll find in this trattoria outfitted with marble-topped tables and trompe l'oeil murals of Tuscan landscapes. Opened in late 1998 to almost instant acclaim by the same folks who operate Picante Cocina Mexicana (☞ *below*), Mazzini offers a lunch menu of straightforward dishes such as *orecchiette* (ear-shape pasta) with rapini and chili. At dinnertime, the menu expands to include authentic trattoria dishes such as rabbit stuffed with fennel sausage. ⊠ *2826 Telegraph Ave., near Ashby Ave.,* ☎ *415/848–5599. MC, V.*

$ ✕ **Bette's Oceanview Diner.** Buttermilk pancakes that you'll never forget are just one of the specialties at this 1930s-inspired diner, complete with checkered floors and burgundy booths. There are also *huevos rancheros* (Mexican-style scrambled eggs) and lox and eggs for breakfast, and kosher franks and a slew of sandwiches for lunch. The wait for a seat can be long. If you're starving, Bette's To Go, next door, of-

BERKELEY IN THE 1960s: STUDENT ACTIVISM RISES UP

THOSE LOOKING FOR TRACES of Berkeley's politically charged past need go no further than Sather Gate. Both the Free Speech Movement and the fledgling political life of actor-turned-politician Ronald Reagan have their roots here. It was next to Sather Gate, September 30, 1964, that a group of students directly defied the U.C. Berkeley Chancellor's order that all organizations advocating "off campus issues" (e.g., civil rights, nuclear disarmament) keep their information tables off campus. Citation of the tablers brought more than 400 sympathetic students into Sproul Hall that afternoon. They stayed until 3 AM the following morning, setting a precedent of protest that would be repeated in the coming months, with students jamming Sproul Hall in greater numbers each time.

Conservative U.C. president Clark Kerr eventually backed down and allowed student groups to pass out information on campus. By then, the Free Speech Movement had gathered momentum, and the conflict had made a national hero of student leader Mario Savio. Political newcomer Ronald Reagan played on Californians' unease about the unruly Berkeley students in his successful 1966 bid for governor, promising to reign in the "unwashed kooks." Try as he might, the movement continued to grow.

By the end of the 1960s, however, the cohesion of the groups making up the Free Speech Movement had begun to fray. Some members began questioning the efficacy of sit-ins and other nonviolent tactics that had, until then, been the hallmark of Berkeley student protests. The Black Panthers, headquartered just over the border in Oakland, were ascending into the national spotlight, and their "take no prisoners" approach appealed to some of the Berkeley activists who had

seen little come of their efforts to affect national policy.

By 1969 things seemed particularly bleak. Both Robert Kennedy and Martin Luther King Jr. were dead. The student idealism that had worked so well in overpowering administration resistance to free speech on campus seemed powerless to stop the flow of troops heading to Vietnam.

When the university brought in police units to repossess People's Park, a university-owned plot of land at Telegraph Avenue and Haste Street that students and community members had adopted as a park, Berkeley exploded. In the afternoon of May 15, 1969, nearly 6,000 students and residents moved to reclaim the park. In the ensuing riot, police and sheriff's deputies fired both tear gas and buckshot, blinding one observer and killing another. Governor Ronald Reagan, making good on his campaign promises from three years previous, ordered the National Guard into Berkeley. Despite a ban on public assembly, crowds continued to gather and march in the days following the first riot. The park changed hands several times in the following tear gas-filled months, with the fence coming down for final time in 1972.

A LARGE, COLORFUL MURAL on the side of Amoeba Records (at Haste and Telegraph) offers the protestors' version of Park history. Although the area around People's Park and Sather Gate may seem quiet now—with tie-dye T-shirt vendors on Telegraph Avenue providing one of the few visible links to Berkeley's more clamorous past—issues such as affirmative action and tuition fee increases still bring protests to the steps of Sproul.

— Chris Baty

fers takeout. ⊠ *1807 4th St.,* ☎ *510/644–3230. No credit cards. No dinner.*

$ ✕ **Picante Cocina Mexicana.** A no-nonsense, barnlike place, Picante is a find for anyone in search of good Mexican food for a song. The *masa* (flour) is freshly ground for the tortillas and tamales, the salsas are complex, and the combinations are inventive. Try tamales filled with butternut squash and chilies or a simple taco of roasted *poblanos* (peppers) and sautéed onions. Order at the counter and pick up your meal when your number is called. ⊠ *1328 6th St.,* ☎ *510/525–3121. MC, V.*

$$$$ ▥ **Claremont Hotel.** Straddling the Oakland–Berkeley border, the Clare-
★ mont Hotel beckons like a gleaming white castle in the hills. Traveling executives come for the business amenities, including 40 rooms
outfitted with computer terminals, T-1 Internet connections, guest e-
mail addresses, and oversize desks. The Claremont also shines for
leisure travelers, drawing in honeymooners and families alike with its
luxurious suites, therapeutic massages, and personalized yoga work-
outs at the on-site spa. ⊠ *41 Tunnel Rd., at Ashby and Domingo Aves.,
94705,* ☎ *510/843–3000 or 800/551–7266,* ℻ *510/848–6200. 282
rooms. 3 restaurants, 2 bars, in-room data ports, no-smoking floors,
in-room VCRs, 2 pools, spa, dry cleaning, concierge, meeting rooms,
parking (fee). AE, D, DC, MC, V.*

$$$ ▥ **Hotel Durant.** Long the mainstay of parents visiting their children
at U.C. Berkeley, the Hotel Durant is a good option for those who want
to be a short walk from campus and from the restaurants and shops
of Telegraph Avenue. Rooms, accented with dark woods and stately
plaids, are small without feeling cramped. The hotel's bar, Henry's, is
the place for U.C. Berkeley sports fans to congregate after football games.
⊠ *2600 Durant Ave., 94704,* ☎ *510/845–8981,* ℻ *510/486–8336.
140 rooms. Restaurant, bar, no-smoking rooms, room service, laun-
dry service and dry cleaning, business services, meeting rooms, park-
ing (fee). AE, D, DC, MC, V.*

$$–$$$ ▥ **Rose Garden Inn.** The two landmark homes that make up the Rose
Garden Inn were built in the early 1900s by James and John Marshall,
concrete tycoons responsible for laying Berkeley's original sidewalks.
Though the inn has added modern touches to each room (cable tele-
vision and telephones) and grown to incorporate three adjoining homes,
the exquisite feel of a bygone era lingers. Each guest room is unique;
many have fireplaces and some on the upper story come with bay views.
Sale of the property to new owners in 1998 marked a new commit-
ment to refurbish the inn's somewhat worn interior. ⊠ *2740 Telegraph
Ave., 94705,* ☎ *510/549–2145,* ℻ *510/549–1085. 40 rooms. No-smok-
ing rooms, free parking. AE, D, DC, MC, V.*

Oakland

Updated by
Chris Baty and
Sharon Silva

Often overshadowed by San Francisco's beauty and Berkeley's offbeat
antics, Oakland's allure lies in its amazing diversity. Only here can you
find a Nigerian clothing store, a beautifully renovated Victorian home,
a Buddhist meditation center, and a lively salsa club, all within the same
block. Oakland's multifaceted nature reflects its colorful and often tu-
multuous history. Once a cluster of Mediterranean-style homes and gar-
dens that served as a bedroom community for San Francisco, the city
became a hub of shipbuilding and industry almost overnight when the
United States entered World War II. New jobs in the city's shipyards
and factories attracted thousands of new workers, including some of
the first female welders, and the city's neighborhoods became imbued
with a proud but gritty spirit. In the '60s and '70s this intense com-
munity pride gave rise to such militant groups as the Black Panther
Party and the Symbionese Liberation Army but was little match for

the economic hardships and racial tensions that plagued Oakland. In many neighborhoods the reality was wide-spread poverty and gang violence—subjects that dominated the songs of such Oakland-bred rappers as the late Tupac Shakur.

Today Oakland is a mosaic of its past. Affluent types have once again flocked to the city's hillside homes as a warmer and more spacious alternative to San Francisco, while a constant flow of new residents—many from Central America and Asia—ensures continued diversity, vitality, and growing pains. Many neighborhoods to the west and south of downtown remain run-down and unsafe, but a renovated downtown area and the thriving Jack London Square have injected new life into the city. The national visibility from the 1998 election of former California governor Jerry Brown as Oakland mayor further invigorated the city's rising spirits. Despite economic disparities between its separate parts, Oakland is held together by a strong sense of community. Everyday life here centers around the neighborhood, with a main business strip attracting both shoppers and socializers. Some areas, like Piedmont and Rockridge, are perfect places for browsing, eating, or just relaxing between sightseeing trips to Oakland's architectural gems, rejuvenated waterfront, and numerous green spaces.

Numbers in the text correspond to numbers in the margin and on the Oakland map.

★ ❶ One of Oakland's top attractions, the **Oakland Museum of California** is an inviting series of landscaped buildings that display the state's art, history, and natural wonders. The museum is the best possible introduction to a tour of California, and its detailed exhibits can help fill the gaps on a brief visit. The Hall of California Natural Sciences lets you walk through the state's myriad ecosystems, beginning with the screeching gulls and sand dunes of the Pacific Ocean and ending with the coyotes and brush of the Nevada border. A breathtaking film, *Fast Flight,* condenses the trip into five minutes. The museum's rambling Cowell Hall of California History includes everything from Spanish-era armor to a gleaming fire engine that battled the flames in San Francisco in 1906. The Gallery of California Art has an eclectic collection of modern works and early landscapes. Of particular interest are paintings by Richard Diebenkorn, Joan Brown, Elmer Bischoff, and David Park, all members of the Bay Area Figurative School, which flourished here after World War II. The museum also has a bookstore, a pleasant café, and a sculpture garden with a view of the Oakland and Berkeley hills in the distance. ⊠ *1000 Oak St., at 10th St.,* ☎ *510/238-3401.* ⌷ *$6.* ☾ *Wed.–Sat. 10–5, Sun. noon–5.*

❷ A proud reminder of the days when Oakland was a wealthy bedroom community, the **Camron-Stanford House** exudes dignity from its foundation up to its ornate widow's walk. Built in 1876, the Victorian served as the home of the Oakland Museum from 1910 to 1967, and a room containing documents and original artifacts chronicles the museum's history. Six painstakingly redecorated period rooms occupy the upper floor—a tribute to the craftsmanship and dedication that went into the 1978 restoration. ⊠ *1418 Lakeside Dr.,* ☎ *510/836–1976.* ⌷ *$4.* ☾ *Wed. 11–4 and Sun. 1–5.*

❸ **Lake Merritt** is a 155-acre oasis surrounded by parks, with several outdoor attractions on its north side. Joggers and power-walkers charge along the 3-mi path that encircles the lake, and crew teams often glide across the water. Come at sunset to see a string of lanterns create a necklace of golden light along the lakeshore.

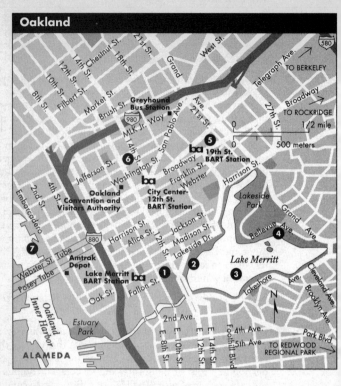

Oakland

4 On the north shore of Lake Merritt, the **Rotary Nature Center and Waterfowl Refuge** is the nesting site of herons, egrets, geese, and ducks in the spring and summer. Migrating birds pass through from September through February, and visitors can watch the birds being fed daily at 3:30 year-round. ⊠ *Perkins St.,* ☎ *510/238–3739.* ☉ *Daily 10–5.*

Given the city's reputation for Victorian and Craftsman homes, visitors to Oakland are generally surprised by the profusion of Art Deco architecture in the downtown neighborhood around the 19th Street BART station. Some of these buildings have fallen into disrepair, but

★ **5** the **Paramount Theatre** (⊠ 2025 Broadway, ☎ 510/465–6400), perhaps the most glorious example of Art Deco architecture in the city if not all the Bay Area, remains open and operating as a venue for concerts and performances of all kinds. For $1 you can take a two-hour tour of the building at 10 AM on the first and third Saturday of each month. When classic films come to the Paramount, the theater recaptures the thrill of movie going in the good old days with a live organ performance, vintage newsreels and cartoons, and the chance to win prizes during the Deco-Win Spin. For performance schedules call the box office or check the free weekly *East Bay Express*.

6 In the midst of Oakland's downtown area, **Preservation Park** is a surprisingly idyllic little business community made up of 14 restored Victorians with tidy, bright green lawns. Wooden benches surrounding a bubbling fountain provide an excellent place to enjoy the architecture and a brief respite from the busy city center.

OFF THE
BEATEN PATH

ELI'S MILE HIGH CLUB – Reputedly the birthplace of West Coast blues, this small, basic club hearkens back to the years just after World War II, when Oakland gave birth to its version of that gritty, hurts-so-bad-I-think-I'm-gonna-die variety of music. Today Eli's continues to bring in live blues bands. A pool table and soul food are additional draws. ⊠ *3629 Martin Luther King Jr. Way,* ☎ *510/655–6661.* 🖅 *$4–$8.* ☉ *Thurs.– Sat. 8 PM–2 AM.*

❼ A former resident of Oakland, Jack London spent many a day boozing and brawling in the waterfront area now called **Jack London Square** (⊠ Embarcadero at Broadway, ☎ 510/814–6000). Home to shops, restaurants, small museums, and historic sites, the square contains a bronze bust of London, author of *The Call of the Wild, The Sea Wolf, Martin Eden,* and other books. The tiny, wonderful **Heinold's First and Last Chance Saloon** (⊠ 56 Jack London Sq., ☎ 510/839–6761), one of London's old haunts, is still serving after 119 years, although it's a little worse for the wear since the 1906 earthquake. London once spent a summer in the nearby **Klondike Cabin,** which was reassembled after being sent from Alaska. Even if you're not a Jack London fan, the square is one of Oakland's livelier areas, particularly on Sunday, when community events like the morning farmers' market take place.

The best local collection of biographical information on Jack London (including letters and photographs) resides in the **History Room** at the Oakland Main Library (⊠ 125 14th St., ☎ 510/238–3222).

Sequoia sempervirens, or coastal redwoods, grow to more than 100 ft tall in **Redwood Regional Park** (☎ 510/562–7275), one of the few spots in the Bay Area that escaped timber-hungry loggers during the 19th century. The park has forested picnic spots and dozens of hiking trails, including the 31-mi **National Skyline Trail,** which links Redwood to four other parks in the Berkeley–Oakland hills. From downtown Oakland take I–580 east toward Hayward, exit at 35th Avenue/MacArthur Boulevard, and then take 35th Avenue east (it will become Redwood Road). Watch for the park entrance on the left, about 3–4 mi down the road.

The upscale neighborhood of **Rockridge** is one of Oakland's most desirable places to live. Explore the tree-lined streets that radiate out from College Avenue just north and south of the BART station for a look at California bungalow architecture at its finest. **College Avenue** is the main shopping strip here. By day it's crowded with shoppers buying fresh flowers, used books, and clothing; by night the same folks are back for dinner and home-brewed ales in the numerous restaurants and pubs. The hub of College Avenue life is **Market Hall** (⊠ 5655 College Ave., ☎ 510/652–4680), an airy European-style marketplace where eight specialty food shops offer everything from Napa Valley wines to garlic goat cheese to organic produce. At the end of College Avenue is the shady campus of the **California College of Arts and Crafts** (⊠ 5213 Broadway Ave., ☎ 510/594–3600). Art students and the general public gather at the college's **Steven Oliver Arts Center**—open weekdays 11 to 5, Wednesday until 9—for cutting-edge exhibits of sculpture, paintings, and mixed media.

Dining and Lodging

$–$$$ ✕ **Oliveto.** Standing smack dab in the heart of Rockridge, this locally renowned restaurant, with respected chef Paul Bertolli at its helm, combines a first-class dining room and casual café. Upstairs, in a sea of subtle Mediterranean tones, diners are treated to imaginative yet restrained Italian cuisine—house-made duck prosciutto, chicken cooked under a brick, swordfish with olives. Downstairs, in the terra-cotta-walled café, everything from an espresso to a pizza to a full-blown Italian meal can be enjoyed at one of the small tables or at the bar. ⊠ *5655 College Ave.,* ☎ *510/547–5356 for restaurant; 510/547–4382 for café. AE, DC, MC, V. No lunch weekends.*

$–$$ ✕ **Autumn Moon Café.** Home-style American café food is served in this friendly spot in a turn-of-the-century house. Enjoy such tantalizing items as roast chicken hash with poached eggs for breakfast, sweet Italian sausage with soft polenta and spinach for lunch, and sea bass with a chipotle-flavored tomato sauce for dinner. A root beer float makes for a delightful finish. ⊠ *3903 Grand Ave.,* ☎ *510/595–3200. MC, V. Closed Mon.*

$ ✕ **Le Cheval Restaurant.** Many Vietnamese restaurants have sprung up in Oakland over the past decade or so, but this is an old favorite of locals and visitors alike. Try the *pho,* Hanoi-style beef noodle soup fragrant with star anise. Less exotic entrées include imperial rolls filled with vegetables and pork, crisp eggy crepes stuffed with shrimp and bean sprouts, or a shrimp and pork salad. At midday, everyone seems to be downing bowls of noodles topped with marinated grilled meats and chili-laced fish sauce. Finish your meal with a Vietnamese-style filtered coffee. ⊠ *1007 Clay St.,* ☎ *510/763–8495. MC, V. No lunch Sun.*

$$$ 🏨 **Clarion Suites Lake Merritt.** Built in 1927, the Clarion Suites was restored in 1992 to its original Mediterranean Art Deco splendor. Hidden behind an unassuming entryway are a stunning lobby and lounge with 16-ft ceilings, mohair and velvet sofas, and walls decorated in period shades of pewter, ivory, cobalt, and crimson. Beyond the lounge lies the Terrace Room, a spacious dining area enclosed on three sides by glass and wrought-iron pillars. The views of Lake Merritt from here are unparalleled. Unfortunately the rooms are less splendid than the lobby and lounge, though many come equipped with kitchenettes, honor bars, and a desk stocked with everything from paper clips to correction fluid. ⊠ *1800 Madison, 94612,* ☎ *510/832–2300,* 𝔽𝔸𝕏 *510/832–7150. 51 rooms. Restaurant, in-room data ports, kitchenettes, no-smoking rooms, laundry service and dry cleaning, business services, meeting rooms, parking (fee). AE, D, MC, V.*

$$$ 🏨 **Waterfront Plaza Hotel.** The waterfront views and Jack London
★   Square's vibrant collection of shops and restaurants make the neighborhood one of the most appealing in Oakland. Yet even without the lively surroundings, this thoroughly modern hotel would rank among the best in the city. Despite its large size, the ever-friendly staff and management put immense effort into making guests' stays comfortable—perks include VCRs, hair dryers, twice-daily housekeeping, and ironing essentials in every room. ⊠ *10 Washington St., in Jack London Square, 94607,* ☎ *510/836–3800 or 800/729–3638,* 𝔽𝔸𝕏 *510/832–5695. 144 rooms. Restaurant, in-room data ports, no-smoking rooms, room service, outdoor pool, exercise room, laundry service and dry cleaning, concierge, business services, meeting rooms, parking (fee). AE, D, DC, MC, V.*

$$ 🏨 **Executive Inn at Embarcadero Cove.** Though north-facing rooms have an unappealing view of the freeway and can be somewhat noisy, the Executive Inn's location between the Oakland airport and downtown Oakland is convenient for travelers who plan to limit their explorations largely to the East Bay. To make up for its removed location, the Executive Inn provides complimentary shuttle service to the Oakland airport, BART stations, and Jack London Square. The generic pastel pink-and-green decor is nothing special, but all rooms on the building's south side have peaceful views overlooking the waters of the Oakland Estuary. ⊠ *1755 Embarcadero (off I–880 at 16th St. exit), 94606,* ☎ *510/536–6633 or 800/346–6331,* 𝔽𝔸𝕏 *510/536–6006. 149 rooms. No-smoking rooms, outdoor pool, outdoor hot tub, exercise room, laundry service and dry cleaning, business services, meeting rooms, airport shuttle, free parking. AE, D, DC, MC, V.*

East Bay Essentials

Arriving and Departing

BY CAR

Take I–80 east across the Bay Bridge. For Berkeley, take the University Avenue exit through downtown Berkeley to the campus or take the Ashby Avenue exit and turn left on Telegraph Avenue to the traditional campus entrance; there is a parking garage on Channing Way. For Oakland, take I–580 off the Bay Bridge to the Grand Avenue exit for Lake Merritt. To reach downtown and the waterfront, take I–980 from I–580 and exit at 12th Street. Both trips take about 30 minutes, longer during rush hour.

BY TRAIN

BART trains (☎ 415/992–2278) make stops in downtown Berkeley and in several parts of Oakland, including Rockridge. Use the Lake Merritt station for the Oakland Museum and southern Lake Merritt, the Oakland City Center–12th Street station for downtown, and the 19th Street station for the Paramount Theater and the north side of Lake Merritt. From the Berkeley (not North Berkeley) station it's a five-minute walk on Center Street to the western edge of campus. Both trips take from 30 to 45 minutes one-way.

Visitor Information

Berkeley Convention and Visitors Bureau (⌂ 2015 Center St., 94704, ☎ 510/549–8710). **Oakland Convention and Visitors Authority** (⌂ 550 10th St., Suite 214, 94607, ☎ 510/839–9000).

THE INLAND PENINSULA

Updated by
Amy
McConnell

Less glamorous than so-called "marvelous Marin" and the bohemian East Bay cities of Berkeley and Oakland, the Inland Peninsula is often passed over by visitors to the Bay Area. Many associate the area with the blandness and urban sprawl that have long been synonymous with Silicon Valley. Such associations are justified only in part. Much of the area between Santa Clara County and San Francisco *is* clogged with modern office complexes and strip-mall shopping centers, but the peninsula also has lovely rolling farmlands, redwood forests, and historic mansions.

Palo Alto is home to Stanford University, which occupies 8,200 acres of former farmland. Downtown, a hub of upscale restaurants and shops cater to a new class of high-tech elite as well as the university crowd. The wealthy residential community of Woodside harbors one of California's few remaining grand country houses, Filoli, as well as countless hiking and biking trails. Throughout the rest of the inland peninsula, former country estates built by the mining and transportation "bonanza kings" of the 19th century lie hidden in the hills, waiting to be discovered by those who care to look.

Much of your first impression of this area will depend on where and when you enter. Take the 30-mi stretch of Highway 101 from San Francisco along the eastern side of the peninsula and you'll see office complex after shopping center after business tower—and you'll likely get caught in horrific morning and evening commuter traffic. On the west side, however, I–280 takes you past picturesque rolling hills, lakes, and reservoirs.

Palo Alto

Palo Alto's main attraction is the Eden-like campus of Stanford University, an 8,200-acre expanse of grass-covered hills that was once part of founder Leland Stanford's farm. Downtown Palo Alto is now a hotbed of trendy restaurants, shops, and attractions catering to the glut of high-income peninsula residents as well as the university crowd. Wander up and down University Avenue and the surrounding side streets and you'll discover Wolfgang Puck's star-studded Spago, the historic Stanford Theatre, a 1920s-style movie palace founded and financed by Hewlett Packard Jr., and even a Barbie Hall of Fame. Just down the road, the Stanford Shopping Center is one of the Bay Area's best. A bit farther afield, the Stanford Linear Accelerator and the Hewlett-Packard garage attract those who hope to learn the secrets of high-tech success by osmosis.

Stanford University, 30 mi south of San Francisco, has its roots among the peninsula's estates. Originally the property was former California governor Leland Stanford's farm for breeding horses. For all its stature as one of the nation's leading universities, Stanford is still known as "The Farm." Founded and endowed by Leland and Jane Stanford in 1885 as a memorial to their son, Leland Jr., who died of typhoid fever, the university opened in 1891. Frederick Law Olmsted conceived the plan for the grounds and Romanesque sandstone buildings, joined by arcades and topped by red-tile roofs. Variations on this style persist in newer buildings, which, along with playing fields, cover about 1,200 acres of the 8,200-acre campus. The center of the university is the inner quadrangle, a group of 12 original classroom buildings later joined by Memorial Church, whose facade and interior walls are covered with mosaics of biblical scenes.

The university is organized into seven schools made up of 70 departments. In addition, there are several institutes on campus, including the Hoover Institution on War, Revolution, and Peace, which is a research center and library. The 285-ft **Hoover Tower** is a landmark and tourist attraction; an elevator ($2) leads to an observation deck that provides sweeping views of the area.

Except for the central cluster of buildings, the Stanford campus is remarkably uncongested—enrollment is only about 14,000—although certain areas, such as the Clock Tower and White Plaza, are a constant stream of students on bicycles and in-line skates. Free one-hour **walking tours** leave daily at 11 and 3:15 from the Visitor Information Center (☎ 650/723–2560 or 650/723–2053) in front of Memorial Hall on Serra Street, opposite Hoover Tower. The main campus entrance, Palm Drive, is an extension of University Avenue from Palo Alto. Lined with majestic palm trees and leading directly to the main quadrangle, this entrance will give you a full perspective of Stanford's unique California mission–Romanesque architecture and its western Ivy League ambience.

★ After a 10-year closure for structural repairs necessitated by the 1989 earthquake, the Stanford Museum, now named the **Iris and B. Gerald Cantor Center for Visual Arts,** is bigger and better than ever. Although it's no longer the world's largest privately owned museum, as it was when it opened in 1894, it is still a major repository for one of the most comprehensive and varied art collections in the Bay Area. Works span the centuries as well as the globe, from pre-Columbian to modern, including the world's largest collection—180—of Rodin sculptures outside of Paris, many of them displayed in the outdoor sculpture garden. (Don't miss the awe-inspiring complete reproductions of the *Gates of Hell.*) Other highlights include a bronze Buddha from the Ming dynasty, wooden masks and carved figurines from 18th- and 19th-century Africa, paintings by Georgia O'Keeffe, and sculpture by Willem de Kooning and Bay Area artist Robert Arneson. ✉ *Lomita Dr. and*

Museum Way, off Palm Dr. at Stanford University, ☎ 650/723–4177.
🖃 *Free.* ⊙ *Wed.–Sun. 11–5, Thurs. until 8. Rodin Sculpture Garden
tours Sat. 11, Sun. 3.*

For a look at some less-traditional art, seek out the inconspicuous **Papua
New Guinea Sculpture Garden,** tucked into a small, heavily wooded
plot of land. The garden is filled with tall, ornately carved wooden poles,
drums, and carved stones—all created on location by 10 artists from
Papua New Guinea who spent six months here in 1994. A Stanford
anthropology professor proposed the idea for the garden. Detailed
plaques explain the concept and the works themselves. ✉ *Santa Teresa
St. and Lomita Dr.* 🖃 *Free.*

"Barbie mimics society. Whatever we've done, she's done," says Eve-
lyn Burkhalter, founder of the **Barbie Hall of Fame.** She's assembled
the largest collection of Barbie dolls on public display in the world,
with 16,000 plastic figures in residence. Don't miss the infamous Talking Math Barbie, who says, "Math is *so hard.*" ✉ *433 Waverly St., at
University Ave.,* ☎ 650/326–5841. 🖃 *$6.* ⊙ *Tues.–Fri. 1:30–4:30, Sat.
10–noon and 1:30–4:30.*

Though it doesn't look like much, the **Hewlett-Packard garage** is a good
place to get a sense of the humble origins of one of the world's largest
technology companies. It all started in this one-car garage, where former Stanford freshman roommates William Hewlett and David Packard
put their heads together back in the 1930s. The rest is history. Today,
the Hewlett-Packard garage is a California State Landmark. ✉ *367
Addison Ave.*

Two-hour tours of the **Stanford Linear Accelerator Center (SLAC)** reveal the workings of the 2-mi-long electron accelerator, which is used
for elementary-particle research. Call for reservations and times. ✉ *Sand
Hill Rd., 2 mi west of main campus,* ☎ 650/926–2204.

Dining and Lodging

$$$–$$$$ ✕ **Spago.** Silicon Valley's best and brightest have made a hit out of
Wolfgang Puck's splashy, dashing Spago. The fare is inventive Cali-
fornian, the service flawless. Flat breads, bread sticks, whole wheat bread,
and a loaf made of scallions and pine nuts will tide you over until the
first course—perhaps Hudson Valley foie gras served with Yukon gold
potatoes and fig marmalade—arrives. Dinner might include barbecued
free-range squab with herbed risotto and caramelized fennel or tamarind-
glazed rack of lamb. The tasty desserts are artistically presented affairs.
✉ *265 Lytton Ave.,* ☎ *650/833–1000. Reservations essential. AE, D,
DC, MC, V. No lunch weekends.*

$$$ ✕ **Zibibbo.** This lively restaurant's eclectic menu includes selections from
★ an oak-fired oven, rotisserie, grill, and oyster bar. Service is family-style,
with large platters placed in the center of the table—all the better to
taste just a bite of the skillet-roasted mussels, Swiss chard tart with goat
cheese and currants, leg of lamb with chickpea–tomato tagine, and more.
The aesthetic is as flashy as the menu. The two-story Victorian house
is full of nooks and crannies. You can sit in the garden, glassed-in atrium,
upstairs loft, or middle dining room, or cozy up to the exhibition
kitchen counter or high-ceilinged bar. ✉ *430 Kipling St.,* ☎ *650/328–
6722. AE, DC, MC, V.*

$$–$$$ ✕ **Crescent Park Grill.** It's a little removed from the liveliest part of Uni-
versity Avenue, but this sophisticated restaurant has a scene of its
own, with jazz on Wednesday and Saturday nights and a big open
kitchen. The imaginative seasonal menu makes choosing difficult. Try
the grilled pork chop with roasted squash, red chard, and balsamic onions
or seared monkfish with crispy potatoes and leeks. Desserts have the

same kind of seasonal appeal. In the fall, you might find warm choco-late soufflé cake with dried cherry-zinfandel sauce. ⊠ *546 University Ave.,* ☎ *650/326–0111. AE, MC, V. Closed Sun. No dinner Sat.*

$$–$$$ ✕ **Evvia.** An innovative California-influenced Greek menu and a stun-
  ★ ning interior insure that Evvia always packs in a crowd. A large fire-place, hand-painted pottery, and a big bar area with colorful backlit glassware make this one of Palo Alto's most inviting restaurants. Though the menu is written out in Greek, there's an unmistakable California influence in dishes like *lahanika pilafi,* risotto with butternut squash, mint, and leeks; and *psari sta karvouna,* mesquite-grilled striped bass with herbs and braised greens. ⊠ *420 Emerson St.,* ☎ *650/326–0983. Reservations essential. AE, DC, MC, V. No lunch weekends.*

$$–$$$ ✕ **L'Amie Donia.** Chef-owner Donia Bijan, who made a name for her-self at San Francisco's Sherman House and Brasserie Savoy, has deco-rated her utterly charming French bistro in sunny yellow and soothing blue. Her menus, which reflect the seasons, focus on the rustic, flavorful fare that one might find in the French countryside: roast beets with warm goat cheese and walnuts, rabbit with mustard sauce, or pan-roasted veal chop with an almond crust. ⊠ *530 Bryant St.,* ☎ *650/323–7614. Reservations essential. AE, D, MC, V. Closed Sun.–Mon. No lunch.*

$$ ✕ **Il Fornaio Cucina Italiana.** In a gorgeous Italianate setting on the ground floor and back patio of the Garden Court Hotel, Il Fornaio has a ca-sually rustic look, with food as the visual focus. Buy gourmet fare to go or stay here to sample superb antipasti and pasta, or pizzas and cal-zones baked to perfection in a wood-burning oven. The café area just inside the front door is a nice stop for coffee and snacks, and counter service makes for quick meals while watching the cooking. ⊠ *520 Cow-per St.,* ☎ *650/853–3888. AE, DC, MC, V.*

$$ ✕ **Nola.** With a lantern-lit central courtyard and a whimsical, folk art–filled interior, this New Orleans–inspired restaurant has a festive mood. The food is California-Cajun: grilled Cajun pork chop on garlic mashed potatoes with braised red chard and sweet apple coulis; citrus-glazed ono medallions on white-corn polenta with grilled vegetables. Almost all the wines are served by the glass as well as by the bottle. Save room for the house-made beignets. ⊠ *535 Ramona St.,* ☎ *650/328–2722. AE, DC, MC, V. No lunch weekends.*

$ ✕ **Pasta?** All the pastas here are under $7. What's more, it's very good food—nothing fancy, but made with fresh seasonal ingredients and pre-sented with care. In addition to standard pasta dishes like salmon fet-tuccine, there are always a few lighter selections served with light oil and no cheese or salt. A handful of meat and fish entrées, such as pork medallions with Chianti sauce, are priced well below $10. Naturally, the place does a brisk business with students. ⊠ *326 University Ave.,* ☎ *650/328–4585. MC, V.*

$ ✕ **Pluto's.** The space-age name and design have nothing to do with the earthly pleasures of Pluto's fresh, custom-made salads, sandwiches, and hot meals. Service is quasi-buffet-style. Grab a "personal guest check" (menu), make your choices from any of the food stations, and the server will process your card to determine how much you owe. Choose greens with a choice of eight fixings such as grilled fennel or roasted peppers, or build your own sandwich with a base of marinated flank steak or grilled eggplant, and add extras like caramelized onions or garlic mayo. Be prepared for crowds and a high noise level. ⊠ *482 University Ave.,* ☎ *650/853–1556. MC, V.*

$ ✕ **Vicolo.** A favorite Bay Area pizza chain, Vicolo specializes in gourmet combinations: goat cheese and caramelized onion, asparagus and field mushrooms, escarole and feta. There's even a winter vegetable pizza made with roasted butternut squash, sautéed kale, and walnuts. Sal-ads make a perfect accompaniment, or even a full meal if you throw in a slice of focaccia. The atmosphere here is no-frills; the narrow, cavernous room has painted cement walls. The outdoor tables are nice on sunny days, if you're lucky enough to snag one. ⊠ *473 University Ave.,* ☎ *650/324–4877. MC, V.*

$$$$ 🏨 **Garden Court Hotel.** This stylish boutique hotel has a European flair.
★ From the outside it looks like an Italian villa, complete with columns and arches, a dormer roof, and balconies dressed up with bougainvillea. The inside is even more appealing, from the intimate, slate blue–color lobby to the tasteful, sunlight-filled rooms, each with a two- or four-poster bed with comforter. Every room has a private terrace looking out on a beautiful central courtyard filled with potted plants. On the ground floor of the building are shops and restaurants, including Il Fornaio (☞ *above*), which provides 24-hour room service. Book well in advance, as the hotel often fills up with wedding parties. ⊠ *520 Cowper St., 94301,* ☎ *650/322–9000 or 800/824–9028,* ℻ *650/324–3609. 62 rooms. Restaurant, bar, in-room data ports, room service, in-room VCRs, exercise room, laundry service, concierge, business services. AE, D, DC, MC, V.*

$$$$ 🏨 **Stanford Park Hotel.** The original oil paintings, antiques, tapestries, and forest-green color scheme of this stately hotel make it feel more like a hunt club in the English countryside than a business hotel in Silicon Valley. A fireplace, skylights, and oversize chairs invite guests to linger in the cavernous lobby. Rooms are equally welcoming, with fireplaces, vaulted ceilings, English yew-wood armoires, and the requisite framed hunting scenes. The Duck Club Restaurant carries on the hunting motif with a regional American menu with a fair share of game. Outside, a heated pool and hot tub are enclosed in a landscaped courtyard surrounded by lush greenery. ⊠ *100 El Camino Real, 94025,* ☎ *650/322–1234 or 800/368–2468,* ℻ *650/322–0975. 163 rooms. Restaurant, bar, lobby lounge, in-room data ports, minibars, outdoor pool, exercise room, laundry service, concierge, business services, meeting room. AE, DC, MC, V.*

$$$–$$$$ 🏨 **Sheraton Hotel Palo Alto.** From the front, this Sheraton looks like any other business hotel. But step inside and you'll discover one of Palo Alto's loveliest havens of tranquility: A koi pond winds its elaborate course all the way from the pool area through landscaped gardens. (Request an even-numbered room for a better view of the pond.) The hotel is amazingly quiet considering its site on a busy intersection. Rooms are standard-issue business style, with all the amenities you'd expect. ⊠ *625 El Camino Real, 94301,* ☎ *650/328–2800 or 800/874–3516,* ℻ *650/327–7362. 350 rooms. Restaurant, lounge, in-room data ports, no-smoking floors, room service, pool, exercise room, coin laundry, laundry service, concierge, business services, meeting rooms. AE, D, DC, MC, V.*

$$$–$$$$ 🏨 **The Victorian on Lytton.** Only a block from downtown Palo Alto, this inn caters to business travelers who want comfort and amenities without teddy bears and lace. Innkeepers Susan and Maxwell Hall gutted the building—a former apartment building—and completely configured the interior to accommodate spacious rooms, some with canopy beds. Complimentary breakfast is ordered the night before and brought to your room in the morning. ⊠ *555 Lytton Ave., 94301,* ☎ *650/322–8555,* ℻ *650/322–7141. 10 rooms. No-smoking rooms. AE, MC, V.*

$–$$$ 🏨 **Cowper Inn.** In a quiet, residential neighborhood five minutes from
★ downtown Palo Alto, this former Victorian home is one of the least expensive lodging options in the area, and it's charming to boot. Each of the 14 rooms is unique, but all have handmade quilts. Shared-bath rooms are as low as $65. The cozy parlor has a brick fireplace, piano, and a big window looking out on tree-lined Cowper Street. Breakfast includes homemade breads and fresh-squeezed orange juice; guests are invited to help themselves to almonds and sherry throughout the day.

✉ *705 Cowper St., 94301,* ☎ *650/327–4475,* ⌷ *650/329–1703. 14 rooms. Breakfast room, piano. MC, V.*

Shopping

The **Stanford Shopping Center,** one of the Bay Area's first shopping centers, remains one of its best. In addition to an excellent selection of such upscale stores as Ralph Lauren, Smith & Hawken, Crate & Barrel, and Bloomingdale's, you'll find some irresistible eateries here. ✉ *180 El Camino Real (take Sand Hill Rd. east off I–280 or Embarcadero Rd. west off Hwy. 101),* ☎ *650/617–8585.*

Woodside

Just west of Palo Alto, Woodside is a tiny, rustic town where weekend warriors stock up on espresso and picnic fare before charging off on their mountain bikes. Blink once and you're past the town center. The main draw here is the wealth of surrounding lush parks and preserves.

One of the few great country houses in California that remains intact in its original setting is **Filoli,** in Woodside. Built between 1915 and 1917 for wealthy San Franciscan William B. Bourn II, it was designed by Willis Polk in a Georgian Revival style, with redbrick walls and a tile roof. The name is Bourn's acronym for "fight, love, live." As interesting to visitors as the house—once the setting of the television series *Dynasty*—are the 16 acres of formal gardens. These were planned and developed over a period of more than 50 years and preserved for the public when the last private owner, Mrs. William P. Roth, deeded Filoli to the National Trust for Historic Preservation.

The gardens rise south from the mansion to take advantage of the natural surroundings of the 700-acre estate and its vistas. Among the designs are a sunken garden. In the middle of it all is a charming teahouse designed in the Italian Renaissance style. From June through September Filoli hosts a monthly series of Sunday afternoon jazz concerts. Bring a picnic or buy a box lunch; Filoli provides tables, sodas, wine, fruit, and popcorn. In December the mansion is festively decorated for a series of holiday events: brunches, afternoon teas, Christmas concerts, and more. ✉ *Cañada Rd. near Edgewood Rd.,* ☎ *650/364–2880.* ⌷ *$10.* ⊙ *Mid-Feb.–Oct., Tues.–Sat. for guided and self-guided tours. Reservations essential for guided tours.*

One peninsula oddity unknown even to most residents is the **Pulgas Water Temple,** where exquisitely groomed grounds surround a Romanesque temple and a reflecting pool. Walk past the temple up the steps of the columned circular temple to feel the power of the water as it thunders deafeningly under your feet. Look up to the top of the columns and read the inscription from the Bible's Isaiah: I GIVE WATER IN THE WILDERNESS AND RIVERS IN THE DEEP, TO GIVE DRINK TO MY PEOPLE. The temple commemorates the massive underground pipeline project of the early 1930s that channeled water from Hetch Hetchy near Yosemite to the Crystal Springs Reservoir on the peninsula. ✉ *Cañada Rd., 1½ mi north of Edgewood Rd.,* ☎ *650/872–5900.* ⌷ *Free.* ⊙ *Weekdays 9:30–4.*

Dining

$$–$$$ ✕ **Village Pub.** "Pub" is a misnomer for this stylishly simple dining room. Instead of basic pub grub, you'll find contemporary dishes like seared scallops with foie gras and salmon with ginger-shrimp dumplings. ✉ *2967 Woodside Rd., ¾ mi from I–280W,* ☎ *650/851–1294. AE, D, DC, MC, V. No lunch weekends.*

$ ✕ **Bucks in Woodside.** You'll either be amused or turned off by the eccentric decor of this casual restaurant. Giant plastic alligators, Elvis paintings, a human-size Statue of Liberty model, and framed computer chips on the walls make a not-so-subtle aesthetic statement. The menu is a grab bag of crowd pleasers: basic soups, sandwiches, burgers, and salads. For breakfast there's a "U-do-it" omelet in addition to other more standard choices. ⊠ *3062 Woodside Rd.,* ☎ *650/851–8010. AE, MC, V.*

$ ✕ **Woodside Bakery and Café.** Stop by the bakery section for a cup of hot cocoa and a fresh-baked pastry, or sit in the café for a glass of wine and a light meal. Everything is fresh and well presented. The menu tends toward light, seasonal dishes such as fresh pastas and salads. But you'll also find more substantial entrées like grilled swordfish with cranberry relish. ⊠ *3052 Woodside Rd.,* ☎ *650/851–0812. AE, MC, V.*

Inland Peninsula Essentials

Arriving and Departing

BY CAR

By **car** the most pleasant direct route down the peninsula is I–280, the Junipero Serra Freeway, which passes along Crystal Springs Reservoir. For Stanford University, exit at Sand Hill Road and drive east. Turn right on Arboretum Drive, then right again on Palm Drive, which leads to the center of campus. U.S. 101, also known as the Bayshore Freeway, is more direct but also more congested; from there take University Avenue or Embarcadero Road west to Stanford. For Woodside take the Woodside Road exit and drive west.

BY TRAIN

CalTrain (☎ 800/660–4287) runs from 4th and Townsend streets to Palo Alto ($4 each way); from there take the free **Marguerite shuttle bus** (☎ 650/723–9362) to the Stanford campus and the Palo Alto area. Buses run about every 15 minutes 6 AM–8 PM and are timed to connect with trains and public transit buses.

Visitor Information

Palo Alto Chamber of Commerce (⊠ 325 Forest Ave., 94301, ☎ 650/324–3121). **Woodside Town Hall** (⊠ 2955 Woodside Rd., 94062, ☎ 650/851–6790).

SAN MATEO COUNTY COAST

Updated by
Chris Baty and
Sharon Silva

Although the San Mateo County Coast is only a few miles from the inland peninsula and San Francisco, its undeveloped hills, rugged coastline, and quaint towns and inns are worlds away from urban sprawl, strip shopping centers, and traffic congestion. Set out from San Francisco down scenic Highway 1, hugging the twists and turns of the coast, or venture 11 mi west from I–280 near San Mateo, over hilly Highway 92. As you wind your way past Christmas tree farms, pumpkin patches, and rural flower growers, you'll find that the pace of life is slower here than in the rest of the Bay Area.

The towns along the coast were founded in 1769 when Spanish explorer Gaspar de Portola arrived. After the Mexican government gained control, the land was used for agriculture by ranchers who provided food to San Francisco's Mission Dolores. Soon, lighthouses and ships were being built to facilitate the transport of goods to San Francisco. You can still visit the short, squat Point Montara Lighthouse in Montara, 8 mi north of Half Moon Bay, or the 115-ft Pigeon Point Lighthouse, one of the tallest on the West Coast, 7 mi south of Pescadero.

Most towns that dot the coast are no more than a few blocks long, with just enough room for a couple of B&Bs, restaurants, and boutiques or galleries. Beyond the towns are the beautiful coastal beaches—the area's lifeblood.

Half Moon Bay

The largest and most visited of the coastal communities, Half Moon Bay is nevertheless a tiny town with a population of fewer than 10,000. The town's hub, **Main Street,** is lined with five blocks of small crafts shops, art galleries, and outdoor cafés, many housed in renovated 19th-century structures. Half Moon Bay comes to life on the third weekend in October, when 300,000 people gather for the **Half Moon Bay Art and Pumpkin Festival** (☎ 650/726–9652).

The 4-mi stretch of **Half Moon Bay State Beach** (⊠ Hwy. 1, west of Main St., ☎ 650/726–8819) is perfect for long walks, kite flying, and picnic lunches, though the 50°F water and dangerous currents prevent most visitors from swimming.

The coastal communities can easily be explored on two wheels. The **Bicyclery** (⊠ 101 Main St., ☎ 650/726–6000) has bike rentals and will provide information on organized rides up and down the coast. If you prefer to go it alone, try the 3-mi bike trail that leads from Kelly Avenue in Half Moon Bay to Mirada Road in Miramar.

Built in 1928 after two horrible shipwrecks on the point, the **Point Montara Lighthouse** still has its original light keeper's quarters from the late 1800s. Gray whales pass this point during their migration from November through April, so bring your binoculars. The lighthouse is also a youth hostel known for its outdoor hot tub at ocean's edge. ⊠ 16th St. at Hwy. 1, Montara, ☎ 650/728–7177. ⊙ Call for hrs, tours, and lodging rates.

Dining and Lodging

$–$$ ✕ **Pasta Moon.** The sight of the wood-burning oven tips off diners to the thin-crust pizzas that are served in this small restaurant. The kitchen also turns out handmade pastas, a wonderful crisp-skinned roast chicken, and a variety of roasted meats. ⊠ 315 Main St., ☎ 650/726–5125. MC, V.

$–$$ ✕ **San Benito House.** Tucked inside a historic inn in the heart of Half Moon Bay, this homey operation prepares memorable sandwiches with bread baked in the restaurant's oven and sells them, deli style, for a picnic by the sea. Candlelight dinners feature fresh fish and house-made pastas. ⊠ 356 Main St., ☎ 650/726–3425. MC, V. No lunch. No dinner Mon.–Wed.

$–$$ ✕ **Two Fools.** The kitchen tosses together big organic salads and packs contemporary burritos with a healthy mix of ingredients. A slice of old-fashioned American meat loaf topped with caramelized onions is sandwiched in a house-made bun at lunchtime. Locals stop here regularly for takeout at lunch and dinnertime. Weekend brunch draws people touring the coast. ⊠ 408 Main St., ☎ 650/712–1222. MC, V. No lunch weekends.

$$$–$$$$ ▥ **Mill Rose Inn.** Perhaps the most decadent B&B in the entire Bay Area, the Mill Rose Inn pampers guests with in-room fireplaces, brass beds stacked high with down comforters, decanters of sherry and brandy on the tables, in-room coffee and cocoa, and baskets of fruit and candies. Room rates include a lavish champagne breakfast and afternoon snacks. ⊠ 615 Mill St., 94019, ☎ 650/726–8750, ﬀ 650/726–3031. 4 rooms, 2 suites. No-smoking rooms, refrigerators, in-room VCRs. AE, D, DC, MC, V.

$$–$$$$ ▥ **Old Thyme Inn.** Rooms in this charming Queen Anne Victorian house have been comfortably decorated, each with an herb motif. The more

Finally, a travel companion that doesn't snore on the plane or eat all your peanuts.

MCI WORLDCOM   WorldPhone®

123 456 7891 2345
J.D. SMITH

When traveling, your MCI WorldCom Card is the best way to keep in touch. Our operators speak your language, so they'll be able to connect you back home—no matter where your travels take you. Plus, your MCI WorldCom Card is easy to use, and even earns you frequent flyer miles every time you use it. When you add in our great rates, you get something even more valuable: peace-of-mind. So go ahead. Travel the world. MCI WorldCom just brought it a whole lot closer.

You can even sign up today at www.mci.com/worldphone or ask your operator to make a collect call to 1-410-314-2938.

EASY TO CALL WORLDWIDE

1 Just dial the WorldPhone access number of the country you're calling from.
2 Dial or give the operator your MCI WorldCom Card number.
3 Dial or give the number you're calling.

Australia ◆ To call using OPTUS To call using TELSTRA	1-800-551-111 1-800-881-100
Bahamas/Bermuda	1-800-888-8000
British Virgin Islands	1-800-888-8000
Costa Rica ◆	0-800-012-2222
Denmark	8001-0022
Norway ◆	800 -19912
India For collect access	000-127 000-126
United States/Canada	1-800-888-8000

For your complete WorldPhone calling guide, dial the WorldPhone access number for the country you're in and ask the operator for Customer Service. In the U.S. call 1-800-431-5402.

◆ Public phones may require deposit of coin or phone card for dial tone.

EARN FREQUENT FLYER MILES

AmericanAirlines®
A'Advantage®

Continental Airlines
OnePass

△ Delta Air Lines
SkyMiles®

◢ MILEAGE PLUS.
United Airlines

U·S AIRWAYS
DIVIDEND MILES

MCI WorldCom, its logo and the names of the products referred to herein are proprietary marks of MCI WorldCom, Inc. All airline names and logos are proprietary marks of the respective airlines. All airline program rules and conditions apply.

MCI WORLDCOM

Distinctive guides packed with up-to-date expert advice
and smart choices for every type of traveler.

Fodor's. For the world of ways you travel

expensive rooms have fireplaces and whirlpool tubs. Antiques, fresh flowers, a homemade breakfast, in-room sherry, and afternoon snacks make this a lovely place to spend a relaxing weekend. ⊠ *779 Main St., 94019,* ☎ *650/726–1616,* FAX *650/726–6394. 7 rooms. No-smoking rooms. AE, D, MC, V.*

$$ ⌂ **The Goose and Turrets.** Knickknacks from the international travels of innkeepers Raymond and Emily Hoche-Mong fill the shelves here, and the common area with a wood-burning stove is like an art and history museum. A full home-cooked breakfast, afternoon goodies, and homemade chocolate truffles are sure to make anyone feel at home. ⊠ *835 George St., 94037,* ☎ *650/728–5451. 5 rooms. Breakfast room, no-smoking rooms, boccie. AE, D, DC, MC, V.*

Pescadero

Walking down Stage Road, Pescadero's main street, it's hard to believe you're only 30 minutes from Silicon Valley. The few short blocks that comprise the downtown area could almost serve as the backdrop for a western movie, with Duarte's Tavern serving as the centerpiece. In fact, Pescadero, some 16 mi south of Half Moon Bay, was reportedly larger 100 years ago than it is today. This is a good place to stop for a bite or to browse for antiques housed in what looks like a converted barn. The town's real attraction, though, is its proximity to beaches and spectacular hiking.

If a quarantine is not in effect (watch for signs), from November through April you can look for mussels at **Pescadero State Beach,** where sandy expanses, tidal pools, and rocky outcroppings form one of the coast's more scenic beaches. Barbecue pits and tables attract many picnicking families. Across Highway 101 at the **Pescadero Marsh Natural Preserve,** hikers can spy on birds and other wildlife by following any of the trails that crisscross 600 acres of marshland. Early spring and fall are the best times to visit. ☎ *650/879–2170.* ☞ *Free; parking $5.* ☉ *Daily 8–sunset.*

If you prefer mountain trails to sand dunes, head for **Pescadero Creek County Park,** a 7,500-acre expanse of shady, old-growth redwood forests, grasslands, and mountain streams. The park is actually composed of three smaller ones: Heritage Grove Redwood Preserve, Sam McDonald Park, and San Mateo Memorial County Park. At 6.4 mi, the Old Haul Road Trail runs the length of the park. Campsites cost $15 per night. ☎ *650/879–0238.* ☞ *$4 per car.*

OFF THE **SAN GREGORIO** – In addition to beautiful scenery and expansive state
BEATEN PATH beaches, this area is home to the idiosyncratic **San Gregorio General Store** (⊠ Rte. 84 at Stage Rd., 1 mi east of Hwy. 1, ☎ 650/726–0565). Part old-time saloon, part hardware store, part grocery, the store has been a fixture in town for the past 121 years; the current Spanish-style structure replaced the original wood building when it burned down in 1930. Come to browse through the hodgepodge items—camp stoves, books, and boots, to name just a few—or to listen to Irish music and bluegrass on weekend afternoons.

Dining

$–$$ ✕ **Duarte's Tavern.** This 19th-century roadhouse serves simple American fare, with locally grown vegetables and fresh fish as standard items. Don't pass up the famed house artichoke soup or the old-fashioned berry pie à la mode. Breakfasts of eggs, bacon, sausage, and hotcakes are hearty here. ⊠ *202 Stage Rd.,* ☎ *650/879–0464. MC, V.*

En Route   At the south end of the coast is the 115-ft **Pigeon Point Lighthouse,** one of the tallest on the West Coast. Built in 1872, it has been used as a backdrop in numerous TV shows and commercials. The light from the 8,000-pound Fresnel lens can be seen 20 mi at sea. The former coast guard quarters now serve as a youth hostel. ⊠ *Pigeon Point Rd. and Hwy. 1,* ☎ *650/879–2120.* ☞ *$2.* ☉ *Weekends 11–4; guided tours 10–3.*

Año Nuevo State Reserve

At the most southerly point of the San Mateo County Coast, Año Nuevo is the world's only approachable mainland rookery for elephant seals. If you know you'll be in the area between mid-December and March, make reservations early for a 2½-hour guided walking tour to view the huge (up to 3 tons), fat, furry elephant seals mating or birthing, depending on the time of year. Tours proceed rain or shine, so dress for anything. From April to November there's less excitement, but you can still watch the seals lounging on the beach. The visitor center has a fascinating film and exhibits, and there are plenty of hiking trails in the area. ⊠ *Hwy. 1 south of Pigeon Pt. (take Hwy. 1 south from Pescadero),* ☎ *650/879–0227; tour reservations 800/444–4445.* ☞ *$4; parking $5.* ☉ *Tours leave every 15 mins 8:45–3.*

San Mateo County Coast Essentials

Arriving and Departing

Public transportation to this area is limited, so it's best to drive. To get to Half Moon Bay, take Highway 1, also known as the Coast Highway, south along the length of the San Mateo coast. A quicker route is via I–280, the Junipero Serra Freeway; follow it south as far as Highway 92, where you can turn west toward the coast. To get to Pescadero, drive south 16 mi on Highway 1 from Half Moon Bay. For Año Nuevo continue south on Highway 1 another 12 mi.

BY BUS

SamTrans (☎ 800/660–4287) buses travel to Half Moon Bay from the Daly City BART station. Another bus connects Half Moon Bay with Pescadero. Each trip takes approximately one hour. Call for schedules since departures are infrequent.

Visitor Information

California State Parks Bay Area District Office (⊠ 250 Executive Park Blvd., Suite 4900, San Francisco 94134, ☎ 415/330–6300). **Half Moon Bay Chamber of Commerce** (⊠ 520 Kelly Ave., 94019, ☎ 650/726–8380).

ON AND AROUND THE BAY

Around the bay are miles of shoreline parks and wildlife refuges, easily accessible but almost never seen by travelers on the busy Bayshore and East Shore freeways. Yerba Buena Island provides the center anchorage for the Bay Bridge. It is connected by a causeway to man-made Treasure Island, which has a military museum and relics of the island's 1939 Golden Gate International Exposition. Excursions are available to the Farallon Islands, 23 mi outside the Golden Gate, where wildlife is abundant. Other boating excursions explore the bay and the delta's maze of waterways as far as Stockton and Sacramento. Back on land, about an hour's drive northeast of San Francisco, the town of Benicia, once the state capital, has been meticulously restored. Across Carquinez Strait is the former home of naturalist John Muir.

Yerba Buena and Treasure Islands

Every day 250,000 people pass through **Yerba Buena Island** on their way across the San Francisco–Oakland Bay Bridge, yet the island remains a mystery to most of them. Yerba Buena and the adjacent Treasure Island are primarily military bases, but they are accessible to the public. **Treasure Island** provides a superb bay-level view of the San Francisco skyline.

Wildlife Refuges

Recently developed wildlife refuges provide welcome access to the bay's shore, which can appear to be a congested commercial strip from surrounding freeways. Among the best of the free public parks is **Coyote Point Nature Museum** (☎ 650/342–7755), just off U.S. 101 south of San Francisco Airport, open from Tuesday through Saturday 10–5 and Sunday noon–5. The **Baylands Nature Interpretive Center** (☎ 650/329–2506), open Tuesday–Wednesday 10–5, Thursday–Friday 2–5, and weekends 1–5, is in the marshes at the east end of Embarcadero Road in Palo Alto. The **San Francisco Bay National Wildlife Refuge** (☎ 510/792–0222) is on Thornton Avenue in Fremont, at the east end of Dumbarton Bridge/Highway 84; it is open Tuesday–Sunday 10–5. On West Winton Avenue, at the east end of San Mateo Bridge/Highway 92, the **Hayward Regional Shoreline** contains the Cogswell marsh—the largest marsh restoration project on the West Coast. It is open daily 6 AM–sunset; for guided walks call the Interpretive Center (☎ 510/881–6751).

Another major wildlife center, outside the bay, is the **Gulf of the Farallones National Marine Sanctuary.** Though the islands are off-limits to visitors, rare nesting birds and passing seals and whales are visible from cruise boats. The Oceanic Society Expeditions (☎ 415/474–3385) operates cruises on weekends and on select weekdays from June to November. The fare is $65.

Benicia and Martinez

The historic port city of **Benicia** is worth a detour for travelers on I–80 between San Francisco and Sacramento. The old town center is on 1st Street, and at the foot of the street there is a fishing pier with a view through Carquinez Strait to San Pablo Bay. Benicia was named for the wife of General Mariano Vallejo, who owned the surrounding 99,000 acres. It was the state capital in 1852 and 1853, and the handsome brick Greek Revival **capitol** has been splendidly restored. ⊠ *1st and W. G Sts.,* ☎ *707/745–3385.* ➮ *$2.* ☉ *Daily 10–5.*

The Federal-style **Fischer-Hanlon Home,** next door to the capitol, is closed to the public, but visitors are invited to wander through the home's gardens. Nearby are scattered historic buildings, art galleries, crafts workshops, and antiques stores. The **Chamber of Commerce** (⊠ 601 1st St., ☎ 707/745–2120) distributes a guide to the old waterfront district—including a list of former brothels. The **Union Hotel** (⊠ 401 1st St., ☎ 707/746–0100) has been brilliantly restored; its restaurant is the area's finest.

Just across Carquinez Strait from Benicia is **Martinez,** another historic port city that has become increasingly industrial. Martinez is said to be the birthplace of the martini, which according to legend was first called the "Martinez cocktail" and was later slurred into its present designation. Atop a hill and surrounded by orchards and gardens is the **John Muir National Historic Site,** the carefully restored Victorian-era residence of conservationist John Muir. ⊠ *Alhambra Ave. at Hwy. 4,* ☎ *925/228–8860.* 🖭 *$2.* ⊙ *Wed.–Sun. 10–4:30.*

Six Flags Marine World

One of northern California's most popular attractions, this 160-acre wildlife and theme park has been a phenomenal success since moving in 1986 from a crowded site south of San Francisco to Vallejo, about an hour's drive northeast. Animals of the sea, air, and land perform in shows, roam in natural habitats, and stroll among park visitors with their trainers. Among the animal stars are killer whales, dolphins, camels, elephants, sea lions, chimpanzees, and a troupe of human water-skiers (April–October). The 1998 addition of roller coasters, water rides, and bumper cars has further added to the huge crowds of kids and their tired parents trekking to the park from San Francisco and its suburbs.

Owned by the Marine World Foundation, a nonprofit organization devoted to educating the public about the world's wildlife, the park is a family attraction, with entertaining but informative shows and close-up looks at exotic animals. For additional sightseeing, visitors can reach the park on a high-speed ferry from San Francisco, a trip that offers unusual vistas through San Francisco and San Pablo bays. ⊠ *Marine World Pkwy., Vallejo,* ☎ *707/643–6722.* 🖭 *$27.95.* ⊙ *Summer, daily 10–10; fall and spring, Fri., Sat., and Sun. 10–8; closed winter.*

On and Around the Bay Essentials

Arriving and Departing

BY BUS AND TRAIN

You can use public transportation to get to Marine World; for all other destinations you'll need a car. **Greyhound Lines** (☎ 800/231–2222) runs buses from downtown San Francisco to Vallejo. You can take a **BART** train (☎ 650/992–2278) to the El Cerrito Del Norte station and transfer to the **Vallejo Transit line** (☎ 707/648–4666) to reach Marine World.

BY CAR

To get to Treasure Island, take the Bay Bridge to the Treasure Island exit. For Benicia, take the I–780 exit in Vallejo, then Benicia's East 2nd Street exit. For Marine World, take I–80 east to Marine World Parkway in Vallejo. The trip takes an hour each way. Parking is $5 at the park.

BY FERRY

During Marine World's operating season, high-speed **Blue and Gold Fleet** (☎ 415/705–5444) ferries depart throughout the day for Marine World from Pier 39 at Fisherman's Wharf; the trip takes one hour. One-way tickets cost $7.50.

Visitor Information

Benicia Chamber of Commerce (⊠ 601 1st St., 94510, ☎ 707/745–2120). **Martinez Area Chamber of Commerce** (⊠ 620 Las Juntas St., 94553, ☎ 925/228–2345).

8 THE SOUTH BAY

The South Bay contains old-fashioned neighborhoods, abundant green hills, and the prestigious corporate corridors of Silicon Valley—all within minutes of each other. To the surprise of many visitors, the world's high-tech capital is wonderfully multifaceted, with some of the Bay Area's finest restaurants and shops. No longer a nondescript suburb of San Francisco, San Jose and its environs have grown up and blossomed into a lively metropolis with a proud identity.

By Therese
Iknoian

Updated by
Lotus Abrams

SAN JOSE IS THE SOUTH BAY'S best-kept secret, and only now is it finally enjoying the respect it deserves. Not only is San Jose's population larger than that of San Francisco, its older sister to the north, San Jose now has its own ballet, symphony, repertory theater, nationally recognized museums, downtown nightlife, and exclusive hotels. The South Bay's strong job market and low crime rate, as well as its warm, sunny climate, make it a desirable place to live. You won't find cloaks of fog clinging all day on this end of the peninsula.

Likely, your motive in visiting the South Bay will be to see Silicon Valley, the birthplace of the world's tiny chips and circuits that support the Information Superhighway. Though this is admittedly the center of high-tech research and the corporate headquarters of such giants as Apple, Sun Microsystems, Oracle, and Hewlett-Packard, Silicon Valley is more a state of mind than a place—an attitude held by the legions of software engineers, programmers, and computer-philes who call the area home. Of course you can still visit the true birthplace of Silicon Valley, but that tour actually takes you to the peninsula and the garage where Hewlett and Packard began developing the technology that became the backbone for the computer companies of today.

More enlightening is a trip through the increasingly visitor-friendly towns of the South Bay. Look beyond what seems to be an endless sprawl of office parks, intertwined highways, shopping centers, and high-rises, and you'll find such diverse towns as Santa Clara, with its 200-year-old mission; Saratoga, with its fine antiques stores and French restaurants; Campbell, whose quaint town center boasts a finely renovated historic mansion and a classic melodrama theater; and San Jose—the third-largest city in both California and on the West Coast—with its burgeoning core, its many micro-neighborhoods, and a growing ribbon of urban green connecting the city from north to south. Take a weekend, rent a car, open the windows or fold down the top, and head south.

Pleasures and Pastimes

Dining

It used to be that for a really world-class dining experience, South Bay foodies would head to San Francisco. No longer. Today some of the country's greatest chefs recognize the South Bay's appeal and have opened trendy bistros and eateries, especially in San Jose's revitalized downtown. Dining might be a notch more casual than in San Francisco—and a notch less expensive, too—but that doesn't mean you won't need reservations.

The South Bay offers a rich selection of ethnic restaurants. Explore the sushi and noodle houses in San Jose's Japantown, or venture into East San Jose for some of the best tacos and tamales north of the border. Don't be afraid of small store-front restaurants, especially in such micro-neighborhoods as Willow Glen, or in such small towns as Campbell. They can offer friendly service, great food, and terrific value. For dining price ranges, *see* Chapter 2.

Galleries and Museums

With the opening in late 1998 of the Tech Museum of Innovation in downtown San Jose, the South Bay's arts scene is nearly complete. San Jose has modern art and children's museums, and in Santa Clara there are computer-oriented museums and sites. Be sure to check for special musical events—from chamber music to acoustic jazz—at the San Jose

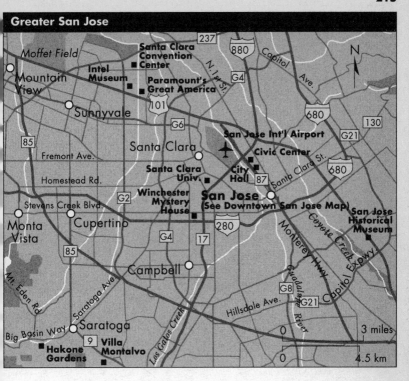

Greater San Jose

Museum of Art. Note that many museums are open late the third Thursday of each month.

Lodging

Plan ahead, because during the week many hotels are heavily booked by Silicon Valley business travelers up to two weeks in advance. The market is so hot that such chains as Wyndham, DoubleTree, and Crowne Plaza have moved in and renovated older facilities at a furious pace. Ironically, many business- and convention-oriented hotels can be nearly empty on weekends, when rates plummet and package deals abound. If you have a car, also consider smaller hotels in such outlying areas as Campbell, along The Alameda in Santa Clara, or on Stevens Creek Boulevard in San Jose or Santa Clara. Don't spend a lot of time hunting for a quaint bed-and-breakfast. There are only a few in the South Bay, and we've listed the nicest ones. For lodging price ranges, *see* Chapter 3.

Parks and Historic Homesteads

The South Bay—once known not for computers, but for its blossoming fruit orchards and vineyards—works hard to preserve its parklands and turn-of-the-century homesteads. The Winchester Mystery House (☞ Exploring San Jose, *below*) may be the best-known site, but look beyond the tales of ghosts to see the sprawling farm house it once was. You can also visit former vineyards and historic homes in the surrounding hills, notably Villa Montalvo and the Mountain Winery in Saratoga, or the Mirassou Winery to the east of downtown San Jose.

A 3-mi ribbon of green called the Guadalupe River Park runs through downtown San Jose, connecting such major sites as the Children's Museum and the Arena. New playgrounds and sculpture gardens make this a popular spot for families.

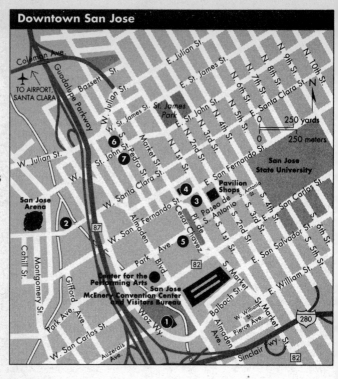

Downtown San Jose

Spectator Sports

Depending on the sporting season, you can take your pick of local major-league franchises, including soccer and ice hockey (☞ Spectator Sports, *below*).

EXPLORING THE SOUTH BAY

San Jose

55 mi south of San Francisco on U.S. 101 or I–280.

In 1777, as New England colonists were just beginning America's war for independence, El Pueblo de San Jose de Guadalupe became California's first civil settlement under Spanish rule, with a total population of 66. The Spanish-era precursor to modern San Jose was situated near the Guadalupe River, only a short distance from today's city hall.

California's first legislature met in a two-story adobe building on a site facing Plaza de Cesar Chavez, now occupied by the luxurious Fairmont Hotel. There, they planned and prepared for California's admission to the Union in 1850. Unfortunately for San Jose, the state capital moved several time before finding a permanent home in Sacramento.

Nowadays this plaza—minus the legislature—is the heart of San Jose's long-planned downtown renaissance, which has finally come to fruition and allowed the South Bay's capital to blossom. In the last few years the downtown has become a major destination for entertainment, arts, nightlife, and sports at the San Jose Sports Arena. At the same time, such businesses as IBM and Adobe Systems have set up here. Strikingly modern architecture now coexists with finely restored 19th-century and mission-style buildings.

The Guadalupe River Park, a 3-mi belt of trees and gardens, connects the downtown area with the Children's Discovery Museum to the south. Eventually the trail will extend to the San Jose International Airport to the north and will include even more parks and playgrounds. A 21-mi urban light-rail system links the downtown to the business district and Paramount's Great America to the north and to various suburbs and malls to the south. San Jose's downtown can be easily explored by foot, with side trips by light-rail, but visitors still need a car to get to outlying communities and such sights as the Egyptian Museum and the Winchester Mystery House.

A Good Tour

Numbers in the text correspond to numbers in the margin and on the Downtown San Jose map.

Much of downtown San Jose can be toured easily on foot. Start at the **Children's Discovery Museum** ① and be sure to wander around the outside of this outrageously purple building. Crossing through the surrounding park, take a stroll through the "herd" of larger-than-life animal sculptures facing San Carlos Street. The nearby steps lead down to Guadalupe Creek and a parallel walking path; a good detour leads north to the San Jose Arena and the **Guadalupe River Park** ②, with a carousel and children's playground.

Back at the sculpture park, continue east on San Carlos Street into the heart of downtown San Jose. Immediately on the left is the Center for the Performing Arts, home to the city's ballet and symphony. San Jose's McEnery Convention Center and the Visitors Center are across the road.

Continue down San Carlos Street and turn left on Market Street; ahead is Plaza de Cesar Chavez. On the square's northeast corner are the must-see **San Jose Museum of Art** ③ and adjacent **Cathedral Basilica of St. Joseph** ④. On the square's western edge at Park Avenue is the **Tech Museum of Innovation** ⑤, with its children-friendly hands-on exhibits.

Follow Market Street north from the plaza and turn left on Santa Clara Street. For a glimpse of the historic Hotel De Anza, walk four blocks ahead to the corner of North Almaden Boulevard. Otherwise walk one block, turn right on San Pedro Street, and continue two blocks—past the sidewalk cafés and restaurants—to St. John Street and turn left. The **Fallon House** ⑥ will be on your right, the **Peralta Adobe** ⑦ on your left. At this point, you can turn around and go east three blocks on St. John Street and board the light-rail to return to downtown.

TIMING

The above downtown walk can be completed easily in about two hours. However, if you decide to spend time in the museums or at a café along San Pedro Street, give yourself at least four hours.

Sights to See

④ **Cathedral Basilica of St. Joseph.** The Renaissance-style cathedral, built in 1877, is completely restored and has extraordinary stained-glass windows and murals. The multidome cathedral occupies the site where a small adobe church served the first residents of the Pueblo of San Jose in 1803. ⊠ *90 S. Market St.,* ☎ *408/283–8100.*

① **Children's Discovery Museum.** An angular purple building across the creek from the convention center at the rear of the Discovery Meadow park, the museum exhibits interactive installations on science, the humanities, and the arts. Children can dress up in period costumes, create art from recycled materials, or play on a real fire truck. The park is also a favorite site for school and family picnics, and kids can crawl all over the oversize animal sculptures, loosely nicknamed "The Parade of Animals." ⊠ *180 Woz Way, at Auzerais St.,* ☎ *408/298–5437.* ⊡ *$6.* ☉ *Tues.–Sat. 10–5, Sun. noon–5.*

★ **Egyptian Museum and Planetarium.** Owned by the Rosecrucian Order, the museum exhibits the West Coast's largest collection of Egyptian and Babylonian antiquities, including mummies and an underground replica of a rock tomb. The museum's entrance is a reproduction of the Avenue of Ram Sphinxes from the Temple at Karnak in Egypt. The complex is surrounded by a garden filled with palms, papyrus, and other plants recalling ancient Egypt. The planetarium offers programs like the popular "Celestial Nile," which describes the significant role astrology played in ancient Egyptian myths and religions. ⊠ *1342 Naglee Ave., at Park Ave.,* ☎ *408/947–3636.* ⊡ *$7 museum, $4 planetarium.* ☉ *Daily 10–5, planetarium weekdays only.*

❻ Fallon House. San Jose's seventh mayor, Thomas Fallon, built this Victorian mansion in 1855. The house's period-decorated rooms can be viewed on a 90-minute tour that includes the Peralta Adobe (☞ *below*) and a screening of a video about the two houses. Tickets are sold beside the Fallon House at the City Store gift shop, which carries books on local history. ⊠ *175 W. St. John St.,* ☎ *408/993–8182.* ⊡ *$6 (includes admission to Peralta Adobe).* ☉ *Guided tours Tues.–Sun. noon–5.*

🖑 **❷ Guadalupe River Park.** This downtown park includes the Arena Green, next to the sports arena, with a carousel, children's playground, and artwork honoring five champion figure skaters from the area. By early 2000, an interactive park is scheduled to open one block south on San Fernando Street. The design will encourage children to learn how rivers function, with plenty of hands-on displays plus swings, slides, a mist fountain, and water jets. The River Park path, which will someday stretch for 3 mi, starts at the Children's Discovery Museum and runs north, ending at the Arena Green.

Heritage Rose Garden. The newer of the city's two rose gardens, completed in 1994, has won national acclaim for its 5,000 rose bushes and trees on 4 acres. A quiet retreat, the garden has benches perfect for a break or picnic, and is alongside the still-developing Historic Orchard, which houses fruit trees indigenous to the Santa Clara Valley. ⊠ *Taylor and Spring Sts.,* ☎ *408/298–7657.* ⊡ *Free.*

Municipal Rose Garden. Originally installed in 1931, the Municipal Rose Garden is one of several outstanding green spaces in the city's urban core. You'll find 5.5 acres of roses with 4,000 shrubs and trees in 189 well-labeled beds, as well as marvelous walkways, fountains, and trellises. Some of the neighboring homes in the Rose Garden district date back to the city's founding fathers. ⊠ *Naglee and Dana Aves.,* ☎ *408/277–4191.* ⊡ *Free.*

❼ Peralta Adobe. California pepper trees shade the circa-1797 last remaining structure from the pueblo that was once San Jose. The whitewashed two-room home has been furnished to interpret life in the first Spanish civil settlement in California and during the Mexican rancho era. ⊠ *184 W. St. John St.,* ☎ *408/993–8182.* ⊡ *$6 (includes admission to Fallon House).* ☉ *Guided tours Tues.–Sun. noon–5.*

San Jose Historical Museum. On the outskirts of downtown San Jose, occupying 25 acres of Kelley Park, this outdoor "museum" highlights the history of San Jose and Santa Clara Valley. Visitors can see 28 historic and reconstructed buildings, hop a historic trolley, observe letterpress printing, and buy ice cream and candy at O'Brien's. ⊠ *1600 Senter Rd., at Phelan Ave.,* ☎ *408/287–2290.* ⊡ *$6.* ☉ *Tues.–Sun. noon–5.*

3 **San Jose Museum of Art.** In a four-part collaboration with New York's Whitney Museum, the San Jose Museum of Art is exploring the development of 20th-century American art with exhibits of pieces from the Whitney Museum's permanent collection. The series will run through June of 2000, including works by American artists Georgia O'Keeffe, Edward Hopper, and John Marin. Housed in a former post office building, the museum also has a permanent collection that includes paintings, large-scale multimedia installations, photographs, and sculptures by local and nationally known artists. ⊠ *110 S. Market St.,* ☎ *408/294–2787.* ☞ *$7, free 1st Thurs. of month.* ☉ *Tues.– Wed. and Fri.–Sun. 10–5, Thurs. 10–8.*

NEED A BREAK? **Caffe La Pastaia,** with two downtown locations, is the perfect stop for coffee or a light meal. The branch inside the San Jose Museum of Art (⊠ 110 S. Market St., ☎ 408/287–1970) occupies a tower with windows overlooking Plaza de Cesar Chavez. The second branch is in the Hotel De Anza (⊠ 233 W. Santa Clara St., ☎ 408/286–2626).

★ **5** ☕ **Tech Museum of Innovation.** San Jose's nationally recognized museum of technology moved to a new, much larger building in October of 1998, designed by renowned architect Ricardo Legorreta of Mexico City. The museum now has plenty of space for its high-tech and hands-on exhibits, allowing visitors to discover and demystify such disciplines as multimedia, communications, biotechnology, robotics, and space exploration. Another new feature is the 299-seat Hackworth IMAX Dome Theater. ⊠ *201 S. Market St., at Park Ave.,* ☎ *408/294–8324.* ☞ *$8 for museum or IMAX, $13.50 for both.* ☉ *Tues.–Sun. 10–5 (until 6 PM Memorial Day–Labor Day, until 8 PM the 3rd Thurs. of each month).*

Winchester Mystery House. Perhaps San Jose's best-known site, the mystery house, which is on the National Register of Historic Places, is 3 mi west of downtown. Convinced that spirits would harm her if construction ever stopped, firearms heiress and house owner Sarah Winchester constantly added to her house. For 38 years, beginning in 1884, she kept hundreds of carpenters working around the clock, creating a bizarre 160-room Victorian labyrinth with stairs going nowhere and doors that open into walls. The brightly painted house is a favorite family attraction, and though the grounds are no longer dark and overgrown, the place retains an air of mystery. Explore the house on a 65-minute daytime tour or come on a Friday the 13th for an evening flashlight tour. ⊠ *525 S. Winchester Blvd., between Stevens Creek Blvd. and I–280,* ☎ *408/247–2101.* ☞ *$13.95.* ☉ *Guided tours Nov.–Feb., daily 9:30–4; Mar.–Oct., hrs vary, call ahead.*

OFF THE BEATEN PATH **CAMPBELL** – Buried in the heart of metropolitan Santa Clara County 10 minutes south of San Jose on Highway 17, the town of Campbell has a small-town center with a friendly, neighborhood mood. Within a couple of blocks are the city hall, an old cannery that now houses offices, and a handful of galleries, boutiques, and restaurants.

A favorite local hangout is **Orchard Valley Coffee,** where the large-pane front windows open wide on spring and summer days. It's also an Internet café where you can rent computer time and check your e-mail. The café keeps its cozy feel with well-worn pillows and benches you feel comfortable putting your feet up on. The menu includes light meals, salads, soups, and pastries. ⊠ 349 E. Campbell Ave., ☎ 408/374–2115. D, MC, V.

On Campbell's Civic Center Plaza, the historic Tudor Revival **Ainsley House** gives a glimpse of South Bay life in the 1920s and '30s. This structure was moved in one piece from its previous location a half mile away, after descendants of the owners, the valley's founding canner, donated it to the city for preservation. ⊠ *300 Grant St.,* ☎ *408/866–2119.* ▨ *$6.* ☉ *Guided tours Thurs.–Sun., noon–4; gardens open daily sunrise–sunset.*

Dining and Lodging

$$$–$$$$ ★ ✕ **Emile's.** Swiss chef and owner Emile Mooser's menu is a blend of classical European and contemporary Californian influences. Specialties include house-cured gravlax, rack of lamb, fresh game, and Grand Marnier soufflé. Mooser is an expert at matching food and wine. He'll gladly make a selection from his restaurant's extensive list for you. The interior is distinguished by romantic lighting, stunning floral displays, and an unusual leaf sculpture on the ceiling. ⊠ *545 S. 2nd St.,* ☎ *408/289–1960. AE, D, DC, MC, V. Closed Sun.–Mon. No lunch Tues.–Thurs. and Sat.*

$$–$$$$ ✕ **Scott's Seafood Grill & Bar.** This downtown restaurant also has locations in San Francisco and Palo Alto. Its large windows and sixth-floor location provide diners with great views of San Jose. You can choose from favorites like Boston clam chowder and lobster, and more unusual dishes like charbroiled ahi tuna with wasabi lemon butter and grilled salmon with a Thai chile-citrus glaze and orange-tomatillo relish. There are also a few chicken and steak choices, for non–seafood eaters. ⊠ *185 Park Ave.,* ☎ *408/971–1700. AE, D, DC, MC, V. No lunch weekends.*

$$$ ✕ **A.P. Stump's.** This elegant newcomer opened in the fall of 1998. With its tin ceilings, dramatic lighting, and gold- and copper-toned walls, this restaurant's extravagant interior is well matched to the food. Chef-partner Jim Stump offers creative dishes on his frequently changing menu, which may include sesame ahi with bok choy and soba noodle cake or molasses-glazed pork chop with huckleberry sauce. Deserts are equally innovative, like the dark chocolate and coconut mousse, and the caramelized champagne sabayon. ⊠ *163 W. Santa Clara St.,* ☎ *408/292–9928. AE, D, DC, MC, V. Closed Sun. No lunch Sat.*

$$$ ✕ **Paolo's.** A longtime meeting ground for South Bay notables, Paolo's sponge-painted interior is as contemporary as any in San Jose. Duck and delicate handmade pastas are among the appealing, up-to-the-moment offerings. At lunchtime the dining room is a sea of suits, with bankers and brokers entertaining clients. ⊠ *333 W. San Carlos St.,* ☎ *408/294–2558. AE, D, DC, MC, V. Closed Sun. No lunch Sat.*

$$–$$$ ✕ **Bella Mia.** Locals love this restaurant for its elegant interior and good Italian food. There are plenty of fresh pastas to choose from, like salmon ravioli in tomato dill sauce and pasta carbonara, as well as flatbread pizzas. You can also choose from a number of grilled entrées, like spit-roasted chicken and citrus-grilled pork chops. If you can, get a table outside in the brick-walled patio. Trailing vines, a bubbling fountain, and outdoor heating make it a pleasant place to eat year-round. ⊠ *58 S. First St.,* ☎ *408/280–1993. AE, D, DC, MC, V.*

$$–$$$ ✕ **Blake's Steakhouse and Bar.** Blake's fully satisfies the carnivore while managing not to neglect even the staunchest non–beef eater. Uncluttered and tranquil for a steak house, the restaurant offers intimate high-back booths, some with a view of bustling San Pedro Square. Order any cut of beef you fancy, as well as roasted fowl and charbroiled fish. ⊠ *17 N. San Pedro Sq.,* ☎ *408/298–9221. AE, D, DC, MC, V.*

$$–$$$ ✕ **The Glen.** This rustic yet elegant neighborhood spot is a great place to spend an evening. Start with dinner: The menu has some standard choices like grilled chicken breast on rice or swordfish linguine in a

black pepper-lemon sauce. But there are also a few creative choices, like a sushi selection that includes the Caribbean Jerk Roll, with grilled jerk prawns, mango, and avocado. After dinner enjoy the large double-sided rock fireplace in the full bar, or play pool on one of 12 handmade pool tables. ⊠ *1180 Lincoln Ave., Willow Glen,* ☎ *408/288–9422, AE, MC, V. No lunch.*

$$–$$$ ✕ **The Grill on the Alley.** The Fairmont Hotel's coolly elegant restaurant, with its crisp, white tablecloths, gleaming hardwood floors, and black leather upholstered chairs and booths, has the same owners as the popular Beverly Hills location. The American grill–style menu features broiled seafood and meats, pasta, and American classics like chicken pot pie, meat loaf, and mashed potatoes with gravy. The long dark wood bar is a great spot for a martini. ⊠ *172 S. Market St.,* ☎ *408/294–2244, AE, D, DC, MC, V. No lunch weekends.*

$$–$$$ ✕ **Spiedo Ristorante.** This restaurant is the sister of the San Mateo restaurant by the same name, well known for its northern Italian cuisine. High ceilings and split-level dining help create a simple yet elegant decor. Start your meal off with antipasti or the butter lettuce salad with Gorgonzola, grilled apple rings, cherry tomatoes, caramelized walnuts, and a walnut vinaigrette. Entrées include mesquite-grilled fillet of beef served with a brandy-mushroom sauce, mesquite rotisserie dishes, pastas, and pizzas baked in an oak-burning oven. ⊠ *151 W. Santa Clara St.,* ☎ *408/971–6096. AE, D, DC, MC, V. No lunch Sun.*

$–$$$ ✕ **Pagota.** The selections here are standard rather than innovative, but the decor of this Chinese restaurant in the Fairmont Hotel is stunning. The high ceilings, towering pillars, and huge flower arrangement in the center of the room contrast nicely with the intimate booths that ring the perimeter with their tiny red lanterns. The menu offers favorites like spring rolls, mu shu pork, wonton soup, and cashew chicken. ⊠ *170 S. Market St.,* ☎ *408/998–3955. AE, D, DC, MC, V. Closed Sun. No lunch.*

$$ ✕ **Menara Moroccan Restaurant.** The food is only part of the reason to come here for a leisurely meal. Arched entryways, lazily spinning ceiling fans, and a tiled fountain all lend to the exotic decor. Dine on jewel-toned cushions around low tables, feasting on lamb with honey, delicately spiced chicken kabobs, or hare with paprika. You can choose from five multi-course dinners—all include couscous, salad, flaky b'stilla pastry, dessert, and sweet mint tea. A nightly belly dancing performance completes the experience. ⊠ *41 E. Gish Rd.,* ☎ *408/453–1983. AE, D, MC, V. No lunch.*

$$ ✕ **71 Saint Peter.** This could easily be the best restaurant in San Jose.
★ The selection is somewhat small, but each dish is prepared with care, from the grilled halibut served with a mango-papaya salsa and Thai chile beurre blanc, to the penne pasta with roasted chicken, Portobello mushroom, and red peppers in a garlic-basil broth. The ceramic-tile floors and wood-beam ceiling add rustic touches to the warm, elegant atmosphere. You can watch chef/owner Mark Tabak at work in the glass-walled kitchen. ⊠ *71 N. San Pedro St.,* ☎ *408/971–8523,* FAX *408/938–3440. AE, D, DC, MC, V. Closed Sun. No lunch Sat.*

$–$$ ✕ **Chez Sovan.** This Cambodian jewel is a wonderful addition to the South Bay dining scene. The original San Jose branch, which serves only lunch, stands in a rather homely stretch of town, but the Campbell location offers a pleasant setting in addition to its satisfying food. The spring rolls are delectable at both addresses, as are the noodle dishes, grilled meats, and flavorful curries. ⊠ *923 N. 13th St.,* ☎ *408/287–7619;* ⊠ *2425 S. Bascom Ave., Campbell,* ☎ *408/371–7711. AE, MC, V. No lunch Sun. at San Jose location.*

$–$$ ✕ **Gordon Biersch Brewery Restaurant.** An early link in the fast-growing chain of brew-pubs of the same name, this movers'-and-shakers' scene is so busy on Friday night that the waitstaff hands out beepers to would-be diners so they can be signaled when their table is ready. Twenty- and thirtysomethings make up most of the crowd. They happily feast on the kitchen's legendary garlic fries, lemon roast chicken, specialty pastas, and burgers. ⊠ *33 E. San Fernando St.,* ☎ *408/294–6785. AE, D, DC, MC, V.*

$ ✕ **Aqui.** This Willow Glen spot is not your typical Mexican restaurant. Its strip-mall exterior gives way to hammered copper doors, comfortable booths, and a creative menu. Mexican favorites like burritos can be ordered with grilled ahi and a wasabi vinaigrette or teriyaki steak and grilled onions. There are also a number of flatbread dishes with a variety of toppings, including turkey and chipotle dressing. There is patio seating in the back. ⊠ *1145 Lincoln Ave.,* ☎ *408/995–0381. No reservations. MC, V.*

$ ✕ **Arena Garden Restaurant.** Aficionados of the Vietnamese soup called *pho* will find this former drive-in fast-food joint a welcome way station, less than a quarter-mile from the sports arena. The soup—rice noodles and meats in a broth fragrant with star anise and other exotic spices—is a classic of northern Vietnam. It arrives in oversize bowls, along with a plate of fresh mint and bean sprouts and a bottle of chili sauce. You can also order Chinese and Thai dishes, meatless soups, and dry rice dishes topped with grilled seafood. Diners receive free parking at the sports arena when the bill comes to $10 or more, a great deal since arena parking costs at least $7. ⊠ *735 The Alameda,* ☎ *408/288–9900. D, MC, V.*

$ ✕ **The Old Spaghetti Factory.** This downtown classic features, of course, spaghetti. The large, cavernous space feels like an old saloon, with worn wood floors and richly colored fringed lamps hanging from the ceiling. There are plenty of sauce variations for your spaghetti including mushroom, white clam, and marinara. Other pasta dishes include ravioli, tortellini, and lasagna. There's nothing unusual here, just basic, good pasta. Don't forget an order of the garlic cheese bread. ⊠ *51 N. San Pedro St.,* ☎ *408/288–7488,* ℻ *408/288–5241. AE, D, DC, MC, V. No lunch weekends.*

$ ✕ **Peggy Sue's.** Settle into a red vinyl booth amid posters of Elvis and Marilyn for a burger and a malt at this classic hamburger joint. As you tap your toes to '50s tunes, peruse the menu and you'll find 19 different takes on the hamburger, from the simple cheeseburger to more creative variations, like the La Bamba burger with hot pepper cheese and grilled pineapple. A modern twist allows you to substitute any burger for a Gardenburger, turkey burger, or chicken. ⊠ *29 N. San Pedro St.,* ☎ *408/298–6750,* ℻ *408/298–6740. AE, D, DC, MC, V.*

$ ✕ **Senora Emma's.** This taqueria serves up large and tasty portions of nachos, tacos, burritos, and quesadillas as well as full meals. You can help yourself to several kinds of salsas, limes, and jalapenos at the salsa bar, and get a margarita at the full bar. The interior of this restaurant may be nothing special to look at, but there's a great sidewalk patio that offers terrific people-watching opportunities. ⊠ *177 N. Santa Clara St.,* ☎ *408/279–3662. AE, MC, V.*

$ ✕ **White Lotus.** The Southeast Asian–influenced meatless dishes at this slightly worn restaurant are deliciously prepared using fresh ingredients. Choose from an extensive menu of vegetable and meat-substitute dishes, like soft, chewy pan-fried rice noodles with tofu and crisp vegetables, curry "chicken," or spicy garlic eggplant. Start your meal with an order of crunchy imperial rolls or the tangy sweet and sour soup. ⊠ *80 N. Market St.,* ☎ *408/977–0540. DC, MC, V. Closed Sun.*

$ ✕ **Willow Street Wood-Fired Pizza.** What began as a quaint "secret"
★ pizzeria in the Willow Glen neighborhood just south of downtown has become one of the best and trendiest spots in the South Bay. Order an individual wood-fired pizza with classic cheese or try something less mun-

dane, such as chicken Brie or artichoke and goat cheese. Moderate appetites can share a large salad and a pizza and be perfectly happy. Reservations are accepted only for parties of eight or more, but smaller parties can call ahead to secure a spot on the waiting list. ⊠ *1072 Willow St.,* ☎ *408/971–7080;* ⊠ *1554 Saratoga Ave.,* ☎ *408/871–0400;* ⊠ *20 S. Santa Cruz Ave., Los Gatos,* ☎ *408/354–5566. AE, MC, V.*

$$$$ 🏨 **Crowne Plaza.** Downtown near the McEnery Convention Center, this former Holiday Inn completed renovations in the spring of 1998. The hotel decor and restaurant feature a tasteful Mediterranean theme; there is a 24-hour fitness center. Rooms are well stocked with extras like terry robes and fine-quality soaps. ⊠ *282 Almaden Blvd., 95110,* ☎ *408/998–0400 or 800/227–6963,* ℻ *408/289–9081. 239 rooms. Restaurant, bar, café, in-room data ports, no-smoking floors, room service, sauna, exercise room, concierge, concierge floors, business services, meeting rooms. AE, D, DC, MC, V.*

$$$$ 🏨 **DoubleTree Hotel.** This full-service hotel's sprawling lobby is filled with activity—restaurants, a gift shop, and plenty of comfortable seating areas. Large desks, modem lines, voice mail, and even portable telephones that work anywhere in the hotel make the rooms practical for business travelers. ⊠ *2050 Gateway Pl., 95110,* ☎ *408/453–4000 or 800/222–8733,* ℻ *408/437–2898. 495 rooms, 10 suites. Restaurant, bar, café, coffee shop, sushi bar, in-room data ports, no-smoking floors, refrigerators, room service, pool, beauty salon, hot tub, sauna, exercise room, nightclub, concierge floors, business services, airport shuttle. AE, MC, V.*

$$$$ 🏨 **Fairmont Hotel.** Affiliated with the famous San Francisco hotel of
★ the same name, this downtown gem offers the utmost in luxury and sophistication. Get lost in the lavish lobby sofas under dazzling chandeliers or dip your feet in the fourth-floor pool, making rings in the exotic palms mirrored in the water. Rooms have every imaginable comfort, from down pillows and custom-designed comforters to oversize bath towels changed twice a day. ⊠ *170 S. Market St., at Fairmont Pl., 95113,* ☎ *408/998–1900 or 800/527–4727,* ℻ *408/227–1648. 541 rooms. 3 restaurants, lobby lounge, no-smoking floors, room service, pool, health club, business services. AE, D, DC, MC, V.*

$$$$ 🏨 **Hotel De Anza.** This lushly appointed art deco hotel has hand-painted ceilings, a warm coral and green color scheme, and an enclosed terrace with towering palms and dramatic fountains. Business travelers will appreciate the many amenities, including a full-service business center and personal voice-mail services. ⊠ *233 W. Santa Clara St., 95113,* ☎ *408/286–1000 or 800/843–3700,* ℻ *408/286–0500. 91 rooms, 9 suites. Restaurant, in-room data ports, minibars, in-room VCRs, exercise room, nightclub. AE, D, DC, MC, V.*

$$$$ 🏨 **Hyatt Sainte Claire.** The first American hotel to utilize an earthquake-protective roller system when it was built in 1926, the Sainte Claire has survived decades of quakes without a whimper. An extensive renovation in 1992 restored its high ceilings, classic chandeliers, and courtyard lined in Spanish tiles, as well as the magnificent painted ceiling in the Palm Room parlor. Many rooms have a colorful night-sky theme. ⊠ *302 S. Market St., 95113,* ☎ *408/885–1234 or 800/233–1234,* ℻ *408/977–0403. 162 rooms. Restaurant, café, in-room data ports, minibars, nightclub, meeting room. AE, D, DC, MC, V.*

$$$–$$$$ 🏨 **Campbell Inn.** There are plenty of reasons to stay 10 minutes from downtown San Jose at this creekside inn in Campbell. You can play tennis, swim in the pool, ride one of the inn's bicycles on a nearby trail, or simply relax in the lobby, with large comfortable chairs and a fireplace. Suites have whirlpool tubs and saunas, and all room rates include a complimentary breakfast buffet. ⊠ *675 E. Campbell Ave., Campbell, 95008,* ☎ *408/374–4300 or 800/582–4449,* ℻ *408/379–0695. 85 rooms, 10 suites. In-room data ports, no-smoking rooms, re-*

frigerators, outdoor pool, outdoor hot tub, 1 tennis court, bicycles, airport shuttle. AE, D, DC, MC, V.

$$$–$$$$ 🏨 **The Hensley House.** This is the only B&B in downtown San Jose, with rooms in either a Victorian or neighboring Craftsman-style house. The antiques-decorated rooms have thoughtful touches like robes, feather mattresses, and down comforters and pillows. They are also equipped for business travelers with in-room modem lines and a fax machine in every room. The complimentary breakfast frequently includes chorizo and eggs or quiche and homemade bread. ⊠ 456 N. 3rd St., 95112, ☎ 408/298–3537 or 800/498–3537, FAX 408/298–4676. 11 rooms, 4 suites. Breakfast room, in-room data ports. AE, D, DC, MC, V.

$$$ 🏨 **Arena Hotel.** This hotel near the San Jose Arena has plenty of bonuses that other city hotels don't. Every room has a 4-ft-square whirlpool tub, CD player, VCR, and kitchenette with a sink, microwave, and refrigerator. The hotel has a library of more than 100 video tapes to choose from. A full breakfast is complimentary. ⊠ 817 The Alameda, 95162, ☎ 408/294–6500 or 800/954–6835, FAX 408/294–6585. 84 rooms, 3 suites. Breakfast room, no-smoking rooms, kitchenettes, room service, in-room VCRs, business services, meeting rooms. AE, D, DC, MC, V.

$$$ 🏨 **Courtyard by Marriott.** Close to the airport, this hotel is designed primarily for business travelers. After a long day, the lobby lounge with its toasty fireplace and full bar is a pleasant place to relax. Don't miss the inviting pool area surrounded by greenery and a wooden gazebo. ⊠ 1727 Technology Dr., 95110, ☎ 408/441–6111 or 800/321–2211, FAX 408/441–8039. 139 rooms, 12 suites. Restaurant, in-room data ports, no-smoking floors, pool, hot tub, exercise room, business services, meeting rooms. AE, D, DC, MC, V.

$$$ 🏨 **Hanford Hotel.** Palm trees surround this appealing low-rise hotel. The large rooms are pleasantly decorated in pastels and include a few extras like in-room voice mail and reclining chairs. A complimentary breakfast is included either at the hotel or at the neighboring restaurant. The hotel is close to the airport, light-rail, and two major freeways. ⊠ 1755 N. First St., 95112, ☎ 408/453–3133 or 800/793–9121, FAX 408/452–1849. 183 rooms, 3 suites. Breakfast room, in-room safes, no-smoking rooms, pool, hot tub, exercise room, coin laundry, business services, meeting rooms, airport shuttle. AE, D, DC, MC, V.

$$$ 🏨 **Homewood Suites Hotel.** Business travelers who require a long stay will appreciate the services at this hotel. These suites feel more homey and less formal than most hotel rooms, and the building looks more like an apartment complex than a traditional hotel. Each room has a full kitchen complete with pots and pans, and a complementary grocery shopping service is available. The rates include a daily breakfast buffet and light dinner. Some suites have wood-burning fireplaces. Local phone calls are free. ⊠ 10 W. Trimble Rd., 95131, ☎ 408/428–9900 or 800/225–5466, FAX 408/428–0222. 140 suites. Breakfast room, snack bar, kitchenettes, refrigerators, pool, exercise room, coin laundry, business services, meeting room, airport shuttle. AE, DC, MC, V.

$$$ 🏨 **Radisson Plaza Hotel.** This hotel near the airport has an elegant charm that many of the newer hotels in San Jose lack. The lobby is decorated with Victorian antiques, polished wood work, and ornate chandeliers. Rooms are on the small side, but they are beautifully decorated with Victorian-style dark wood furniture and elegant gold-frame mirrors. Suites have whirlpool tubs. ⊠ 1471 N. Fourth St., 95112, ☎ 408/452–0200 or 800/333–3333, FAX 408/437–8819. 185 rooms, 8 suites. Restaurant, bar, in-room data ports, no-smoking rooms, room service, pool, hot tub, exercise room, airport shuttle. AE, D, DC, MC, V.

$$$ 🏨 **San Jose Hilton and Towers.** Though the lobby at this conveniently located hotel appears a little dark and formal, rooms are generously

sized. Some have terrific views of San Jose and the hills beyond. The top two floors are concierge levels, with complimentary breakfast and refreshments. ✉ *300 Almaden Blvd., 95110,* ☎ *408/287–2100 or 800/445–8667,* FAX *408/947–4488. 340 rooms, 15 suites. Restaurant, bar, in-room data ports, no-smoking floors, outdoor pool, hot tub, exercise room, concierge, concierge floor, business services, meeting rooms. AE, D, DC, MC, V.*

$$$ 🏨 **Sundowner Inn.** Just off U.S. 101 north of San Jose, this contemporary hotel offers full services for business travelers. There are 500 complimentary video tapes to choose from; there's also a library full of best-sellers you can borrow. A complimentary breakfast buffet is served poolside. ✉ *504 Ross Dr., Sunnyvale 94089,* ☎ *408/734–9900 or 800/223–9901,* FAX *408/747–0580. 92 rooms, 13 suites. Restaurant, no-smoking rooms, pool, sauna, exercise room, laundry service, meeting room. AE, D, DC, MC, V.*

$$$ 🏨 **Wyndham Hotel.** Everything in this lobby is big—from the winding staircase to the giant potted palms and dramatic high ceilings. Warm terra-cotta tones prevail and give the hotel a Mediterranean feel. Moderate-size rooms have views of the surrounding hills. Although it's not downtown, the hotel is across the street from the light-rail. ✉ *1350 N. First St., 95112,* ☎ *408/453–6200 or 800/538–6818,* FAX *408/437–9693. 355 rooms, 5 suites. Restaurant, in-room data ports, no-smoking floors, room service, pool, exercise room, concierge floor, business services. AE, D, DC, MC, V.*

$$-$$$ 🏨 **The Briar Rose Bed & Breakfast Inn.** This charming bed-and-breakfast is set on nearly half an acre of gardens in a restored 1875 Victorian farmhouse. There are plenty of thoughtful touches in the rooms, like antique furniture and feather mattresses, and a lovely front parlor with a marble fireplace. The complimentary breakfast often includes quiche, pancakes, waffles, or omelets. Groups of five or more can enjoy afternoon tea in the garden or back parlor with advance reservations. ✉ *897 E. Jackson St., 95112,* ☎ *408/279–5999,* FAX *408/279–4534. 5 rooms, 1 suite. Breakfast room, in-room data ports. AE, DC, D, MC, V.*

$$ 🏨 **Days Inn.** There's nothing fancy about these motel-style accommodations, but there is a pool, hot tub, and a complimentary Continental breakfast. The hotel is about 5 mi from downtown. ✉ *4170 Monterey Rd., 95111,* ☎ *408/224–4122 or 800/329–7466,* FAX *408/224–4177. 34 rooms. No-smoking rooms, refrigerators, pool, hot tub. AE, D, DC, MC, V.*

Nightlife and the Arts

Because of its size, it's not surprising that San Jose offers Silicon Valley's richest mix of performing arts and other cultural attractions. The city's calendar is packed with everything from film and jazz festivals to crafts fairs and national-class sports events. There are many nightclubs and dance floors within the larger hotels, as well as a burgeoning cluster of small clubs in an area called SoFA—the South of First Area—along 1st and 2nd streets south of San Carlos Avenue.

NIGHTLIFE

Try **Big Lil's Barbary Coast Dinner Theater** (✉ 157 W. San Fernando St., ☎ 408/295–7469) for a fresh take on the Old West; it serves up comedy, melodrama, and ribs on Friday and Saturday evenings. Just west of downtown, the **Garden City Lounge** (✉ 360 S. Saratoga Ave., ☎ 408/244–3333) has free jazz nightly. **Agenda** (✉ 399 S. 1st St., ☎ 408/287–3991) is one of the most popular night spots downtown, with a restaurant on the main floor, a bar upstairs, and a nightclub on the bottom floor. Pick up a pool cue at trendy **South First Billiards** (✉ 420 S. 1st St., ☎ 408/294–7800), in the SoFA conglomeration of clubs.

Mirassou Vineyards (⊠ 3000 Aborn Rd., ☎ 408/274–4000) organizes elegant eight-course candlelight dinners, accenting food and wine pairings ($95 per person). Dinners are offered every spring and fall. Call ahead for a schedule.

THE ARTS

BASS (☎ 408/998–2277) sells tickets to many art events.

The **Center for Performing Arts** (⊠ 255 Almaden Blvd., ☎ 408/277–3900) is the city's main performance venue. **American Musical Theatre of San Jose** (☎ 408/453–7108), the **San Jose Symphony** (☎ 408/288–2828), and the **San Jose Cleveland Ballet** (☎ 408/288–2800) perform at the center.

The **San Jose Repertory Theatre** (⊠ 101 Paseo de San Antonio, ☎ 408/291–2255) occupies a contemporary four-story, 528-seat theater, dubbed "The Blue Box" because of its angular blue exterior.

Outdoor Activities and Sports

BEACHES

About 45 minutes south of San Jose on Highway 17 is the **Santa Cruz Beach Boardwalk**—part Asbury Park and part Coney Island—with its huge weekend crowds of sun-scorched surfers and Bay Area residents. The mile-long boardwalk, lined with rides, amusements, arcades, and a miniature golf course, runs along Beach Street. ⊠ *400 Beach St. (take Hwy. 17 south to Ocean St., follow signs)*, ☎ *831/423–5590; 831/426–7433 for recorded information.* ☜ *$18.95.* ☉ *Memorial Day–Labor Day, daily; Labor Day–Memorial Day, weekends; call for hrs.*

GOLF

The **San Jose Municipal Golf Course** (⊠ 1560 Oakland Rd., ☎ 408/441–4653) is an 18-hole course. The **Cinnabar Hills Golf Club** (⊠ 23600 McKean Rd., ☎ 408/323–5200) is a 27-hole course that opened in 1998.

SPECTATOR SPORTS

Known to area sports fans as the Shark Tank or, simply, the Tank, the 17,483-seat **San Jose Arena** (⊠ Santa Clara St. at Autumn St., ☎ 408/287–9200; 408/998–2277 for tickets) looks like a giant hothouse, with its glass entrance, shining metal armor, and skylight ceiling. In addition to hosting a national tennis tour, the Sybase Open in early February, basketball games, music concerts, ice-skating shows, and other events, the arena is home to the National Hockey League's **San Jose Sharks**. Call **BASS** (☎ 408/998–2277) for tickets.

The **San Jose Clash** (☎ 408/985–4625) brought major league soccer to the Bay Area in 1996. Look for the team in San Jose's **Spartan Stadium** (⊠ 7th St. between E. Alma Ave. and E. Humboldt St.); at other times of the year they host qualifying games for international soccer competitions.

The **Hellyer Velodrome** (⊠ 985 Hellyer Ave., ☎ 408/226–9716) hosts bicycle races of all levels between May and August on Friday evening from 7:30 to 10. Admission is $5. The velodrome was built in 1961 and is the only one in northern California. It attracts national-class cyclists and Olympians in training.

WALKING AND CYCLING

The paved 9-plus-mi **Los Gatos Creek Trail** spans San Jose, Campbell, and Los Gatos, with one staging area with parking and rest rooms on Gilman Street and Campbell Avenue.

Shopping

The malls of Silicon Valley are a mind-blowing maze of shopping habitats, including **Eastridge Mall** (⊠ Capitol Expressway and Tully Rd.,

☎ 408/274–0360), **Valley Fair Shopping Center** (✉ 2855 Stevens Creek Blvd., Santa Clara/San Jose, ☎ 408/248–4450), and **Vallco Fashion Park** (✉ 10123 N. Wolfe Rd., Cupertino, ☎ 408/255–5660).

Originally opened in 1960 with 20 sellers, the **San Jose Flea Market** is part Mexican *mercado* (market), part carnival, and part garage sale. Some 2,700 vendors spread over 120 acres sell handicrafts, leather, jewelry, furniture, produce, and more. Be sure to examine merchandise before buying. ✉ *1590 Berryessa Rd., between Hwys. 680 and 101,* ☎ *408/453–1110.* ⌸ *Free; parking $5 weekends, $1 weekdays.* ⏱ *Wed.– Sun. dawn–dusk.*

The **Prime Outlets at Gilroy** (✉ 681 Leavesley Rd., ☎ 408/842–3729 or 800/980–7467) are located in Gilroy, 45 minutes south of San Jose. Bargain shoppers will find discounts of up to 75% on clothing and gear by Esprit, Brooks Brothers, Anne Klein, Nike, and Eddie Bauer.

Santa Clara

40 mi south of San Francisco on U.S. 101, 4 mi west of San Jose on Hwy. 82.

Santa Clara's offerings include two major attractions at opposite ends of the sightseeing spectrum: Mission Santa Clara de Asis, founded in 1777, and Paramount's Great America, northern California's answer to Disneyland. Although many visitors head straight to the amusement park, Santa Clara has plenty of history and is worthy of a brief visit—despite the sprawling shopping malls and sterile business parks. The old part of the city borders the west side of Santa Clara University. In these neighborhoods there are some exemplary examples of Victorian homes, some well preserved, some fallen into disrepair.

Santa Clara University, founded in 1851 by Jesuits, was California's first college. The campus's **de Saisset Art Gallery and Museum** has a permanent collection that includes California mission artifacts and a full calendar of temporary exhibits. ✉ *500 El Camino Real,* ☎ *408/ 554–4528.* ⌸ *Free.* ⏱ *Tues.–Sun. 11–4.*

In the center of Santa Clara University's campus is the **Mission Santa Clara de Asis,** the 8th of 21 California missions founded under the direction of Father Junípero Serra and the first to honor a woman. The mission's present site was the fifth chosen, after the first four were flooded by the Guadalupe River and destroyed by earthquakes. In 1926 the permanent mission chapel was destroyed by fire. Roof tiles of the current building, a replica of the original, were salvaged from earlier structures, which dated from the 1790s and 1820s. Early adobe walls and a spectacular rose garden with 4,500 roses—many classified as antiques—remain as well. Part of a wooden **Memorial Cross** from 1777 is set in front of the Santa Clara Mission church. ✉ *500 El Camino Real,* ☎ *408/ 554–4023.* ⌸ *Free.* ⏱ *Daily 1–sundown for self-guided tours.*

Ⓒ At **Paramount's Great America** 100-acre theme park, on the edge of San Francisco Bay, each section recalls a familiar part of North America: Hometown Square, Yukon Territory, Yankee Harbor, County Fair, and Orleans Place. Popular attractions include the "Drop Zone Stunt Tower," the tallest free-fall ride in North America; the "Vortex," a stand-up roller coaster; a *Top Gun* movie–theme roller coaster, whose cars travel along the outside of a 360-degree loop track; Xtreme Skyflyer, which lifts you by harness more than 17 stories high and drops you back to earth at 60 mph; and "Nickelodeon Splat City," 3 acres of obstacle courses apparently designed for kids who love to get wet and dirty. "Kidzville," a town site for kids with interactive rides, opened in 1999. The park is served by Santa Clara County Transit and the Fremont BART station. ⊠ *Great America Pkwy. between U.S. 101 and Hwy. 237 (6 mi north of San Jose)*, ☎ *408/988–1776.* ▨ *$32.99; parking $6.* ☉ *Mid-Mar.–May and Sept.–Oct., weekends; June–Aug., daily; opens 10 AM, closing times vary with season. AE, D, MC, V.*

Visitors to the **Intel Museum** can learn how computer chips are made and follow the development of Intel Corporation's microprocessor, memory, and systems product lines. Guided tours are available by reservation. ⊠ *Robert Noyce Bldg., 2200 Mission College Blvd.,* ☎ *408/765–0503.* ▨ *Free.* ☉ *Weekdays 8–5.*

The **Carmelite Monastery** is a fine example of Spanish Ecclesiastical architecture. Built in 1917, it's on the grounds of a historic ranch crossed by shady walkways and dotted with benches perfect for quiet contemplation. The grounds are open Monday through Saturday 6:30–5, Sunday 8–5. Mass, open to the public, is held at 7:15 AM Monday through Saturday and 10:30 AM on Sunday. ⊠ *1000 Lincoln St.,* ☎ *408/296–8412.* ▨ *Free.*

From the Carmelite Monastery a stroll up Lincoln Street will bring you to Civic Center Park. Here a **statue of St. Clare,** patron saint of Santa Clara, rises out of a fountain. The sculpture was cast in Italy in 1965 by Anne Van Kleeck, who used an ancient wax process. It was then shipped around Cape Horn and dedicated on this site in 1985. ⊠ *Civic Center Park, Lincoln St. at El Camino Real.*

Skylights cast natural light for viewing the exhibitions in the **Triton Museum of Art.** A permanent collection of 19th- and 20th-century sculpture by artists from the Bay Area is displayed in the garden, which you can see through a curved-glass wall at the rear of the building. Inside there are rotating exhibits of contemporary works in a variety of media and a permanent collection of 19th- and 20th-century American artists, many from California. In 1999, the museum's permanent Native American collection went on display for the first time. ⊠ *1505 Warburton Ave.,* ☎ *408/247–3754.* ▨ *$2 suggested donation.* ☉ *Tues. 10–9, Wed.–Sun. 10–5.*

The tiny **Santa Clara Historic Museum** exhibits artifacts and photos that trace the history of the region. ⊠ *1509 Warburton Ave.,* ☎ *408/248–2787.* ▨ *Free.* ☉ *Sun. 1–4.*

Walk over to the grounds of **city hall** to see noted San Francisco sculptor Benny Bufano's primitive *Universal Child,* facing the museum. The 85-ft statue depicts the children of the world standing as one.

The **Harris-Lass Historic Museum** is built on Santa Clara's last farmstead. A restored house, summer kitchen, and barn convey a sense of life on the farm from the early 1900s through the 1930s. Guided tours take place every half hour until 3:30. ⊠ *1889 Market St.,* ☎ *408/249–7905.* ▨ *$3.* ☉ *Weekends noon–4.*

Dining and Lodging

$$–$$$ ✕ **Birk's.** Silicon Valley's businesspeople come to this sophisticated American grill to unwind after a hard day of paving the way to the future. High-tech sensibilities will appreciate the modern open kitchen and streamlined, multilevel dining area—yet the menu is traditional, strong on steaks and chops with a California flair. Try the smoked prime rib, served with garlic mashed potatoes and creamed spinach. ⊠ *3955 Freedom Circle, at U.S. 101 and Great America Pkwy.,* ☎ *408/980–6400. AE, D, DC, MC, V. No lunch weekends.*

$$ ✕ **Mio Vicino.** Mio's is a small, bare-bones, checkered-tablecloth Italian bistro in Old Santa Clara, with the same sense of warmth and friendli-

ness you might find in an Italian grandmother's kitchen. The menu includes a long list of classic and contemporary pastas—and if you don't see it on the menu, just ask. The house specialties are shellfish pasta and chicken cannelloni. ✉ *1290 Benton St.,* ☎ *408/241–9414;* ✉ *384 E. Campbell Ave., Campbell,* ☎ *408/378–0335. MC, V. No lunch weekends.*

$ ✕ **Su's Mongolian BBQ.** People familiar with Mongolian barbecue know that you don't come for the atmosphere of folding chairs, old Formica tables, and a poster listing employee rights. Instead you come for the food, which is cheap, tasty, and served in all-you-can-eat portions. The real treat is filling a bowl with your choice of thinly sliced, flash-frozen meats, then topping it with a combination of vegetables and spices, oyster sauce, and hot chilies. Hand the bowl to a chef at the stand-up griddle and, moments later, a delicious stir-fry is handed back to you. ✉ *1111 El Camino Real,* ☎ *408/985–2958. MC, V. No lunch weekends.*

$$$$ ▨ **Embassy Suites.** This upper-end chain hotel is ideal for Silicon Valley business travelers and families bound for Great America. Every room in the hotel is a two-room suite, equipped with a microwave and refrigerator. Guests receive complimentary cooked-to-order breakfasts and evening beverages. Inquire about free tickets to the Winchester Mystery House in San Jose. ✉ *2885 Lakeside Dr., 95054,* ☎ *408/496–6400 or 800/362–2779,* ⨳ *408/988–7529. 257 suites. Restaurant, lounge, in-room data ports, no-smoking rooms, room service, pool, sauna, hot tub, exercise room, meeting rooms, airport shuttle, free parking. AE, D, DC, MC, V.*

$$$ ▨ **Biltmore Hotel & Suites.** This hotel's central Silicon Valley location makes it a popular choice for business travelers. Other attractions are a microbrew-pub, espresso bar, and 16 meeting rooms. Suite accommodation includes a complimentary breakfast. ✉ *2151 Laurelwood Rd., 95054,* ☎ *408/988–8411 or 800/255–9925,* ⨳ *408/988–0225. 98 rooms, 164 suites. Restaurant, lounge, in-room data ports, no-smoking rooms, pool, hot tub, health club, meeting rooms, airport shuttle, free parking. AE, D, DC, MC, V.*

$$ ▨ **Madison Street Inn.** At this refurbished Queen Anne Victorian, a complimentary full breakfast and afternoon refreshments are served on a brick garden patio with a bougainvillea-draped trellis. The inn has the distinct look of a private home, with a green-and-red-trim facade. ✉ *1390 Madison St., 95050,* ☎ *408/249–5541,* ⨳ *408/249–6676. 6 rooms, 4 with bath. No-smoking rooms, pool, hot tub, meeting rooms. AE, D, DC, MC, V.*

Nightlife and the Arts

AMC Mercado 20 (✉ 3111 Mission College Blvd., ☎ 408/919–0248), Northern California's largest movie complex, features "love seat" chairs with retractable handles as well as stadium seating, with every row at least 18 inches higher than the one in front. Digital sound and a shopping complex with trendy restaurants promises a thoroughly enjoyable movie experience.

Backbeat (✉ 777 Lawrence Expressway, ☎ 408/241–0777) is a club for South Bay twenty- and thirtysomethings. The happy-hour buffet, included in the cover charge ($5–$12), isn't your typical chips, dips, and buffalo wings, but a tasty spread of main dishes, salads, and fresh breads. Music is from the '70s, '80s, and '90s, and there's a large dance floor, a private cigar club, and a private suite for up to 12 people. A strict dress code doesn't allow jeans, work boots, sweats, or any "overly revealing clothing."

ComedySportz (✉ 3428 El Camino Real, ☎ 408/985–5233) is a comedy club where teams of professional comedians square off in a contest of improvisation Thursday to Saturday nights.

Saratoga

50 mi south of San Francisco on I–280, 10 mi southwest of San Jose on I–280 or Hwy. 85.

A 10-mi detour southwest from San Jose's urban core puts you in the heart of Saratoga, at the foot of the Santa Cruz Mountains. Once an artists' colony, the town is now home to many Silicon Valley CEOs whose mansions dot the hillsides. Spend a slow-paced afternoon exploring Big Basin Way, the ⅓-mi main drag of the Village, as the downtown area is locally known. Here you'll find antiques stores, galleries, gift shops, and a handful of worthwhile restaurants. Or, for a quick driving tour of the hills with their sweeping valley views, drive south out of town on Big Basin Way, which becomes Highway 9. After about 1½ mi take a right on Pierce Road, toward the Mountain Winery.

Built in 1912 by former governor James Phelan, **Villa Montalvo** is a striking white mansion presiding over an expansive lawn. Inside there's an art gallery with changing exhibits by local artists and artists-in-residence (call ahead to make sure an exhibit is on). You can picnic and lounge on the lawn. Additional draws are a gift shop and 175-acre park with several hiking trails. ⊠ *15400 Montalvo Rd.,* ☎ *408/961–5800.* ☑ *Free.* ⊙ *Park: daily 9–5. Gallery: Thurs.–Fri. 1–4, weekends 11–4.*

One of the most peaceful and meditative attractions in the area is the Zen-style **Hakone Gardens,** nestled on a steep hillside just south of downtown. Designed in 1918 by Aihara Naoharu, who had been an imperial gardener in Japan, the gardens have been carefully maintained, with koi (carp) ponds and sculptured shrubs. ⊠ *21000 Big Basin Way,* ☎ *408/741–4994.* ☑ *Free; parking $5, free 1st Tues. of month.* ⊙ *Weekdays 10–5, weekends 11–5.*

Dining and Lodging

$$–$$$$ ✕ **La Fondue.** Waiters here come out with trays of condiments—pesto and Cajun spices are among the most popular—to mix into your appetizer cheese fondue tableside. Next you'll receive a pot of boiling wine or broth (never oil) in which to cook the meat or vegetable of your choice; try wild game or tender filet mignon. If you can manage it, finish off with a pot of chocolate fondue. Ask to sit in the star room in back if you're in an outlandish mood: Its tie-dye ceiling drapings and gold stars are sure to make an impression. ⊠ *14510 Big Basin Way,* ☎ *408/867–3332. Reservations essential. AE, D, MC, V. No lunch.*

$$$ ✕ **Sent Sovi.** This small, flower-draped restaurant, housed in a quaint
★ cottage on Saratoga's quiet main street, takes its name from a six-century-old Catalan cookbook. Chef and co-owner David Kinch offers a small, regularly changing menu of refined European fare. You might find potato-wrapped sea bass with wild mushrooms and red wine broth, spice-glazed roast quail stuffed with gingerbread, or napoleon of lobster salad with toasted cumin crackers. Desserts are equally tantalizing, especially a hazelnut waffle with silky caramel sauce. A five-course tasting menu will let you sample more widely from Kinch's remarkable repertoire. ⊠ *14583 Big Basin Way,* ☎ *408/867–3110. AE, MC, V. Closed Mon. No lunch.*

$$–$$$ ✕ **Bella Saratoga.** This local favorite is a hit for weekend jazz brunches and hearty Italian meals. Pastas are made fresh. Other specialties are grilled seafood and all kinds of meats. Come at night to enjoy the elegant Victorian ambience, or on a sunny afternoon for a quiet snack on the outdoor porch. ⊠ *14503 Big Basin Way,* ☎ *408/741–5115. Reservations essential for weekend brunch. AE, D, MC, V.*

$$$–$$$$ ▥ **Inn at Saratoga.** Though this five-story European-style inn is only 10 minutes from San Jose, its aura of calm makes it feel far from busy

Silicon Valley. All rooms have secluded sitting alcoves overlooking a peaceful creek, and the sun-dappled patio provides a quiet retreat. Modern business conveniences are available but discreetly hidden. The entire hotel is no-smoking. ⊠ 20645 4th St., 95070, ☎ 408/867–5020; 800/338–5020; 800/543–5020 in CA; ℻ 408/741–0981. 42 rooms, 3 suites. Business services, meeting room. AE, DC, MC, V.

\$\$–\$\$\$ 🏨 **Saratoga Oaks Lodge.** This small and cozy inn occupies a historic site that was once the tollgate to a private road heading over the Santa Cruz mountains. Originally little more than a rough-and-tumble campground, the Saratoga Oaks has since progressed from a tent-cabin resort to a motel to today's fully renovated lodge. Each room comes equipped with a microwave and refrigerator; some have fireplaces and steam baths. ⊠ 14626 Big Basin Way, 95070, ☎ 408/867–3307, ℻ 408/867–6765. 15 rooms, 5 suites. In-room data ports, refrigerators, no-smoking rooms. AE, D, MC, V.

Nightlife and the Arts

The **Plumed Horse** (⊠ 14555 Big Basin Way, ☎ 408/867–4711) is known for good contemporary jazz.

Summer concerts at **Villa Montalvo** (⊠ 15400 Montalvo Rd., Saratoga, ☎ 408/961–5858 for tickets) are performed on an intimate outdoor stage where seats give you a sweeping view of the valley—particularly spectacular at sunset. There's also a carriage house where concerts are performed throughout the rest of the year. In addition to the concerts at the villa itself, a summer concert series takes place at the Mountain Winery in the hills above Saratoga.

Outdoor Activities and Sports

Garrod Farms Stables (⊠ 22600 Mount Eden Rd., ☎ 408/867–9527) provides horse and pony rentals.

Shopping

Bit-O-Country (⊠ 14527 Big Basin Way, ☎ 408/867–9199) carries just what the name implies: countrified knickknacks that range from handmade pillows and scented candles to cookie cutters and greeting cards. Stock up on dishes, linens, home accessories, and gifts at **The Butter Paddle** (⊠ 14510 Big Basin Way, ☎ 408/867–1678), where all profits are donated to the local Eastfield Ming Quong Foundation for abused and troubled children. **Corinthian Corners** (⊠ 14416 Big Basin Way, ☎ 408/867–4630) is an antiquarian's dream, with baskets of estate jewelry, fine European furniture, and grandfather clocks worth up to \$12,500. You might find a dusty carousel horse in a back corner.

South Bay Essentials

Arriving and Departing

BY BUS AND TRAIN

CalTrain (☎ 800/660–4287) runs from 4th and Townsend streets in San Francisco to Santa Clara's Railroad and Franklin streets stop near the university (\$4.75 one-way) and to San Jose's Rod Diridon station (\$5.25 one-way). The trip to Santa Clara takes approximately 1¼ hours; the trip to San Jose takes about 1½ hours. A **shuttle** (☎ 408/321–2300) links downtown San Jose to the CalTrain station, across from the Arena, every 20 minutes during morning and evening commute hours.

BY CAR

By **car,** the quickest route to San Jose from San Francisco is I–280. From there take the Guadalupe Parkway (also known as Highway 87) north, then the Santa Clara Street exit east for the most direct route to downtown San Jose. For Saratoga, take Highway 85 south from I–280 before you reach San Jose, then take the Saratoga/Sunnyvale Road exit and drive south, following the signs.

To reach Santa Clara, take U.S. 101 and exit south on San Tomas Expressway; turn left on El Camino Real (also labeled Highway 82 on maps, though few locals call it that). To avoid the often-heavy commuter traffic on U.S. 101, use Highway 280 during rush hours. From I–280, just before the San Jose exit, take I–880 north to The Alameda, which becomes El Camino Real (Highway 82); turn left off the exit ramp and follow the signs to Santa Clara.

To reach Saratoga, take I–280 south to Highway 85, and follow Highway 85 south toward Gilroy. Exit on Saratoga–Sunnyvale Road, go south, and follow the signs to the Village—about 2½ mi. Signs will also direct you to Hakone Gardens and Villa Montalvo.

BY PLANE

San Jose International Airport (⊠ 1661 Airport Blvd. off Hwy. 87, ☎ 408/277–4759) is served by most major airlines. **South & East Bay Airport Shuttle** (☎ 408/559–9477) transports visitors to and from the airport.

Getting Around

In San Jose **light-rail trains** run 24 hours a day and serve most major attractions, shopping malls, historic sites, and downtown. Trains run every 10 minutes weekdays from 6 AM to 8 PM, and vary during weekends and late-night hours from every 15 minutes to once an hour. Tickets are valid for two hours; they cost $1.10 one-way or $2.50 for a day pass. Historic trolleys operate in downtown San Jose from 10:30 to 5:30 during the summer and on some holidays throughout the year. Buy tickets for both the light-rail and the trolleys at vending machines in any transit station. For more information call or visit the **Downtown Customer Service Center** (⊠ 2 N. 1st St., San Jose, ☎ 408/321–2300).

Valley Transportation Authority (☎ 408/321–2300 or 800/894–9908) buses run efficiently, although not as frequently as a visitor might like. Operators can help you plan routes.

Guided Tours

A **Historical Walking Tour** of downtown San Jose is detailed in a brochure available from the Convention and Visitors Bureau. The self-guided walk leads you past the 14 historical buildings described in the brochure.

Visitor Information

The **San Jose Convention and Visitors Bureau** offers information on the entire South Bay. The bureau has two offices within a few blocks of each other, one in the lobby of the San Jose McEnery Convention Center, and the other just down the street; both supply events calendars and information about housing, tours, and other activities. ⊠ 150 W. San Carlos St., 95110, ☎ 408/977–0900. ☺ Weekdays 8–5:30, weekends 11–5; and ⊠ 333 W. San Carlos St., Suite 1000, 95110, ☎ 408/295–9600. ☺ Weekdays 8–5.

San Jose Convention and Visitors Bureau information hot line (☎ 408/295–2265). **Santa Clara Chamber of Commerce and Convention and Visitors Bureau** (⊠ 1850 Warburton Ave., 95050, ☎ 408/244–8244). **Saratoga Chamber of Commerce** (⊠ 20460 Saratoga–Los Gatos Rd., 95070, ☎ 408/867–0753).

9 THE WINE COUNTRY

You don't have to be a wine enthusiast to appreciate the mellow beauty of Napa and Sonoma counties, whose rolling hills and verdant vineyards resemble those of Tuscany and Provence. Here, among state-of-the-art wineries, fabulous restaurants, and luxury hotels where mud baths and massage are daily rituals, you just might discover that life need have no nobler purpose than enjoying the fruits of the earth.

Updated by
Marty
Olmstead

N 1862, AFTER AN EXTENSIVE TOUR of the wine-producing areas of Europe, Count Agoston Haraszthy de Mokcsa reported a promising prognosis about his adopted California: "Of all the countries through which I passed, not one possessed the same advantages that are to be found in California. . . . California can produce as noble and generous a wine as any in Europe; more in quantity to the acre, and without repeated failures through frosts, summer rains, hailstorms, or other causes."

The "dormant resources" that the father of California's viticulture saw in the balmy days and cool nights of the temperate Napa and Sonoma valleys are in full fruition today. The wines produced here are praised and savored by connoisseurs throughout the world. The area also continues to be a proving ground for the latest techniques of grape growing and wine making.

Ever more competitive, vintners constantly hone their skills, aided by the scientific know-how of graduates of the nearby University of California at Davis and by the practical knowledge of the grape growers. They experiment with high-density vineyard planting, canopy management (to control the amount of sunlight that reaches the grapes), and filtration of the wine.

For many, wine making is a second career. Any would-be wine maker can rent the cumbersome, costly machinery needed to stem and press the grapes. Many say making wine is a good way to turn a large fortune into a small one, but that hasn't deterred the doctors, former college professors, publishing tycoons, art dealers, and others who come here to try their hand at it.

In 1975 Napa Valley had no more than 20 wineries; today there are more than 240. In Sonoma County, where the web of vineyards is looser, there are well over 150 wineries, and development is now claiming the cool Carneros region, at the head of the San Francisco Bay, deemed ideal for growing the chardonnay grape. Within these combined regions of the Wine Country, at least 120 wineries have opened in the last six years alone. Nowadays individual grape growers produce their own wines instead of selling their grapes to larger wineries. As a result, smaller "boutique" wineries harvest excellent, reasonably priced wines that have caught the attention of connoisseurs and critics, while the larger wineries consolidate land and expand their varietals.

This state-of-the-art viticulture has also given rise to a gastronomic renaissance. Inspired by the creative spirit that produces the region's great wines, esteemed chefs are opening restaurants in record numbers, making culinary history in the process.

In addition to great food and wine, you'll find a wealth of California history in the Wine Country. The town of Sonoma is filled with remnants of Mexican California and the solid, ivy-covered, brick wineries built by Haraszthy and his disciples. Calistoga is a virtual museum of Steamboat Gothic architecture, replete with the fretwork and clapboard beloved of Gold Rush prospectors and late 19th-century spa goers. St. Helena is home to a later architectural fantasy, the beautiful art nouveau mansion of the Beringer brothers. The latter-day postmodern extravaganza of Clos Pegase is in Calistoga.

The area's natural beauty draws a continuous flow of tourists—from the spring, when the vineyards bloom yellow with wild mustard, to the fall, when the grapes are ripe. Haraszthy was right: This is a chosen place.

Pleasures and Pastimes

Dining

Many star chefs from urban areas throughout the United States have migrated to the Wine Country, drawn by the area's renowned produce and world-class wines—the products of fertile soil and near-perpetual sun. As a result of this marriage of imported talent and indigenous bounty, food now rivals wine as the principal attraction of the region.

Higher quality has, of course, meant higher prices. However, those on a budget will also find appealing inexpensive eateries. High-end delis offer superb picnic fare, and brunch is a cost-effective strategy at pricey restaurants.

With few exceptions (which are noted in individual restaurant listings), dress is informal. Where reservations are indicated as essential, you may need to reserve a week or more ahead. During the summer and early fall harvest seasons you may need to book several months ahead. For dining price ranges, *see* Chapter 2.

Galleries and Museums

More and more artists and art dealers are discovering the Napa Valley as a showplace for original works of art. Internationally famous artists and local artists exhibit their work side by side in galleries that showcase artistic styles to suit every taste. Shows at most galleries are scheduled throughout the year, and exhibitions change frequently.

Hot-Air Ballooning

Day after day, colorful balloons fill the morning sky high above the Wine Country's valleys. To aficionados, peering down at vineyards from the vantage point of the clouds is the ultimate California experience. Balloon flights take place soon after sunrise, when the calmest, coolest time of day offers maximum lift and soft landings. Prices depend on the duration of the flight, number of passengers, and services. Some companies provide such extras as pickup at your lodging or champagne brunch after the flight. Expect to spend about $175 per person.

Lodging

In a region where first-class restaurants and wineries attract connoisseurs from afar, it's no surprise that elegant lodgings have sprung up to accommodate them. Ranging from quaint to utterly luxurious, the area's many inns, hotels, and spas are usually exquisitely appointed. Most local bed-and-breakfasts have historic Victorian and Spanish architecture and serve a full breakfast highlighting local produce. The newer hotels and spas are often state-of-the-art buildings offering such comforts as massage treatments or spring water–fed pools. Many house world-class restaurants or are a short car ride away from gastronomic bliss.

Not surprisingly, a stay in the Wine Country is expensive. Since Santa Rosa is the largest population center in the area, it has the largest selection of rooms, many at moderate rates. Try there if you've failed to reserve in advance or have a limited budget. Many B&Bs are fully booked long in advance of the summer season, and small children are often discouraged as guests. For all accommodations in the area, rates are lower on weeknights and about 20% less in the winter. For lodging price ranges, *see* Chapter 3.

Spas and Mud Baths

Mineral water soaks, mud baths, and massage are rejuvenating local traditions. Calistoga, known worldwide as the Hot Springs of the West, is famous for its warm, spring water–fed mineral tubs and mud baths full of volcanic ash. Sonoma, St. Helena, and other towns also have full-service spas.

Wine Tasting

Wine tasting can be an educational, fascinating, and even mysterious ritual. The sight of polished glasses and uniquely labeled bottles lined up in a row, the tour guide's commentary on the character of each wine, the decadent mood of the vineyards with their full-to-bursting grapes—all combine to create an anticipation that's gratified with the first sip of wine. Learning about the origin of the grapes, the terraces on which they're grown, the weather that produced them, and the methods by which they're transformed into wine will give you a new understanding and appreciation of wine—and a great afternoon (or all-day) diversion. For those new to the wine tasting game, Mondavi (☞ Oakville, *below*) and Korbel Champagne Cellars (☞ Healdsburg, *below*) give general tours geared toward teaching novices the basics on how wine and champagne are made and what to look for when you taste.

There are more than 400 wineries in Sonoma and Napa, so it pays to be selective when planning your visit. Better to mix up the wineries with other sights and diversions—a picnic, trips to local museums, a ride in a hot-air balloon—than attempt to visit too many in one day. Unless otherwise noted, the wineries in this chapter are open daily year-round and charge no fee for admission, tours, or tastings.

Exploring the Wine Country

Numbers in the text correspond to numbers in the margin and on the Wine Country map.

Great Itineraries

The Wine Country is comprised of two main areas: the Napa Valley and the Sonoma Valley. Five major paths cut through both valleys: U.S. 101 and Highways 12 and 121 through Sonoma County, and Highway 29 north from Napa. The 25-mi Silverado Trail, which runs parallel to Highway 29 north from Napa to Calistoga, is a more scenic, less crowded route with a number of distinguished wineries.

Because the Wine Country is expansive, it's best to plan smaller, separate trips over the course of several days. You can get a feel for the area's towns and vineyards by taking to the open road over a weekend. Along the way you can stop at a winery or two, have a picnic lunch, and watch the countryside glide past your windshield. With four or five days you'll be able to explore more towns and wineries and also indulge in dining adventures. You might even bike the Silverado Trail or fish the Russian River. A full week will allow time for all of the above, plus pampering at the region's hot springs and mud baths, a round of golf, and a hot-air balloon ride.

IF YOU HAVE 2 DAYS

Start at the circa-1857 **Buena Vista Carneros Winery** ㉙. From there, take Highway 12 north to the Oakville Grade to historic 🏛 **St. Helena,** taking time to admire the views of Sonoma and Napa valleys from the Mayacamas Mountains. After lunch in St. Helena, take the 30-minute tour of **Beringer Vineyards** ㉑. The next day drive to **Calistoga** for an early morning balloon ride, an afternoon trip to the mud baths, and a visit to **Clos Pegase** ㉖ before heading back to St. Helena for dinner at Greystone—the Culinary Institute of America's beautiful West Coast campus and highly acclaimed restaurant.

IF YOU HAVE 4 DAYS

Concentrate on the Napa Valley, starting at Yountville and traveling north to Calistoga. Make your first stop in **Oakville,** where the circa-1880s Oakville Grocery—once a Wells Fargo Pony Express stop—is indisputably the most popular place for picnic supplies. Enjoy the picnic grounds at **Robert Mondavi** ⑫ before touring the winery and tasting the wine. If time permits, spend the night in the town of ⊞ **Rutherford** and visit either **Frog's Leap** ⑰ or the **Niebaum–Coppola Estate** ⑲, or continue north to ⊞ **St. Helena.** Take a look at the Silverado Museum and visit the shopping complex surrounding the **Freemark Abbey Winery** ㉓. On the third day drive to ⊞ **Calistoga** for a balloon ride before heading north to Old Faithful Geyser of California, then continue on to Robert Louis Stevenson State Park, which encompasses the summit of Mount St. Helena. On the fourth day take Highway 29 just north of Calistoga proper, head west on Petrified Forest Road and then south on Calistoga Road, which runs into Highway 12. Follow Highway 12 southeast to **Glen Ellen** for a taste of the Sonoma Valley. Visit Jack London State Historic Park, then loop back north on Bennett Valley Road to beautiful **Matanzas Creek Winery** ㉟ in Santa Rosa.

IF YOU HAVE 7 DAYS

Begin in the town of **Sonoma,** whose colorful plaza and mission evoke early California's Spanish past. Afterward, head north to ⊞ **Glen Ellen** and the Valley of the Moon. Picnic and explore the grounds at Jack London State Historic Park. Next morning visit **Kenwood Vineyards** ㉝ before heading north to ⊞ **Healdsburg** in Dry Creek Valley via Santa Rosa and U.S. 101. In this less-trafficked haven of northern Sonoma County, a host of "hidden" wineries—including **Ferrari-Carano Winery** ㊴—lie nestled in the woods along the roads. Spend the night in **Healdsburg.** On the third day cross over into Napa Valley—take Mark Springs Road east off U.S. 101's River Road exit and follow the signs on Porter Creek Road to Petrified Forest Road to Highway 29. Spend the day (and the night) in the quaint town of ⊞ **Calistoga,** noted for its mud baths and mineral springs. Wake up early on the fourth day for a balloon ride. If you're feeling energetic, take to the Silverado Trail for a bike ride with stops at **Cuvaison** ㉕, **Stag's Leap Wine Cellars** ⑩, and **Clos du Val** ⑧. On day five, visit the galleries, shops, and eateries of St. Helena before heading to the Oakville Grocery, a must-see (and must-taste) landmark. Spend the night and visit the wineries in ⊞ **Rutherford.** On day six, explore nearby **Yountville,** stopping for lunch at one of its many acclaimed restaurants before heading up the hill to the **Hess Collection Winery and Vineyards** ⑥, on Mt. Veeder, where a brilliant art collection and excellent wines may keep you occupied for hours. Splurge on dinner at Domaine Chandon. On your last day return to the town of Sonoma via the Carneros Highway, stopping for a look at how brandies are made at the **RMS Brandy Distillery** ③, then moving on to the landmark **Buena Vista Carneros Winery** ㉙, or **Gloria Ferrer Champagne Caves** ②.

When to Tour the Wine Country

"Crush," the term used to indicate the season when grapes are picked and crushed, usually takes place in September or October, depending on the weather. From September until December the entire Wine Country celebrates its bounty with street fairs and festivals. The Napa Valley Wine Festival takes place the first weekend in November. The Sonoma County Harvest Fair, with its famous grape stomp, is held the first weekend in October. Golf tournaments, wine auctions, and art and food fairs occur throughout the fall.

In season (April–October), Napa Valley draws crowds of tourists, and traffic along Highway 29 from St. Helena to Calistoga is often backed up on weekends. The Sonoma Valley, Santa Rosa, and especially Healdsburg are less crowded. In season and over holiday weekends it's best to book lodging, restaurant, and winery reservations well in advance. Many wineries give tours at specified times and require appointments.

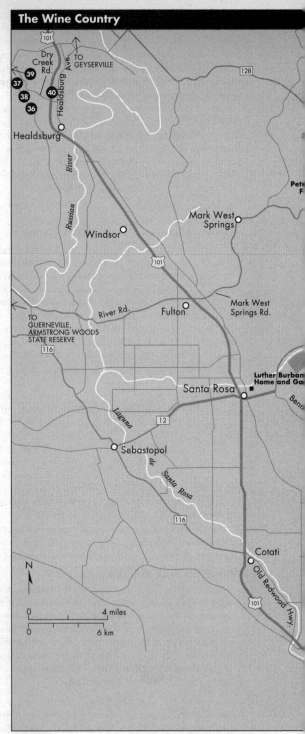

The Wine Country

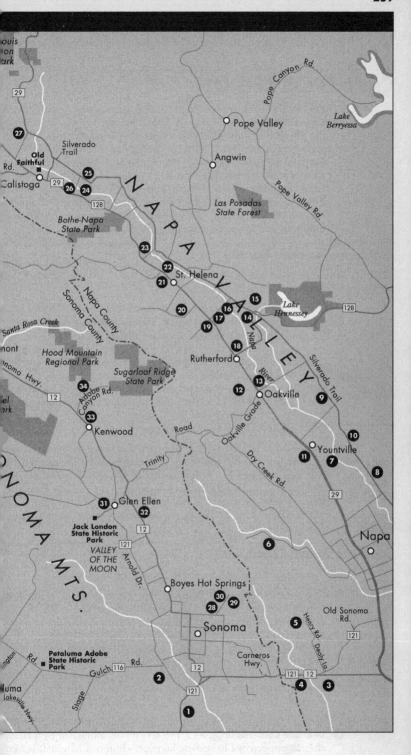

To avoid crowds, visit the Wine Country during the week and get an early start in the morning (most wineries open around 10). Pack a sun hat, since summer is usually hot and dry, and autumn can be even hotter.

CARNEROS REGION

One of the most important viticultural areas in the Wine Country straddles southern Sonoma and Napa counties. The Carneros region has a long, cool growing season tempered by maritime breezes and lingering fogs off the San Pablo Bay—optimum slow-growing conditions for pinot noir and chardonnay grapes. So exotic looking are the misty Carneros marshlands that Francis Ford Coppola chose them as the location for scenes of the Mekong Delta in his 1979 movie *Apocalypse Now.* When the sun is shining, however, Carneros looks like a sprawling and scenic expanse of quintessential wine country, where wildflower meadows and vineyards stretch toward the horizon.

Southern Sonoma County

36 mi from San Francisco, north on U.S. 101, east on Hwy. 37, and north on Hwy. 121.

① Sam Sebastiani, of the famous Sebastiani family, decided to strike out on his own and with his wife, Vicki, opened **Viansa.** Reminiscent of a Tuscan villa, the winery's ocher-color building is surrounded by olive trees and overlooks the valley. The varietals produced here depart from the traditionally Californian and include muscat canelli and nebbiolo. The Italian Marketplace on the hillside premises sells delicious specialty sandwiches and salads to complement Viansa's Italian-style wines. The on-site Wine Country Visitor Center has brochures and information. ✉ *25200 Arnold Dr., Sonoma County,* ☎ *707/935–4700.* ☉ *Daily 10–5. Tours by appointment.*

② The array of sparkling and still wines at **Gloria Ferrer Champagne Caves** originated with a 700-year-old stock of Ferrer grapes. The method here is to age the wines in a "cava," or cellar, where several feet of earth maintain a constant temperature—an increasingly popular alternative to temperature-controlled warehouses. ✉ *23555 Carneros (Hwy. 121)* ☎ *707/996–7256.* ⌸ *Tasting fees vary.* ☉ *Daily 10:30–5:30. Tours hourly 11–4.*

Southern Napa County

7 mi east of Hwy. 121/Hwy. 116 junction on Hwy. 121/12.

③ Learn the history and folklore of rare alembic brandy at the **RMS Brandy Distillery.** Tours include an explanation of the double-distillation process, which eliminates all but the finest spirits for aging; a view of the French-built alembic pot stills that resemble Aladdin's lamp; a trip to the atmospheric oak barrel house, where taped chants create an otherworldly mood; and a sensory evaluation of vintage brandies (no tasting allowed, by law). ✉ *1250 Cuttings Wharf Rd., Napa (from Domaine Carneros, head 1 mi east on Carneros Hwy.),* ☎ *707/253–9055,* ⅁ *707/253–0116.* ☉ *Apr.–Oct., daily 10–5; Nov.–Mar., daily 10:30–4:30. Tours on the hr.*

④ **Domaine Carneros** occupies a 138-acre estate dominated by a classic château inspired by Champagne Taittinger's historic Château de la Marquetterie in France. Carved into the hillside beneath the winery, Domaine Carneros's cellars produce sparkling wines reminiscent of the Taittinger style and using only Carneros grapes. At night the château is a glowing beacon rising above the dark vineyards. By day activity buzzes throughout the visitor center, the touring and tasting rooms, and the kitchen and dining room, where private luncheons and dinners emphasize food and wine pairings. ⊠ *1240 Duhig Rd., Napa,* ☎ *707/257–0101,* FAX *707/257–3020.* 🍽 *Tasting fees vary.* ☉ *Mon.– Thurs. 10:30–5, Fri.–Sun. 10:30–6. Tours Mon.–Thurs. at 11, 1, and 3; Fri.–Sun. hourly 11–3.*

THE NAPA VALLEY

The Napa Valley is the undisputed capital of American wine production, with more than 240 wineries. Famed for its unrivaled climate and neat rows of vineyards, the area is made up of small, quirky towns whose Victorian Gothic architecture—narrow, gingerbread facades and pointed arches—is reminiscent of a distant world. Calistoga feels like an Old West frontier town, with wooden-plank storefronts and people in cowboy hats. St. Helena is posh, with tony shops and elegant restaurants. Yountville is small, concentrated, and redolent of American history, yet fast becoming an up-to-the-minute culinary hub.

With long country roads winding through the region, bicycling is a popular pastime. For rentals try **Napa Valley Bike Tours and Rentals** (⊠ 4080 Byway E, Napa, ☎ 707/255–3377, FAX 707/255–3380).

Napa

8 mi from Cuttings Wharf Rd. to downtown Napa, east on Hwy. 121/ 12, north on Hwy. 29; 46 mi from San Francisco, east and north on I–80 to Hwy. 37 west to Hwy. 29 north.

Although the city of Napa doesn't offer much in the way of attractions yet, plans are underway for a new food and wine center and a restored opera house. The oldest town in the Napa Valley—established in 1848— it also claims an advantageous location. Most destinations in both the Napa and Sonoma valleys are easily accessible from here. For those seeking an affordable alternative to the hotels and B&Bs in the heart of the Wine Country, Napa is a good option. But choose lodgings on the north side of town near Yountville. Parts of Napa are downright seedy.

⑤ Bunkered into a scenic Carneros hilltop, **Codorniu Napa** produces California sparkling wines distinguished by a higher percentage of chardonnay grapes than most sparklings (a 50–50 blend of chardonnay and pinot noir). ⊠ *1345 Henry Rd., north off Old Sonoma Rd. and Dealy La.,* ☎ *707/224–1668,* FAX *707/224–1672.* ☉ *Daily 10–5. Tours daily; times vary.*

★ ⑥ The **Hess Collection Winery and Vineyards** is a delightful discovery on a hilltop 9 mi northwest of Napa (don't give up; the road leading to the winery is long and winding). Within the simple, rustic limestone structure, circa 1903, you'll find Swiss owner Donald Hess's personal art collection, including works by such contemporary European and American artists as Robert Motherwell, Francis Bacon, and Frank Stella. Cabernet sauvignon is the real strength here, though Hess also produces some fine chardonnays. The winery and the art collection are open for self-guided tours. ⊠ *4411 Redwood Rd., west off Hwy. 29,* ☎ *707/255–1144,* FAX *707/253–1682.* ☉ *Daily 10–4.*

⑦ The winery at **Trefethen Vineyards** was built in 1886. Today it's the only wooden, gravity-powered winery in Napa. Trefethen is known for its reserve cabernet as well as its 1993 merlot, available only on the premises. ⊠ *1160 Oak Knoll Ave., off Hwy. 29,* ☎ *707/255–7700.* ☉ *Daily 10–4:30. Tours by appointment.*

8 **Clos du Val,** founded by French owner Bernard Portet, produces a celebrated reserve cabernet. It also makes zinfandel, pinot noir, merlot, sangiovese, and chardonnay. Although the winery itself is austere, the French-style wines age beautifully. ⊠ *5330 Silverado Trail,* ☎ *707/259-2200.* 🖭 *Tasting fee $5.* ☉ *Daily 10–5. Tours by appointment.*

9 Small **Pine Ridge** makes estate-bottled wines, including chardonnay, cabernet, and merlot. Tours include barrel tastings in the winery's caves. ⊠ *5901 Silverado Trail,* ☎ *707/253–7500,* 🅵🅰🆇 *707/253–1493.* ☉ *Daily 11–5. Tours by appointment at 10:15, 1, and 3.*

Dining and Lodging

$$$ ✕ **Silverado Country Club.** There are two restaurants and a bar and grill at this large, famous resort. The elegant Vintner's Court, with California–Pacific Rim cuisine, serves dinner only; there is a seafood buffet on Friday night and a champagne brunch on Sunday. Royal Oak serves steak and seafood for dinner nightly. The bar and grill is open for breakfast and lunch year-round. In the summer lunch offerings include an outdoor barbecue with chicken and hamburgers. ⊠ *1600 Atlas Peak Rd. (follow signs to Lake Berryessa),* ☎ *707/257–0200. Reservations essential. AE, D, DC, MC, V. Vintner's Court closed Mon.-Tues. No dinner Sun.*

$–$$ ✕ **Bistro Don Giovanni.** Even in winter, the valley views from the covered patio here are extraordinary. The wine list at the restaurant of Giovanni and Donna Scala is as locally representative as their menu is eclectic. Don't miss the individual pizzas cooked in a wood-burning oven, the handmade pastas, or the focaccia sandwiches concealing grilled vegetables. The terra-cotta tile floors and high ceilings create a casual Mediterranean feel. ⊠ *4110 St. Helena Hwy. (Hwy. 29),* ☎ *707/224–3300. AE, D, MC, V.*

$–$$ ✕ **Celadon.** Venture into downtown Napa for chef-owner Greg Cole's creative and enticing food. Dishes like flash-fried calamari with a chipotle chili and ginger glaze and small tasting plates such as a large crab cake laced with whole-seed mustard sauce make this an ideal place to sample contemporary cuisine accompanied by any of a dozen wines available by the glass. ⊠ *1040 Main St.,* ☎ *707/254–9690. AE, MC, V. Closed Sun.*

$$$–$$$$ 🏨 **Silverado Country Club and Resort.** This luxurious if somewhat staid 1,200-acre property in the hills east of Napa has cottages, kitchen apartments, and one- to three-bedroom efficiencies, many with fireplaces. With two golf courses, nine pools, and 23 tennis courts, it's a place for serious sports enthusiasts and anyone who enjoys the conveniences of a full-scale resort. ⊠ *1600 Atlas Peak Rd. (6 mi east of Napa via Hwy. 121), 94558,* ☎ *707/257–0200 or 800/532–0500,* 🅵🅰🆇 *707/257–2867. 277 condo units. 3 restaurants, bar, 9 pools, 2 18-hole golf courses, 23 tennis courts, bicycles. AE, D, DC, MC, V.*

$$ 🏨 **Chateau Hotel.** Despite the name, this is a pretty simple motel with only the barest nod to France. Clean rooms, a great location, Continental breakfast, facilities for travelers with disabilities, and discounts for senior citizens make up for its lack of charm. ⊠ *4195 Solano Ave. (west of Hwy. 29, exit at Trower Ave.), 94558,* ☎ *707/253–9300; 800/253–6272 in CA,* 🅵🅰🆇 *707/253–0906. 115 rooms. Refrigerators, pool, hot tub. AE, D, DC, MC, V.*

Nightlife and the Arts

In 1995, former telecommunications tycoon and vintner William Jarvis and his wife transformed a historic stone winery building in downtown Napa into the **Jarvis Conservatory,** an excellent venue for baroque French ballet and Spanish operetta known as zarzuela. Performances open to the public are held in conjunction with workshops and festivals centered on these two art forms. ⊠ *1711 Main St.,* ☎ *707/255–5445.* ☉ *Regular shows scheduled 1st Sat. of month; call for ticket prices and listing of other shows.*

Outdoor Activities and Sports

FISHING
You can fish from the banks of the Napa River at **John F. Kennedy Park** (⊠ 2291 Streblow Dr., ☎ 707/257–9529). There are also picnic facilities and barbecue pits. Call ahead for river conditions.

GOLF
The 18-hole **Chardonnay Club** (⊠ 2555 Jameson Canyon Rd., ☎ 707/257–8950) course is a favorite among Bay Area golfers. The greens fee, $65 weekdays and $85 weekends, includes a cart. Within the vicinity of the Silverado Trail, the **Silverado Country Club** (⊠ 1600 Atlas Peak Rd., ☎ 707/257–0200) has two challenging 18-hole courses with a beautiful view at every hole. The greens fee is $120, including a cart; you must be a guest to play.

TENNIS
Vintage High School (⊠ 1375 Trower Ave.) maintains eight public tennis courts. **Napa High School** (⊠ 2474 Jefferson St.) maintains six tennis courts with coin-operated night lights. Call the Napa Valley School District (☎ 707/253–3715) for information.

Yountville

13 mi north of the town of Napa on Hwy. 29.

Yountville has become the valley's boomtown, with two new hotels and two new restaurants opening in 1998, plus a host of shops and wineries. Another attraction is **Vintage 1870** (⊠ 6525 Washington St., ☎ 707/944–2451), a 26-acre complex of boutiques, restaurants, and gourmet stores. The vine-covered brick buildings were built in 1870 and housed a winery, livery stable, and distillery. The original mansion of the property is now the popular Mexican-style **Compadres Bar and Grill**. Nearby is the **Pacific Blues Café**, housed in the train depot Samuel Brannan built in 1868 for his privately owned Napa Valley Railroad. At **Yountville Park** there's a picnic area with tables, barbecue pits, and a view of grapevines.

At the intersection of Madison and Washington streets, Yountville's quaint and historic **Washington Square** was the town's original main square. Today it's a complex of boutiques and family-style restaurants. **Pioneer Cemetery,** the final resting place of the town's founder, George Yount, is across the street from Washington Square.

⑩ In 1995, the World Wine Championships gave **Stag's Leap Wine Cellars** a platinum award for its 1990 reserve chardonnay, designating it the highest-ranked premium chardonnay in the world. The winery's proprietary red table wine, Cask 23, consistently earns accolades as well. ⊠ *5766 Silverado Trail,* ☎ *707/944–2020.* ⌦ *Tasting fee $3.* ☉ *Daily 10–4. Tours by appointment.*

⑪ French-owned **Domaine Chandon** claims one of Yountville's prime pieces of real estate, on a knoll west of downtown. Tours of the sleek, modern facilities on the beautifully maintained property include sample flutes of the méthode champenoise sparkling wine. Champagne is $3.70–$6.75 per glass, hors d'oeuvres are complimentary, and an elegant restaurant beckons. ⊠ *California Dr., west of Hwy. 29,* ☎ *707/944–2280.* ☉ *Nov.–Feb., daily 11–6; Mar.–Oct., 11–8. Tours on the hr.*

Dining and Lodging

$$$$ ✕ **French Laundry.** Napa Valley's most acclaimed restaurant can be found
★ inside an old converted brick building on a residential street corner.
The prix fixe menus, which include four or five courses, always include
two or three additional surprises—little bitefuls—to start, such as a tiny
ice cream cone filled with salmon tartare or a quail egg sandwiched
between a crown of caviar and a base of brioche. Your meal thus
launched, a full three hours will likely pass before you reach dessert.
Chef Thomas Keller, with two coveted James Beard awards on his man-
tel, doesn't lack for admirers. Reservations are hard won and not accepted more than two months in advance, but lunch is a little easier
to come by. ✉ *6640 Washington St.,* ☎ *707/944–2380. Reservations
essential. AE, MC, V. Closed 1st 2 wks in Jan.; lunch hrs and days vary
with the season.*

$$$–$$$$ ✕ **Domaine Chandon.** This large, formal dining room is decorated in
shades of gray and green with gold accents, as if to match the oak trees
outside. Wrought-iron grapevines twist through the railings that un-
obtrusively define spacious dining areas. Typical dishes, such as rack
of lamb or Sonoma duck breast, blend continental and California
cuisines. The dining room looks out over acres of vineyards and na-
tive oaks. When the weather is good, try for a seat on the tree-shaded
terrace, an ideal spot for sipping a glass of bubbly and admiring its
source. Don't be surprised to encounter a wedding party in full swing
almost anytime of the year. ✉ *California Dr. (take Yountville exit off
Hwy. 29 toward Veterans' Home),* ☎ *707/944–2892. Reservations es-
sential. AE, D, DC, MC, V. No dinner Mon.–Tues. Apr.–Oct.*

$$$ ✕ **Brix.** Overlooking vineyards and the Mayacamas Mountains, the
spacious yellow-and-green dining room invites you to sit back and enjoy
the East–West menu. Scallops are served with a Thai lime-butter sauce,
and salmon is flavored with a light soy glaze. A wood-fired oven is used
for cooking pizzas. Desserts receive an Asian accent as well, with a gin-
ger crème brûlée among the offerings. ✉ *7377 St. Helena Hwy.,* ☎
707/944–2749. AE, D, DC, MC, V.

$$–$$$ ✕ **Bistro Jeanty.** In 1998 Philippe Jeanty, who put Domaine Chandon's
restaurant on the map, opened his own restaurant with a menu inspired
by the cooking of his French childhood. His traditional cassoulet will
warm those nostalgic for bistro cooking, while classic coq au vin rises
above the ordinary with the infusion of a spicy red wine sauce. The scene
here is Gallic through and through with a small bar and a handful of
tables in a crowded room. French graphic posters festoon the walls along
with photographs of beaming and obviously well-fed chefs. The wait-
staff, some French and some American, are not as knowledgeable, especially about the wine list, as they should be. ✉ *6510 Washington St.,*
☎ *707/944–0103. MC, V. Closed last wk of Jan., 1st wk of Feb.*

$$–$$$ ✕ **Bouchon.** Thomas and Joseph Keller, flush with the success of their
French Laundry, opened a second restaurant in the fall of 1998. And
for the sake of everyone in their business (including fellow restaurant
employees who work very late), they're keeping it open from 7 AM until
2 AM. On their French country menu, typical courses include *steak frites,*
leg of lamb, and sole meunière—served amid elegant antique chandeliers and a snazzy zinc bar. ✉ *6534 Washington St.,* ☎ *707/944–
8037. AE, MC, V.*

$$ ✕ **Mustards Grill.** Everyone's favorite Napa Valley restaurant, Mus-
★ tards attracts winemakers and other locals as well as hungry tourists.
Grilled fish, steak, local fresh produce, and an impressive wine list are
the trademarks of this boisterous bistro with a black-and-white mar-
ble floor and upbeat artwork. The thin, crisp, golden onion rings are
addictive. ✉ *7399 St. Helena Hwy., 1 mi north of Yountville,* ☎ *707/
944–2424,* FAX *707/944–0828. Reservations essential. D, DC, MC, V.*

$ ✕ **The Diner.** An unpretentious classic, this breakfast-centric eatery has local sausages and house potatoes that are not to be missed. Healthful versions of Mexican and American classics are served for dinner. ⌷ *6476 Washington St.,* ☎ *707/944–2626. No credit cards. Closed Mon.*

$$$$ ⌷ **Napa Valley Lodge.** Balconies, covered walkways, and a red tile roof imbue this inn with the ambience of a hacienda. The large pool area is landscaped with lots of greenery. Many spacious second-floor rooms have vineyard views. Fresh brewed coffee, Continental breakfast, and the morning paper are complimentary. ⌷ *2230 Madison St., at Hwy. 29,* ☎ *707/944–2468 or 800/368–2468,* ⌷ *707/944–9362. 55 rooms. Refrigerators, pool, hot tub, sauna, exercise room. AE, D, DC, MC, V.*

$$$$ ⌷ **Vintage Inn.** Accommodations in this luxurious inn are arranged in two-story villas throughout the 3½-acre property. All the spacious rooms have fireplaces, whirlpool baths, refrigerators, private verandas or patios, hand-painted fabric bedspreads, window seats, and shuttered windows. Guests are treated to a welcome bottle of wine, Continental breakfast with champagne, and afternoon tea. ⌷ *6541 Washington St., 94599,* ☎ *707/944–1112 or 800/351–1133,* ⌷ *707/944–1617. 80 rooms. Refrigerators, pool, hot tub, tennis court, bicycles. AE, D, DC, MC, V.*

$$$–$$$$ ⌷ **La Residence.** Even though it's within feet of the St. Helena Highway, "La Res," as it's known, is secluded and romantic enough to make you feel as if you've flown to France, or at least New Orleans. The hotel is housed in two buildings: the Mansion, a renovated 1870s Gothic Revival manor house built by a riverboat captain from New Orleans; and Cabernet Hall, a French-style barn. Both buildings overlook a pool, a manicured garden, and towering oak trees that bathe the entire property in shade. The spacious rooms have period antiques, fireplaces, and double French doors opening onto verandas or patios. ⌷ *4066 St. Helena Hwy. (Hwy. 29), 4 mi south of Yountville,* ☎ *707/253–0337,* ⌷ *707/253–0382. 20 rooms. Dining room, pool, hot tub, business services. AE, DC, MC, V.*

$$$ ⌷ **Petit Logis.** In 1997 Jay and Judith Caldwell remodeled a row of shops into a small, charming one-story inn. Wall murals and 11-ft ceilings infuse each unique room with a European elegance. Breakfast, included in the room rate, is offered at one of two nearby restaurants. ⌷ *6527 Yount St., 94599,* ☎ *707/944–2332. 5 rooms. MC, V.*

Hot-Air Ballooning

Balloons Above the Valley (⌷ Box 3838, Napa 94558, ☎ 707/253–2222; 800/464–6824 in CA) is a reliable organization. Also try **Napa Valley Balloons** (⌷ Box 2860, Yountville 94599, ☎ 707/944–0228; 800/253–2224 in CA).

Oakville

2 mi west of Yountville on Hwy. 29.

There are three reasons to visit the town of Oakville: its grocery store, its scenic mountain grade, and its magnificent, highly exclusive winery. The **Oakville Grocery** (⌷ 7856 St. Helena Hwy.), built in the late 1880s to serve as a grocery store and Wells Fargo Pony Express stop, carries gourmet foods and difficult-to-find wines. Custom-packed picnic baskets are a specialty. Along the mountain range that divides the Napa and Sonoma valleys, the **Oakville Grade** is a twisting half-hour route with breathtaking views of both valleys. Though the surface of the road is good, it can be difficult to negotiate at night, and trucks are advised not to attempt it at any time.

⑫ At **Robert Mondavi,** the most famous winery in the nation, visitors are encouraged to take the 60-minute production tour with complimentary tasting, before trying the reserve reds ($1–$5 per glass). In-depth three- to four-hour tours and gourmet lunch tours are also popular. Afterward, visit the art gallery, or stick around for a summer concert. ⊠ *7801 St. Helena Hwy., Oakville,* ☎ *707/259–9463.* ⊙ *Daily 9–5. Tours by appointment.*

⑬ **Opus One,** the combined venture of famed California wine maker Robert Mondavi and French baron Philippe Rothschild, is famed for its vast (1,000 barrels side by side on a single floor) semicircular barrel cellar modeled on the Château Mouton Rothschild winery in France. The futuristic building is the work of the same architects who built San Francisco's Transamerica Pyramid. The state-of-the-art facilities produce about 20,000 cases of ultrapremium Bordeaux-style red wine from grapes grown in the estate's own vineyards and in the surrounding Oakville appellation. ⊠ *7900 St. Helena Hwy.,* ☎ *707/963–1979, FAX 707/944–1753.* 🎫 *Tasting fee $25.* ⊙ *Daily 10–3:30. Tours by appointment.*

Rutherford

1 mi northwest of Oakville on Hwy. 29.

From a fast-moving car, Rutherford is a quick blur of dark forest, a rustic barn or two, and maybe a country store. Then it's gone. But don't speed by this tiny hamlet. With its singular microclimate and soil, this is an important viticultural center.

⑭ A joint venture of Mumm—the French champagne house—and Seagram, **Mumm Napa Valley** is considered one of California's premier sparkling-wine producers. Its Napa Brut Prestige and ultrapremium Vintage Reserve are the best known. The excellent tour and comfortable tasting room are two more good reasons to visit. An art gallery contains a permanent exhibit of photographs by Ansel Adams that record the wine-making process. ⊠ *8445 Silverado Trail,* ☎ *707/942–3434.* 🎫 *Tasting fees vary.* ⊙ *May–Oct., daily 10:30–6; Nov.–Apr., daily 10–5. Tours daily 11–4.*

⑮ The wine at **Rutherford Hill Winery** is aged in French oak barrels stacked in more than 30,000 square ft of caves—one of the largest such facilities in the nation. Tours of the caves can be followed by a picnic in oak, olive, or madrone orchards. ⊠ *200 Rutherford Hill Rd., off the Silverado Trail,* ☎ *707/963–7194.* 🎫 *Tasting fees vary.* ⊙ *Daily 10–5. Tour times vary seasonally; call ahead.*

⑯ **Caymus Vineyards** is run by wine master Chuck Wagner, who started making wine on the property in 1972. His family, however, had been farming the land (grapes and plums) since 1906. Today a 100% cabernet sauvignon special selection is the winery's claim to fame. Caymus also turns out a superior white, the Conundrum Proprietary, made of an unusual blend of grapes—sauvignon blanc, semillon, chardonnay, muscat canelli, and viognier. ⊠ *8700 Conn Creek Rd.,* ☎ *707/963–4204.* ⊙ *Daily 10–4:30. No tours.*

⑰ **Frog's Leap** is the perfect place for wine novices to begin their education. Owners John and Julie Williams maintain a sense of humor and a humble attitude that translates into an informative and satisfying experience. They also happen to produce some of the finest zinfandel, cabernet sauvignon, and sauvignon blanc in the Wine Country. Call ahead for directions. There is no tasting room. ⊠ *8815 Conn Creek Rd.,* ☎ *707/963–4704.* ⊙ *Tours by appointment.*

18 **Beaulieu Vineyard** utilizes the same wine-making process, from crush to bottle, as it did the day it opened in 1900. The winery's cabernet is a benchmark of the Napa Valley. The Georges du Latour Private Reserve (1994 and 1995 both received high scores from major wine publications) remains a collector's favorite. ⊠ *1960 St. Helena Hwy. (Hwy. 29),* ☎ *707/963–2411.* ▨ *Tasting fee $18 in Reserve Room.* ◷ *Daily 10–5. Tours daily 11–4.*

In the 1970s, filmmaker Francis Ford Coppola bought the old Niebaum estate, a part of the then-world-famous Inglenook estate. He resurrected an early Inglenook-like quality red with his first bottle of Rubicon, released in 1985. Since then, **Niebaum-Coppola Estate** has consistently received high ratings, and in 1995 Coppola purchased the other half of the Inglenook estate, the ancient, ivy-covered château and an additional 95 acres of land. When you're through touring the winery, take a look at the Coppola movie memorabilia, which includes Don Corleone's desk and chair from *The Godfather* and costumes from *Dracula.* ⊠ *1991 St. Helena Hwy. (Hwy. 29),* ☎ *707/963–9099.* ▨ *Tasting fee $7.50.* ◷ *Daily 10–5. Tours daily; times vary.*

Dining and Lodging

$$$$ ✕▥ **Auberge du Soleil.** This stunning property, terraced on a hill stud-
★ ded by olive trees, offers some of the valley's best views. The hotel's renowned restaurant has a frequently changing menu that emphasizes local produce and also includes such unusual specialties as roasted lobster sausage and rosemary-roasted rack of lamb. Slow-roasted garlic with homemade pretzels and pan-seared salmon sandwiches are standouts on the moderately priced bar menu. Guest rooms, except for the most expensive ones, run a bit small; all are decorated with a nod to the spare side of Southwestern style. ⊠ *180 Rutherford Hill Rd. (off Silverado Trail just north of Rte. 128), 94573,* ☎ *707/963–1211 or 800/348–5406,* FAX *707/963–8764. 50 rooms. Restaurant, pool, hot tub, massage, steam room, 3 tennis courts, exercise room. AE, D, DC, MC, V.*

$$$–$$$$ ▥ **Rancho Caymus Inn.** California-Spanish in style, this cozy inn has well-maintained gardens and large suites with kitchens and whirlpool baths. Well-chosen details include beehive fireplaces, tile murals, stoneware basins, and llama-hair blankets. ⊠ *1140 Rutherford Rd. (junction of Hwys. 29 and 128), 94573,* ☎ *707/963–1777 or 800/845–1777,* FAX *707/963–5387. 26 rooms. DC, MC, V. 2-night minimum Apr.–Nov.*

St. Helena

2 mi northwest of Oakville on Hwy. 29.

By the time Charles Krug planted grapes in St. Helena around 1860, quite a few vineyards already existed. Today the town beckons visitors with its abundant selection of wineries—many of which lie along the route from Yountville to St. Helena—and restaurants, including Greystone on the West Coast campus of the Culinary Institute of America. Arching sycamore trees bow across Main Street (Highway 29) to create a pleasant, shady drive.

20 Known for its barrel-fermented chardonnay, the family-owned **Flora Springs** winery tasting room is housed in a lovely old stone building. The actual winery is a couple of miles away. ⊠ *677 St. Helena Hwy. S (Hwy. 29),* ☎ *707/967–8032.* ▨ *Tasting fee $3.* ◷ *Mon.–Sat. 10–4.*

Arguably the most beautiful winery in the Napa Valley, the 1876
21 **Beringer Vineyards** is also the oldest continuously operating one. In 1883 the Beringer brothers, Frederick and Jacob, built the Rhine House Mansion, where tastings are now held among Belgian art nouveau hand-carved oak and walnut furniture and stained-glass windows. Tours, given

every 30 minutes, include a visit to underground wine tunnels made of volcanic ash that were dug by Chinese laborers during the 19th century. ⊠ *2000 Main St.,* ☎ *707/963–4812.* ⊙ *Daily 9:30–4; summer hrs sometimes extend to 5. Tours daily every 30 mins.*

㉒ **Charles Krug Winery** opened in 1861 when Count Haraszthy loaned Krug a small cider press. Today, it is run by the Peter Mondavi family. The gift shop stocks everything from gourmet food baskets with grape-shape pasta to books about the region and its wines. The joint tasting and tour fee is $3. ⊠ *2800 N. Main St.,* ☎ *707/963–5057.* ⊙ *Daily 10:30–5:30. Tours 11:30, 1:30, and 3:30.*

㉓ **Freemark Abbey Winery,** originally called the Tychson Winery after Josephine Tychson, the first woman to establish a winery in California, has long been known for its cabernets, whose grapes come from the fertile Rutherford Bench. All other wines are estate grown, including a much-touted late-harvest riesling. ⊠ *3022 St. Helena Hwy. N,* ☎ *707/963–9694.* ⊙ *Daily 10–4:30. Tour daily at 2.*

Grapeseed mudwraps and Ayurvedic-inspired massages performed by two attendants are among the trademarks of the upscale **Health Spa Napa Valley** (⊠ 1030 Main St., ☎ 707/967–8800), which has a pool and a health club. Should your treatments leave you too limp to operate your car, you can walk to Tra Vigne and other St. Helena restaurants.

For some nonalcoholic sightseeing, visit the **Silverado Museum,** next door to the public library. Its Robert Louis Stevenson memorabilia consists of more than 8,000 artifacts, including first editions, manuscripts, and photographs. ⊠ *1490 Library La.,* ☎ *707/963–3757.* ☎ *Free.* ⊙ *Tues.–Sun. noon–4.*

The **Culinary Institute of America,** the country's leading school for chefs, set up its West Coast headquarters in the century-old Greystone Winery, the former site of the Christian Brothers Winery and a national historic landmark. The CIA campus consists of 30 acres of herb and vegetable gardens, a 15-acre merlot vineyard, and a Mediterranean-inspired restaurant (☞ Wine Spectator Greystone Restaurant, *below*) that's open to the public. Also on the property are a well-stocked culinary store, a quirky corkscrew and winepress museum, and a culinary library. Cooking demonstrations are occasionally scheduled for nonstudents. ⊠ *2555 Main St.,* ☎ *800/333–9242,* ⨳ *707/967–1113.*

Dining and Lodging

$$$–$$$$ ✕ **Terra.** A romantic restaurant housed in a century-old stone foundry, Terra is especially known for its exquisite Mediterranean-inspired dishes, many with Asian touches. The sweetbreads ragout and osso buco are memorable, as are many of the fish dishes. Save room for desserts. ⊠ *1345 Railroad Ave.,* ☎ *707/963–8931. Reservations essential. MC, V. Closed Tues. No lunch.*

$$–$$$ ✕ **Showley's.** Often overlooked by tourists intent on the latest hot spot, this local favorite is well worth a little detour from the beaten path. Garlic chicken and roasted monkfish with garlic mashed potatoes are among the recommended items on the changing menu here. Starters are equally well prepared, especially the chili *en nogada,* made with pork, pine nuts, and chutney and served with a walnut–crème fraîche sauce. ⊠ *1327 Railroad Ave.,* ☎ *707/963–1200. AE, D, MC, V. Closed Mon.*

$$–$$$ ✕ **Wine Spectator Greystone Restaurant.** This restaurant, housed in the handsome old Christian Brothers' winery, is run by the Culinary Institute of America. Century-old stone walls house a large and bustling restaurant, with cooking, baking, and grilling stations in full view. The

menu has a Mediterranean spirit and emphasizes such small plates as bruschetta topped with wild mushrooms and *muhammara*, a spread of roasted red peppers and walnuts. ⊠ *2555 Main St.,* ☎ *707/967–1010. AE, DC, MC, V.*

$$ ✕ **Brava Terrace.** Vegetables plucked straight from the restaurant's own garden are used to enliven chef Fred Halpert's trademark New American cuisine. Brava has a comfortably casual ambience with a full bar, a large stone fireplace, a romantic outdoor terrace overlooking a shady brook, and a heated deck with views of the valley floor and Howell Mountain. ⊠ *3010 St. Helena Hwy. (Hwy. 29), ½ mi north of downtown St. Helena,* ☎ *707/963–9300. Reservations essential. AE, D, DC, MC, V. Closed Wed. Nov.–Apr. and last 2 wks of Jan.*

$$ ✕ **Tra Vigne.** This Napa Valley fieldstone building has been transformed
★ into a striking trattoria with a huge wood bar, high ceilings, and plush banquettes. Homemade mozzarella, olive oil and vinegar, and house-cured pancetta and prosciutto contribute to a mouth-watering tour of Tuscan cuisine. Although getting a table without a reservation is sometimes difficult, drop-ins can dine at the bar. The outdoor courtyard in summer is a sun-splashed Mediterranean vision of striped umbrellas and awnings, crowded café tables, and rustic pots overflowing with flowers. On occasion, the kitchen has been maddeningly inconsistent. ⊠ *1050 Charter Oak Ave., off Hwy. 29,* ☎ *707/963–4444. Reservations essential in dining room. D, DC, MC, V.*

$$$$ ✕🏨 **Meadowood Resort.** Secluded at the end of a semi-private road, this 256-acre resort has accommodations in a rambling country lodge and several bungalow suites. For the popular Sunday brunch (nonguests welcome), refined French cuisine with a California twist is served à la carte or as part of a prix fixe menu in either a dining room with a cathedral ceiling, a fireplace, and greenery or outdoors on a terrace overlooking the golf course. The Grill, a less formal, less expensive Meadowood restaurant, serves a lighter menu of pizzas and spa food for breakfast and lunch (and early dinners on Friday and Saturday). ⊠ *900 Meadowood La., 94574,* ☎ *707/963–3646 or 800/458–8080,* 𝔽𝔸𝕏 *707/963–5863. 40 rooms, 45 suites. 2 restaurants (reservations essential), bar, room service, 2 pools, hot tub, massage, sauna, steam room, 9-hole golf course, 7 tennis courts, croquet, health club. AE, D, DC, MC, V.*

$$$–$$$$ 🏨 **Harvest Inn.** The larger-than-average rooms at this Tudor-esque inn are on the dark side, but the lushly landscaped grounds are lovely. Most rooms have wet bars, refrigerators, antique furnishings, and fireplaces. Pets are allowed in certain rooms for a $20 fee. Complimentary breakfast is served in the breakfast room and on the patio overlooking the vineyards. ⊠ *1 Main St., 94574,* ☎ *707/963–9463 or 800/950–8466,* 𝔽𝔸𝕏 *707/963–4402. 55 rooms. Refrigerators, 2 pools, hot tub. AE, D, DC, MC, V.*

$$$–$$$$ 🏨 **Wine Country Inn.** Surrounded by a pastoral landscape of hills, old
★ barns, and stone bridges, this is a peaceful New England–style retreat. Rural antiques fill all the rooms, most of which overlook the vineyards with either a balcony, patio, or deck. Most rooms have fireplaces, and some have private hot tubs. A hearty country breakfast is served buffet style in the sun-splashed common room, and wine tastings are scheduled in the afternoon. ⊠ *1152 Lodi La. (off Hwy. 29), 94574,* ☎ *707/963–7077,* 𝔽𝔸𝕏 *707/963–9018. 24 rooms. Pool, hot tubs. MC, V.*

$–$$$ 🏨 **El Bonita Motel.** A cute motel with such pleasant touches as window boxes and landscaped grounds, the conveniently located El Bonita has relatively elegant furnishings with muted pastel walls and floral upholstery. ⊠ *195 Main St. (Hwy. 29), 94574,* ☎ *707/963–3216 or 800/541–3284,* 𝔽𝔸𝕏 *707/963–8838. 41 rooms. Pool. AE, MC, V.*

Shopping

Handcrafted candles made on the premises are for sale at the **Hurd Beeswax Candle Factory** (⌂ 3020 St. Helena Hwy. N, ☎ 707/963–7211). Bargain hunters will delight in the many designer labels for sale at the **Village Outlet Stores** complex on St. Helena Highway, across the street from Freemark Abbey Winery. **On the Vine** (⌂ 1234 Main St., ☎ 707/963–2209) presents wearable art and unique jewelry inspired by food and wine themes.

At **I. Wolk Gallery** (⌂ 1235 Main St., ☎ 707/963–8800) you'll find works by established and emerging artists from New York, Chicago, Los Angeles, and Santa Fe—everything from abstract and contemporary realist paintings to high-quality works on paper and sculpture. The **Gallery on Main Street** (⌂ 1359 Main St., ☎ 707/963–3350), one of the oldest in the region, features oils, watercolors, ceramics, and etchings by northern California artists. Visit **My Favorite Things** (⌂ 1289 Main St., ☎ 707/963–0848) for memorable keepsakes and unusual home accessories. **Dean and Deluca** (⌂ 607 St. Helena Hwy., ☎ 707/967–9980), a branch of the famous Manhattan store, is crammed with everything you need in the kitchen, including terrific produce and deli items, as well as a huge wine selection.

Calistoga

3 mi northwest of St. Helena on Hwy. 29.

In addition to its wineries, Calistoga is noted for its mineral water, hot mineral springs, mud baths, steam baths, and massages. The Calistoga Hot Springs Resort was founded in 1859 by maverick entrepreneur Sam Brannan, whose ambition was to found "the Saratoga of California." He tripped up the pronunciation of the phrase at a formal banquet—it came out "Calistoga"—and the name stuck.

The **Sharpsteen Museum** has a magnificent diorama of the Calistoga Hot Springs Resort in its heyday. Other exhibits document Robert Louis Stevenson's time in the area and the career of museum founder Ben Sharpsteen, an animator at the Walt Disney studio. ⌂ *1311 Washington St.,* ☎ *707/942–5911.* 🖭 *Free.* ☉ *May–Oct., daily 10–4; Nov.–Apr., daily noon–4.*

Indian Springs, an old-timey spa, has been pumping out 212-degree water from its three geysers for more than a century. The place offers some of the best bargains on mud bathing and short massages, and has a large mineral-water pool for guests. The spa has 16 cottages with studio or one-bedroom units and a larger structure with three bedrooms. ⌂ *1712 Lincoln Ave.,* ☎ *707/942–4913.* ☉ *Daily 9–7. Reservations recommended for spa treatments.*

㉔ **Sterling Vineyards** sits on a hilltop to the east of Calistoga, its pristine white Mediterranean-style buildings reached by an enclosed gondola from the valley floor. The view from the tasting room is superb, and the gift shop is one of the best in the valley. ⌂ *1111 Dunaweal La.,* ☎ *707/942–3300.* 🖭 *Tram $6.* ☉ *Daily 10:30–4:30.*

㉕ **Cuvaison** specializes in chardonnay, merlot, and cabernet sauvignon for the export market. Two small picnic areas on the grounds look out over Napa Valley. ⌂ *4550 Silverado Trail,* ☎ *707/942–6266.* 🖭 *Tasting fees vary.* ☉ *Daily 10–5. Tours by appointment.*

★ ㉖ Designed by postmodern architect Michael Graves, **Clos Pegase** is a one-of-a-kind structure packed with unusual art objects from the collection of art book publisher and owner Jan Shrem. Works of art even appear in the underground wine tunnels. ⊠ *1060 Dunaweal La.,* ☎ *707/942–4981.* ☉ *Daily 10:30–5. Tours at 11 and 2.*

㉗ **Château Montelena** is a vine-covered stone French château constructed circa 1882 and set amid Chinese-inspired gardens, complete with a man-made lake with gliding swans and islands crowned by Chinese pavilions. Château Montelena produces award-winning chardonnays and cabernet sauvignons. ⊠ *1429 Tubbs La.,* ☎ *707/942–5105; 800/222–7288 outside the Bay Area.* 🎫 *Tasting fees vary.* ☉ *Daily 10–4. Tours by reservation at 11 and 2.*

☾ Many families bring children to Calistoga to see **Old Faithful Geyser of California** blast its 60-ft tower of steam and vapor about every 40 minutes (the pattern is disrupted during heavy rains or if there's an earthquake in the offing). One of just three regularly erupting geysers in the world, it is fed by an underground river that heats to 350°F. The spout usually lasts three minutes. Picnic facilities are available. ⊠ *1299 Tubbs La., 1 mi north of Calistoga,* ☎ *707/942–6463.* 🎫 *$6.* ☉ *During daylight savings time, daily 9–6; winter, daily 9–5.*

☾ The **Petrified Forest** contains the remains of the volcanic eruptions of Mount St. Helena 3.4 million years ago. The force of the explosion uprooted the gigantic redwoods, covered them with volcanic ash, and infiltrated the trees with silica and minerals, causing petrifaction. Explore the museum, then picnic on the grounds. ⊠ *4100 Petrified Forest Rd., 5 mi west of Calistoga,* ☎ *707/942–6667.* 🎫 *$4.* ☉ *Daily 10–5 (until 6 in summer).*

☾ **Robert Louis Stevenson State Park,** on Highway 29, 3 mi northeast of Calistoga, encompasses the summit of Mount St. Helena. It was here, in the summer of 1880, in an abandoned bunkhouse of the Silverado Mine, that Stevenson and his bride, Fanny Osbourne, spent their honeymoon. The stay inspired Stevenson's "The Silverado Squatters," and Spyglass Hill in *Treasure Island* is thought to be a portrait of Mount St. Helena. The park's 3,000 acres are mostly undeveloped except for a fire trail leading to the site of the bunkhouse—which is marked with a marble tablet—and to the summit beyond.

Dining and Lodging

$$–$$$ ✕ **All Seasons Café.** Bistro cuisine takes a California spin in this sun-filled setting with marble tables and a black-and-white checkerboard floor. The seasonal menu includes organic greens, wild mushrooms, local game birds, and house-smoked beef, as well as homemade breads, desserts, and ice cream from an on-site ice cream plant. The café shares space with a well-stocked wine shop. ⊠ *1400 Lincoln Ave.,* ☎ *707/942–9111. MC, V. No lunch Wed.*

$$–$$$ ✕ **Catahoula Restaurant and Saloon.** This sleek restaurant, named after
★ Louisiana's state dog, is the brainchild of chef Jan Birnbaum, whose credentials include stints at the Quilted Giraffe in New York and Campton Place in San Francisco. Using a large wood-burning oven, Birnbaum turns out such dishes as spicy gumbo with andouille sausage and chocolate s'mores cooked over a wood fire. The large barroom opposite the dining room has its own menu of small plates, which are ideal for sampling Birnbaum's kitchen wizardry. ⊠ *Mount View Hotel, 1457 Lincoln Ave.,* ☎ *707/942–2275. Reservations essential. MC, V. Closed Tues. and Jan.*

$$–$$$ ✕ **Wappo Bar and Bistro.** This colorful restaurant is an adventure in international dining with a menu ranging from Asian noodles and Thai shrimp curry to chile rellenos to Turkish mezze. ⊠ *1226 S. Washington St.,* ☎ *707/942–4712. AE, MC, V.*

$$ ✕ **Calistoga Inn.** Grilled meat and fish for dinner and soups, salads, and sandwiches for lunch are prepared with flair at this microbrewery with a tree-shaded outdoor patio. ⊠ *1250 Lincoln Ave.,* ☎ *707/942–4101. AE, MC, V.*

$–$$ ✕ **Pacifico.** Technicolor ceramics and subtropical plants adorn this Mexican restaurant that serves Oaxacan and other fare. ⊠ *1237 Lincoln Ave.,* ☎ *707/942–4400. MC, V.*

$$$$ ▨ **Cottage Grove Inn.** These 16 elegant and contemporary cottages are shaded by elm trees. Rooms have skylights and plush furnishings. Fireplaces, CD players, VCRs, two-person hot tubs, and front porches with wicker rocking chairs add to the coziness. Spas and restaurants are within walking distance. Rates include Continental breakfast and afternoon wine and cheese. ⊠ *1711 Lincoln Ave., 94515,* ☎ *707/942–8400 or 800/799–2284,* 𝔽𝔸𝕏 *707/942–2653. 16 rooms. Breakfast room, refrigerators, in-room VCRs. AE, D, DC, MC, V.*

$$$–$$$$ ▨ **Mount View Hotel.** The Mount View is one of the valley's most historic resorts. A full-service European spa offers state-of-the-art pampering, and three cottages are each equipped with a private redwood deck, Jacuzzi, and wet bar. Catahoula's saloon adds to the allure. ⊠ *1457 Lincoln Ave., 94515,* ☎ *707/942–6877,* 𝔽𝔸𝕏 *707/942–6904. 33 rooms. Restaurant, pool, spa. AE, MC, V.*

$$$ ▨ **Brannan Cottage Inn.** This pristine Victorian cottage with lacy white fretwork, large windows, and a shady porch is the only one of Sam Brannan's 1860 resort cottages still standing on its original site. Rooms have private entrances, and elegant stenciled friezes of stylized wildflowers cover the walls. A full breakfast is included. ⊠ *109 Wapoo Ave., 94515,* ☎ *707/942–4200. 6 rooms. Breakfast room. MC, V.*

$$$ ▨ **Meadowlark Country House.** The ambience is decidedly laid-back and sophisticated at this inn surrounded by 20 hillside acres just north of downtown Calistoga. Innkeeper Kurt Stevens prides himself on being helpful but not intrusive. The main house, built in 1886, and a newer building down a gravel path hold unfussy but country-stylish rooms. Rates include a full breakfast. ⊠ *601 Petrified Forest Rd.,* ☎ *707/942–5651 or 800/942–5651,* 𝔽𝔸𝕏 *707/942–5023. 7 rooms. Breakfast room, pool, hot tub, sauna. MC, V.*

$–$$$ ▨ **Calistoga Spa Hot Springs.** The spa's no-nonsense motel-style rooms have kitchenettes stocked with utensils and coffeemakers, which makes them popular with families and travelers on a budget. (There's a supermarket a block away). The on-premises spa includes mineral baths, mud baths, three pools, and a hot tub. There's a two-night minimum on weekends (three nights on holiday weekends). ⊠ *1006 Washington St., 94515,* ☎ *707/942–6269,* 𝔽𝔸𝕏 *707/942–4214. 57 rooms. Snack bar, kitchenettes, 2 pools, wading pool, hot tub, spa, meeting room. MC, V.*

Outdoor Activities and Sports

BIKING

Getaway Adventures and Bike Shop (⊠ 1117 Lincoln Ave., ☎ 707/942–0332) rents bikes and conducts winery and other bike tours.

GLIDING, HOT-AIR BALLOONING

The **Calistoga Balloon Adventures** (☎ 707/942–2282 or 800/333–4359) charters early morning flights (exact times vary) out of Calistoga or, depending on weather conditions, St. Helena, Oakville, or Rutherford. The company's deluxe balloon flight ($165 per person) includes a catered brunch finale at the Marriott in Napa or the Cafe Sarifornia in Calistoga. Pilots are well versed in Napa Valley lore.

TENNIS

Near the center of town, at the intersection of **Stevenson and Grant streets,** are four courts with night lighting.

Shopping

For connoisseurs seeking extraordinary values, the **All Seasons Café Wine Shop** (⊠ 1400 Lincoln Ave., ☎ 707/942–6828) is a true find. A wine shop inside the **Calistoga Depot** (⊠ 1458 Lincoln Ave., ☎ 707/942–5556), California's second-oldest existing train depot, carries 500 vintages.

SONOMA COUNTY

While the Napa Valley is upscale and elegant, Sonoma Valley is rustic and unpretentious. Its name is Miwok Indian for *many moons*. Other Sonoma County valleys, such as Alexander, Dry Creek, and Russian River, are equally haunting in their beauty and just as prolific in their production of award-winning wines. Here, family-run wineries treat visitors like friends, and tastings are usually free. Cool marine air from the Russian River helps vintners grow their vines because it allows for more sun while leaving the soil rockier. This agricultural mix forces the vines to root deeper, producing intensely flavored grapes that translate into especially complex reds. The Sonoma countryside—from inland to coastal valleys—also provides excellent opportunities for hiking, biking, camping, boating, and fishing.

Sonoma

14 mi west of Napa on Hwy. 12; 45 mi from San Francisco, north on U.S. 101, east on Hwy. 37, and north on Hwy. 121/12.

Sonoma is the oldest town in the Wine Country. Its historic town plaza is the site of the last and the northernmost of the 21 missions established by the Franciscan order of Father Junípero Serra. The central plaza also includes the largest group of old adobes north of Monterey. The **Mission San Francisco Solano,** whose chapel and school were used to bring Christianity to the Native Americans, is now a museum with a fine collection of 19th-century watercolors. ⊠ *114 Spain St. E,* ☎ *707/938–1519.* ⌸ *$2, includes the Sonoma Barracks on the central plaza and General Vallejo's home, Lachryma Montis (☞ below).* ☾ *Daily 10–5.*

❷❽ Originally planted by Franciscans of the Sonoma Mission in 1825, the **Sebastiani Vineyards** were bought by Samuele Sebastiani in 1904. Red wines are king here. To complement them, Sylvia Sebastiani has recorded her good Italian home cooking in a family recipe book, *Mangiamo.* ⊠ *389 4th St. E,* ☎ *707/938–5532.* ☾ *Daily 10–5. Tours 10–4:30.*

❷❾ **Buena Vista Carneros Winery** (follow signs from the plaza) is the oldest continually operating winery in California. It was here, in 1857, that Count Agoston Haraszthy de Mokcsa laid the basis for modern California wine making, bucking the conventional wisdom that vines should be planted on well-watered ground by instead planting on well-drained hillsides. Chinese laborers dug tunnels 100 ft into the hillside, and the limestone they extracted was used to build the main house. The winery, which is surrounded by redwood and eucalyptus trees, has a specialty food shop, an art gallery, and picnic areas. ⊠ *18000 Old Winery Rd., off Napa Rd.,* ☎ *707/938–1266.* ☾ *Daily 10:30–4:30. Tour daily at 2.*

❸❿ **Ravenswood** is literally dug into the mountains like a bunker and famous for its legendary zinfandel. The merlot should be tasted as well. From late May through Labor Day the winery serves barbecued chicken and ribs ($5–$10) in the vineyards to complement its hearty wines. ⊠

18701 Gehricke Rd., off E. Spain St., ☎ *707/938–1960.* ☺ *Daily 10–4:30. Tours by appointment at 10:30.*

A tree-lined driveway leads to **Lachryma Montis,** which General Mariano G. Vallejo, the last Mexican governor of California, built for his large family in 1851; the state purchased the home in 1933. The Victorian Gothic house is secluded in the midst of beautiful gardens. Opulent Victorian furnishings, including a white-marble fireplace in every room, are particularly noteworthy. ✉ *W. Spain St., near 3rd St. E,* ☎ *707/938–1519.* 🎫 *$2.* ☺ *Daily 10–5. Tours by appointment.*

Dining and Lodging

$$–$$$ ✕ **Babette's.** Chef Daniel Patterson serves memorable six-course, prix fixe dinners just six months of the year in an intimate formal dining room on one of Sonoma's charming paseos. His menus offer three choices for each course, including such tantalizing combinations as quail breast on a bed of watercress and quinoa, or raw scallops dressed simply with olive oil and lemon juice. The café menu, which is served every day year round in an adjoining room, features cassoulet with house-made sausage and other rustic fare. The restaurant's hours vary from season to season, so call ahead. ✉ *464 1st St.,* ☎ *707/939–8921. MC, V. Restaurant closed Sun.–Mon. and Dec.–Apr.*

$$–$$$ ✕ **Freestyle.** Another restaurant venture by the group behind such successes as San Francisco's Rubicon and New York's Tribeca Grill and Nobu, this offbeat restaurant has a field day with local fish and produce. The appetizer taste of the day showcases a single ingredient prepared three distinctive ways—prawns, for example, in gumbo, grilled and served with salsa, and deep-fried tempura-style. Main courses such as steak with grilled Portobello mushrooms are often hearty, as are the desserts. ✉ *522 Broadway,* ☎ *707/996–9916. AE, DC, MC, V. Closed Tues. No lunch Mon.*

$$ ✕ **La Salette.** Chef-owner Manny Azevedo, born in the Azores and raised in Sonoma, found culinary inspiration in his wide-ranging travels. The flavors of his dishes, such as Mozambique prawns with tomatoes and grilled plantains and salt cod baked with white onions, stand strong while complementing each other. Sophisticated paintings and sculpture enliven the off-white walls in this restaurant, which has patio seating for balmy evenings. The service is demurely self-assured. There's something about having a Portuguese dish explained by a native of that country that gives diners a feeling of confidence. ✉ *18625 Hwy. 12,* ☎ *707/938–1927. MC, V.*

$$ ✕ **Ristorante Piatti.** A beautiful room opens onto one of the finest patios in the valley at this, the first in a minichain of California trattorias. Pizza from the wood-burning oven and northern Italian specials (spit-roasted chicken, ravioli with lemon cream) are served in a rustic Italian setting with an open kitchen and bright wall murals, or on the terrace. ✉ *El Dorado Hotel, 405 1st St. W,* ☎ *707/996–2351. AE, MC, V.*

$ ✕ **The Café.** Overstuffed booths, ceiling fans, and an open kitchen give this bistro an informal feel. Country breakfasts, pizza from the wood-burning oven, and tasty Californian renditions of northern Italian cuisine are the specialties. The menu includes several spa cuisine options. ✉ *Sonoma Mission Inn, 18140 Sonoma Hwy., 2 mi north of Sonoma on Hwy. 12 at Boyes Blvd.,* ☎ *707/938–9000. AE, DC, MC, V.*

$ ✕ **La Casa.** Whitewashed stucco and red tiles evoke Old Mexico at this restaurant just around the corner from Sonoma's plaza. There's bar seating, a patio, and an extensive menu of traditional Mexican food: chimichangas and snapper Veracruz for entrées, sangria to drink, and flan for dessert. The food is not the world's best, but locals love the casual atmosphere and the margaritas. ✉ *121 E. Spain St.,* ☎ *707/996–3406. AE, DC, MC, V.*

$$$–$$$$ ✕⌂ **Sonoma Mission Inn & Spa.** This 1920s resort blends Mediterranean and old-style California architecture for a look that's early Hollywood. The town, Boyes Hot Springs, has lagged behind the inn in gentrification. Still, guests come from afar to use the hotel's extensive spa facilities and treatments—including a pool that's heated by warm mineral water pumped from underground wells—and also for the gourmet and classic spa food served at the Grille and at the less formal Café (☞ *above*). Thirty suites in a secluded, tree-shaded area have verandas or patios, whirlpools, and fireplaces. At press time, an extensive renovation was underway. ✉ *18140 Hwy. 12 (2 mi north of Sonoma at Boyes Blvd.), Box 1447, 95476,* ☎ *707/938–9000 or 800/358–9022; 800/862–4945 in CA;* FAX *707/996–5358. 198 rooms, 30 suites. 2 restaurants, 2 bars, coffee shop, 2 pools, hot tub, spa. AE, DC, MC, V.*

$$$–$$$$ ⌂ **Thistle Dew Inn.** The public rooms of this turn-of-the-century Victorian home a half block from Sonoma Plaza are filled with collector's-quality Arts and Crafts furnishings. Owners Larry and Norma Barnett live on the premises, and Larry prepares creative, sumptuous breakfasts and hors d'oeuvres in the evening. Four of the six rooms have private entrances and decks, and all have queen-size beds with antique quilts, private baths, and air-conditioning. Some rooms have fireplaces; some have whirlpools. Welcome bonuses include a hot tub and free use of the inn's bicycles. ✉ *171 W. Spain St., 95476,* ☎ *707/938–2909; 800/382–7895 in CA. 6 rooms. Breakfast room, bicycles. AE, MC, V.*

$$–$$$ ⌂ **El Dorado Hotel.** A modern hotel in a remodeled old building, El Do-
★ rado has unusually spare and simple accommodations. Rooms reflect Sonoma's Mission era, with Mexican-tile floors and white walls. The best rooms are Numbers 3 and 4, which have big balconies overlooking Sonoma Plaza. ✉ *405 1st St. W, 95476,* ☎ *707/996–3030 or 800/ 289–3031,* FAX *707/996–3148. 26 rooms. Restaurant, pool. AE, MC, V.*

$$ ⌂ **Vineyard Inn.** Built as a roadside motor court in 1941, this inn with red-tile roofs brings a touch of Mexican village charm to an otherwise lackluster and somewhat noisy location at the junction of two main highways. Set across from two vineyards, it's the closest lodging to Sears Point Raceway. Rooms have queen-size beds, and Continental breakfast is included. ✉ *23000 Arnold Dr. (at junction of Hwys. 116 and 121), 95476,* ☎ *707/938–2350 or 800/359–4667,* FAX *707/938–2353. 9 rooms, 4 suites. Breakfast room. AE, MC, V.*

Nightlife and the Arts

The **Sebastiani Theatre** (☎ 707/996–2020), on historic Sonoma Square, schedules first-run movies. Every Sunday in August and September **Shakespeare at Buena Vista** (☎ 707/938–1266) brings the Bard to Sonoma. Performances are best enjoyed with a picnic lunch and a bottle of wine.

Shopping

Several shops in the four-block **Sonoma Plaza** attract food lovers from miles around. Serious picnickers stop at the **Sonoma French Bakery** (✉ Sonoma Plaza, 466 1st St. E, ☎ 707/996–2691), famous for its sourdough bread and cream puffs. **The Sonoma Cheese Factory** (✉ Sonoma Plaza, 2 Spain St., ☎ 707/996–1000), run by the same family for four generations, makes Sonoma Jack cheese and the tangy Sonoma Teleme. Great swirling baths of milk and curds are visible through the windows, along with flat-pressed wheels of cheese.

Glen Ellen

7 mi north of Sonoma on Hwy. 12.

Jack London lived in the Sonoma Valley for many years. The craggy, quirky, and creek-bisected town of Glen Ellen commemorates him with place names and nostalgic establishments. **Jack London Village** (⊠ 14301 Arnold Dr., ☎ 707/935–1240) has many interesting shops like **The Ranch Store** (☎ 707/935–2311), which carries garden art, local farm foods, handmade quilts, and rustic furnishings. The **Jack London Bookstore** (⊠ 14300 Arnold Dr., ☎ 707/996–2888), across the street from Jack London Village, carries many of London's books. The century-old **London Lodge** (⊠ 13740 Arnold Dr., ☎ 707/996–3100) has a brooding, nostalgic appeal.

In the hills above Glen Ellen—known as the Valley of the Moon—lies **Jack London State Historic Park.** London's collection of South Seas and other artifacts are on view at the House of Happy Walls, a museum of London's effects. The ruins of Wolf House, which London designed and which mysteriously burned down just before he was to move in, are close to the House of Happy Walls. London is buried on the property. ⊠ 2400 London Ranch Rd., ☎ 707/938–5216. ☞ Parking $6. ☉ Park, daily 9:30–5; museum, daily 10–5.

Two million cases of wine are bottled annually in this area. As you drive along Highway 12, you'll see orchards and rows of vineyards flanked by oak-covered mountain ranges. One of the best-known local wineries is **Benziger Family Winery,** which specializes in premium estate and Sonoma County wines. Benziger's Imagery Series is a low-volume release of unusual red and white wines distributed in bottles with art labels by well-known artists from all over the world. Free, educational tram tours through the vineyards depart several times a day, weather permitting. ⊠ 1883 London Ranch Rd., ☎ 707/935–3000. ☞ Tasting fees vary. ☉ Daily 10–4:30. Tours every ½ hr, Mar.–Sept., 9:30–5; Oct.–Feb., 9:30–4.

Arrowood Vineyards is neither as old nor as famous as some of its neighbors, but wine makers and critics are quite familiar with the excellent handcrafted wines produced here. The feel is more New England farmhouse than California wine estate. The winery's harmonious architecture overlooking the Valley of the Moon earned it an award from the Sonoma Historic Preservation League, and the wine-making equipment is state-of-the-art. ⊠ 14347 Sonoma Hwy., ☎ 707/938–5170. ☉ Daily 10–4:30. Tours by appointment.

Dining and Lodging

$$ ✕ **The Girl & the Fig.** Mustard-yellow walls, mismatched yellow chairs, and changing art exhibits set a bohemian tone here. The food, which may include apricot-glazed poussin or grilled pork tenderloin with a ginger-fig sauce, is almost overshadowed by a unique wine list focusing largely on regional Rhône-style varietals. Many wines are available by the glass or in flights, for easy sampling. ⊠ 13690 Arnold Dr., ☎ 707/938–3634. AE, MC, V.

$$$–$$$$ 🏨 **Beltane Ranch.** On a slope of the Mayacamas range on the eastern side of the Sonoma Valley lies this 100-year-old house built by a retired San Francisco madam. Beltane Ranch, surrounded by miles of trails through oak-studded hills, is part of a working cattle and grape-growing ranch—the nearby Kenwood Winery has a chardonnay made from the ranch's grapes. The Wood family, who have lived on the premises since 1936, have stocked the comfortable living room with dozens of books on the area. The rooms, all with private baths and antique furniture, open onto the building's wraparound porch. The cottage apartment, created out of the gardener's quarters, has a sitting room. ⊠ 11775 Sonoma Hwy. (Hwy. 12), 95442, ☎ 707/996–6501. 5 rooms. Tennis court, hiking, horseshoes. No credit cards.

$$$–$$$$ 🏨 **Gaige House Inn.** Built in the 19th century as a personal residence, the Gaige House was bought in 1996 by owners who have added chic,

contemporary rooms to the mix of older, more traditional accommodations on the two main floors. A large pool surrounded by a green lawn, striped awnings, white umbrellas, and magnolias conjure a manicured Hamptons-like glamour right in the middle of rustic Glen Ellen. The first-rate country breakfast is served in a bright dining room downstairs or on the terrace. ✉ *13540 Arnold Dr., 95442,* ☎ *707/935–0237 or 800/935–0237,* FAX *707/935–6411. 13 rooms. Breakfast room, pool, outdoor hot tub. AE, D, MC, V.*

$$–$$$ ⊞ **Glenelly Inn.** Just outside the hamlet of Glen Ellen, this sunny little establishment, built as an inn in 1916, offers all the comforts of home—including a hot tub in the garden. Innkeeper Kristi Hallamore serves breakfast in front of the common room's cobblestone fireplace and provides local delicacies in the afternoon. On sunny mornings guests may eat outside under the shady oak trees. ✉ *5131 Warm Springs Rd., 95442,* ☎ *707/996–6720,* FAX *707/996–5227. 8 rooms. Breakfast room, outdoor hot tub. MC, V.*

Kenwood

3 mi north of Glen Ellen on Hwy. 12.

Kenwood has a historic train depot and several restaurants and shops that specialize in locally produced goods. Its inns, restaurants, and winding roads nestle in soothing bucolic landscapes.

㉝ The beautifully rustic grounds at **Kenwood Vineyards** complement the attractive tasting room and artistic bottle labels. Although Kenwood produces all premium varietals, the winery is best known for its Jack London Vineyard reds—pinot noir, zinfandel, merlot, and a unique Artist Series cabernet. Most weekends the winery offers a free food and wine pairing. ✉ *9592 Sonoma Hwy., Kenwood,* ☎ *707/833–5891.* ⊙ *Daily 10–4:30. No tours.*

㉞ **Landmark Vineyards.** The landscaping and design of this boutique winery, established by the heirs of John Deere are as classical as its winemaking methods. Those methods include two fermentations in French oak barrels and the use of the yeasts present in the skins of the grapes to create the wine rather than the addition of manufactured yeasts. Landmark's Damaris Reserve and Overlook chardonnays have been particularly well received, as has the winery's Grand Detour pinot noir. The winery's first claret was introduced in 1998. ✉ *101 Adobe Canyon Rd., off Sonoma Hwy.,* ☎ *707/833–1144 or 800/452–6365.* ⊙ *Daily 10–4:30. No tours.*

Dining

$$–$$$ ✕ **Kenwood Restaurant & Bar.** One of the enduring favorites in an area known for fine dining, this is where Napa and Sonoma chefs eat on their nights off. Indulge in California country cuisine in the sunny, South of France–style dining room or head through the French doors to the patio for a memorable view of the vineyards. ✉ *9900 Hwy. 12,* ☎ *707/833–6326. MC, V. Closed Mon.*

$ ✕ **Café Citti.** The aroma of garlic envelops the neighborhood whenever the Italian chef-owner is roasting chickens at this homey roadside café. The variety of deli items, hot pastas, and soups makes this a good budget stop. ✉ *9049 Hwy. 12,* ☎ *707/833–2690. MC, V.*

Santa Rosa

8 mi northwest of Kenwood on Hwy. 12.

Santa Rosa is the Wine Country's largest city and a good bet for moderately priced hotel rooms, especially for those who have not reserved in advance.

The **Luther Burbank Home and Gardens** commemorates the great botanist who lived and worked on these grounds for 50 years, single-handedly developing the modern techniques of hybridization. Arriving as a young man from New England, he wrote: "I firmly believe . . . that this is the chosen spot of all the earth, as far as nature is concerned." The Santa Rosa plum, Shasta daisy, and lily of the Nile agapanthus are among the 800 or so plants he developed or improved. In the music room of his house, a Webster's Dictionary of 1946 lies open to a page on which the verb "burbank" is defined as "to modify and improve plant life." ⊠ *Santa Rosa and Sonoma Aves.,* ☎ *707/524–5445.* ⊞ *Gardens free; guided tours of house and greenhouse $2.* ☉ *Gardens Nov.–Mar., daily 8–5; Apr.–Oct., daily 8–7. Tours Apr.–Oct., Wed.–Sun. 10–4.*

★ ㉟   **Matanzas Creek Winery** specializes in three varietals—sauvignon blanc, merlot, and chardonnay. All three have won glowing reviews from various magazines. Huge windows in the visitor center overlook a field of 3,100 tiered and fragrant lavender plants. Acres and acres of gardens planted with unusual grasses and plants from all over the world have caught the attention of horticulturists. After you taste the wines, ask to see the self-guided garden tour book before taking a stroll. ⊠ *6097 Bennett Valley Rd.,* ☎ *707/528–6464.* ☉ *Daily 10–4:30. Tours by appointment.*

Dining and Lodging

$$$ ✕ **John Ash & Co.** The first Wine Country restaurant to tout locally grown ingredients in the 1980s, John Ash has maintained its status despite the departure of its namesake chef in 1991. With patio seating outside and a cozy fireplace indoors, the slightly formal restaurant looks like a Spanish villa amid the vineyards. A café menu offers bites between meals. ⊠ *4330 Barnes Rd. (River Rd. exit west from Hwy. 101),* ☎ *707/527–7687. Weekend reservations essential. AE, MC, V. No lunch Mon.*

$$–$$$ ✕ **Cafe Lolo.** This casual but sophisticated spot is the territory of chef and co-owner Michael Quigley, who has singlehandedly made downtown Santa Rosa a culinary destination. His dishes stress fresh ingredients and an eye to presentation. Don't pass up the chocolate kiss, an individual cake with a wonderfully soft, rich center. ⊠ *620 5th St.,* ☎ *707/576–7822. AE, MC, V. Closed Sun. No lunch Sat.*

$–$$$ ✕ **Mistral.** As Mediterranean as the wind for which it's named, Mistral is a warm and gracious restaurant that tries to make everybody happy. The extensive menu ranges from braised mahimahi to grilled pork tenderloin and offers a wide-ranging wine list to match. If you like to drink by the glass, the range of types and prices available here will please you. ⊠ *1229 N. Dutton Ave.,* ☎ *707/578–4511. AE, D, DC, MC, V. No lunch weekends.*

$ ✕ **Mixx.** Great service and an eclectic mix of dishes define this small restaurant with large windows, booth and table seating, high ceilings, and Italian blown-glass chandeliers. House-made ravioli, grilled Cajun prawns, and lamb curry are among the favorites of the many regular customers. All the dishes are based on locally grown ingredients and served with Napa Valley wine. ⊠ *135 4th St., at Davis (behind the mall on Railroad Sq.),* ☎ *707/573–1344. AE, MC, V. No lunch weekends.*

$$$–$$$$ ☷ **Vintner's Inn.** Set on 50 acres of vineyards, this French provincial inn has large rooms, many with wood-burning fireplaces, and a trellised sundeck. Breakfast is complimentary, and the close-by John Ash & Co. restaurant (☞ *above*) tempts guests to other meals. Guests are entitled to discount passes to an affiliated health club, and VCRs can be rented for a small fee. ⊠ *4350 Barnes Rd. (River Rd. exit west from U.S. 101), 95403,* ☎ *707/575–7350 or 800/421–2584,* ℻ *707/575–1426. 44 rooms. Restaurant, hot tub. AE, DC, MC, V.*

$$$ ⊞ **Fountaingrove Inn.** A redwood sculpture and a wall of cascading
★ water distinguish the lobby at this elegant, comfortable inn. All rooms
have work spaces with modem jacks. A buffet breakfast is complimentary,
and there's also an elegant restaurant with a piano player and a stel-
lar menu. Guests have access to a nearby 18-hole golf course, a tennis
court, and a health club, all for an additional fee. Golf packages are
available, as are discounts for senior citizens. ⊠ *101 Fountaingrove
Pkwy. (near U.S. 101), 95403,* ☎ *707/578–6101 or 800/222–6101,*
℻ *707/544–3126. 126 rooms. Restaurant, in-room data ports, room
service, pool, hot tub, meeting rooms. AE, D, DC, MC, V.*

$$ ⊞ **Los Robles Lodge.** This pleasant, relaxed motel overlooks a pool that's
set into a grassy landscape. Pets are allowed, except in executive rooms.
Some rooms have whirlpools. ⊠ *1985 Cleveland Ave. (Steele La. exit
west from Hwy. 101), 95401,* ☎ *707/545–6330 or 800/255–6330,* ℻
*707/575–5826. 100 rooms. Restaurant, coffee shop, lounge, pool,
outdoor hot tub, coin laundry. AE, DC, MC, V.*

Nightlife and the Arts

The **Luther Burbank Performing Arts Center** (⊠ 50 Mark West Springs
Rd., ☎ 707/546–3600) presents concerts, plays, and other performances by locally and internationally known artists. For symphony, ballet, and other live theater performances throughout the year, call the
Spreckels Performing Arts Center (☎ 707/584–1700 or 707/588–3434)
in Rohnert Park. **SRT** (Summer Repertory Theatre; ⊠ 1501 Mendocino
Ave., ☎ 707/527–4307) presents classic and contemporary plays.

Outdoor Activities and Sports

GOLF

The **Fountaingrove Country Club** (⊠ 1525 Fountaingrove Pkwy., ☎
707/579–4653) has an 18-hole course. The greens fee, which includes
a mandatory cart, runs $35–$70 depending on time of day and day of
week. **Oakmont Golf Club** (⊠ west course: 7025 Oakmont Dr., ☎ 707/
539–0415; ⊠ east course: 565 Oak Vista Ct., ☎ 707/538–2454) has
two 18-hole courses. The greens fee is $24–$32, plus $20 for an op-
tional cart.

HOT-AIR BALLOONING

For views of the ocean coast, the Russian River, and San Francisco on
a clear day, **Sonoma Thunder Wine Country Balloon Safaris** (☎ 707/
538–7359 or 800/759–5638) operates out of Santa Rosa, although many
flights actually originate outside Healdsburg. The cost is $175 per per-
son, including a champagne brunch at a hilltop winery.

Healdsburg

17 mi north of Santa Rosa on U.S. 101.

The countryside around Dry Creek Valley and Healdsburg is a fantasy
of pastoral bliss, beautifully overgrown and in constant repose. Alongside the relatively untrafficked roads, country stores offer just-plucked
fruits and vine-ripened tomatoes. Wineries here are barely visible,
tucked behind groves of eucalyptus or hidden high on fog-shrouded
hills.

Healdsburg itself is centered by a fragrant plaza surrounded by shade
trees, appealing antiques shops, and restaurants. A whitewashed bandstand is the venue for free summer concerts, where the music ranges
from jazz to bluegrass. For a free map of the area, contact **Russian River
Wine Road** (⊠ Box 46, Healdsburg 95448, ☎ 707/433–6782).

36 **Dry Creek Vineyard,** whose fumé blanc is an industry landmark, is also
earning notice for its reds, especially zinfandels and cabernets. Flow-

ering magnolia and redwood trees provide an ideal setting for picnics. ⊠ *3770 Lambert Bridge Rd.,* ☏ *707/433–1000.* ⊘ *Daily 10:30–4:30. Tours by appointment.*

㊲ An unassuming winery in a wood and cinder-block barn, **Quivira** produces some of the most interesting wines in Dry Creek Valley. Though it is known for its exquisitely balanced and fruity zinfandel, it also makes a superb blend of red varietals called Dry Creek Cuvée. ⊠ *4900 W. Dry Creek Rd.,* ☏ *707/431–8333.* ⊘ *Daily 10–4:30. Tours by appointment.*

㊳ The boutique winery **A. Rafanelli,** owned by third-generation vintner Dave Rafanelli and his wife Patty, has been in operation since 1906. Zinfandel and cabernet are the only wines produced here; the 1995 zinfandel won high marks from *The Wine Spectator.* ⊠ *4685 Dry Creek Rd.,* ☏ *707/433–1385.* ⊘ *Daily 10–4. Tours by appointment.*

㊴ Noted for its beautiful Italian villa–style winery and visitor center (the breezy courtyard is covered with every kind of flower imaginable), **Ferrari-Carano Winery** produces chardonnays, fumé blancs, and merlots. Tours take you between the rows of grape vines right into the vineyards themselves. ⊠ *8761 Dry Creek Rd.,* ☏ *707/433–6700.* ⊘ *Daily 10–5. Tours by appointment.*

㊵ **Simi Winery.** Giuseppe and Pietro Simi, two brothers from Italy, began growing grapes in Sonoma in 1876. Though their winery's operations are strictly high-tech these days, its tree-studded entrance area and stone buildings recall a more genteel era. The tour highlights the winery's rich history. ⊠ *16275 Healdsburg Ave. (take Dry Creek Rd. exit off U.S. 101),* ☏ *707/433–6981.* ⊘ *Daily 10–4:30. Tours at 11, 1, and 3.*

OFF THE **CLOS DU BOIS –** Ten mi north of Healdsburg on Highway 116, these
BEATEN PATH vineyards produce the fine estate chardonnays of the Alexander and Dry Creek valleys that have been mistaken for great French wines. ⊠ *19410 Geyserville Ave., Geyserville,* ☏ *707/857–3100 or 800/222–3189.* ⊘ *Daily 10–4:30. No tours.*

Dining and Lodging

$$ ✕ **Bistro Ralph.** In a town where good restaurants rarely seem to last, Ralph Tingle has sustained success with his California home-style cuisine, serving up a small menu that changes weekly. The stark industrial setting includes a stunning wine rack of graceful curves fashioned in metal and wood. Take a seat at the bar and chat with the locals, who love this place just as much as out-of-towners do. ⊠ *109 Plaza St., off Healdsburg Ave.,* ☏ *707/433–1380. Reservations essential. MC, V. No lunch weekends.*

$$$–$$$$ 🏨 **Healdsburg Inn on the Plaza.** This 1900 brick building on the town plaza has a bright solarium and a roof garden. The rooms, most with fireplaces, are spacious, with quilts and pillows piled high on antique beds. In the bathrooms claw-foot tubs are outfitted with rubber ducks. Full breakfast, afternoon coffee and cookies, and early evening wine and popcorn are included. ⊠ *110 Matheson St., Box 1196, 95448,* ☏ *707/433–6991. 10 rooms. Breakfast room. MC, V.*

$$$–$$$$ 🏨 **The Honor Mansion.** This photogenic 1883 Italianate Victorian opened in 1994 to rave reviews for its interior decor. Antiques, feather beds, and fancy water bottles add a luxurious ambience to the rooms in the main house. A separate cottage is available in the rear, and two suites were added in 1999. Full breakfast is included. ⊠ *14891 Grove St., 95448,* ☏ *707/433–4277 or 800/554–4667;* ⊞ *707/431–7173. 8 rooms. Breakfast room, pool, hot tub. D, MC, V.*

$$$–$$$$ 🏨 **Madrona Manor.** The oldest continuously operating inn in the area, this 1881 Victorian mansion, surrounded by 8 acres of wooded and landscaped grounds, provides a storybook setting. Sleep either in the splendid three-story mansion, the carriage house, or one of two separate cottages. Mansion rooms are recommended: All nine have fireplaces, and five contain the antique furniture of the original owner. ⊠ *1001 Westside Rd. (take central Healdsburg exit from U.S. 101, turn left on Mill St.), Box 818, 95448,* ☎ *707/433–4231 or 800/258–4003,* FAX *707/433–0703. 21 rooms. Restaurant, pool. AE, D, DC, MC, V.*

$$ 🏨 **Best Western Dry Creek Inn.** Continental breakfast and a bottle of wine are complimentary at this three-story Spanish Mission–style motel, and there's also a coffee shop next door. Midweek discounts are available, and direct bus service from San Francisco's airport can be arranged. ⊠ *198 Dry Creek Rd., 95448,* ☎ *707/433–0300 or 800/222–5784;* FAX *707/433–1129. 102 rooms. Pool, hot tub, coin laundry. AE, D, DC, MC, V.*

Outdoor Activities and Sports

Take a swim at the outdoor pool, or rent a canoe for a float trip down the Russian River at **Memorial Beach Park,** open from Memorial Day to Labor Day.

Shopping

Oakville Grocery (⊠ 124 Matheson St., ☎ 707/433–3200) has a bustling Healdsburg branch filled with wine, produce, and deli items. Head to **Salami Tree** (⊠ 304 Center St., ☎ no phone) for picnic supplies. **Tip Top Liquor Warehouse** (⊠ 90 Dry Creek Rd., ☎ 707/431–0841) has a large selection of local wines, including some hard-to-find labels.

Every Saturday morning from early May to October, Healdsburg locals gather at the open-air **Farmers' Market** (⊠ North Plaza parking lot, North and Vine Sts., ☎ 707/431–1956) to pick up supplies from local producers of vegetables, fruits, flowers, cheeses, and olive oils.

OFF THE BEATEN PATH   **KORBEL CHAMPAGNE CELLARS** – In order to be called champagne, a wine must be made in the French region of Champagne or technically it's just like any other bubbly—a sparkler. But despite the objections of the French, champagne has entered the lexicon of California wine makers, and many refer to their sparkling wines as champagne. Whatever you call it, Korbel produces a tasty, reasonably priced wine and now produces its own beer as well, which is available at a brew-pub on the premises. The wine tour, one of the best in Sonoma County, clearly explains the process of making sparkling wine. The winery's 19th-century buildings and gorgeous rose gardens are a delight in their own right. ⊠ *13250 River Rd., Guerneville,* ☎ *707/887–2294.* ☺ *Oct.–Apr., daily 9–4:30; May–Sept., daily 9–5. Tours on the hr 10–3.*

THE WINE COUNTRY ESSENTIALS

Arriving and Departing

By Bus
Greyhound (☎ 800/231–2222) runs buses from the Transbay Terminal at 1st and Mission streets in San Francisco to Sonoma and Santa Rosa.

By Car
From San Francisco, cross the Golden Gate Bridge, go north on U.S. 101, east on Highway 37, and north and east on Highway 121. For

Sonoma wineries, head north at Highway 12; for Napa's, turn left (to the northwest) when Highway 121 runs into Highway 29.

From Berkeley and other East Bay towns, take I–80 north to Highway 37 west to Highway 29 north. From points north of the Wine Country, take U.S. 101 south to Geyserville and follow Highway 128 southeast into the Napa Valley.

Getting Around

By Bus
Sonoma County Area Transit (☎ 707/585–7516) and **Napa Valley Transit** (☎ 707/255–7631) both provide transportation between towns in their respective Wine Country counties.

By Car
Although traffic on the two-lane country roads can be heavy, the best way to get around the sprawling Wine Country is by private car. Rentals are available at the airports and in San Francisco, Oakland, Sonoma, Santa Rosa, and Napa.

The **Rider's Guide** (⊠ 484 Lake Park Ave., Suite 255, Oakland 94610, ☎ 510/653–2553) produces tapes about the history, landmarks, and wineries of the Sonoma and Napa valleys that you can play in your car (maps also provided). The tapes are available at some local Bay Area bookstores and can also be ordered directly from Rider's Guide for $12.95, plus $2.50 postage.

Contacts and Resources

B&B Reservation Agencies
Bed & Breakfast Exchange (⊠ 1407 Main St., Suite 102, St. Helena, ☎ 707/942–5900). The **Bed & Breakfast Association of Sonoma** (⊠ 3250 Trinity Rd., Glen Ellen, ☎ 800/969–4667). **The Wine Country Bed & Breakfast Inns of Sonoma County** (☎ 707/433–4667; 800/354–4743 for brochure). **Wine Country Reservations** (☎ 707/257–7757).

Emergencies
Ambulance (☎ 911). **Police** (☎ 911).

Guided Tours
Full-day guided tours of the Wine Country usually include lunch and cost about $50. The guides, some of whom are winery owners themselves, know the area well and may show you some lesser-known cellars. Reservations are usually required.

Gray Line (⊠ 350 8th St., San Francisco 94103, ☎ 415/558–9400) has bright red double-decker buses that tour the Wine Country. **Great Pacific Tour Co.** (⊠ 518 Octavia St., San Francisco 94102, ☎ 415/626–4499) operates full-day tours of Napa and Sonoma, including a summer picnic lunch and a winter restaurant lunch, in passenger vans that seat 14. **HMS Travel Group** (⊠ 707 4th St., Santa Rosa 95404, ☎ 707/526–2922 or 800/367–5348) offers customized tours of the Wine Country for six or more people, by appointment only. The **Napa Valley Wine Train** (⊠ 1275 McKinstry St., Napa 94559, ☎ 707/253–2111 or 800/427–4124) allows you to enjoy lunch, dinner, or weekend brunch on one of several restored 1915 Pullman railroad cars that run between Napa and St. Helena. Dinner costs $70, lunch $65, brunch $57; per-person prices include train fare, meals, tax, and service. On weekend brunch trips and weekday lunch trips you can ride a special "Deli" car for $27.50. In winter service is sometimes limited to Thursday through Sunday; call ahead.

Visitor Information

Napa Valley Conference and Visitors Bureau (✉ 1310 Napa Town Center, Napa 94559, ☎ 707/226–7459). The **Redwood Empire Association** (✉ The Cannery, 2801 Leavenworth St., 2nd Floor, San Francisco 94133, ☎ 415/543–8334). **Sonoma County Tourism Program** (✉ 401 College Ave., Santa Rosa 95401, ☎ 707/524–5789). **Sonoma Valley Visitors Bureau** (✉ 453 First St., Sonoma 95476, ☎ 707/996–1090).

10 BACKGROUND AND ESSENTIALS

Portrait of San Francisco

Books and Videos

Smart Travel Tips A to Z

SPLENDOR IN THE FOG

That visitors will envy San Franciscans is a given—at least, so say Bay Area residents, who tend to pity anyone who did not have the foresight to settle here. (There's probably never been a time when the majority of the population was native born.) Their self-satisfaction may surprise some, considering how the city has been battered by fires and earthquakes from the 1840s onward, most notably in the 1906 conflagration and again in 1989, when the Loma Prieta earthquake rocked the city's foundations and caused serious damage to the Marina District as well as to numerous local freeways. Since its earliest days San Francisco has been a phoenix, the mythical bird that periodically dies in flame to be reborn in greater grandeur.

Its latest rebirth has occurred in SoMa, the neighborhood south of Market Street, where the Yerba Buena Gardens development has taken shape with the world-class SFMOMA (San Francisco Museum of Modern Art) at its heart—transforming a formerly seedy neighborhood into a magnet of culture. As a peninsula city, surrounded on three sides by water, San Francisco grows from the inside out. Its blighted areas are improved, not abandoned. The museum development's instant success—measured by a huge influx of residents, suburban commuters, and international visitors—perfectly exemplifies this tradition.

In its first life San Francisco was little more than a small, well-situated settlement. Founded by Spaniards in 1776, it was prized for its natural harbor, so commodious that "all the navies of the world might fit inside it," as one visitor wrote. Around 1849 the discovery of gold at John Sutter's sawmill in the nearby Sierra foothills transformed the sleepy little settlement into a city of 30,000. Millions of dollars' worth of gold was panned and blasted out of the hills, the impetus for the development of a western Wall Street. Fueled by the 1859 discovery of a fabulously rich vein of silver in Virginia City, Nevada, San Francisco became the West Coast's cultural fulcrum and major transportation hub, and its population soared to 342,000. In 1869 the transcontinental railway was completed, linking the once-isolated western capital to the East. San Francisco had become a major city of the United States. Of course the boom was not without its price. Gambling and violent crime were rampant, destructive fires flared up on an almost daily basis, and immigrant railroad workers suffered cruelly under multifarious anti-Chinese laws.

San Francisco has long been a bastion of what it likes to refer to as "progressive politics." The Sierra Club, founded here in 1892 by John Muir, has its national headquarters on Polk Street. The turn-of-the-century "yellow journalism" of William Randolph Hearst's *San Francisco Examiner* gave way to such leftish publications as *Mother Jones* magazine and today's left-of-center weekly newspapers. Political contentiousness has sometimes led to violence, most notably in 1978 when the city's liberal mayor, George Moscone, and its first gay supervisor, Harvey Milk, were assassinated by a vindictive right-wing ex-supervisor.

However, despite a boomtown tendency toward raucousness and a sad history of anti-Asian discrimination, the city today prides itself on its tolerance. Consider the makeup of the city's chief administrative body, the 11-member Board of Supervisors. Chinese, Hispanics, gays, blacks, and women have all been representatives. The mix, everybody knows, is what makes San Francisco.

Loose, tolerant, and even licentious are words that are used to describe San Francisco. Bohemian communities thrive here. As early as the 1860s the Barbary Coast—a collection of taverns, whorehouses, and gambling joints along Pacific Avenue close to the waterfront—was famous, or infamous. North Beach, the city's Little Italy, became the home of the beat movement in the 1950s (Herb Caen, the city's best-known columnist, coined the term beatnik). Lawrence Ferlinghetti's City Lights, a bookstore and publishing house that still stands on Columbus Avenue, brought out, among other titles, Allen Ginsberg's *Howl* and *Kaddish*. Across Broadway a plaque identifies the Condor as the site of the nation's first topless and bottomless performances. In the '60s the Free Speech Movement began at the University of California at Berkeley, and Stanford's David Harris, who went to prison for defying the draft, numbered among the nation's most famous student leaders. In October 1965 Allen Ginsberg introduced the term *flower power*, and the Haight-Ashbury district became synonymous with hippiedom, giving rise to such legendary bands as Jefferson Airplane and the Grateful Dead. Thirty years later the Haight's history and its name still draw neo-hippies, as well as new wavers with black lips and blue hair, and some rather menacing skinheads. Transients make panhandling one of Haight Street's major business activities, and the potential for crime and violence after dark has turned many of the liberal residents into unlikely law-and-order advocates. Still, most remain committed to keeping the Haight the Haight.

Southwest of the Haight is the one-time Irish neighborhood known as the Castro, which during the 1970s became identified with gay and lesbian liberation. Castro Street is dominated by the elaborate Castro Theatre, a 1922 vision in Spanish baroque style, which presents first-run art and independent films with occasional revivals of Hollywood film classics. (The grand old pipe organ still plays during intermissions, breaking into "San Francisco" just before the feature begins.) There's been much talk, most of it exaggerated, about how AIDS has "chastened" and "matured" the Castro. The disease *has* spawned the creation of AIDS education, treatment, and care-giving networks, such as Shanti and Project Open Hand, models for the rest of the nation. The Castro is still an effervescent neighborhood, and—as housing everywhere has become more and more scarce—an increasingly mixed one. At the same time, gays, like Asians, are moving out of the ghetto and into neighborhoods all around the city.

I n terms of both geography and culture, San Francisco is about as close as you can get to Asia in the continental United States. The first great wave of Chinese immigrants came as railroad laborers. Chinese workers quickly became the target of race hatred and discriminatory laws. Chinatown—which began when the Chinese moved into old buildings that white businesses seeking more fashionable locations had abandoned—developed as a refuge, as much as anything else. It is still a fascinating place to wander and a good bet for late-night food, but it's not the whole story by any means. The Asian community, which now accounts for a fifth of San Francisco's population, reaches into every San Francisco neighborhood and particularly into the Sunset and Richmond districts, west toward the ocean. There was heavy Japanese immigration earlier in this century, but most of it went to southern California, where organized labor had less of a foothold and where there were greater opportunities for Asian workers. Still, San Francisco has its Japantown, with the Japan Center complex and a handful of shops and restaurants. Working hard to establish themselves over the decades, today Asian-Americans of every persuasion are at the highest levels of the city's elected and appointed government and in leadership positions in San Francisco's business, medical, and educational communities.

Geographically, San Francisco is the thumbnail on a 40-mi thumb of land, the San Francisco Peninsula, which stretches northward between the Pacific Ocean and San Francisco Bay. Hemmed in on three sides by water, its land area (less than 50 square mi) is relatively small. The population, at about 750,000, is small, too. Technically speaking, it's only California's fourth-largest city, behind Los Angeles, San Diego, and nearby San Jose. But that statistic is misleading: The Bay Area, extending from the bedroom communities north of Oakland and Berkeley south through the peninsula and the San Jose area, is really one continuous megacity, with San Francisco as its heart.

Not so many centuries ago the area that was to become San Francisco was a windswept, virtually treeless, and, above all, sandy wasteland. Sand even covered the hills. The sand is still there, but—except along the ocean—it's well hidden. City hall is built on 80 ft of it. The westerly section of the city seems flat only because sand has filled in the contours of the hills.

The hills that remain are spectacular. They provide vistas all over the city. Nothing is more common than to find yourself staring out toward Angel Island or Alcatraz, or across the bay at Berkeley and Oakland. The hills also made cable cars a necessity early on. The city's two bridges, which are almost as majestic as their surroundings, had their 50th birthdays in 1986 and 1987. The Golden Gate Bridge, which crosses to Marin County, got a bigger party, but the San Francisco–Oakland Bay Bridge got a better present: a necklace of lights along its spans. They were supposed to be temporary, but the locals were so taken with the glimmer that bridge boosters started a drive to make them permanent. Radio DJs and newspaper columnists put out daily appeals, drivers gave extra quarters to the toll takers, various corporations put up shares, and now—nearly one million dollars later—the lights on the Bay Bridge shine nightly.

First-time visitors to San Francisco sometimes arrive with ideas about its weather gleaned from movie images of sunny California or from a misinformed 1967 song that celebrated "a warm San Franciscan night." Sunny, perhaps. Warm—not likely. That's *southern* California. (A perennially popular T-shirt quotes Mark Twain's alleged remark: "The coldest winter I ever spent was a summer in San Francisco.") Still, it almost never freezes here, and heat waves are equally rare. Most San Franciscans come to love the climate, which is genuinely temperate—sufficiently welcoming for the imposing row of palms down the median of Dolores Street but seldom warm enough for just a T-shirt at night. The coastal stretch of ocean may look inviting, but the surfers you sometimes see along Ocean Beach are wearing wet suits (though the beach can be fine for sunning). And, of course, there's the famous fog—something that tourists tend to find more delightful than do the residents. It's largely a summer phenomenon: San Francisco's real summer begins in September, when the fog lifts and the air warms up for a while. November brings on the rains.

Victorian architecture is as integral to the city as fog and cable cars. Bay-windowed, ornately decorated Victorian houses—the ahistorical, multicolor paint jobs that have become popular make them seem even more ornate—are the city's most distinguishing architectural feature. They date mainly from the latter part of Queen Victoria's reign, 1870 to the turn of the century. In those three decades San Francisco more than doubled in population (from 150,000 to 342,000); the transcontinental railway, linking the once-isolated western capital to the East, had been completed in 1869. That may explain the exuberant confidence of the architecture.

Another measure of the city's exuberance is its many festivals and celebrations. The Lesbian, Gay, Bisexual, and Transgendered Pride Parade and Celebration held each June, vies with the Chinese New Year's Parade, an annual February event, as the city's most elaborate. They both get competition from Japantown's Cherry Blossom Festival, in April; the Columbus Day

268

Portrait

and St. Patrick's Day parades; Carnaval, held in the Hispanic Mission District in May; and the May Day march, a labor celebration in a labor town. The mix of ethnic, economic, social, and sexual groups can be bewildering, but the city's residents—whatever their origin—face it with aplomb and even gratitude. Nearly everyone smiles on the fortunate day they arrived on this windy, foggy patch of peninsula.

WHAT TO READ & WATCH BEFORE YOU GO

Books

While many novels have San Francisco settings, they don't come any better than *The Maltese Falcon,* by Dashiell Hammett, the founder of the hard-boiled school of detective fiction. First published in 1930, Hammett's books continue to be readily available in new editions, and the details about the fog, the hills, and the once-seedy offices south of Market continue to be accurate.

Another standout is Vikram Seth's *Golden Gate,* a novel in verse about life in San Francisco and Marin County in the early '80s. Others are John Gregory Dunne's *The Red White and Blue,* Stephen Longstreet's *All or Nothing* and *Our Father's House,* and Alice Adams's *Rich Rewards.* Many of the short stories in Adams's collection, *To See You Again,* have Bay Area settings.

Two books that are filled with interesting background information on the city are Richard H. Dillon's *San Francisco: Adventurers and Visionaries* and *San Francisco: As It Is, As It Was,* by Paul C. Johnson and Richard Reinhardt.

For anecdotes, gossip, and the kind of detail that will make you feel almost like a native San Franciscan, get hold of any of the books by the late and much-loved San Francisco *Chronicle* columnist Herb Caen: *Baghdad-by-the-Bay, Only in San Francisco,* *One Man's San Francisco,* and *San Francisco: City on Golden Hills.* Armistead Maupin's soap opera–style *Tales of the City* stories are set in San Francisco; you can read them or watch them on video.

Videos

Films shot in San Francisco in the 1990s include *Mrs. Doubtfire, Basic Instinct, The Rock, Metro, The Presidio,* and *The Game.* Among the older films about the city, *San Francisco,* starring Clark Gable and Spencer Tracy, re-creates the 1906 earthquake with outstanding special effects. In *Escape from Alcatraz,* Clint Eastwood plays the prisoner who allegedly escaped from the famous jail on a rock in the San Francisco Bay. Eastwood also starred in the Dirty Harry film series, which takes place around the Bay Area. *The Times of Harvey Milk,* about San Francisco's first openly gay elected official, won the Academy Award for best documentary feature in 1984. Alfred Hitchcock immortalized Mission Dolores and the Golden Gate Bridge in *Vertigo,* the eerie story of a detective with a fear of heights, starring Jimmy Stewart and Kim Novak. A few other noteworthy films shot in San Francisco are *Dark Passage,* with Humphrey Bogart; *Foul Play,* with Chevy Chase and Goldie Hawn; and the 1978 remake of *Invasion of the Body Snatchers.*

ESSENTIAL INFORMATION

AIR TRAVEL

Heavy fog is infamous for causing chronic delays in and out of San Francisco. Travelers heading to the East and South Bay should make every effort to fly into either the Oakland or San Jose airports. The Oakland airport, which is easy to navigate and is accessible by public transit, is a good alternative to San Francisco's airport.

BOOKING YOUR FLIGHT

When you book **look for nonstop flights** and **remember that "direct" flights stop at least once.** Try to avoid connecting flights, which require a change of plane.

CARRIERS

Airlines from all around the world and the nation fly into the San Francisco area, so you'll likely have many flights from which to choose.

➤ MAJOR AIRLINES: **America West** (☎ 800/235–9292) to Oakland, San Francisco. **American** (☎ 800/433–7300) to Oakland, San Francisco. **Continental** (☎ 800/523–3273) to Oakland, San Francisco. **Delta** (☎ 800/221–1212) to Oakland, San Francisco. **Northwest** (☎ 800/225–2525) to San Francisco. **Southwest** (☎ 800/435–9792) to Oakland, San Francisco. **TWA** (☎ 800/892–4141) to San Francisco. **United** (☎ 800/241–6522) to Oakland, San Francisco. **US Airways** (☎ 800/428–4322) to San Francisco.

➤ SMALLER AIRLINES: **Midwest Express** (☎ 800/452–2022) to San Francisco. **Reno Air** (☎ 800/736–6247) to San Francisco.

➤ FROM THE U.K.: **British Airways** (☎ 0345/222–111). **United** (☎ 0845/844–4777). **Virgin Atlantic** (☎ 01293/747–747). **TWA** (☎ 0181/815–0707). **American** (☎ 0345/789–789) flies via New York, Boston, or Chicago, and **Delta** (☎ 0800/414–767) flies via Atlanta or Cincinnati.

CHECK-IN & BOARDING

Assuming that not everyone with a ticket will show up, airlines routinely overbook planes. When that happens, airlines ask for volunteers to give up their seats. In return these volunteers usually get a certificate for a free flight and are rebooked on the next flight out. If there are not enough volunteers, the airline must choose who will be denied boarding. The first to get bumped are passengers who checked in late and those flying on discounted tickets, so **get to the gate and check in as early as possible,** especially during peak periods.

Always **bring a government-issued photo ID to the airport.** You may be asked to show it before you are allowed to check in.

CUTTING COSTS

The least-expensive airfares to San Francisco must usually be purchased in advance and are nonrefundable. It's smart to **call a number of airlines, and when you are quoted a good price, book it on the spot**—the same fare may not be available the next day. Always **check different routings** and look into using different airports. Travel agents, especially low-fare specialists (☞ Discounts & Deals, *below*), are helpful.

Consolidators are another good source. They buy tickets for scheduled international flights at reduced rates from the airlines, then sell them at prices that beat the best fare available directly from the airlines, usually without restrictions. Sometimes you can even get your money back if you need to return the ticket. Carefully read the fine print detailing penalties for changes and cancellations, and **confirm your consolidator reservation with the airline.**

When you **fly as a courier** you trade your checked-luggage space for a ticket deeply subsidized by a courier service. There are restrictions on when you can book and how long you can stay.

➤ CONSOLIDATORS: **Cheap Tickets** (☎ 800/377–1000). **Up & Away Travel** (☎ 212/889–2345). **Discount Airline Ticket Service** (☎ 800/576–1600). **Unitravel** (☎ 800/325–2222). **World Travel Network** (☎ 800/409–6753).

ENJOYING THE FLIGHT

For more legroom **request an emergency-aisle seat.** Don't sit in the row in front of the emergency aisle or in front of a bulkhead, where seats may not recline. If you have dietary concerns, **ask for special meals when booking.** These can be vegetarian, low-cholesterol, or kosher, for example. On long flights, try to maintain a normal routine, to help fight jet lag. At night **get some sleep.** By day **eat light meals, drink water** (not alcohol), and **move around the cabin** to stretch your legs.

FLYING TIMES

Flying time is 6 hours from New York, 4 hours from Chicago, 1 hour from Los Angeles, 3½ hours from Dallas, 10 hours from London, and 15 hours from Sydney.

HOW TO COMPLAIN

If your baggage goes astray or your flight goes awry, complain right away. Most carriers require that you **file a claim immediately.**

➤ AIRLINE COMPLAINTS: **U.S. Department of Transportation Aviation Consumer Protection Division** (✉ C-75, Room 4107, Washington, DC 20590, ☎ 202/366–2220). **Federal Aviation Administration Consumer Hotline** (☎ 800/322–7873).

AIRPORTS & TRANSFERS

The major gateway to San Francisco is **San Francisco International Airport** (SFO), just south of the city, off U.S. 101. Several domestic airlines serve **Oakland Airport (OAK)**, which is across the bay but not much farther away from downtown San Francisco (via I–880 and I–80), although rush-hour traffic on the Bay Bridge may make travel times longer. Several domestic airlines serve **San Jose International Airport (SJC)**, which is about 40 mi south of San Francisco.

➤ AIRPORT INFORMATION: **San Francisco International Airport** (☎ 650/761–0800). **Oakland International Airport** (☎ 510/577–4000). **San Jose International Airport** (☎ 408/277–4759).

TRANSFERS

FROM SAN FRANCISCO INTERNATIONAL AIRPORT: A taxi ride from SFO to downtown costs about $30. Airport shuttles are inexpensive and efficient. The SFO Airporter ($10) picks up passengers at baggage claim (lower level) and serves selected downtown hotels. SuperShuttle stops at the upper-level traffic islands and takes you from the airport to anywhere within the city limits of San Francisco. It costs from $10 to $12 depending on your destination. Inexpensive shuttles to the East Bay (among them Bayporter Express) also depart from SFO's upper-level traffic islands; expect to pay around $20. The cheapest way to get from the airport to San Francisco is via SamTrans Bus 7B (55 minutes; $2.20) and 7F (35 minutes; $3; only one small carry-on bag permitted) to San Francisco or Bus 3X to the Colma BART train station (☞ BART, *below*). Board the SamTrans buses on the upper (departures) level.

To get to downtown San Francisco from the airport, take U.S. 101 north to the Civic Center (9th Street), 7th Street, or 4th Street exit. If you're headed to the Embarcadero or Fisherman's Wharf, take I–280 north (the exit is to the right, just past 3Com Park) and get off at the 4th Street/King Street exit. King Street becomes the Embarcadero a few blocks east of the exit. The Embarcadero winds around the waterfront to Fisherman's Wharf.

FROM OAKLAND INTERNATIONAL AIRPORT: A taxi from Oakland's airport to downtown San Francisco costs between $30 and $35. America's Shuttle, Bayporter Express, and other shuttles serve major hotels and provide door-to-door service to the East Bay and San Francisco. Marin Door to Door serves Marin County for a flat $50 fee. The best way to get to San Francisco via public transit is to take the AIR BART bus ($2) to the Coliseum/Oakland International Airport BART station (BART fares vary depending on where you're going; the ride to downtown San Francisco costs $2.75).

If you're driving from Oakland International Airport, take Hegenberger Road east to I–880 north to I–80 west.

FROM SAN JOSE INTERNATIONAL AIRPORT: A taxi from the airport to downtown San Jose costs about $12 (a taxi to San Francisco costs about $100). South & East Bay Airport Shuttle transports visitors to the South Bay and East Bay. A shuttle to downtown San Jose costs $15. VIP Shuttle provides service from the airport in San Jose to downtown San Francisco for $69.

To get to downtown San Jose from the airport, take Airport Boulevard east to Highway 87 south. To get to San Francisco from the airport, take Airport Boulevard east to Highway 87 south to I–280 north.

➤ TAXIS & SHUTTLES: **America's Shuttle** (☎ 510/841–0272). **Bayporter Express** (☎ 415/467–1800). **Marin Door to Door** (☎ 800/540–4815). **SFO Airporter** (☎ 415/495–8404). **South & East Bay Airport Shuttle** (☎ 408/559–9477). **SuperShuttle** (☎ 415/558–8500). **VIP Airport Shuttle** (☎ 408/885–1800 or 800/235–8847).

BART

You can use Bay Area Rapid Transit (BART) trains to reach Oakland, Berkeley, Concord, Richmond, Fremont, Martinez, and Dublin/Pleasanton. Trains also travel south from San Francisco as far as Daly City and Colma. Fares range from $1.10 to $4.45; trains run until midnight.

➤ BART: **Bay Area Rapid Transit** (☎ 650/992–2278).

BIKE TRAVEL

San Francisco's famous hills present a big challenge for bike riders, but you'll still see plenty of residents riding through the city. The Embarcadero, Marina Green, and Golden Gate Park are popular cycling areas.

➤ BIKE RENTALS: **Start to Finish** (☎ 415/202–9830 or ☎ 415/243–8812). **Park Cyclery** (☎ 415/751–7368).

BOAT & FERRY TRAVEL

Several ferry lines run out of San Francisco. Blue and Gold Fleet operates a number of lines, including a Golden Gate cruise, service to Alcatraz and Angel Island, and ferries to Sausalito and Tiburon; tickets can be purchased at Pier 39 and Pier 41. Golden Gate Ferry runs seven days a week to and from Sausalito and Larkspur, leaving from behind the San Francisco Ferry Building on the Embarcadero. The Oakland/Alameda Ferry operates seven days a week between Alameda's Main Street Ferry Building and San Francisco's Pier 39 and the Ferry Building; tickets may be purchased onboard.

➤ FERRY LINES: **Golden Gate Ferry** (☎ 415/923–2000). **Blue and Gold Fleet** (☎ 415/705–5555). **Oakland/Alameda Ferry** (☎ 510/522–3300).

BUS TRAVEL

The San Francisco Municipal Railway, or Muni, operates light rail vehicles, the F Market historic streetcar line, trolley buses, and the world-famous cable cars. Light rail travels along Market Street to the Mission District and Noe Valley (J line), the Ingleside district (K line), and the Sunset District (L, M, and N lines). Muni provides 24-hour service to all areas of the city.

On buses and streetcars, the fare is $1. Exact change is required, and dollar bills are accepted in the fare boxes. For all Muni vehicles other than cable cars, 90-minute transfers are issued free upon request at the time the fare is paid. Transfers are valid for a single ride in any direction.

Cable car fares are $2 for a one-way trip. The conductors can make change for up to $20, but transfers are neither issued nor accepted for cable car service.

CUTTING COSTS

A $6 pass good for unlimited travel all day on all routes can be purchased on the cable cars. Also, one-day ($6), three-day ($10), or seven-day ($15) Passports can be purchased at several outlets, including the cable car ticket booth at Powell and Market streets and the Visitors Information Center downstairs in Hallidie Plaza. The Passports are not only good for unlimited Muni travel, but are also good for discounts at visitor attractions in San Francisco, including the museums in Golden Gate Park. Currently, cable car ticket machines are not being used.

➤ BUS INFORMATION: **AC Transit** (☎ 510/839–2882) serves the East Bay. **Golden Gate Transit** (☎ 415/923–2000) serves Marin County. **San Francisco Municipal Railway System (Muni)** (☎ 415/673–6864) operates many routes within San Francisco.

CABLE CARS

Don't miss the sensation of moving up and down some of San Francisco's steepest hills in a small, open-air, clanging cable car. Move toward one quickly as it pauses, wedge yourself into any available space, and hold on!

The fare (for one direction) is $2. You can buy tickets onboard (exact change is preferred) or at the kiosks at the cable car turn-arounds located at Hyde and Beach streets and Powell and Market streets.

The Powell-Mason line and the Powell-Hyde line begin at Powell and Market streets near Union Square and terminate at Fisherman's Wharf. The California Street line runs east and west from Market Street near the Embarcadero to Van Ness Avenue. Along the Powell Street lines, you'll find the cable car museum at Washington and Mason streets—a short walk down the hill from the California Street line.

CALTRAIN

CalTrain connects San Francisco to Palo Alto, San Jose, and Santa Clara. Trains leave the city at 4th and Townsend streets. One-way fares run $3.75–$5.25. Trips last 1–1½ hours.

➤ CALTRAIN: **CalTrain** (☎ 800/660–4287).

CAMERAS & PHOTOGRAPHY

Early afternoon is the best time to avoid the fog in your photos—though you may want visual memories of the fog blanketing the city. The views from Coit Tower and Fisherman's Wharf offer plenty of photo-taking opportunities. Of course, don't miss a shot of the Golden Gate Bridge and a cable car.

➤ PHOTO HELP: **Kodak Information Center** (☎ 800/242–2424). *Kodak Guide to Shooting Great Travel Pictures,* available in bookstores or from Fodor's Travel Publications (☎ 800/533–6478; $16.50 plus $4 shipping).

EQUIPMENT PRECAUTIONS

Always **keep your film and tape out of the sun.** Carry an extra supply of batteries, and **be prepared to turn on your camera or camcorder** to prove to security personnel that the device is real. Always **ask for hand inspection of film,** which becomes clouded after successive exposures to airport X-ray machines, and **keep videotapes away from metal detectors.**

CAR RENTAL

Unless you plan on making excursions into Marin County, the East Bay, the South Bay, or the Wine Country, **avoid renting a car.** First see how well suited the cable cars are to this city of hills, how well the Muni buses and streetcars get you around every neighborhood, and how efficiently BART delivers you to the East Bay.

Rates in San Francisco begin at $36 a day and $123 a week for an economy car with air-conditioning, an automatic transmission, and unlimited mileage. This does not include tax on car rentals, which is 8.25%. For budget cars, stick to companies like Reliable. If you're looking to rent a BMW, Corvette, or Ford Explorer, try Sunbelt. Major hotels charge as much as $28 per day for parking.

➤ MAJOR AGENCIES: **Alamo** (☎ 800/327–9633; 0181/759–6200 in the U.K.). **Avis** (☎ 800/331–1212; 800/879–2847 in Canada; 02/9353–9000 in Australia; 09/525–1982 in New Zealand). **Budget** (☎ 800/527–0700; 0144/227–6266 in the U.K.). **Dollar** (☎ 800/800–4000; 0181/897–0811 in the U.K., where it is known as Eurodollar; 02/9223–1444 in Australia). **Hertz** (☎ 800/654–3131; 800/263–0600 in Canada; 0181/897–2072 in the U.K.; 02/9669–2444 in Australia; 03/358–6777 in New Zealand). **National InterRent** (☎ 800/227–7368; 0345/222525 in the U.K., where it is known as Europcar InterRent).

CUTTING COSTS

To get the best deal **book through a travel agent who will shop around.** Also **price local car-rental companies,** although the service and maintenance may not be as good as those of a major player. Remember to ask about required deposits, cancellation penalties, and drop-off charges if you're planning to pick up the car in one city and leave it in another. If you're traveling during a holiday period, also make sure that a confirmed reservation guarantees you a car.

➤ LOCAL AGENCIES: **Reliable** (☎ 415/928–4414). **Sunbelt** (☎ 415/772–1919).

INSURANCE

When driving a rented car you are generally responsible for any damage to or loss of the vehicle as well as for any property damage or personal injury that you may cause. Before you rent see what coverage your personal auto-insurance policy and credit cards already provide.

For about $15 to $20 per day, rental companies sell protection, known as a collision- or loss-damage waiver (CDW or LDW), that eliminates your liability for damage to the car. Some states, including California, have capped the price of the CDW and LDW. In most states you don't need a CDW if you have personal auto insurance or other liability insurance. However, **make sure you have enough coverage to pay for the car.** If you do not have auto insurance or an umbrella policy that covers damage to third parties, purchasing liability insurance and a CDW or LDW is highly recommended.

REQUIREMENTS & RESTRICTIONS

In San Francisco you must be 21 to rent a car, and rates may be higher if you're under 25. You'll pay extra for child seats (about $3 per day), which are compulsory for children under five, and for additional drivers (about $2 per day). Non-U.S. residents will need a reservation voucher, a passport, a driver's license, and a travel policy that covers each driver, in order to pick up a car.

SURCHARGES

Before you pick up a car in one city and leave it in another **ask about drop-off charges or one-way service fees,** which can be substantial. Note, too, that some rental agencies charge extra if you return the car before the time specified in your contract. To avoid a hefty refueling fee **fill the tank just before you turn in the car,** but be aware that gas stations near the rental outlet may overcharge.

CAR TRAVEL

Driving in San Francisco can be a challenge because of the hills, one-way streets, and traffic. Take it easy, remember to **curb your wheels** when parking on hills, and **use public transportation** or **cab it** whenever possible.

Rush hour takes places from 7 to 10 in the morning and 4:30 to 6:30 in the evening. Bridge traffic is erratic but generally remains fairly congested during the day and on weekends.

Market Street runs west from the ferry building to the Castro. The major east–west streets north of Market are **Geary Boulevard** (it's called Geary Street until Van Ness Avenue), which runs to the Pacific Ocean; **Fulton Street,** which begins at the back of the Opera House and continues along the north side of Golden Gate Park to Ocean Beach; and **Fell Street,** the left two lanes of which cut through Golden Gate Park and empty into **Lincoln Boulevard.** The latter continues on the park's south side to the ocean.

Among the major north–south streets are **Divisadero,** which becomes Castro Street at Duboce Avenue and continues past Cesar Chavez Street; **Van**

Ness Avenue (it becomes South Van Ness Avenue a few blocks south of City Hall); and **Park Presidio Boulevard,** which empties into **19th Avenue.**

PARKING

This is a great city for walking and a terrible city for parking. On certain streets, parking is forbidden during rush hours. **Look for the warning signs;** illegally parked cars are towed. Downtown parking lots are often full and most are expensive. (The city-owned Sutter-Stockton, Ellis-O'Farrell, and 5th and Mission garages have the most reasonable rates in the downtown area.) Finding a spot in North Beach at night can be exceedingly difficult; try the five-level 766 Vallejo Garage.

➤ GARAGES: Ellis-O'Farrell Garage (⊠ 123 O'Farrell St., at Stockton St., ☎ 415/986–4800). **Embarcadero Center Garage** (⊠ 1–4 Embarcadero, between Battery and Drumm Sts., ☎ 800/733–6318). **5th and Mission Garage** (⊠ 833 Mission St., at 5th St., ☎ 415/982–8522). **Opera Plaza Garage** (⊠ 601 Van Ness Ave., at Turk St., ☎ 415/771–4776). **Pier 39 Garage** (⊠ 2550 Powell St., at the Embarcadero, ☎ 415/705–5418). **Portsmouth Square Garage** (⊠ 733 Kearny St., at Clay St., ☎ 415/982–6353). **766 Vallejo Garage** (⊠ 766 Vallejo St., at Powell St., ☎ 415/989–4490). **Sutter-Stockton Garage** (⊠ 444 Stockton St., at Sutter St., ☎ 415/982–7275). **The Wharf Garage** (⊠ Fisherman's Wharf, 350 Beach St., at Taylor St., ☎ 415/921–0226).

ROAD MAPS

The detailed Thomas Bros. Maps of San Francisco are sold at bookstores throughout the city. If you're an American Automobile Association or Canadian Automobile Association member, you can drop by the headquarters of its local affiliate, the California State Automobile Association, and pick up city maps. The San Francisco Convention and Visitors Bureau storefront on the lower level of Hallidie Plaza also has maps.

➤ MAPS: California State Automobile Association (⊠ 150 Van Ness Ave., at Hayes St., ☎ 415/565–2012). San Francisco Convention and Visitors Bureau (⊠ Hallidie Plaza, lower level, 5th and Powell Sts., ☎ 415/974–6900).

RULES OF THE ROAD

The use of seat belts is required in California. The speed limit on city streets is 25 mi per hour unless posted otherwise. A right turn on a red light after stopping is legal unless posted otherwise.

CHILDREN IN SAN FRANCISCO

The City by the Bay is made for kids—from the awesome hills to the ferries to the cable cars. Wherever you go in San Francisco, you're bound to find kid-friendly activities. If you are renting a car don't forget to **arrange for a car seat** when you reserve.

BABY-SITTING

Bay Area Child Care (☎ 650/991–7474) will come to your hotel room.

FLYING

If your children are two or older **ask about children's airfares.** As a general rule, infants under two not occupying a seat fly at greatly reduced fares or even for free.

Experts agree that it's a good idea to use safety seats aloft for children weighing less than 40 pounds. Airlines set their own policies: U.S. carriers usually require that the child be ticketed, even if he or she is young enough to ride free, since the seats must be strapped into regular seats. Do **check your airline's policy about using safety seats during takeoff and landing.** And since safety seats are not allowed just everywhere in the plane, get your seat assignments early.

When reserving, **request children's meals or a freestanding bassinet** if you need them. But note that bulkhead seats, where you must sit to use the bassinet, may lack an overhead bin or storage space on the floor.

LODGING

Most hotels in San Francisco allow children under a certain age to stay in their parents' room at no extra charge, but others charge for them as extra adults; be sure to **find out the cutoff age for children's discounts.**

SIGHTS & ATTRACTIONS

Places that are especially good for children are indicated by a rubber duckie icon in the margin.

CONCIERGES

Concierges, found in many hotels, can help you with theater tickets and dinner reservations. A good one with connections may be able to get you seats for a hot show or prime-time dinner reservations at the restaurant of the moment. You can also turn to your hotel's concierge for help with travel arrangements, sightseeing plans, services ranging from aromatherapy to zipper repair, and emergencies. And, **always tip** a concierge who has been of assistance.

CONSUMER PROTECTION

Whenever shopping or buying travel services in San Francisco, **pay with a major credit card** so you can cancel payment or get reimbursed if there's a problem. If you're doing business with a particular company for the first time, **contact your local Better Business Bureau and the attorney general's offices** in your state and the company's home state, as well. Have any complaints been filed? Finally, if you're buying a package or tour, always **consider travel insurance** that includes default coverage (☞ Insurance, *below*).

➤ LOCAL BBBs: **Council of Better Business Bureaus** (✉ 4200 Wilson Blvd., Suite 800, Arlington, VA 22203, ☎ 703/276–0100, FAX 703/525–8277).

CUSTOMS & DUTIES

When shopping, **keep receipts** for all purchases. Upon reentering the country, **be ready to show customs officials what you've bought.** If you feel a duty is incorrect or object to the way your clearance was handled, note the inspector's badge number and ask to see a supervisor. If the problem isn't resolved, write to the appropriate authorities, beginning with the port director at your point of entry.

IN AUSTRALIA

Australia residents who are 18 or older may bring home $A400 worth of souvenirs and gifts (including jewelry), 250 cigarettes or 250 grams of tobacco, and 1,125 ml of alcohol (including wine, beer, and spirits). Residents under 18 may bring back $A200 worth of goods. Prohibited items include meat products. Seeds, plants, and fruits need to be declared upon arrival.

➤ INFORMATION: **Australian Customs Service** (Regional Director, ✉ Box 8, Sydney, NSW 2001, ☎ 02/9213–2000, FAX 02/9213–4000).

IN CANADA

Canadian residents who have been out of Canada for at least 7 days may bring home C$500 worth of goods duty-free. If you've been away less than 7 days but more than 48 hours, the duty-free allowance drops to C$200; if your trip lasts 24–48 hours, the allowance is C$50. You may not pool allowances with family members. Goods claimed under the C$500 exemption may follow you by mail; those claimed under the lesser exemptions must accompany you. Alcohol and tobacco products may be included in the 7-day and 48-hour exemptions but not in the 24-hour exemption. If you meet the age requirements of the province or territory through which you reenter Canada, you may bring in, duty-free, 1.14 liters (40 imperial ounces) of wine or liquor *or* 24 12-ounce cans or bottles of beer or ale. If you are 16 or older you may bring in, duty-free, 200 cigarettes and 50 cigars. Check ahead of time with Revenue Canada or the Department of Agriculture for policies regarding meat products, seeds, plants, and fruits.

You may send an unlimited number of gifts worth up to C$60 each duty-free to Canada. Label the package UNSOLICITED GIFT—VALUE UNDER $60. Alcohol and tobacco are excluded.

➤ INFORMATION: **Revenue Canada** (✉ 2265 St. Laurent Blvd. S, Ottawa, Ontario K1G 4K3, ☎ 613/993–0534; 800/461–9999 in Canada).

IN NEW ZEALAND

Homeward-bound residents 17 or older may bring back $700 worth of souvenirs and gifts. Your duty-free allowance also includes 4.5 liters of wine or beer; one 1,125-ml bottle of spirits; and either 200 cigarettes, 250 grams of tobacco, 50 cigars, or a combination of the three up to 250 grams. Prohibited items include meat products, seeds, plants, and fruits.

➤ INFORMATION: **New Zealand Customs** (Custom House, ⊠ 50 Anzac Ave., Box 29, Auckland, ☎ 09/359–6655, FAX 09/359–6732).

IN THE U.K.

From countries outside the EU, you may bring home, duty-free, 200 cigarettes or 50 cigars; 1 liter of spirits or 2 liters of fortified or sparkling wine or liqueurs; 2 liters of still table wine; 60 ml of perfume; 250 ml of toilet water; plus £136 worth of other goods, including gifts and souvenirs. If returning from outside the EU, prohibited items include meat products, seeds, plants, and fruits.

➤ INFORMATION: **HM Customs and Excise** (⊠ Dorset House, Stamford St., Bromley Kent BR1 1XX, ☎ 0171/202–4227).

IN THE U.S.

Non-U.S. residents ages 21 and older may import into the United States 200 cigarettes or 50 cigars or 2 kilograms of tobacco, 1 liter of alcohol, and gifts worth $100. Meat products, seeds, plants, and fruits are prohibited.

➤ INFORMATION: **U.S. Customs Service** (inquiries, ⊠ 1300 Pennsylvania Ave. NW, Washington, DC 20229, ☎ 202/927–6724; complaints, ⊠ Office of Regulations and Rulings, 1300 Pennsylvania Ave. NW, Washington, DC 20229; registration of equipment, ⊠ Resource Management, 1300 Pennsylvania Ave. NW, Washington, DC 20229, ☎ 202/927–0540).

DINING

RESERVATIONS & DRESS

Reservations are always a good idea: we mention them only when they're essential or are not accepted. Book as far ahead as you can, and reconfirm as soon as you arrive. We mention dress only when men are required to wear a jacket or a jacket and tie.

DISABILITIES & ACCESSIBILITY

California is a national leader in making attractions and facilities accessible to travelers with disabilities. Since 1982, the state building code has required that all construction for public use include access for people with disabilities. State laws more than a decade old provide special privileges, such as license plates allowing special parking spaces, unlimited parking in time-limited spaces, and free parking in metered spaces. Identification from states other than California is honored.

➤ LOCAL RESOURCES: **San Francisco Convention and Visitors Bureau** (⊠ Box 429097, San Francisco 94142-9097, ☎ 415/974–6900, 415/392–0328 TTY) publishes a free *San Francisco Lodging Guide* that spells out which hotels are up to ADA requirements. **California State Coastal Conservancy** (⊠ Publications Dept., 1330 Broadway, Suite 1100, Oakland 94612, ☎ 510/286–1015) publishes the free booklet "Wheelchair Riders Guide to San Francisco Bay and Nearby Shorelines."

LODGING

When discussing accessibility with an operator or reservations agent **ask hard questions.** Are there any stairs, inside *or* out? Are there grab bars next to the toilet *and* in the shower/tub? How wide is the doorway to the room? To the bathroom? For the most extensive facilities meeting the latest legal specifications **opt for newer accommodations.**

PARKS

The National Park Service provides a Golden Access Passport for all national parks free of charge to those who are medically blind or have a permanent disability; the passport covers the entry fee for the holder and anyone accompanying the holder in the same private vehicle as well as a 50% discount on camping and various other user fees. Apply for the passport in person at a national recreation facility that charges an entrance fee; proof of disability is required.

SIGHTS & ATTRACTIONS

Major attractions in San Francisco are wheelchair accessible, including the elevator to Coit Tower, Alcatraz, ferries, and the museums.

TRANSPORTATION

All Bay Area Rapid Transit (BART) stations are equipped with elevators, as well as wheelchair-accessible rest rooms, phones, and drinking fountains. Travelers with disabilities are entitled to a Bay Region Transit Discount Card, which offers savings of up to 75% off normal BART fares. Muni trains are wheelchair accessible, but not all Muni buses are.

➤ BART: **Bay Area Rapid Transit Passes Office** (☎ 510/464–7133).

➤ COMPLAINTS: **Disability Rights Section** (✉ U.S. Department of Justice, Civil Rights Division, Box 66738, Washington, DC 20035-6738, ☎ 202/514–0301; 800/514–0301; 202/514–0301 TTY; 800/514–0301 TTY, FAX 202/307–1198) for general complaints. **Aviation Consumer Protection Division** (☞ Air Travel, *above*) for airline-related problems. **Civil Rights Office** (✉ U.S. Department of Transportation, Departmental Office of Civil Rights, S-30, 400 7th St. SW, Room 10215, Washington, DC 20590, ☎ 202/366–4648, FAX 202/366–9371) for problems with surface transportation.

TRAVEL AGENCIES

In the United States, although the Americans with Disabilities Act requires that travel firms serve the needs of all travelers, some agencies specialize in working with people with disabilities.

➤ TRAVELERS WITH MOBILITY PROBLEMS: **Access Adventures** (✉ 206 Chestnut Ridge Rd., Rochester, NY 14624, ☎ 716/889–9096), run by a former physical-rehabilitation counselor. **Flying Wheels Travel** (✉ 143 W. Bridge St., Box 382, Owatonna, MN 55060, ☎ 507/451–5005 or 800/535–6790, FAX 507/451–1685). **Hinsdale Travel Service** (✉ 201 E. Ogden Ave., Suite 100, Hinsdale, IL 60521, ☎ 630/325–1335).

➤ TRAVELERS WITH DEVELOPMENTAL DISABILITIES: **New Directions** (✉ 5276 Hollister Ave., Suite 207, Santa Barbara, CA 93111, ☎ 805/967–2841 or 888/967–2841, FAX 805/964–7344).

DISCOUNTS & DEALS

Be a smart shopper and **compare all your options** before making decisions. A plane ticket bought with a promotional coupon from travel clubs, coupon books, and direct-mail offers may not be cheaper than the least expensive fare from a discount ticket agency. And always keep in mind that what you get is just as important as what you save.

DISCOUNT RESERVATIONS

To save money **look into discount-reservations services** with toll-free numbers, which use their buying power to get a better price on hotels, airline tickets, even car rentals. When booking a room, always **call the hotel's local toll-free number** (if one is available) rather than the central reservations number—you'll often get a better price. Always ask about special packages or corporate rates.

➤ AIRLINE TICKETS: ☎ **800/FLY–4–LESS.** ☎ **800/FLY–ASAP.**

➤ HOTEL ROOMS: **Accommodations Express** (☎ 800/444–7666). **Central Reservation Service (CRS)** (☎ 800/548–3311). **Hotel Reservations Network** (☎ 800/964–6835). **Players Express Vacations** (☎ 800/458–6161). **Quikbook** (☎ 800/789–9887). **Room Finders USA** (☎ 800/473–7829). **RMC Travel** (☎ 800/245–5738). **Steigenberger Reservation Service** (☎ 800/223–5652).

PACKAGE DEALS

Don't confuse packages and guided tours. When you buy a package, you travel on your own, just as though you had planned the trip yourself. Fly/drive packages, which combine airfare and car rental, are often a good deal. In cities, ask the local visitor's bureau about hotel packages that include tickets to major museum exhibits or other special events.

EMERGENCIES

➤ DOCTORS & DENTISTS: **Davies Medical Center Physician Referral Service** (☎ 415/565–6333). **1–800–DENTIST** (☎ 800/336–8478). **St. Luke's Hospital Physician Referral Service** (☎ 415/821–3627). San

Francisco Dental Society Referral Service (☎ 415/421–1435).

➤ EMERGENCY SERVICES: For **police, fire, or ambulance,** telephone 911.

➤ HOSPITALS: Two hospitals with 24-hour emergency rooms are **San Francisco General Hospital** (⊠ 1001 Potrero Ave., ☎ 415/206–8000) and the **Medical Center at the University of California, San Francisco** (⊠ 505 Parnassus Ave., at 3rd Ave., near Golden Gate Park, ☎ 415/476–1000). **Physician Access Medical Center** (⊠ 26 California St., ☎ 415/397–2881) is a drop-in clinic in the Financial District, open weekdays 7:30–4:30. **Access Health Care** (☎ 415/565–6600) provides drop-in medical care at Davies Medical Center, Castro Street at Duboce Avenue, weekdays 8–8.

➤ 24-HOUR PHARMACIES: Several **Walgreens Drug Stores** have 24-hour pharmacies (⊠ 498 Castro, at 18th St., ☎ 415/861–3136; ⊠ 25 Point Lobos, near 42nd Ave. and Geary St., ☎ 415/386–0736; and ⊠ 3201 Divisadero St., at Lombard St., ☎ 415/931–6417). The downtown Walgreens pharmacy (⊠ 135 Powell St., near Market St., ☎ 415/391–7222) is open weekdays 8–8, Saturday 9–5, and Sunday 10–6.

GAY & LESBIAN TRAVEL

San Francisco's credentials as a gay-friendly destination are impeccable. The Castro District is ground zero for the lesbian and gay community, but gay-owned shops and nightlife are sprinkled throughout town.

➤ LOCAL RESOURCES: *Fodor's Gay Guide to the USA* (available in bookstores, or contact Fodor's Travel Publications, ☎ 800/533–6478; $20). The *Bay Area Reporter* (☎ 415/861–5019) is a weekly gay paper.

➤ GAY- AND LESBIAN-FRIENDLY TRAVEL AGENCIES: **Different Roads Travel** (⊠ 8383 Wilshire Blvd., Suite 902, Beverly Hills, CA 90211, ☎ 323/651–5557 or 800/429–8747, FAX 323/651–3678). **Kennedy Travel** (⊠ 314 Jericho Turnpike, Floral Park, NY 11001, ☎ 516/352–4888 or 800/237–7433, FAX 516/354–8849). **Now Voyager** (⊠ 4406 18th St., San Francisco, CA 94114, ☎ 415/626–1169

or 800/255–6951, FAX 415/626–8626). **Yellowbrick Road** (⊠ 1500 W. Balmoral Ave., Chicago, IL 60640, ☎ 773/561–1800 or 800/642–2488, FAX 773/561–4497). **Skylink Travel and Tour** (⊠ 1006 Mendocino Ave., Santa Rosa, CA 95401, ☎ 707/546–9888 or 800/225–5759, FAX 707/546–9891), serving lesbian travelers.

HEALTH

DIVERS' ALERT

Do not fly within 24 hours of scuba diving.

MEDICAL PLANS

No one plans to get sick while traveling, but it happens, so **consider signing up with a medical-assistance company.** Members get doctor referrals, emergency evacuation or repatriation, hot lines for medical consultation, cash for emergencies, and other assistance.

HOLIDAYS

Major national holidays include New Year's Day; Martin Luther King Jr. Day (3rd Mon. in Jan.); President's Day (3rd Mon. in Feb.); Memorial Day (last Mon. in May); Independence Day; Labor Day (1st Mon. in Sept.); Thanksgiving Day (4th Thurs. in Nov.); Christmas Eve and Christmas Day; and New Year's Eve.

Tourist season in San Francisco runs from May to October. Fall is the busiest time. Plan on calling at least several weeks ahead for weekend dining and lodging reservations.

INSURANCE

The most useful travel insurance plan is a comprehensive policy that includes coverage for trip cancellation and interruption, default, trip delay, and medical expenses (with a waiver for preexisting conditions).

Without insurance you will lose all or most of your money if you cancel your trip, regardless of the reason. Default insurance covers you if your tour operator, airline, or cruise line goes out of business. Trip-delay covers expenses that arise because of bad weather or mechanical delays. Study the fine print when comparing policies.

Always **buy travel policies directly from the insurance company**; if you buy it from a cruise line, airline, or tour operator that goes out of business you probably will not be covered for the agency or operator's default, a major risk. Before you make any purchase **review your existing health and home-owner's policies** to find what they cover away from home.

➤ TRAVEL INSURERS: In the U.S. **Access America** (⌂ 6600 W. Broad St., Richmond, VA 23230, ☎ 804/285–3300 or 800/284–8300), **Travel Guard International** (⌂ 1145 Clark St., Stevens Point, WI 54481, ☎ 715/345–0505 or 800/826–1300). In Canada **Voyager Insurance** (⌂ 44 Peel Center Dr., Brampton, Ontario L6T 4M8, ☎ 905/791–8700; 800/668–4342 in Canada).

➤ INSURANCE INFORMATION: In the U.K. the **Association of British Insurers** (⌂ 51–55 Gresham St., London EC2V 7HQ, ☎ 0171/600–3333, FAX 0171/696–8999). In Australia the **Insurance Council of Australia** (☎ 03/9614–1077, FAX 03/9614–7924).

LODGING

The lodgings we list are the cream of the crop in each price category. We always list the facilities that are available—but we don't specify whether they cost extra. When pricing accommodations, always ask what's included and what costs extra.

Properties indicated by an ✕⌂ are lodging establishments whose restaurant warrants a special trip.

Assume that hotels operate on the European Plan (EP, with no meals) unless we specify that they use the Continental Plan (CP, with a Continental breakfast daily), Modified American Plan (MAP, with breakfast and dinner daily), or the Full American Plan (FAP, with all meals).

APARTMENT RENTALS

If you want a home base that's roomy enough for a family and comes with cooking facilities **consider a furnished rental.** These can save you money, especially if you're traveling with a group. Home-exchange directories sometimes list rentals as well as exchanges.

➤ INTERNATIONAL AGENTS: **Europa-Let/Tropical Inn-Let** (⌂ 92 N. Main St., Ashland, OR 97520, ☎ 541/482–5806 or 800/462–4486, FAX 541/482–0660). **Hometours International** (⌂ Box 11503, Knoxville, TN 37939, ☎ 423/690–8484 or 800/367–4668). **Interhome** (⌂ 1990 N.E. 163rd St., Suite 110, Miami Beach, FL 33162, ☎ 305/940–2299 or 800/882–6864, FAX 305/940–2911). **Rent-a-Home International** (⌂ 7200 34th Ave. NW, Seattle, WA 98117, ☎ 206/789–9377, FAX 206/789–9379). **Vacation Home Rentals Worldwide** (⌂ 235 Kensington Ave., Norwood, NJ 07648, ☎ 201/767–9393 or 800/633–3284, FAX 201/767–5510). **Hideaways International** (⌂ 767 Islington St., Portsmouth, NH 03801, ☎ 603/430–4433 or 800/843–4433, FAX 603/430–4444; membership $99).

B&BS

San Francisco's bed-and-breakfast inns run the gamut from the traditional room to let in a residential home to palatial digs like the Archbishop's Mansion or the Sherman House (☞ Lodging *in* Chapter 3 for details about these two properties).

➤ RESERVATION SERVICES: **Bed and Breakfast California** (☎ 650/696–1690 or 800/872–4500). **Bed and Breakfast San Francisco** (☎ 415/479–1913 or 800/452–8249).

HOME EXCHANGES

If you would like to exchange your home for someone else's **join a home-exchange organization,** which will send you its updated listings of available exchanges for a year and will include your own listing in at least one of them. It's up to you to make specific arrangements.

➤ EXCHANGE CLUBS: **HomeLink International** (⌂ Box 650, Key West, FL 33041, ☎ 305/294–7766 or 800/638–3841, FAX 305/294–1448; $88 per year). **Intervac U.S.** (⌂ Box 590504, San Francisco, CA 94159, ☎ 800/756–4663, FAX 415/435–7440; $83 per year).

HOSTELS

No matter what your age you can **save on lodging costs by staying at hostels.** In some 5,000 locations in more than 70 countries around the world, Hostelling International (HI), the umbrella group for a number of national youth-hostel associations, offers single-sex, dorm-style beds and, at many hostels, couples rooms and family accommodations. Membership in any HI national hostel association, open to travelers of all ages, allows you to stay in HI-affiliated hostels at member rates (one-year membership is about $25 for adults; hostels run about $10–$25 per night). Members also have priority if the hostel is full; they're eligible for discounts around the world, even on rail and bus travel in some countries.

➤ ORGANIZATIONS: **Australian Youth Hostel Association** (✉ 10 Mallett St., Camperdown, NSW 2050, ☎ 02/9565–1699, FAX 02/9565–1325). **Hostelling International—American Youth Hostels** (✉ 733 15th St. NW, Suite 840, Washington, DC 20005, ☎ 202/783–6161, FAX 202/783–6171). **Hostelling International—Canada** (✉ 400–205 Catherine St., Ottawa, Ontario K2P 1C3, ☎ 613/237–7884, FAX 613/237–7868). **Youth Hostel Association of England and Wales** (✉ Trevelyan House, 8 St. Stephen's Hill, St. Albans, Hertfordshire AL1 2DY, ☎ 01727/855215 or 01727/845047, FAX 01727/844126). **Youth Hostels Association of New Zealand** (✉ Box 436, Christchurch, ☎ 03/379–9970, FAX 03/365–4476). Membership in the U.S. $25, in Canada C$26.75, in the U.K. £9.30, in Australia $44, in New Zealand $24.

HOTELS

Most of the major chains have properties in or near San Francisco. All hotels listed have private bath unless otherwise noted.

➤ TOLL-FREE NUMBERS: **Adam's Mark** (☎ 800/444–2326). **Baymont Inns** (☎ 800/428–3438). **Best Western** (☎ 800/528–1234). **Choice** (☎ 800/221–2222). **Clarion** (☎ 800/252–7466). **Colony** (☎ 800/777–1700). **Comfort** (☎ 800/228–5150). **Days Inn** (☎ 800/325–2525). **Doubletree and Red Lion Hotels** (☎ 800/222–8733). **Embassy Suites** (☎ 800/362–2779). **Fairfield Inn** (☎ 800/228–2800). **Forte** (☎ 800/225–5843). **Four Seasons** (☎ 800/332–3442). **Hilton** (☎ 800/445–

8667). **Holiday Inn** (☎ 800/465–4329). **Howard Johnson** (☎ 800/654–4656). **Hyatt Hotels & Resorts** (☎ 800/233–1234). **Inter-Continental** (☎ 800/327–0200). **La Quinta** (☎ 800/531–5900). **Le Meridien** (☎ 800/543–4300). **Marriott** (☎ 800/228–9290). **Nikko Hotels International** (☎ 800/645–5687). **Omni** (☎ 800/843–6664). **Quality Inn** (☎ 800/228–5151). **Radisson** (☎ 800/333–3333). **Ramada** (☎ 800/228–2828). **Renaissance Hotels & Resorts** (☎ 800/468–3571). **Ritz-Carlton** (☎ 800/341–3333). **ITT Sheraton** (☎ 800/325–3535). **Sleep Inn** (☎ 800/221–2222). **Westin Hotels & Resorts** (☎ 800/228–3000). **Wyndham Hotels & Resorts** (☎ 800/822–4200).

MONEY MATTERS

Prices throughout this guide are given for adults. Substantially reduced fees are almost always available for children, students, and senior citizens. For information on taxes, *see* Taxes, *below*.

ATMS

ATMs are widely available all throughout San Francisco.

➤ ATM LOCATIONS: **Cirrus** (☎ 800/424–7787). **Plus** (☎ 800/843–7587) for locations in the U.S. and Canada, or visit your local bank.

CREDIT CARDS

Throughout this guide, the following abbreviations are used: **AE**, American Express; **D**, Discover; **DC**, Diner's Club; **MC**, MasterCard; and **V**, Visa.

➤ REPORTING LOST CARDS: To report lost or stolen credit cards, call the following toll-free numbers: **American Express** (☎ 800/327–2177); **Discover Card** (☎ 800/347–2683); **Diners Club** (☎ 800/234–6377); **MasterCard** (☎ 800/307–7309); and **Visa** (☎ 800/847–2911).

NATIONAL PARKS

Look into discount passes to save money on park entrance fees. The Golden Eagle Pass ($50) gets you and your companions free admission to all parks for one year. (Camping and parking are extra.) Both the Golden Age Passport ($10), for those 62 and older, and the Golden Access Passport (free), for travelers with disabilities, entitle holders to free entry to all national parks, plus 50% off fees for the use of many park facilities and services. You must show proof of age and of U.S. citizenship or permanent residency (such as a U.S. passport, driver's license, or birth certificate) and, if requesting Golden Access, proof of disability. All three passes are available at all national park entrances where entrance fees are charged. Golden Eagle and Golden Access passes are also available by mail.

➤ PASSES BY MAIL: **National Park Service** (⊠ National Capitol Area Office, 1100 Ohio Dr. SW, Washington, DC 20242, ☎ 202/208–4747).

PACKING

When packing for a vacation in the San Francisco Bay Area, **prepare for temperature variations.** An hour's drive can take you up or down many degrees, and the variation from daytime to nighttime in a single location is often marked. Take along sweaters, jackets, and clothes for layering as your best insurance for coping with variations in temperature. Include shorts or cool cottons for summer, and always tuck in a bathing suit, since many lodgings have pools and hot tubs. Bear in mind, though, that **the city can be chilly at any time of the year,** especially in summer, when the fog is apt to descend and stay.

Although casual dressing is a hallmark of the California lifestyle, men will need a jacket and tie for many good restaurants in the evening, and women will be more comfortable in something dressier than regulation sightseeing garb.

In your carry-on luggage **bring an extra pair of eyeglasses or contact lenses** and **enough of any medication you take** to last the entire trip. You may also want your doctor to write a spare prescription using the drug's generic name, since brand names may vary from country to country. In luggage to be checked, **never pack prescription drugs or valuables.** To avoid customs delays, carry medications in their original packaging. And don't forget to copy down and carry addresses of offices that handle refunds of lost traveler's checks.

CHECKING LUGGAGE

How many carry-on bags you can bring with you is up to the airline. Most allow two, but not always, so make sure that everything you carry aboard will fit under your seat, and get to the gate early. Note that if you have a seat at the back of the plane, you'll probably board first, while the overhead bins are still empty.

If you are flying internationally, note that baggage allowances may be determined not by piece but by weight—generally 88 pounds (40 kilograms) in first class, 66 pounds (30 kilograms) in business class, and 44 pounds (20 kilograms) in economy.

Airline liability for baggage is limited to $1,250 per person on flights within the United States. On international flights it amounts to $9.07 per pound or $20 per kilogram for checked baggage (roughly $640 per 70-pound bag) and $400 per passenger for unchecked baggage. You can buy additional coverage at check-in for about $10 per $1,000 of coverage, but it excludes a rather extensive list of items, shown on your airline ticket.

Before departure **itemize your bags' contents** and their worth, and label the bags with your name, address, and phone number. (If you use your home address, cover it so that potential thieves can't see it readily.) Inside each bag **pack a copy of your itinerary.** At check-in **make sure that each bag is correctly tagged** with the destination airport's three-letter code. If your bags arrive damaged or fail to arrive at all, file a written report with the airline before leaving the airport.

PASSPORTS & VISAS

➤ U.K. CITIZENS: **U.S. Embassy Visa Information Line** (☎ 01891/200–290; calls cost 49p per minute, 39p per minute cheap rate) for U.S. visa information. **U.S. Embassy Visa Branch** (⊠ 5 Upper Grosvenor Sq., London W1A 1AE) for U.S. visa information; send a self-addressed, stamped envelope. Write the **U.S. Consulate General** (⊠ Queen's House, Queen St., Belfast BTI 6EO) if you live in Northern Ireland. Write the **Office of Australia Affairs** (✉ 59th fl., MLC Centre, 19-29 Martin Pl., Sydney NSW 2000) if you live in Australia. Write the **Office of New Zealand Affairs** (✉ 29 Fitzherbert Terr., Thorndon, Wellington) if you live in New Zealand.

PASSPORT OFFICES

The best time to apply for a passport or to renew is during the fall and winter. Before any trip, check your passport's expiration date, and, if necessary, renew it as soon as possible.

➤ AUSTRALIAN CITIZENS: **Australian Passport Office** (☎ 131–232).

➤ CANADIAN CITIZENS: **Passport Office** (☎ 819/994–3500 or 800/567–6868).

➤ NEW ZEALAND CITIZENS: **New Zealand Passport Office** (☎ 04/494–0700 for information on how to apply; 04/474–8000 or 0800/225–050 in New Zealand for information on applications already submitted).

➤ U.K. CITIZENS: **London Passport Office** (☎ 0990/210–410) for fees and documentation requirements and to request an emergency passport.

REST ROOMS

Public rest rooms are located in forest-green kiosks at Pier 39, on Market Street at Powell Street, at Castro and Market streets, and at the Civic Center. The fee to use the facilities is 25¢. Most of the public garages (☞ Garages, *above*) have rest rooms, and there are usually lobby-level rest rooms in large hotels.

SAFETY

Those flying with a laptop computer should **be on the lookout for scam artists at the airport.** The ruse typically involves a pair who wait until your computer case is on the X-ray belt, then step through the portal and set off an alarm. While security checks that person for contraband—forcing you to wait—their partner walks off with your computer.

Be wary of solicitations at the airport. Recently, airline travelers have complained of harassment by solicitors, including some who pose as airport officials asking unsuspecting foreign passengers for "airport taxes," which don't exist. Officials have begun cracking down on all charities—some of which are legitimate—by allowing them to accept only checks or credit cards.

Like many cities on the West Coast, San Francisco is a magnet for the down and out. Be prepared to hear some hard luck stories. While most are no threat to the traveler, some street people are more aggressive than others and can persist in their pleas for cash until if feels like harassment. If you feel uncomfortable, don't reach for your wallet.

Use common sense and **avoid certain neighborhoods late at night**—the Tenderloin, Civic Center plaza, parts of the Mission (around 14th Street, for example, or south of 24th to Army Street), and the Lower Haight—especially if you're walking alone.

SENIOR-CITIZEN TRAVEL

To qualify for age-related discounts **mention your senior-citizen status up front** when booking hotel reservations (not when checking out) and before you're seated in restaurants (not when paying the bill). When renting a car ask about promotional car-rental discounts, which can be cheaper than senior-citizen rates.

➤ EDUCATIONAL PROGRAMS: **Elderhostel** (✉ 75 Federal St., 3rd fl., Boston, MA 02110, ☎ 877/426–8056, ℻ 877/426–2166).

SIGHTSEEING TOURS

In addition to bus and van tours of the city, most tour companies run excursions to various Bay Area and Northern California destinations such as Marin County and the Wine Country, as well as farther-flung areas such as Monterey and Yosemite. City tours generally last 3½ hours and cost $25–$30. Golden Gate Tours offers bay cruises ($38) as well as standard city bus tours. In addition to their bay cruises, Gray Line offers city tours in motorcoaches and motorized cable cars ($16–$32); Great Pacific Tours conducts their city tours (starting at $32).

➤ TOUR COMPANIES: **Golden Gate Tours** (☎ 415/788–5775). **Gray Line Tours** (☎ 415/558–9400). **Great Pacific Tour** (☎ 415/626–4499). **Tower Tours** (☎ 415/434–8687).

WALKING TOURS

Tours of various San Francisco neighborhoods generally cost $15–$35. Some tours have culinary themes: Lunch and snacks are often included. Trevor Hailey leads a popular "Cruising the Castro" tour focusing on the history and development of the city's gay and lesbian community. Cookbook author Shirley Fong-Torres and her team lead a tour through Chinatown—"Chinatown with the Wok Wiz," with stops at Chinese herbal markets and art studios. The Chinese Culture Center leads a Chinatown heritage walk and a culinary walk for groups of four or more only. City Guides, a free service sponsored by the San Francisco Public Library, offers the greatest variety of walks, including Chinatown, North Beach, Coit Tower, Pacific Heights mansions, Japantown, Haight-Ashbury, historic Market Street, the Palace Hotel, and downtown roof gardens and atriums. Schedules are available at the San Francisco Visitors Center at Powell and Market streets and at library branches. Javawalk explores the San Francisco's historic ties to coffee while visiting a few of San Francisco's more than 300 cafés. Victorian Home Walk is a low-impact amble through some of the city's less traveled neighborhoods. Learn about the different styles of Victorian buildings while exploring Pacific Heights and Cow Hollow.

➤ TOUR OPERATORS: **Trevor Hailey** (☎ 415/550–8110). **Chinatown with the "Wok Wiz"** (☎ 415/981–8989). **Chinese Culture Center** (☎ 415/986–1822). **City Guides** (☎ 415/557–4266). **Javawalk** (☎ 415/673–9255). **Victorian Home Walk** (☎ 415/252–9485).

SMOKING

Most hotels and motels have no-smoking rooms; in larger establishments entire floors are reserved for nonsmokers. Most bed-and-breakfast inns do not allow smoking on the premises.

In 1998 the California state legislature passed a law banning smoking in all indoor public spaces, including bars and nightclubs. Smoking is also prohibited in all restaurants and many other public places.

STUDENTS

To save money, **look into deals available through student-oriented travel agencies.** To qualify you'll need a bona fide student ID card. Members of international student groups are also eligible.

➤ STUDENT IDs & SERVICES: **Council on International Educational Exchange** (CIEE, ✉ 205 E. 42nd St., 14th fl., New York, NY 10017, ☎ 212/822–2600 or 888/268–6245, FAX 212/822–2699) for mail orders only, in the U.S. **Travel Cuts** (✉ 187 College St., Toronto, Ontario M5T 1P7, ☎ 416/979–2406 or 800/667–2887) in Canada.

TAXES

The sales tax in San Francisco is 8.5%. The tax on hotel rooms is 14%.

TAXIS

It can be difficult to hail a passing cab in some neighborhoods, but downtown—especially near major hotels (or at their taxi stands)—and along major streets like Haight and Castro streets, or destination points like SoMa and North Beach, flagging down a taxi shouldn't be a problem. Sometimes, it can be preferable to duck into a bar or restaurant and call one of the many cab companies for pick-up.

Taxis in San Francisco charge $1.70 for the first mile, $1.80 for each additional mile, and 30¢ per minute in stalled traffic.

➤ TAXI COMPANIES: **City Wide Cab** (☎ 415/920–0700; San Francisco). **Yellow Cab** (☎ 415/626–2345; San Francisco).

TELEPHONES

AREA CODES

The 415 area code is used in San Francisco and Marin County. The area code south of San Francisco on the Peninsula is 650. San Jose and

other South Bay cities use 408. Oak-
and and Berkeley use 510, and a new
925 area code covers the area east of
the Oakland Hills, from Walnut
Creek to Concord to Moraga. The
area code in the Wine Country is 707.

COUNTRY CODES

The country code for the United
States is 1.

DIRECTORY & OPERATOR INFORMATION

Dial 411 for information in the 415
area code. Dial 1, the area code, and
555–1212 for information outside the
city.

INTERNATIONAL CALLS

Dial 011+country code+city
code+number. The country code for
Australia is 61; New Zealand, 64; and
the United Kingdom, 44. To reach
Canada, dial 1+area code+number.

LOCAL CALLS

Dial only the seven-digit phone number (and not the area code) for all
local calls.

LONG-DISTANCE CALLS

Competitive long-distance carriers
make calling within the United States
relatively convenient and let you
avoid hotel surcharges. By dialing an
800 number, you can get connected to
the long-distance company of your
choice.

➤ LONG-DISTANCE CARRIERS: **AT&T**
(☎ 800/225–5288). **MCI** (☎ 800/
888–8000). **Sprint** (☎ 800/366–
2255).

TIPPING

At restaurants, a 15% tip is standard
for waiters; up to 20% may be ex-
pected at more expensive establishments. The same goes for taxi drivers,
bartenders, and hairdressers. Coat-
check operators usually expect $1;
bellhops and porters should get 50¢
to $1 per bag; hotel maids in upscale
hotels should get about $1 per day of
your stay. On package tours, conductors and drivers usually get $10 per
day from the group as a whole; check
whether this has already been figured
into your cost. For local sightseeing
tours, you may individually tip the
driver-guide $1 if he or she has been
helpful or informative. Ushers in
theaters do not expect tips.

TOURS & PACKAGES

On a prepackaged tour or independent vacation everything is prear-
ranged so you'll spend less time
planning—and often get it all at a
good price.

BOOKING WITH AN AGENT

Travel agents are excellent resources.
But it's a good idea to collect
brochures from several agencies because some agents' suggestions may be
influenced by relationships with tour
and package firms that reward them
for volume sales. If you have a special
interest **find an agent with expertise in
that area**; ASTA (☞ Travel Agencies,
below) has a database of specialists
worldwide.

Make sure your travel agent knows
the accommodations and other services of the place they're recommend-
ing. Ask about the hotel's location,
room size, beds, and whether it has a
pool, room service, or programs for
children, if you care about these. Has
your agent been there in person or
sent others whom you can contact?

Do some homework on your own,
too: Local tourism boards can provide information about lesser-known
and small-niche operators, some of
which may sell only direct.

BUYER BEWARE

Each year consumers are stranded or
lose their money when tour operators—even large ones with excellent
reputations—go out of business. So
check out the operator. Ask several
travel agents about its reputation, and
try to **book with a company that has a
consumer-protection program.** (Look
for information in the company's
brochure.) In the United States, members of the National Tour Association
and United States Tour Operators
Association are required to set aside
funds to cover your payments and
travel arrangements in case the company defaults. It's also a good idea to
choose a company that participates in
the American Society of Travel Agent's
Tour Operator Program (TOP); ASTA
will act as mediator in any disputes
between you and your tour operator.

Remember that the more your package or tour includes the better you can predict the ultimate cost of your vacation. Make sure you know exactly what is covered, and **beware of hidden costs.** Are taxes, tips, and transfers included? Entertainment and excursions? These can add up.

➤ TOUR-OPERATOR RECOMMENDATIONS: **American Society of Travel Agents** (☞ Travel Agencies, *below*). **National Tour Association** (NTA, ✉ 546 E. Main St., Lexington, KY 40508, ☎ 606/226–4444 or 800/682–8886). **United States Tour Operators Association** (USTOA, ✉ 342 Madison Ave., Suite 1522, New York, NY 10173, ☎ 212/599–6599 or 800/468–7862, FAX 212/599–6744).

GROUP TOURS

Among companies that sell tours to San Francisco, the following are nationally known, have a proven reputation, and offer plenty of options. The classifications below represent different price categories, and you'll probably encounter these terms when talking to a travel agent or tour operator. The key difference is usually in accommodations, which run from budget to better, and better-yet to best.

➤ DELUXE: **Globus** (✉ 5301 S. Federal Circle, Littleton, CO 80123-2980, ☎ 303/797–2800 or 800/221–0090, FAX 303/347–2080).

➤ BUDGET: **Cosmos** (☞ Globus, *above*).

PACKAGES

Like group tours, independent vacation packages are available from major tour operators and airlines. The companies listed below offer vacation packages in a broad price range.

➤ AIR/HOTEL/CAR: **American Airlines Vacations** (☎ 800/321–2121). **Delta Vacations** (☎ 800/872–7786). **United Vacations** (☎ 800/328–6877). **US Airways Vacations** (☎ 800/455–0123).

➤ HOTEL ONLY: **SuperCities** (✉ 139 Main St., Cambridge, MA 02142, ☎ 800/333–1234).

➤ CUSTOM PACKAGES: **Amtrak Vacations** (☎ 800/321–8684).

➤ FROM THE U.K.: **British Airways Holidays** (✉ Astral Towers, Betts Way, London Rd., Crawley, West Sussex RH10 2XA, ☎ 01293/723–121). **Jetsave** (✉ Sussex House, London Rd., East Grinstead, West Sussex RH19 1LD, ☎ 01342/327–711). **Key to America** (✉ 1–3 Station Rd., Ashford, Middlesex TW15 2UW, ☎ 01784/248–777). **Kuoni Travel Ltd.** (✉ Kuoni House, Dorking, Surrey RH5 4AZ, ☎ 01306/740–500). **Premier Holidays** (✉ Premier Travel Center, Westbrook, Milton Rd., Cambridge CB4 1YG, ☎ 01223/516–516). **Trailfinders** (✉ 42–50 Earls Court Rd., London W8 6FT, ☎ 020/7937–5400; ✉ 58 Deansgate, Manchester M3 2FF, ☎ 0161/839–6969).

THEME TRIPS

➤ GOLF: **Golf Pacific Coast** (✉ 1267 Saratoga Ave., Ventura, CA 93003, ☎ 800/335–3534).

➤ HORSEBACK RIDING: **Equitour FITS Equestrian** (✉ Box 807, Dubois, WY 82513, ☎ 307/455–3363 or 800/545–0019, FAX 307/455–2354).

➤ WHALE-WATCHING: **Natural Habitat Adventures** (✉ 2945 Center Green Ct., Boulder, CO 80301, ☎ 303/449–3711 or 800/543–8917, FAX 303/449–3712). **Oceanic Society Expeditions** (✉ Fort Mason Center, Bldg. E, San Francisco, CA 94124, ☎ 415/441–1106 or 800/326–7491). **Pacific Sea Fari Tours** (✉ 2803 Emerson St., San Diego, CA 92106, ☎ 619/226–8224).

Also contact **Amtrak**'s Great American Vacations (☎ 800/321–8684).

TRANSPORTATION AROUND SAN FRANCISCO

Within San Francisco it's easy to get around by foot, bus, cable car, or taxi (☞ Bus Travel within San Francisco, Cable Cars, *and* Taxis, *above*). BART provides service to various East Bay destinations, and CalTrain serves the Peninsula (☞ *above*). You'll need a car to get to Marin County, the Wine Country, and beyond.

TRAVEL AGENCIES

A good travel agent puts your needs first. Look for an agency that has been in business at least five years, emphasizes customer service, and has someone on staff who specializes in your destination. In addition **make sure the agency belongs to a professional trade organization.** The American Society of Travel Agents (ASTA), with 27,000 agents in some 170 countries, is the largest and most influential in the field. Operating under the motto "Integrity in Travel," it maintains and enforces a strict code of ethics and will step in to help mediate any agent-client disputes if necessary. ASTA also maintains a Web site that includes a directory of agents. (Note that if a travel agency is also acting as your tour operator *see* Buyer Beware *in* Tours & Packages, *above*.)

➤ LOCAL AGENT REFERRALS: **American Society of Travel Agents** (ASTA, ☎ 800/965–2782 24-hr hot line, ℻ 703/684–8319, www.astanet.com). **Association of British Travel Agents** (⌂ 55–57 Newman St., London W1P 4AH, ☎ 020/7637–2444, ℻ 020/7637–0713). **Association of Canadian Travel Agents** (⌂ 1729 Bank St., Suite 201, Ottawa, Ontario K1V 7Z5, ☎ 613/521–0474, ℻ 613/521–0805). **Australian Federation of Travel Agents** (⌂ Level 3, 309 Pitt St., Sydney 2000, ☎ 02/9264–3299, ℻ 02/9264–1085). **Travel Agents' Association of New Zealand** (⌂ Box 1888, Wellington 10033, ☎ 04/499–0104, ℻ 04/499–0786).

VISITOR INFORMATION

TOURIST INFORMATION

The San Francisco Convention and Visitors Bureau can mail you brochures, maps, and festivals and events listings; or try the bureau's 24-hour fax-on-demand service (☎ 800/220–5747). For information about the Wine Country, redwood groves, and northwestern California, contact the Redwood Empire Association Visitor Information Center (☞ *below*). For $3 they'll send you a visitors guide; or pick one up at the center for $1. You can get information about the South Bay from the San Jose Visitor Information Center (☞ *below*).

➤ CITY: **San Francisco Convention and Visitors Bureau** (⌂ Box 429097, San Francisco 94142-9097, or lower level of Hallidie Plaza at Powell Street cable car turn-around, ☎ 415/974–6900).

➤ METRO AREA: **Berkeley** (⌂ 2015 Center St., 1st fl., Berkeley 94704, ☎ 800/847–4823). **Oakland** (⌂ 550 10th St., Oakland 94607, ☎ 510/839–9000 or 800/262–5526). **San Jose** (⌂ 333 W. San Carlos St., Suite 1000, San Jose 95110, ☎ 408/295–9600 or 800/726–5673). **Santa Clara** (⌂ Box 387, Santa Clara 95052, ☎ 408/244–9660).

➤ WINE COUNTRY: **Redwood Empire Association Visitor Information Center** (⌂ 2801 Leavenworth St., 94133, ☎ 800/200–8334, ℻ 415/394–5994).

➤ STATE: **California Division of Tourism** (⌂ 801 K St., Suite 1600, Sacramento, CA 95814, ☎ 916/322–2882 or ☎ 800/862–2543) has a free visitors guide.

WEB SITES

Do check out the World Wide Web when you're planning. You'll find everything from up-to-date weather forecasts to virtual tours of famous cities. Fodor's Web site, www.fodors.com, is a great place to start your on-line travels.

➤ ACCESS: The **Access-Able Travel Source** site (www.access-able.com) carries information about attractions and restaurants, lodgings, and other establishments that are accessible to travelers with disabilities.

➤ NEWS AND LISTINGS: **The Gate** is an excellent Bay Area resource (www.sfgate.com), with local headline news, daily weather updates, entertainment listings, classified ads, and much more.

If you're hunting for a restaurant, movie and club listings, or even a new job, be sure to browse **The Guardian**, the on-line version (www.sfbg.com) of San Francisco's popular weekly newspaper, the *San Francisco Bay Guardian*.

The smart features on **MetroActive**, the on-line version (www.metroactive.com) of *San Jose Metro*, include guides to nightlife, the arts, dining, and entertainment in the Bay Area, including Silicon Valley and Santa Cruz.

A must-visit for gay and lesbian visitors, the **Q San Francisco** site (www.qsanfrancisco.com/qsf/guide/contents.html) provides nightlife and entertainment listings, accommodation tips, and links to Bay Area gay and lesbian organizations.

The colorful and easy-to-navigate site of *SF Weekly* (www.sfweekly.com) carries news and feature reports plus complete arts and entertainment listings and reviews.

Yahoo!, the popular World Wide Web search engine, maintains an exhaustive site (www.sfbay.yahoo.com) on San Francisco and the Bay Area, with links to hundreds of local businesses and community organizations.

➤ OFFICIAL SITES: In addition to its own travel tips, events calendars, and other resources, the **California Division of Tourism** web site (gocalif.ca.gov) will link you—via the Regions icon—to the web sites of city and regional tourism offices and attractions.

The **National Park Service** site (www.nps.gov) which lists national parks and other lands administered by the park service, has extensive historical, cultural, and environmental information.

The Web site (www.sfvisitor.org) of the **San Francisco Convention and Visitors Bureau** has calendar listings and good maps.

WHEN TO GO

You can **visit San Francisco comfortably any time of year.** The climate here always feels Mediterranean and moderate—with a foggy, sometimes chilly twist. The temperature rarely drops lower than 40°F, and anything warmer than 80°F is considered a heat wave. Be prepared for rain in winter, especially December and January. Winds off the ocean can add to the chill factor, so pack warm clothing. North, east, and south of the city, summers are warmer. Shirt-sleeves and thin cottons are usually fine for the Wine Country.

CLIMATE

➤ FORECASTS: **Weather Channel Connection** (☎ 900/932–8437), 95¢ per minute from a Touch-Tone phone.

The following chart lists the average daily maximum and minimum temperatures for San Francisco.

Jan.	56F	13C	May	64F	17C	Sept.	70F	21C
	46	8		51	10		56	13
Feb.	60F	15C	June	66F	19C	Oct.	69F	20C
	48	9		53	11		55	13
Mar.	61F	16C	July	66F	19C	Nov.	64F	18C
	49	9		54	12		51	10
Apr.	63F	17C	Aug.	66F	19C	Dec.	57F	14C
	50	10		54	12		47	8

FESTIVALS AND SEASONAL EVENTS

➤ JAN.: The **Shrine East-West All-Star Football Classic** takes place at Stanford Stadium (☎ 415/661–0291), 25 mi south of San Francisco in Palo Alto.

➤ JAN.–APR.: **Whale-watching** can be enjoyed throughout the winter, when hundreds of gray whales migrate along the Pacific coast. Contact the San Francisco Convention and Visitor Information Center (☎ 415/391–2000) for details.

➤ FEB.: The **Chinese New Year** celebration in San Francisco's Chinese community, North America's largest, lasts for two weeks, culminating with the Golden Dragon Parade. Contact the **Chinese Chamber of Commerce** (☎ 415/982–3071).

➤ MAR.: On the Sunday closest to March 17, San Francisco's **St. Patrick's Day** celebration includes snake races and a parade through downtown.

➤ APR.: The **Cherry Blossom Festival** (☎ 415/563–2313), an elaborate presentation of Japanese culture and customs, winds up with a colorful parade through San Francisco's Japantown.

➤ MAY: Thousands sign up to run the *San Francisco Examiner* Bay to Breakers Race (☎ 415/777–7770), a 7½-mi route from bay side to ocean side that's a hallowed San Francisco tradition.

➤ MAY: The **San Francisco International Film Festival** (☎ 415/931–3456) draws scads of film buffs, eager to catch the premieres the festival brings to theaters across town.

➤ MAY–JUNE: **Carnaval** (☎ 415/826–1401), held in the Mission District, includes a parade and street festival.

➤ JUNE: The **North Beach Festival** (☎ 415/989–2220), held every Father's Day weekend, transforms Washington Square Park and Grant Avenue into an Italian marketplace, with food, music, and entertainment.

➤ JUNE: **The Lesbian, Gay, Bisexual, and Transgendered Pride Parade and Celebration** (☎ 415/864–3733) winds its way from the Embarcadero to the Civic Center on the third or fourth Sunday of the month.

➤ JULY: The **Fourth of July** celebration, at Crissy Field in the Presidio, features family festivities beginning in mid-afternoon and a fireworks display at 9.

➤ JULY: The **Cable Car Bell-Ringing Championship** (☎ 415/673–6864) is on the third Thursday of July at noon in Union Square.

➤ SEPT.: **A La Carte A La Park** (☎ 415/383–9378) is an opportunity to taste food from the city's best restaurants in the lush environs of Golden Gate Park.

➤ SEPT.: **Opera in the Park** (☎ 415/864–3330) takes place in Golden Gate Park on the Sunday after Labor Day.

➤ SEPT.: The **San Francisco Blues Festival** (☎ 415/979–5588), on the Great Meadow at Fort Mason, is held on the third weekend of September.

➤ OCT.: Beginning the second weekend of the month, **Fleet Week** celebrates the navy's first day in the port of San Francisco with a Blue Angels air show over the bay.

➤ OCT.: On the Sunday closest to Columbus Day, a parade through North Beach kicks off the **Columbus Day** celebration (☎ 415/434–1492).

➤ DEC.: The San Francisco Ballet's rendition of *The Nutcracker* (☎ 415/703–9400) is an elaborate, memorable production.

➤ DEC.: The annual **Sing-It-Yourself Messiah** (☎ 415/759–3410) takes place at St. Ignatius Church during the second week of the month.

INDEX

Icons and Symbols

★   Our special recommendations

✕   Restaurant

🏠   Lodging establishment

✕🏠   Lodging establishment whose restaurant warrants a special trip

🕲   Good for kids (rubber duck)

☞   Sends you to another section of the guide for more information

⊠   Address

☏   Telephone number

🕐   Opening and closing times

🎟   Admission prices

Numbers in white and black circles ③ ❸ that appear on the maps, in the margins, and within the tours correspond to one another.

NOTES

L@@king

© FOR A
great place to go

We know just the place. In fact, it attracts more than 125,000 visitors a day, making it one of the world's most popular travel destinations. It's previewtravel.com, the Web's comprehensive resource for travelers. It gives you access to over 500 airlines, 25,000 hotels, rental cars, cruises, vacation packages and support from travel experts 24 hours a day. Plus great information from Fodor's travel guides and travelers just like you. All of which makes previewtravel.com quite a find.

Preview Travel has everything you need to plan & book your next trip.

air, car & hotel reservations

vacation package & cruises

destination planni & travel tips

24-hour customer service

previewtravel.com

preview
travel

aol keyword: previewtrav
www.previewtravel.com

FODOR'S SAN FRANCISCO

EDITOR: Jennifer Levitsky Kasoff

Contributors: Lotus Abrams, Chris Baty, Lisa Hamilton, Denise M. Leto, Daniel Mangin, Amy McConnell, Andy Moore, Marty Olmstead, Sharon Silva

Editorial Production: Stacey Kulig

Maps: David Lindroth, *cartographer*; Bob Blake and Steven K. Amsterdam, *map editors*

Design: Fabrizio La Rocca, *creative director*; Guido Caroti, *art director*; Jolie Novak, *picture editor*; Melanie Marin, *photo researcher*

Cover Design: Pentagram

Production/Manufacturing: Mike Costa

Database Production: Phebe Brown, Janet Foley, Mark Laroche, Victoria Lu, Andrea Pariser, Priti Tambi, Julie Tomasz, Martin Walsh, Lucy Wu, Alexander Zlotnick

COPYRIGHT

ISBN 0–679–00340–1

ISSN 1525–1829

SPECIAL SALES

IMPORTANT TIP

PHOTOGRAPHY

Corbis/Roger Ressmeyer, *cover*. (Golden Gate Bridge).

David Allen: *14A.*

CalTour: *Robert Holmes, 2 bottom center.*

Rose Pistola: *Carl Duncan, 9D.*

Fine Arts Museums of San Francisco: *Richard Barnes, 2 top right.*

Ghirardelli Square, *3 top left.*

Robert Holmes, *7C, 9A, 10A, 10B, 13B.*

Hunter Public Relations: *Kent Hanson, 2 top left, 9B.*

The Image Bank: *Luis Castañeda, 8A. Gary Cralle, 1. David W. Hamilton, 6B. Michael Melford, 7D. Piecework Productions, 7E, 11B, 13A.*

Kabuki Springs & Spa, *3 bottom left.*

Catherine Karnow, *8B, 9C, 11C, 12A, 12B.*

Kitty Katty's, *2 bottom left.*

Markham Johnson, *12C.*

James Lemass, *8C, 10C.*

Robert Mondavi, *3 top right, 13C.*

James Morley, *15C.*

Perretti & Park Pictures, *15B.*

Pier 39, *3 bottom right.*

San Francisco Convention & Visitors Bureau: *Carol Simowitz, 2 bottom right.*

San Francisco Museum of Modern Art: *Richard Barnes 11D.*

San Francisco Symphony: *Terence McCarthy, 11A.*

David Sanger Photography, *4–5, 6A, 16.*

ABOUT OUR WRITERS

Every Y2K trip is a significant trip. So if there was ever a time you needed excellent travel information, it's now. Acutely aware of that fact, we've pulled out all stops in preparing *Fodor's San Francisco*. To help you zero in on what to see in San Francisco, we've gathered some great color photos of key sights. To show you how to put it all together, we've created great itineraries and neighborhood walks. And to direct you to the places that are truly worth your time and money in this important year, we've rallied the team of endearingly picky know-it-alls we're pleased to call our writers. Having seen all corners of San Francisco, they're real experts on the subjects they cover for us. If you knew them, you'd poll them for tips yourself.

Lotus Abrams has lived in the Bay Area nearly her whole life. She updated the South Bay section and writes for *Sunset* magazine, where she is a fact checker.

Side Trips and A to Z updater **Chris Baty** is a contributor to numerous Fodor's guides. He also writes for the *East Bay Express,* the *San Francisco Weekly,* and his own zine, *Frolic.*

Nightlife, Shopping, and Outdoors updater **Denise M. Leto** is a Berkeley-based writer. Her work has appeared in the *San Francisco Bay Guardian.* She is currently the San Francisco editor of a Web site for business travelers.

Daniel Mangin, who wrote the Exploring section, returned to San Francisco in 1998 after a three-year stint in New York as a senior editor for Fodor's. The former arts editor of the *Bay Area Reporter,* he cowrote Fodor's *Sunday in San Francisco*

and edited *Where Should We Take th Kids? California* and Fodor's *California 1994–99.*

Inland Peninsula updater **Amy McConnel** is a senior travel editor at *Sunset* magazine. She lives in San Francisco.

Lodging updater **Andy Moore** is a nativ southern Californian who has lived i San Francisco for more than 20 years. H is a frequent Fodor's contributor and also an independent filmmaker.

Marty Olmstead updated the Wine Coun try chapter and covers the region for he weekly column in the *Marin Independen Journal* and other publications.

Dining updater **Sharon Silva** is a con tributor to *San Francisco* magazine and Microsoft's *sidewalk.com* on-line city ser vice.

Jennifer Levitsky Kasoff, editor of *Sa Francisco 2000,* believes the City by th Bay is her true home, but for now she' content to live in New York.

Don't Forget to Write

We love feedback—positive and nega tive—and follow up on all suggestions. Sc contact the San Francisco editor a editors@fodors.com or c/o Fodor's, 20 East 50th Street, New York, NY 10022 Have a wonderful trip!

Karen Cure

Karen Cure
Editorial Director